REA's Books Are

They have rescued lots of grades and more!

(continued from previous page)

"Your books have saved my GPA, and quite possibly my sanity. My course grade is now an 'A', and I couldn't be happier."

Student, Winchester, IN

" These books are the best review books on the market. They are fantastic!"

Student, New Orleans, LA

"Your book was responsible for my success on the exam. . . I will look for REA the next time I need help."

Student, Chesterfield, MO

"I think it is the greatest study guide I have ever used!"

Student, Anchorage, AK

"I encourage others to buy REA because of their superiority. Please continue to produce the best quality books on the market."

Student, San Jose, CA

"Just a short note to say thanks for the great support your book gave me in helping me pass the test . . . I'm on my way to a B.S. degree because of you !"

Student, Orlando, FL

MUSIC HISTORY

Charles Stanford, Professor of Music
Cecil Forsyth, Professor of Music

and the Staff of
Research & Education Association,
Carl Fuchs, Chief Editor

Research & Education Association
61 Ethel Road West
Piscataway, New Jersey 08854

Dr. M. Fogiel, Director

SUPER REVIEW®
OF MUSIC HISTORY

Printed in the United States of America

Library of Congress Control Number 2002106287

International Standard Book Number 0-87891-418-8

WHAT THIS Super Review WILL DO FOR YOU

This **Super Review** provides all that you need to know to do your homework effectively and succeed on exams and quizzes.

The book focuses on the core aspects of the subject, and helps you to grasp the important elements quickly and easily.

Outstanding **Super Review** features:

- Topics are covered in historical sequence

- Topics are reviewed in a concise and comprehensive manner

- The material is presented in student-friendly language that makes it easy to follow and understand

- Individual topics can be easily located—fully indexed

- Provides excellent preparation for midterms, finals, and in-between quizzes

- Written by professionals and experts who function as your very own tutors

Dr. Max Fogiel
Program Director

Carl Fuchs
Chief Editor

CONTENTS

CHAPTER   PAGE

I. THE ORIGINS OF MUSIC 3

II. THE EGYPTIANS, ASSYRIANS AND BABYLONIANS, HEBREWS,
ARABIANS, INDIANS, CHINESE 15

III. THE GREEKS 38

IV. ROME AND THE DARK AGES 69

V. SCALES AND NOTES 87

VI. THE LESS DARK AGES 119

VII. DUNSTABLE. DUFAY. DES PRES 144

VIII. THE GOLDEN AGE 158

IX. THE PALACE OF GREENWICH. JANUARY 26, 1595 177

X. SONG AND FOLK-SONG 200

XI. THE SECULAR CENTURY 217

XII. THE EIGHTEENTH CENTURY 233

XIII. THE VIENNESE MASTERS 246

XIV. THE CONTEMPORARIES OF BEETHOVEN AND THE DEVELOPMENT
OF OPERA IN GERMANY, ITALY, AND FRANCE 266

XV. THE POST-BEETHOVEN PERIOD 281

XVI. NATIONALISM. MODERN SCHOOLS 303

XVII. "TWELVE-TONE" MUSIC AND OTHER INNOVATIONS 355

THE CHIEF NAMES IN MUSICAL HISTORY 361

INDEX 373

LIST OF PHOTOS/ILLUSTRATIONS

Etruscan Flute Player/Gerard Terborch's "The Lute"...................................*Frontispiece*

PLATE		PAGE
I.	Ancient Egyptian Harp (Reconstructed)	12
II.	Assyrian Triangular Harp	13
III.	Ancient Harps and Lyres	14
IV.	Hebrew Ritual Trumpets	22a
V.	Biblical Instruments	22b
VI.	Indian Instruments	26a
VII.	Indian Vina	26b
VIII.	Chinese Stone-Chime	32a
IX.	Chinese Instruments	32b
X.	Chinese Sheng	34
XI.	Apollo and Artemis before an Altar	48a
XII.	Apollo and Artemis performing a Libation	48b
XIII.	Organ	76a
XIV.	Hurdy-Gurdy	76b
XV-XVII.	Ancient/Roman Musical Instruments	84-86
XVIII.	Byzantine Notation	100a
XIX.	The Neumes	100b
XX.	Settlement of the Neumes in the Lines	106a
XXI.	Colored Lines with Neumes	106b
XXII.	Evolution of the Clef-Signs	111
XXIII.	Development of Notation	117
XXIV.	A Family of Shawms and Bombards	184a
XXV.	Cornetts	184b
XXVI.	Harpsichord	192a
XXVII.	Chittarone	192b
XXVIII.	Instruments of the Viol Family	194a
XXIX.	A Family of Recorders	194b
XXX-XXXII.	Russian & Irish Folk Instruments	214-216
XXXIII.	Louis XIV of France	220a
XXXIV.	Purcell	220b

LIST OF PHOTOS/ILLUSTRATIONS

PLATE　　　　　　　　　　　　　　　　　　　　　　　　　　　　**PAGE**

XXXV.　　George Frederic Handel 234a

XXXVI.　　Gluck 234b

XXXVII.　　Haydn 248a

XXXVII.　　Franz Joseph Haydn 248b

XXXIX.　　Mozart 252a

XL.　　Wolfgang Amadeus Mozart 252b

XLI.　　Beethoven 256a

XLII.　　Ludwig van Beethoven 256b

XLIII.　　Cherubini 266a

XLIV.　　Gaspare Spontini and Domenico Cimarosa 266b

XLV.　　Rossini 270a

XLVI.　　Carl Maria von Weber 270b

XLVII.　　Felix Mendelssohn Bartholdy 284a

XLVIII.　　Schumann and Madame Schumann 284b

XLIX.　　Robert Schumann 286a

L.　　Brahms 286b

LI.　　Brahms 296a

LII.　　Chopin 296b

LIII.　　Verdi 340a

LIV.　　Giacomo Puccini 340b

LV.　　Philip Glass 360

FLUTE PLAYER, ETRUSCAN, TOMB OF THE LEOPARDS, TARQUINIA

The Lute by Gerard Terborch

CHAPTER 1

The Origins of Music

THE first and fundamental type of music is purely rhythmical. So far as we can tell from records and from the study of primitive peoples it underlies and precedes every other sort of music. It needs no instrument beyond the two knuckles *of a man* and a square foot of "black mother earth." In this and other simple forms it exists as a necessity of life among all primitive peoples: it exists in more elaborate forms as an equal necessity in the lives of the most cultured modern nations.

Let us examine more closely the three words in italics — *of a man*. These are important; for, however low æsthetically we may put the thump of the savage's knuckles, it is not low but very high in the general system of the world. In fact, it marks man off from the rest of creation. The greater number of animals make sounds of some sort under the spur of pain, fear, hunger, or desire. Some even appear to take a pleasure in purposeless noise. For instance, on a calm sunny day a whale will lie near the surface idly beating the water with his tail. Why does he do this? It may be that he finds pleasure in sound; more probably it is only pleasure in muscular movement.

The so-called "songs" of the birds have been cited in this connection. But they are really outside the circle of our argument. It is true that some of them sound rhythmical to us. But this rhythm is involuntary and invariable to the bird. It depends solely on his supplying wind to an already existing and curiously evolved vocal mechanism.

It is voluntary only in the very far-off sense that all evolution finally rests on conscious selection. If each act of the bird's singing were voluntary, and if he could vary his song rhythmically to suit his pleasure, that would be another matter. But that is just what he cannot do. If he could, we should expect to find his whole race only a little lower than man and a great deal above its actually nearest neighbors — the reptiles.

One thing is indeed certain. No animals — not even the highest types of ape — have ever been observed to combine the sounds produced by their own muscular efforts into a series of beats at regular intervals; to combine them for the sake of their own pleasure; and to vary them when so combined. With what feelings of astonishment should we regard an unharnessed carriage-horse begging for entrance to its loose-box, not with the usual indeterminate scrape of its hoof on the cobbles, but with the peremptory rhythm of Beethoven's opening notes in the *C-minor Symphony!* Or a successful cat tapping out a persistent rhythm — a sort of *coda ostinata* — with the mouse in its jaws!

These things, we know, cannot be; and the differences which they imply divide man at his lowest from the rest of creation at its highest. But man has gone farther still. He has a voice. From the earliest specimens of his skull which have been unearthed we know that at first he used his voice, like many other animals, only as a vague and formless expression of his emotions. Like them he howled with pleasure and moaned with pain. So far he was no better than a dog. But, while the beasts of the field stopped at this indeterminate vowelled utterance, man made two long steps forward.

In the first place he found out how to use his lips, his tongue, and his teeth in combination with his throat. He could now not only vary the quality of the sound — or, in other words, choose his vowels — but he could break these up in any way he desired by toneless stoppages. His utterance was no longer merely an expression of his emotions by means of vague wailing cries, but an expression of his intellect by means of recognizable vocal sounds and equally recognizable unvocal sounds. Each little patch of vowel-sound became precise in color; and it could be sharply defined and cut off from its neighbor by a consonant or a group of consonants. In a word, man had invented SPEECH.

No one can tell how many centuries passed before the growing complexities of life forced him to contrive a way of recording his speech. Nor is it necessary to describe in detail what we know of that history. There is one point, however, which we of today can only appreciate with difficulty. To primitive man speech was a puff of breath and, as such, he consciously connected it with the life both of his body and his soul. Imagine, then, the terror with which he viewed an attempt to transfer it to a leaf of birch-bark, to send it on a journey, to allow others a share in its meaning! It was an attack on his own personality, an experiment of impiety, almost of grave danger. Hence the new picture-writing, starting as a thing of magic, became a priestly ritual, and then, changed and simplified in its characters, remained down to our own times a mystery to be jealously guarded from the common people. The word "clerk" with its double meaning resumes this history in five letters.

As we shall see, precisely the same thing happened in music. The mediæval monks were the first to hit upon a music-script at once simple and precise enough to be worth developing. It should have been stripped of its technicalities and extravagances and laid, like an open book, before all. Yet every imaginable obstacle was placed in its path by its own authors. Even at the present day, while the sounds of music are free to anyone with ears, the notation of music is hedged round with many unnecessary difficulties. The musician has still something of the Medicine Man, of the ancient Egyptian Priest, and of the Mediæval Monk in his nature.

The second step which man took interests us more closely. Formerly he was only a howling animal, now he had become a talker. But he still remained a creature of emotions; and these emotions still needed expression. He had the same inner compulsion to lift up his voice under the stress of personal feeling; only he had passed the stage when these feelings could find a satisfactory expression either in pure rhythm or in vague unorganized wailing. His task now was to link up his intellect with his emotions; to join his little patches of consonant-defined vowel — that is to say, the *words* which represented to him material things and abstract ideas — with his rhythm and his changes of pitch. Neither of these could be altered in their nature. Nor did he desire to alter them. The old feeling of satisfaction caused by the throb of his knuckles on the ground and by the rise and fall of his voice still remained in his blood, too deeply rooted to be tampered with. Only he wished to associate them with his new-found speech. And he had to invent ways by which this could be done.

The rhythm was too stubborn a thing to be much changed. At most it could be elaborated or simplified, made more subtle or more direct. But with his voice the plan of action was much less obvious, and it was probably only after centuries of effort that he came to understand distinctly what changes were required.

Theory as to how this change came about is mere guesswork. We may, however, state the result in its broadest outline. In place of an aimless, indeterminate rise and fall in the pitch of his voice, man now had at his command a series of *clearly defined steps*. He had cut out the intermediate sounds and had left himself with a systematized group of musical notes subtly perfect for expressing his emotions in terms of his intellect. Nor did this change cause any violent break with his former methods. The rhythm of the notes, the rise and fall, the loudness and softness of his voice still remained; only they remained organized so that they could be made the basis of an art. Finally, in this long but simple history, man had to learn that both the words and the music could be made to express the same emotional ideas; and, when he had got so far, he had gone beyond the stage of talking and had invented SONG.

The reader must not imagine that these are unimportant

commonplaces. Their very commonness marks their importance. For these three things, rhythm, pitch, and articulation, underlie all musical art and sum up all its possibilities. Music, indeed, may be described as the conventional expression of human feeling by means of *rhythm* (that is to say, idealized gesture) and *melody* (that is to say, idealized emotional cries). And all good music acts as a reminder to mankind of their fundamental significance.

The fourth factor, the musical instrument made by hands, has to some extent altered the outward seeming of the art, but it is more an appearance than a reality. The instrument is made originally to imitate, then to support, then to elaborate the vocal phrase. But, however complex its development, it seeks its justification only on human grounds. This is the case even with the greatest and most standard of all instruments, the pianoforte. A player who tried to refer his phrasing to any other standard than that of the human lungs would soon find himself in difficulties. Instrumental construction, however, is a factor which has played a large part in the history of music. It does not become of great importance to us until the later middle-ages. Still it has always existed. On the material side it is governed by such conditions as the available supply of reeds, wood, and metal, the skill of artificers, and the general wealth of communities. Climate, too, has its effect. For instance, in certain parts of India the hot water-logged air practically forbids the development or even the existence of the whole violin-family.

These are, however, small points. Of greater interest is the relative responsibility of the singer and the instrument for the arrangement of the ancient note-groupings or scales which were invented by the earliest civilizations. Did the singer make his scale and then build the instrument to fit that scale? Or was the instrument built first? The answer to this question is not easy. One might suppose that at the very beginning the singer formed the scale and that the instrument was tuned, as it were, to order. But this easy supposition is by no means supported either by history or by our knowledge of musical methods among primitive peoples.

It is quite likely that the thrumming of the hand on the bow-string may have first suggested musical sound to the ears of the cave-man, but it certainly did not and could not suggest the note-groups or scales whose origin we are now discussing. These note-groups undoubtedly preceded any stringed instruments capable of producing them.

The only instruments indeed which give us a satisfactory explanation of the primitive scales are those which the Greeks and Romans with unerring instinct placed in the hands of Pan and the Satyrs — the river-reeds. They are of universal distribution. They have been used as musical instruments from the earliest times. Their physical nature is such that the simplest mathematical prudence will turn them into sounding-pipes whose scales are those of civilized antiquity and of present-day savagedom.

A river-reed is nothing but a hollow tube whose length is divided transversely at fairly regular intervals by a "knot." When dried it is easily made into one of two different instruments.

If it is cut underneath two successive knots, the result is a *Pan's pipe*. The player blows hard against the rim at the top, and the knot at the bottom acts as a stopper. There is neither hole to "finger" nor reed to set in vibration. It is a "one pipe, one sound" instrument. If the player wishes to make a scale he cuts his reeds of varying lengths, boring vertically (if necessary) through all the knots except the last. He then binds them together and has a *syrinx* or set of *Pan's pipes* — an instrument which has not changed from the days of Marsyas to those of the Punch-and-Judy man. His only requisite besides a knife is a knowledge of the numbers up to 9. For, if he cuts his reeds in the ratio of 9–8–7–6–5, he will have in his hands an instrument giving the pentatonic (five-note) scale — a scale which was probably old in the days of Pindar, and is still in daily use.[1]

The other instrument into which the river-reed can be and always has been turned is the *reed-pipe*. It consists of a single, long, dry reed pierced throughout its whole

[1] Sometimes called the "black-note" or "Chinese" scale. See page 29.

length. At one end is a small strip or tongue of flexible
reed which is held and set in motion by the player's lips.
But this is not a "one pipe, one sound" instrument. It is
bored at intervals with a red-hot point, and the holes so
bored are covered and uncovered at pleasure by the fingers
of the player. He therefore has *a scale* at his disposal.
And the nature of this scale is governed by the disposition
of the holes. The normal tendency is to bore these holes
as nearly equidistant from each other as the exigencies of
the human hand will allow. It is from these borings that all
the ancient Greek scales — diatonic, chromatic, and enharmonic — sprang.[1] And in this way they are the ancestors of
our own scale through the tone-systems of the middle-ages.

On the more general musical question it may be observed
that instruments have always exercised a steady pressure
on the vocal scales which they supported. This can be
seen in the peculiar melodic restrictions of the ancient Greek
kithara; in the repressive influence of the guitar-formalism
on Spanish song; and in the effects of the purely chromatic
orchestra on the nineteenth century opera singer. The melodic freedom of English and Irish folk-music, which has
developed mainly as unaccompanied song, is living testimony on the other side.

These subjects will be dealt with as they come up in turn
for historical discussion. Meanwhile, we must remember that
it is on the organization of these scale-groupings — that is to
say, on the arrangement of their notes with regard to each
other — that the whole history of music primarily depends.
And we may say at once that, as far as Europe and America
are concerned, these scales consist of whole-tones, of half-
tones, and of nothing else. Every note must therefore be
either a whole-tone or a half-tone from its neighbor. The arrangement of these whole-tones and half-tones has, however,
varied continually in the history of music; and the simplest
way of observing these variations is to note the place or
places in a scale where the semitone-interval falls. This is
a matter of great importance; and it is therefore made the

[1] See page 60.

first of the four separate lines along which the history of music is to be studied.

1. Tone-schemes; that is to say, the scales or groupings of notes which have been used by musicians in various ages.

2. The means of communicating music; otherwise voices and instruments.

3. The means of recording music and of making it permanent; in other words, its notation, script, or writing.[1]

4. The development of the music itself, including the lives and works of the great composers.

After what has been said above the reader will easily understand that music itself goes back to a time earlier than its record. Indeed, the first civilizations whose paintings and sculptures we are able to examine were already in possession of a flourishing music. Perhaps we may say that systematic music — its regular practice with voices and instruments — is coeval with civilization. The first stutterings of music are lost to us. All we know is that they come somewhere between the cave-man and the Nile-man of 4000 B.C.

The ancient civilizations which practiced the art of music were the Egyptians, the Assyrians and Babylonians, the Hebrews, the Arabians, the Indians, the Chinese, and the Greeks. Of these the Greeks are by far the most important to us. Not only were their melodies incorporated in the *plain-song* of the Christian church, but the "modes" in which they were originally sung formed, as it were, the raw material from which the monks of a later day hewed their tone-systems. It was to the Greeks, too, that the Italians turned for inspiration in their general musical reform of 1600. The influence of the Egyptians is less intelligible to us only

---

[1] Music can, of course, be handed down from generation to generation without any writing at all. This has probably happened in the case of the earliest Plain-Song and of all Folk-Music. Such music is invariably simple melody. Even when conserved by the church it shows some traces of alteration. Under secular conditions its internal organization often becomes so confused that strict historical classification is impossible. We must remember that "from the early middle-ages till the present day, the traditional music (folk-song) has continued to flow in a sort of underground stream, while the written or professional music has been the main official water-way. The two have constantly joined their currents, and at times the underground stream has actually been in advance of the river overhead."

because we have fewer facts on which to found our judgment. Their credit will probably grow with a greater knowledge on our part. Of this we are certain: their influence was exercised only at second hand through the Greeks.

The Hebrews were especially rich in musical instruments. We owe them something on that score; and there can be little doubt that their Temple-Music was the head-water from which flowed the stream of early Christian *plain-song*. The other ancient nations — Assyrians and Babylonians, Arabians, Indians, and Chinese — are all interesting from the antiquarian standpoint. But they had no effect on our own musical system. A partial exception may be made in the case of the Arabians; for one or two types of instrumental construction, if not native to them, may have found their way into Europe through their country.

We are now in a position to sketch in outline the music of these ancient peoples. But before doing so, it is necessary to classify the great secular changes which, in the course of time, have come over the face of musical history. The best and broadest division, that of Hugo Riemann, breaks up the past 6000 years into three great periods; the ancient, the mediæval, and the modern. Within each of these periods we find a music possessing certain common characteristics; and though the division, at any rate between the ancient and the mediæval, is not marked by any definite event, we can roughly give each a date. The three periods then, with their dates and their main channels of expression, may be set out thus:

ANCIENT	MEDIÆVAL	MODERN
Down to 900 A.D.	From 900 to 1600 A.D.	From 1600 A.D. to the present day.
Voices and Instruments.	Voices.	Voices and Instruments.
Melody only (at most octave-singing and playing).	Polyphony, that is, simultaneous melodies.	Accompanied melody.

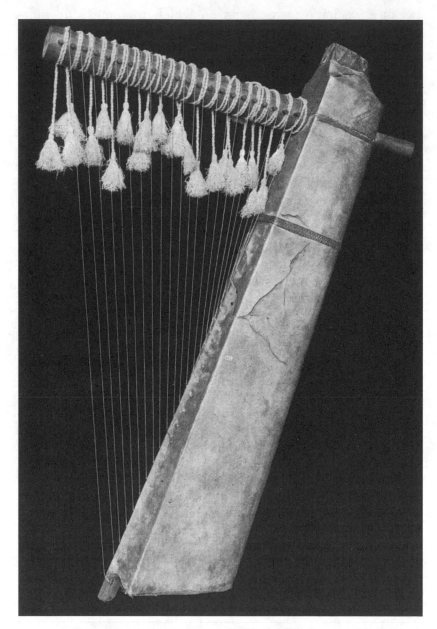

PLATE I. ANCIENT EGYPTIAN HARP (RECONSTRUCTED)

PLATE II. ASSYRIAN TRIANGULAR HARP

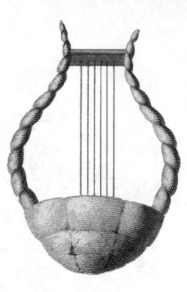

LYRE FROM PICTURE AT HERCULANEUM ABYSINIAN TESTUDO

ANCIENT SINGLE HARP ANCIENT TRIPLE HARP

PLATE III. ANCIENT HARPS AND LYRES

CHAPTER 2

Part I - The Ancient Period
TO 900 A.D.

The Egyptians, Assyrians and Babylonians, Hebrews, Arabians, Indians, Chinese.

THE Egyptians were the first people to cultivate music. Unfortunately no theoretical treatise nor any single note of their music remains. We are therefore not certain as to whether they had either a theory or a notation. We have to fall back on two other sources of information: first, their influence on Greek music; second, their paintings and sculptures.

1. We know that music was practiced on the banks of the Nile from about 4000 B.C. We also know that Pythagoras of Samos founded the Greek music and philosophy, and founded it on his previous studies in Egypt. Pythagoras lived and taught in lower Italy (Croton and Metapontum) about 550 B.C. It is fairly certain that his system, if not purely Egyptian, was at farthest an adaptation of the Egyptian system; and this view is in some sort supported by Greek writers of a later age.

2. Drawings, paintings, and sculptures of musicians and musical instruments exist in profusion, and it is mainly on their silent testimony that we have to rely for information. Furthermore, specimens of Egyptian musical instruments have been continually dug up. Many of these date from the times of the later dynasties; but where the actual instrument agrees in type with the more archaic wall-painting we may make a safe deduction as to its antiquity. The number of instruments represented in Egyptian paintings is large. We shall therefore have to present them without much detail.

In the percussion department the Egyptians had the *tam-*

bourine — an instrument of nearly universal distribution; small two-headed *drums*, about the size and shape of an oyster-barrel; and small hand *kettle-drums*, to be more fully described in the section devoted to Arabian music. Their *sistrum* was a series of narrow jingling plates hung horizontally on a recurved metal frame. Small *bells* were much commoner with them than with the Greeks. Many specimens of Egyptian sistra and bells still exist. Of the latter there are no fewer than 15 examples in the British Museum alone. The Egyptian *cymbals* were made of brass, or of silver and brass mixed, and were used by dancing girls to mark the rhythm of their performance. They varied in diameter from $5\frac{1}{2}$ to 7 inches, and were shaped just like our modern instruments, even to the saucer-like depression in the middle. The plates, however, were flat — not tapered. Tiny finger-tip pairs of cymbals also were in use. These in later ages were carried by the Moors to Spain where they were made of chestnut (castaña) and became known as *castanets*.

In the brass-wind the Egyptians had one or two kinds of straight metal *trumpet* blown with a cup-mouthpiece. These began as short instruments, increased in length, and finally in Roman times became curved. Their wood-wind was rather more complete. They had *cross-flutes* (blown like our modern flutes through a hole in the side) and an end-blown flute called the *nay*. But it is doubtful whether they ever had true reed-instruments, that is, instruments in which the sound was produced by means of the vibration of a single or double-reed held in the player's mouth. It is *possible* that they may have used some sort of simple "squeaker-reed." It is also *possible* that they may have employed reeds not in contact with the player's lips, like those of our modern bagpipe-chanter. But nothing certain is known on these points.

The method of tone-production in the ordinary Egyptian *pipe* is still doubtful. The instrument has been claimed as a true fipple-flute, blown (like our flageolet) by directing the breath through a wooden or ivory beak on to a sharp "lip" cut in the pipe itself. But this is by no means clearly

proved. However that may be, the pipe was a favorite
instrument with them and was sometimes *played in pairs* by
a single musician. What this method of performance implied is matter of speculation. It may have been (1) alternate playing, (2) octave playing, (3) a melody with a
"pedal" either below or above. There is certainly nothing
to show that it meant what we may call "duet playing,"
that is to say the simultaneous performance of two melodies
whether rhythmically distinct or allied. In fact, we may
expand this into the much more general statement that,
throughout the whole of the "Ancient Period," that is to say
down to about 900 A.D., music consisted of nothing but melody — either solo, in unison, or in octaves.[1]

In the string department the Egyptians had no *bowed* instruments, but many of the *plucked* variety. The principal
types were the *lute* and the *harp*. The essentials of the lute-
type are the vaulted, resonating sound-box, the few long
strings which are fingered (or stopped) by the player's left
hand, and stretched from the pegs at the upper end to the
bridge at the lower. The Egyptian lutes conform strictly
to this type and the importance of the invention may be
gauged from the fact that the type remained in artistic use
right down to the seventeenth century of our era. The harp-
type was probably first suggested by the ordinary bow which,
when strung for war or the chase, is practically a one-
stringed twanging instrument. The essentials of the type
are the framework, originally following the lines of the
curved bow, and the many strings which are stretched across
this framework in a series, all of different lengths. The
player's fingers pluck the strings, each of which is employed
to sound only one note — the open note of its full vibrating
length.

The Egyptian harps vary in shape and size. Some have
the archaically simple bow-like form with very few strings.
Others show a size and construction not very different from
those of our modern harps. The curve of the bow has been

[1] See what is said below (pp. 41 to 47) on the Greek pipe (*aulos*) and
double-pipe (*diauloi*).

altered to an acute angle so that the outline of the instrument is triangular. But the "pillar," on which the whole tension of the modern instrument depends, is lacking. A resonating sound-box and a series of pegs for tuning complete the apparatus. Both forms — the three-cornered and the bow-shaped — may be seen in the thirteenth century (B.C.) wall-painting discovered by Bruce. Some of these instruments were of great size — taller even than a tall man.

The illustration (see page 12, Plate I.) is of an elaborately decorated instrument having the triangular shape, but no pillar. The main body of this harp is nothing but a deep wooden resonator covered with parchment. Twenty-two strings run down to this resonator from the upper arm, where they are secured by means of wooden pegs. The absence of the pillar precludes any great tension on the strings; and this accounts for the relatively large size of the sound-box. It is an attempt to improve the playing qualities of the instrument. The date of this specimen is about 1500 B.C.

Practically all the instruments we have mentioned figure in the wall-paintings as if played in ensemble. A deduction of that sort, however, cannot be made. All through the period of antiquity and the whole of the middle-ages — in fact, as late as the Tudors — it was a commonplace of both religious and secular artists to combine their instrumental groups solely according to fancy. We can see much the same fancy at work in the hideous groups of squashed fiddles and drums which "adorn" the outside of the Royal College of Music, London, and the inside of the Æolian Hall, New York. In ancient days, however, the motto usually was "the more, the merrier." To which one might add "the fewer, the better cheer," for some of these combinations make one deaf to look at. It is scarcely necessary to add that such groupings cannot — in the absence of confirmatory evidence — be accepted as history.

It is obvious from the above summary that the Egyptians were a highly musical nation. No people could have called into existence this vast array of instruments except at the prompting of considerable artistic feeling. We know that, besides their use of music for religious purposes, they associated it — perhaps in a somewhat subsidiary and servile manner — with all the chief external events of their lives. From that we may surmise that they had an organized musical system. But, as far as we are concerned, it has vanished.

THE ASSYRIANS AND BABYLONIANS

We now come to the Assyrians and Babylonians, and with regard to them we may repeat what we said of the Egyptians, that we know nothing of their musical system or their notation. Furthermore, their civilization lies wholly out of the track along which ours has slowly marched. The interest of these peoples is therefore only antiquarian; and the most that we can say of their culture is that they possessed musical instruments and apparently associated music with the deeds and pleasures of royalty in somewhat the same servile manner that we have noted in the case of the Egyptians. There is no doubt that they *had* music and plenty of it. One has only to glance round the Assyrian galleries in the British Museum to be sure of that. But we know no more of it than what we can gather from their huge, undetailed, stone carvings.

Still that evidence is first-hand and convincing. Triangular *harps* appear to have been their favorite instrument. In addition they had *trumpets, flutes, drums,* and a sort of primitive ocarina — a *clay flute* with two finger-holes. All these probably came from Egypt. But the Assyrians themselves may have been the inventors of a one-pipe *bagpipe* which afterwards found its way into Greece and became known as the *sumphoneia.*[1] More interesting is their primitive plucked instrument — no more than a square wooden frame with five or six strings — much like the early British *Crwth.*

A question has been raised whether it is to the Ninevite culture that we owe the psaltery and dulcimer. These two

[1] Possibly a phonetic rendering of a lost Assyrian word, and itself the father of the Italian word zampogna (bagpipe).

instruments have a good deal in common. Originally they consisted of a flat board, or perhaps a shallow wooden box, over which was laid a series of strings of different lengths. From its nature it would soon take the form of a truncated isosceles triangle.

This instrument was played in two ways: either by plucking the strings with a plectrum, or by striking them with a hammer. In the former case it was known as a *psaltery:* in the latter, a *dulcimer.* The psaltery was the ancestor of the virginal, spinet, and harpsichord: the dulcimer of the mediæval Irish timpan and the modern pianoforte. The two names, however, are continually confused. And this is natural; for a very slight adjustment was sufficient to turn the one into the other.

It was for long claimed that a dulcimer figured in the stone carving known as "The Procession of King Assurbanipal" (*British Museum*). But Galpin has pointed out that this portion of the slab is a late and faulty restoration necessitated by a crack, and that the instrument is, in fact, nothing but "one of those Trigons or triangular Harps which so frequently occur in these Assyrian bas-reliefs."

The illustration (see page 13, Plate II) shows one of these Assyrian instruments. It is taken from that portion of the Assurbanipal sculptures which represents the king pouring a libation after the lion-hunt. In all essentials this harp is the same as the Egyptian instrument illustrated at page 18. And this can be seen merely by turning the present picture round so that the sound-box stands upright. The detail of the symbolic carved hand at the end of the upper arm is the only difference. This type of small triangular harp is indeed common to the early Asiatic and Nilotic civilizations.

It need scarcely be said that the translators of the English Bible (A. V.) in dealing with Nebuchadnezzar's instruments (Daniel iii) made no pretensions to antiquarian exactness. Their method was merely to substitute an imposing catalogue of English instruments. They also chose, when possible, instruments whose names had something in common with the

original words.   Thus, as Galpin has shown, for the words
"cornet, flute, harp, sackbut, psaltery, dulcimer" we should
probably read "the horn, pipe, lyre, harp, psaltery, and bagpipe."

THE HEBREWS

Like the Assyrians the Hebrews owed a good deal musically to early Egypt.   It would be strange if it were otherwise.   What systematic development they gave to the Egyptian culture we do not know but, in the list of their adopted
instruments, we must include the long straight *trumpets*, the
flute, the *cymbals*, and the *hand kettle-drums*.   The *harp* they
somewhat simplified into the small handy triangular instrument already described.   Both harp and *psaltery* — the
latter in Josephus's time (first century A.D.) a fairly large instrument with 12 strings — were in common use.   The general distinction between the two instruments from the player's
point of view was that the psaltery was plucked by the fingers,
or more commonly by a plectrum, *on one side only;* while
the harp was plucked at discretion *on both sides*.

The Hebrews, however, had far too strongly national a
character to be content with mere adaptations of Egyptian
instruments.   They produced two other types both of great
interest, the *lyre* and the *ram's-horn-trumpet*.

The former was a true lyre whose body followed the lines
of its prototype, the empty carapace of a tortoise.   On either
side rose the curved horns or pillars joined near the top by a
wooden crossbar.   The stringing was of course vertical.   In
form this instrument was much less primitive than the ancient Assyrian lyre or the clumsy British crwth of later times.
Indeed, though its elegance is generally associated nowadays
with Greek poetry, it is fairly certain that the Greeks obtained
their lyre from some Semitic nation, though on its way to
Greece it may have passed through Egypt.[1]

The twisted ram's-horn-trumpet was peculiar to the
Hebrews.   Made from the natural horn, and therefore
roughly conical in form, it was consecrated to the service

[1] See page 47 and Plate XI.

of the Temple and found only in the hands of the priestly Levites. Seven of these instruments — blown under Joshua's directions by seven priests after they had compassed the city seven times on the seventh day — in combination with the shouting of the Israelites, destroyed the wall of Jericho. It is a nice question, and one worth debating in the light of modern musical research, what actually happened on this celebrated occasion.

One of these natural trumpets — made from the horn of the koodoo — is shown in the illustration facing this page (Fig. 1). The other instrument (Fig. 2) is the *shophar*, a trumpet still used in the Hebrew ritual. In shape it closely resembles the ancient Roman *lituus* or augur's wand.[1] This artificial shape as well as the "crinkling" at the bend and at the bell is obtained by heating the natural horn.

As we have already stated, the Jewish Temple Songs formed the basis of the earliest Christian church music. It is, however, true that in various parts of the world these Hebrew melodies were continually altered and adapted to suit local requirements. Hence we find them today in many forms with rather wide differences. Some such process of change and adaptation may have been sanctioned by the first Christians. Nevertheless it is probable that these melodies were preserved in at least as pure a form in the Roman church as elsewhere. We may therefore accept the Catholic Plain-Song as a collection of melodies older than any other in existence. The best opinion is that it was not entirely Hebrew. Snatches of Greek or even Italian folk-music may have been incorporated here and there; and it is at least possible that some of these were purely secular. In other words, the church may have taken into its own service the best songs of the common people. This method was consciously adopted by Luther in the sixteenth century; and in our own day it has been a tower of strength to the Salvation Army.

[1] See page 71.

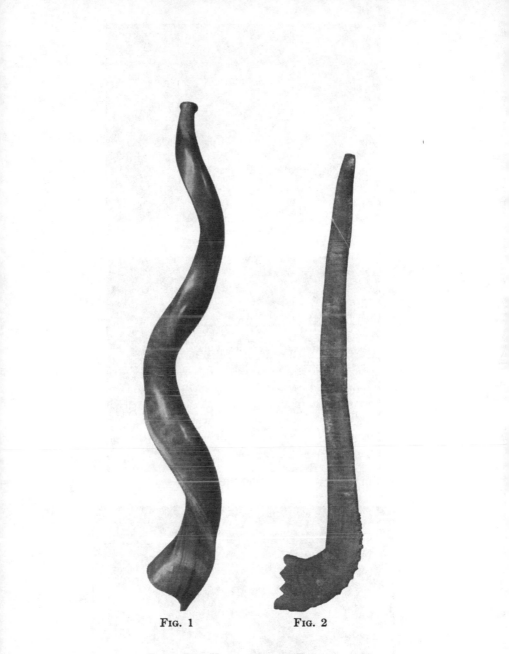

Fig. 1   Fig. 2

Plate IV.   Hebrew Ritual Trumpets

CHATOTSEROT

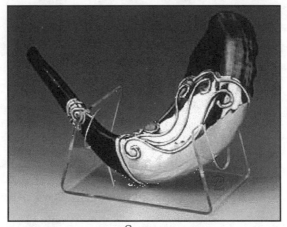

SHOFAR

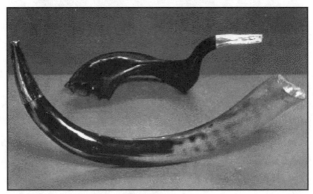

TWO SHOFAR

PLATE V.   BIBLICAL INSTRUMENTS

THE ARABIANS

Arabia appears to have been the musical high-road along which the ancient Egyptian culture passed to India and China. The Arabs themselves were excellent musicians. Furthermore their innate taste for mathematics gave them exactly the right habit-of-mind for discussing the physical bases of music. And their practice kept pace with their theory: for they regularly used an admirable system of unequal temperament in which the octave was split up into seventeen degrees. They fully understood the nature of the diatonic scale and the value of our modern intervals, the fourth, the fifth, and the octave, as well as the major and minor thirds and sixths. Finally they invented an elaborate system of "modes" in which to cast their melodic forms. As was to be expected, their notation was based on numbers.

Most of their instruments came from the Egyptians. Among these we may include the *lutes* and *tambourines* as well as the small pairs of gourds covered with parchment. These primitive *kettle-drums* are still played in Egypt and Arabia. The performer holds them against his chest and obtains an alternation of rhythm by striking one with the flat fingers of his hand and the other with a tough end of dried camel-skin. During the Crusades they found their way into Europe and were adopted as the earliest form of small kettle-drum. In England their Arabic name *Naqqareh* became naturalized into the current fourteenth century word *Nakers*.[1]

It has been claimed that Arabia was the birthplace of that very important musical family, the bowed stringed-instruments. This is not beyond debate. It is unquestioned that the British had, in the very earliest years of our era, a primitive plucked instrument — the *crwth* — which was originally

---

[1] They were afterwards superseded by the big Hungarian cavalry-drums. See page 184. The word *nakers* dropped out of use about 1400, but during the previous century it was common. For instance, "Ay þe nakeryn noyse, notes of pipes, Tymbres & tabornes tulket among" (*Alliterative Poem*, early fourteenth century) ; " þe princes þat war riche on raw Gert nakers strike and trumpes blaw" (From one of Laurence Minot's poems on events in the reign of Edward III. This poem describes the expedition to France and was written before 1352) ; "Pypes, trompes, nakers, and clariouns" (Chaucer, *Knight's Tale*, 1386).

no more than a square wooden frame with five or six strings. It is equally undoubted that, by the eleventh century, the principle of the bow had been applied to the crwth and that the instrument so played figures in early English as *coriun* and in mediæval Latin as *chorus*. Just the same thing happened in Arabia. There the bow was applied to certain *plucked* instruments of the lute kind but, as far as we know, not before the fourteenth century. Research may put back this date, though at present the evidence is in favor of Britain. The argument has been needlessly complicated by the fact that, on the earliest introduction of the *rebec* to Europe (eleventh or twelfth century), its pear-shaped body was recognized as a characteristically Arabian lute-form. It is, however, certain that this lute-form was not at that date bowed in Arabia. It was in Europe. The matter, as we have said, is not quite beyond dispute, but the most satisfactory view is to credit the British with the invention of the bow and with its application to the crwth. The principle, as we know, soon spread over Europe, and it was probably applied by Europeans to an imported Arabian lute.

THE INDIANS

As we have said, ancient India probably received a great part of her musical system from Arabia. For practical purposes she seems to have acclimatized it originally in its simplest form, that of a diatonic scale, probably of A-major. On this, however, she built up in later times a vast theoretical superstructure. The scale was divided into at least twenty-two degrees. Almost any whole-tone could be cut up into quarter-tones or even into eighths. In this way a single pair of octaves might be theoretically 48 notes apart.

It need scarcely be said that this minutely subdivided scale was never in daily use *as a whole*. Parts of it were and are employed by Indian singers; and it is on the selection of the particular notes to be used in the singing-scales that the main effect of Indian music depends. In other words, the Indians have elaborated the Arabian modes into a highly subtle and flexible national system of their own. These modes are known as *rāgs*. They give the singer an almost endless series of scale-lengths which vary between such extremes as the following:

These *rāgs* have been gradually evolved with a very delicate and unfettered sense of melodic expression. Their performance at the present day gives us our only opportunity of realizing what were the musical ideals of ancient pre-harmonic times. No one who has heard Indian song finely rendered can have failed to appreciate its infinite tonal subtlety. The singer has at his choice a nearly unlimited number of *rāgs*. And each of them gives him a vivid and almost personal method of musical expression.[1] We may add that in addition to this modal freedom the Indians have always admitted rhythmical elaborations and complexities of the utmost freedom. As in ancient Greece these were founded on and developed from the prosody and meter of the national poetry.

How many of these Hindostani *rāgs* or modes were in early use we have no means of knowing, but a modern scholar has noted sixty-three at the present day.[2] They can be classified as *pure*, *mixed*, and *altered* — that is to say, those in which the tetrachords[3] were similar, those in which they were dissimilar, and those possessing the alternative B-flat or F-sharp.

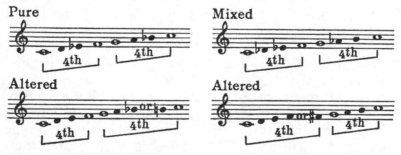

Pure   Mixed

Altered   Altered

[1] See page 58.
[2] Fox Strangways, *The Music of Hindostan*.
[3] See page 50 for explanation of these terms.

The most ancient form of Hindostani song appears to have been the Sāman Chant, a sort of plain-song with a compass of three notes, to which the Rigveda was sung. The evidence on this point is wholly traditional, for the business of music was at all times in the hands of a professional caste; musical practice was passed down orally from father to son, and no notation existed till within the last few centuries. It may be mentioned that the earliest non-legendary Hindu musician of whom we have any account is Jaydeva, who lived in the beginning of the twelfth century of our era. There are, however, over one hundred Sanskrit treatises on theoretical music. The earliest of those is to be found in the *Natyas'āstra*, a work on the drama written by Bharata possibly about 600 A.D. The list continues down to the eighteenth century, and the most important works are the *Sangītaratnākara* of Śārñgadeva (1210–47) and the *Rāgavibodha* of Somanātha (1609).

In the Hindu legends the *drum* is *the* characteristic instrument, associated with all the acts of life. And it remains so to this day. For in India it never becomes, as with us, merely an instrument of accent and climax. It is rather an instrument of "quantity" used as an accompaniment of song to articulate the meter of the poem and to add variety by means of cross-meter. Its two chief types are, and probably always were, the long-drum beaten at both ends either with the hands or with drum-sticks, and the small pairs of right- and left-hand drums, which had their origin in the skin-covered gourd. The other early instruments of the Hindu legend were a *bamboo flute* end-blown and reedless, the *vīnā*, to be presently described, *cymbals, gongs,* metal *horns* and *trumpets,* and various sorts of *pipes* of which very little is known accurately.

From what has been said it will be seen that all the Arabian instruments mentioned above passed over in one form or another to the Indians. The *naqqareh* in especial became standardized there and still remain, as *nāgarī,* the state-drums of the Rajahs. Peculiar to India are the soft-sounding flute, blown by insertion in the player's nostril, and the *vīnā.*

TABLA

MANJIRA

SITAR

TWO NAGADA

PLATE VI. INDIAN INSTRUMENTS

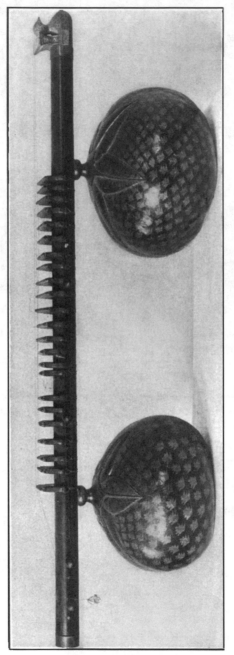

PLATE VII. INDIAN VINA

The latter was originally made of a hollow wooden tube supported on two empty gourds. At one end were the pegs (generally seven), and at the other a raised "claw." The wires ran from this claw or tailpiece to the pegs. But between these wires and the tube itself a number of little brass bridges were interposed. These varied from nineteen to twenty-three or even more. The wires touched only the bridge nearest the pegs; and therefore this bridge acted as a sort of "nut." The remaining bridges were used like the "frets" of the guitar or mandolin. In other words, the player's fingers depressed the wires on to the bridges at pleasure. The nearer the finger approached the "claw" the shorter became the vibrating length of the wire, and consequently the higher the pitch of the note produced. A metal plectrum was used for plucking the strings.

All these details can be clearly seen in the illustration (on the opposite page) of a vīṇā with twenty-three bridges — that is, with twenty-two "frets" and a "nut." The varied spacing of the bridges of course indicates a corresponding variety in the musical intervals. This spacing is not fixed. It can be arranged according to the "mode" in which the player intends to perform. In all the Indian stringed instruments the "setting" of the bridges or "frets" to any particular mode or modal-group is known as *thāṭ* — a word which is used in a secondary sense to classify the typical modes of the various "settings." The lowest note of the vīṇā was the *additional note* [1] of the Greek "complete system" as sung by men's voices:

$$\textbf{\raisebox{0pt}{𝄢}}\ \underline{\quad\quad}$$

It is only necessary to add that the vīṇā has developed into a true lute with a big resonating sound-box. The left-hand stopping apparatus, however, remains essentially as we have described it above. The vīṇā is played in India by professionals, both men and women. Among the former are some artists whose talents command the same respect as those of the best executive musicians in Europe and America.

[1] See page 51.

THE CHINESE

The Chinese themselves say that their music began in the reign of the Emperor Fu Hsi (B.C. 2852). On historical and ethnological grounds this is very probable. At any rate from about the time of the "Yellow Emperor" Huang Ti (B.C. 2697) their musical theory and practice began to assume something of its present form. On the theoretical side there emerged the system of lüs or "fundamental tones" which still forms the basis of Chinese music. This system, simple in itself, has always been associated in the Chinese mind with an apparently tangential series of analogies connecting it with the celestial bodies, the seasons, the elements (earth, fire, water, and so on), the hours of the day, the spirits of the departed, and the points of the compass. But it is to be noted that, with characteristic good taste, the Chinese have always held to an ascetic diatonic ideal in their serious music.

Of the very earliest compositions nothing is left. We know that in B.C. 2255 Shun composed the celebrated piece *Ta Shao* which enchanted the sage Confucius 1600 years later. This memory and a few fanciful theories as to the ultimate principles of music are all that now remain to us.

From very ancient times we learn that the Chinese based their music on a series of lüs. These were 12 tubes of different lengths from 9 inches downwards. They may be regarded as *standards of pitch*. Originally of bamboo, they were afterwards made of some more durable material such as copper, marble, or jade. Various doubtful fables exist to explain their invention; and they all received quaint names such as *Forest Bell, Great Frame, Southern Tube, Old Purified, Answering Bell, Luxuriant Vegetation,* and so on. In practice they gave the 12 chromatic semitones of an octave whose lowest note was somewhat nearer our modern d' than c'. However, it is always customary to explain the system of lüs by reference to our ordinary white-note scale of C-major. At various times four extra lüs were added above this series, and four below. Sometimes the one was in use, sometimes the other. The intervals of the lüs have all been accurately measured. None is in tune with our western scale, whether pure or tempered.

Up to the time of the Yin dynasty (B.C. 1300) only the first five lüs were in use. Numbers 6 and 7 were added during the Chou dynasty (B.C. 1100). But the actual scale in use for Ritual purposes was a C-major scale with a sharp fourth — (F-sharp instead of F-natural). This was in common employment till the rise of the Yüan dynasty founded by Kubla Khan. The intruding Mongols brought with them the F-natural, but afterwards compromised matters with their Chinese subjects by authorizing a scale having both F-sharp and F-natural. The great Ming dynasty in the fifteenth century excluded all half-tones and produced the pentatonic scale:

This is the characteristic Chinese scale *par excellence*. It has neither third nor leading-note. It is neither major nor minor. One may add that Chinese theorists also invented a chromatic series, producing it with curious Chinese ingenuity as a sort of twin-system in which two whole-tone scales were twisted together like the strands of a rope to form a complete whole.

But this remained a theory and no more. It was absolutely unused in both Ritual and Popular music. Finally, it must be mentioned that music in China is and always has been unison-music. The singing is never in harmony. At most the guitar-player is occasionally allowed to touch a fourth, a fifth, or an octave when accompanying the voice. In the Buddhist temples, however, while the singers all pronounce the same words in the same rhythm, each is permitted to use the key most convenient for his own voice. This bald statement naturally covers a somewhat amazing musical practice.

Ritual Music

Chinese music may be divided into *popular* and *religious*. Of the two the former is quite modern and outside the scope of the present study: the latter, which is practically identified with the Confucian Ritual, is ancient and well worth attention. The Chinese have always jealously guarded the purity and the antiquity of their Ritual Music. In its performance they employ certain curious old instruments in a strikingly national way. All the "rubrics" in connection with their religious services were based on strict tradition, and a special board of officers saw to their proper observance.

The ceremonies which we may group together under the heading "ritual" were devoted to the worship of Heaven and Earth at the winter and summer solstices respectively, and of Confucius, with other departed saints and prophets, during the spring and autumn. The emperor was the president of the "Society of the Learned" under whose authority these festivals were held. He was always present in person, or at any rate fictitiously supposed to be present.

The actual Confucian Ceremony at Beijing took place in the vast temple dedicated to the memory of the sage, and was conducted with great splendor and solemnity. The main features of musical interest are the slow "Guiding March" (*tao-yin*), which takes the emperor from and back to the second gate of the temple, and the "Hymn to Confucius."

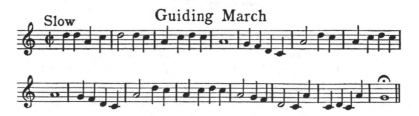

The Hymn was the only one sung while the emperor was actually at the shrine. It consists of six strophes, four of which are accompanied by slow ceremonial dancing. Each strophe is made up of thirty-two long tones in the "white-note" scale of A-minor : each begins with the four notes A—C—D—E, and ends on the tonic. It must be noted, however, that the actual lü in which the Hymn is sung varies according to the lunar calendar. It is a matter not of musical but of astronomical ordinance. To Chinese ears and voices this is not of great importance ; though one cannot help speculating what would be the feelings of an English Cathedral Choir if, when rehearsing for some special service, they received a preliminary order from the Astronomer Royal that all the music was to be transposed up a perfect fifth ! The ancient Hymn is too long to be given in full; but the third strophe, sung during the second offering of the sacrificial animals, will give an idea of its character.

Hymn to Confucius
(Third Strophe)

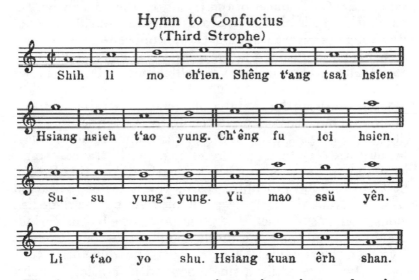

Shih   li   mo   ch'ien. Shêng t'ang tsai hsien

Hsiang hsieh t'ao yung. Ch'êng fu   loi   hsien.

Su - su   yung - yung. Yü   mao   ssŭ   yên.

Li   t'ao   yo   shu. Hsiang kuan êrh shan.

The instrumental accompaniment is ancient and curious. Each strophe is started by a single heavy metal bell, which is immediately answered by a heavy *stone-chime;* two instruments which always work in pairs. The tune itself is played by small gong-chimes combined with small stone-chimes, plucked stringed-instruments, flutes, ocarinas, clappers, and "shêng." At the end of the verse a drum is beaten thrice and answered by two other drums in the manner explained

below.   After the sixth strophe the "tiger-box" is beaten
thrice.   Then follows the second performance of the Guiding
March.   These musical details need "auralizing" to give
them life.   When heard under the conditions of a solemn
night-festival they are said to be extraordinarily impressive.

THE RITUAL INSTRUMENTS

Characteristic of China and perhaps worth western imitation are the L-shaped stone-chimes (*ch'ing*) which were in use
there long before our era.   They are made of a black calcareous
stone, are slung from a cross-bar in a frame, and are struck
with a hammer.   They vary in size from the single big slab
used to start the strophes of the Hymn to the 16-slab instrument with which all the tunes are accompanied.   A one-
note ch'ing is shown in the illustration opposite.

With these stone-chimes are associated large single bells
(*chung*) and groups of sixteen bell-chimes.   These chimes
whether of metal or of stone have been in use since B.C. 2697.
They are tuned to the twelve principal lüs with the addition
of four others either of the lower or the upper series.   The
bell-chime always sounds first and the stone-chime answers.
This business of "starting," "receiving," and "transmitting"
the sound is an orthodox theoretical part of the Ritual.
The Chinese mind probably regards the notes of the sacred
music not from the melodic point of view but as detached
sounds, each one of which is dealt out at leisure by the various
ritual instruments and so is dwelt upon by the worshippers as
a symbolical utterance.   This presents no difficulties to a
people who can identify a single note with a color, a point
of the compass, an element, a planet, and a state-official.

The *shêng* is the most interesting of Chinese instruments.
The body was originally a gourd, but nowadays it is a lac-
quered wooden imitation into which seventeen tubes of five
different lengths are fixed.   The upper parts of these tubes
are of bamboo, the lower of hard wood.   Inside the base of
each tube a small brass tongue or reed — the "vibrating
medium" — is inserted ; and just above each tongue a hole

PLATE VIII.   CHINESE STONE-CHIME

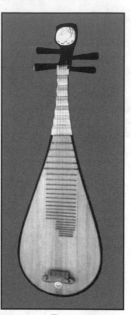

SHENG   ERHU   PIPA

RUAN   LIUQIN

PLATE IX.   CHINESE INSTRUMENTS

or ventage is so pierced in the tube that it must be "stopped" by the fingers before the tongue will sound. The arrangement of the tubes (see illustration) is more for prettiness than for any other reason, as the height of any tube does not necessarily indicate its pitch. In some cases this is modified by the boring of certain other holes which cut off part of the "speaking length" of the tube. Four of the tubes are mute and two are reduplicated. This leaves a scale of eleven notes.

The teapot-like shape of the instrument can be seen in the pictures of three shêng on the next page.

The great peculiarity of the shêng-player is that, unlike all other wind instrumentalists, he plays by sucking in his breath. The strain on lungs and bronchial tubes is said to be great and often to cause disease. In past days great pride was taken in the shêng, so much so that in marriage and funeral ceremonies where a player could not be procured a man was hired to carry a dummy in the procession. Two shên were always used for the Guiding March and six more for the Hymn. These latter, like all the instruments employed, were divided up into two sets of three and placed east and west in the great Hall of Ceremonies. The shêng is the oldest and almost the sole representative of the "free single reed" family of instruments. A single specimen imported into Russia gave the Danish professor Kratzenstein the idea of applying its principle to the organ. His investigations were submitted to the Academy at Petrograd, and their result is the modern harmonium and the accordion.

As with the shêng so with the *ch'in* and the *sê*, no European name is available. Both are ancient plucked string-instruments. The ch'in is essentially a long slightly curved board with seven silk strings which first pass over a bridge and then, after going through seven holes in the board, are secured to a row of nuts on the under-side. The usual method of tone production is by plucking, with all sorts of quick repetitions,

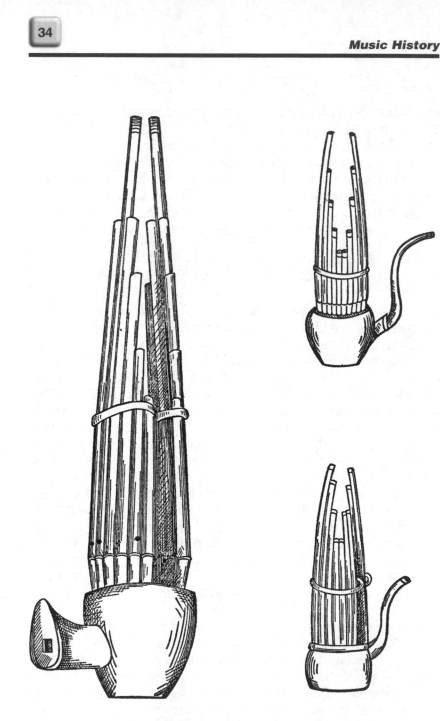

PLATE X.   CHINESE SHÈNG

pushings, and a sort of mandolin tremolo as well. Occasional fifths and octaves are permitted. The ch'in is a very ancient instrument and six have always taken part in the Confucian Ritual, playing the notes of the Hymn with embellishments suggested by the skill of the player. The present tuning is the same as that of the Highland bagpipe, a white-note scale from

The sê is a similar instrument, but it has the peculiarity that, like the ancient Greek *magadis*, it is always played in octaves. It has been made in many sizes and with a varying number of strings from fifty downwards. At the present day it has twenty-five. Four of these *sê* are used in the Ritual Music. Their scale is the ordinary Chinese "white-note pentatonic" from

The flute (*hsiao*), which has now been used in the Ritual Music for over 600 years, is a bamboo instrument scientifically much like our primitive keyless flute. It measures $1\frac{8}{10}$ ft. long, and is provided with an embouchure-hole, five finger-holes, and one thumb-hole. Six of these flutes take part in the sacred music. Their use for secular purposes was officially forbidden. The white-note scale of the *hsiao* runs from

The gong-chimes (*yün-lo*) used in the Guiding March consist of ten little gongs hung in a portable frame and tuned as accurately as possible to a Chinese diatonic scale c' to e''.

Besides the huge ceremonial drum which is placed in the eastern pagoda of the Hall to balance the principal bell in the western, three other smaller drums are used in the Ritual Music. One is a large drum (*ying-ku*) with a single head of parchment about 3 ft. in diameter. It is beaten three times after each verse of the Hymn and each beat is answered by two beats of a slightly smaller double-headed drum known as *tsu-ku*. A smaller drum still (*po-fu*), whose use is forbidden except for religious purposes, answers the two beats of the middle-sized drum with three strokes — one right-handed, one left-handed, and one double-handed.

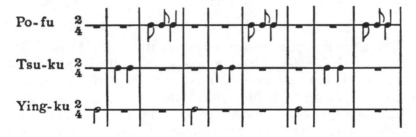

The clappers (*shou-pan*) are long tapered slabs of hard wood about 1½ ft. in length. Each of the six singers in the Hymn is provided with one ; and it is struck at each syllable with the palm of the hand.

The ocarina (*hsüan*) is a cone of baked clay or porcelain pierced with an embouchure-hole and five finger-holes, three in front and two behind. Two hsüan are used in the Confucian service and their scale is as follows :

The last ritual instrument is the *yü* or tiger-box, a conventional tiger of wood *couchant* on a wooden box 3½ ft. in length. Along the tiger's back is a series of 27 saw-like projections. The player strikes the tiger thrice on the head after each strophe of the Hymn, and then runs the stick rapidly three times down the spine.

Besides the above instruments the Chinese possess various others whose use is purely secular. Some are ancient, some modern. We have no space to detail their mechanism ; but for convenience of reference we subjoin the principal types with their Chinese names.

Chinese Name	Description
Ti-tzŭ	An 8-hole transverse flute in common use. One of its holes is used as an embouchure; six are finger-holes, of which one is covered (as in some of the mediæval European instruments) with a thin membrane. Scale, the same as the ritual flute (*hsiao*) but transposed a fourth higher.
Hao-t'ung	A long big-bore instrument of wood, copper-covered, something like our ancient cornett,[1] but with a sliding tube. Used to give one deep solemn note at funerals.
So na	A wooden pipe with a copper bell and a coarse double-reed. It has seven finger-holes in front and a thumb-hole behind. Scale, f' to g''. Used at funerals and weddings.
La-pa	A long military trumpet of copper, giving the fundamental, fifth, octave, and tenth.
P'ai-hsiao	Pan's-pipes of sixteen bamboo tubes, generally mounted on a frame and arranged to sound the twelve principal lüs and the four lüs of the lower series.
Yang-ch'in	"Foreign dulcimer," a trapezoidal box with sixteen sets of wires which are struck by two bamboo rods.
P'i-p'a	"Balloon guitar" (probably ancient). Four strings tuned to c'—f'—g'—c''.
San-hsien	Three-stringed guitar tuned c'—f'—c'', or c'—d'—a'.
Yüeh-ch'in	"Moon guitar" with four strings tuned in unison-pairs to a perfect fifth.
Hu-ch'in	Four-stringed fiddle with a cylindrical body. The silk strings are tuned *alternately* to the same note thus, c'—g'—c'—g'. The fiddler therefore has to pass the hair of his bow *between* the strings before playing.
Ērh-hsien	The ordinary two-stringed Chinese fiddle made of a bit of bamboo and half a cocoanut-shell. Always tuned to a perfect fifth.
Chung	Bells of all sorts from fifty tons downwards. In the manufacture of these the Chinese are unsurpassed by any other nation.
Fêng-ling	Wind-bells, apparently originated in China.
Po	Little cymbals, came to them from Egypt through India. Often used curiously in the theatre. After any special speech to which attention is to be drawn, the player strikes them ten to fifteen times in quick succession.
Ku	Drums of all sizes came from Arabia via central Asia. One kind (the *t'ao-ku*) is played by being twirled when slung in a frame against two balls hung from the barrel.
Pang-ku	An effective little flat wooden drum, hollow at the bottom and skin-covered at the top. Diameter, six inches. It stands on a wooden tripod and is beaten with two hard light sticks as an accompaniment or interpolation to theatrical songs and speeches.

[1] See pages 187–9.

CHAPTER 3

The Greeks

THE earliest European civilization was that of the Greeks. This glorious people stood forth in the sunlight at a time when the tide of oriental civilization seemed to be turning towards the west. Nor did they stand forth on their mountain-tops merely as a bulwark against this flood. They were something more. They were a new fountain-head from which was to spring a new stream, the purer and more majestic river of western thought and western art.

In music they received much from Asiatic and Egyptian sources, but they received it with discrimination. They paid it no homage, but rather surveyed it from the higher ground of a calm and balanced judgment, selecting what was most simple and most subtle for their needs and rejecting the rest. With them music was no longer to be the concern only of priests and warriors or, worse still, an affair of slaves and lights and flagons. They recognized these secondary functions, it is true; but for the first time in history they set up the art before the face of the world as the worthy and honorable pursuit of free men and free minds. By dwelling on this fact we shall better understand the words "the glory that was Greece."

A good deal is known of their music. We can judge of their instruments from innumerable sculptures, paintings, coins, and mosaics, as well as from a few broken specimens still existing; of their tone-system from treatises ancient, mediæval, and modern; of their notation from some four or five fragments — all that has been discovered hitherto. Finally there is a mass of lyric and dramatic poetry written for or to music. The rhythm of this poetry is, of course, the rhythm to which it was sung; and its authors would undoubtedly have regarded its artistic existence *without music* as inconceivable.

We have therefore a certain width of base on which to found our judgment. It must, however, be allowed that there is still considerable difference of opinion, not so much on the theory of the Greeks as on their actual musical procedure. For instance, we can quote with some confidence Aristoxenus's theoretical division of the scale; but when we come down to the simplest physical facts — such as were probably familiar to the street-urchins of 400 B.C. — we begin to face difficulties.

How did the kithara-player fasten his strings? To the little knobs which are represented as running along the cross-bar? How then did he tune them when fastened? By means of the big knob or peg-head at the end of the cross-bar? It seems musically impossible, for that would tighten all the strings at once. What notes did he actually play when accompanying a solo or a chorus? How could he possibly make himself heard at a big outdoor festival? He must have done so; yet we know that, if the wind shifts a point or two at a pageant-performance, even a brass-band becomes inaudible. On what was the crowded audience intent during the progress of a musical performance? Mainly on the poetry? In a purely instrumental performance was it only listening to the tune? Or to the subtly woven rhythms? Or to the harmonics which the player was producing? "Execution" in our sense of the word could scarcely have existed on a seven-stringed lyre or a four-holed pipe. In a vocal performance was the audience enjoying the perfect intonation of intervals smaller than our modern semitone? How was the *aulos* sounded? With a reed like our oboe? Or a beak-mouthpiece like our flageolet? Or neither? What was the use of the "swellings" at the upper end of the pipe?

Most of these questions can only be answered by guesses learned or unlearned. But, in making them, we have to keep one point before our minds. We are separated from the Greek culture not merely by two dozen centuries but by a vast and gradually acquired musical system of our own. And this acts as a distorting-glass between us and them. We cannot accurately express their thought in our notation or recapture their musical sounds on our instruments. The very intervals of their scale — except perhaps the octave, the fifth, and the fourth — have disappeared. It is difficult enough to grasp their attitude towards music: it is doubly difficult to explain it, when grasped, in modern symbols.

GREEK MUSICAL INSTRUMENTS

All the instruments of the earlier Egyptian and Asiatic civilizations were known to the Greeks but, as we have hinted, they were by no means all considered worthy of national adoption. In particular, the Greek mind hated mere size and unnecessary complexity. The big Egyptian harp, for instance, found no favor with them.[1] They asked for essential simplicity and they found it in the *lyre*. This was their national instrument. It was the first to be recognized in their musical competitions; it formed the basis of their tone-system and, to some extent, of their musical nomenclature.

Somewhat later — about the beginning of the sixth century B.C. — a wood-wind instrument, the *aulos*, was admitted to the competitions; but it never attained or even challenged the supremacy of the lyre. Indeed, two hundred years later we find Plato rejecting its use in his ideal city-state.

The last instrument to be included in the competitions was the straight metal trumpet (*salpinx*). This was introduced from Egypt by Phœnician sailors and merchants. The Greeks, however, always looked on it as a strictly military instrument. They associated it with the imposing

---

[1] The *magadis*, a plucked instrument of Asiatic origin, had at least two complete octaves of strings and therefore could be used for the performance of melody in octaves. It was never officially recognized in Greece, and its octave style of performance was always referred to somewhat contemptuously as *magadizing*.

voice and presence of the official herald. Having a lively sense of its limitations, they regarded its inclusion in a *musical* festival much as we regard the inclusion of a weight-lifting contest at an athletic-sports meeting. The man with the biggest physique won the prize.

In addition to these instruments the Greeks acknowledged the *monochord* (*i.e.* single-string) and the *syrinx* (or Pan's pipes). The former was a simple stretched string that passed over a movable bridge: it was employed only for purposes of scientific experiment. The latter was then what it is now, a series of seven little stopped reeds, all differing in length and bound together in order of pitch. The player directed his breath against the sharp edge of the upper (open) end of the pipe. From each pipe he could thus produce only one note. The reader can test this method of tone-production with the cover of a fountain-pen, provided he stops up with his finger the little hole bored in its side. The Greek syrinx [1] was used by shepherds and herdsmen and placed by sculptors in the hands of Pan and the Satyrs.

Neither of these instruments nor the Greek trumpet need detain us further. The aulos and the lyre, however, are important and call for a somewhat detailed description.

The aulos was a wooden pipe originally bored with three or four finger-holes. It was played by one performer either singly or, more often, in couples like the double-pipes of the Egyptians. In the latter case the two pipes are generally, but not always, represented as of different lengths. In spite of the fact that the aulos and the double-aulos figure in many vase-paintings and sculptures, its method of tone production is still doubtful. The finding of certain actual specimens has given us a fair idea as to how the scales were produced. But these two questions are, of course, quite separate.

For long it was supposed that the instrument was blown just like our modern oboe or bassoon by means of a double-reed in the player's lips. This, however, was no more than

[1] The word syrinx had the secondary meaning of the "speaker" or vent-hole used to get the upper octave in a reed-pipe instrument.

an assumption. There is not a shadow of doubt that the later Græco-Roman civilization had a double-reed pipe scarcely distinguishable from a seventeenth century keyless oboe. But it is inconceivable that, if the aulos was played thus, some few of its many representations should not have shown the double-reed clearly. The testimony, however, is all the other way.

Riemann gave his opinion that the aulos was really "a beak-flute exactly like the diapason pipes of the organ." In support of this he adduces the very poor argument that the earliest organ pipes — undoubtedly *flue-pipes* — were called "auloi." But we know from actual specimens in existence that the aulos was *not* a beak-pipe. Riemann also cites an incident which happened at the Pythian games of 448 B.C.[1] An auletes called Midas of Agrigentum, while playing there, broke his mouthpiece. However, he continued playing. The point is that, if the aulos has been a reed-instrument, he would have been compelled to stop; his sound-producing medium would have been gone. But this ignores the fact that in many ages (including the present) reed-instruments have been blown by reeds not in the player's mouth. This is known in every regiment of Highlanders.

Two further points must be noted. In the first place, Riemann's theory presupposes that in the pipe of the aulos a sharp bevel was cut, against which the player could direct his breath. This bevel, which is most conscientiously marked by mediæval artists in their drawings of the recorder and fipple-flute families, simply does not exist in the paintings of Greek instruments. Also we have to notice that the Greeks often depict one, two, or three curious swellings[2] or enlargements at the mouthpiece end of the instrument. What were they for? The suggestion has been abandoned that they altered the pitch; that they were, in fact, used for purposes of transposition. Anyway this would not solve the difficulty now under discussion, as it presumes a sound-

---

[1] The authority is the well-known gloss on Pindar (*Pyth.* XII.).
[2] Called respectively the *hŏlmos* and the *huphŏlmĭŏn* (ὁλμος, ὑφόλμιον).

producing medium still nearer the lips. The mechanical difficulties, too, practically put it out of court.

It is at least as probable that the sound-producing medium was placed inside the "swelling" we have just mentioned. It actually was there in some members of the mediæval shawm-bombard family, the ancestors of our bassoons and oboes.[1] If that were so, in the case of the aulos the reed might be either a single-reed (as in the bagpipe drones), a double-reed (as in the bagpipe-chanter), or a rectangular free-single-reed (as in the Chinese shêng). The third suggestion is no more than a guess, but guesses have their value where all is so uncertain. An instrument of this kind would be much more effective than a flue-pipe in outdoor competitions and theatrical performances. It would also offer a quite natural explanation of Midas's not very wonderful feat. The "swelling" broke off and left the reed exposed, but lying flat in its aperture at right-angles to the line of the pipe. He continued to play by putting the upper half-inch of the pipe itself into his mouth. All he needed was to breathe quickly when blowing and to keep his lips tightly closed round the broken top. This makeshift would be quite impracticable to a player suddenly confronted with an ordinary double-reed exposed through an accident to the outer chamber.

We have already mentioned the Egyptians' double-pipe and our ignorance of their musical method. The same difficulties occur in the case of the Greek *diauloi*. What was the object of using two pipes equal or unequal in length? Of the three explanations offered on page 17 we may certainly put aside that of "octave playing." Were they used as "a drone bass and a melody above" or in "alternation"?

Of these the former appears at first sight the more likely. Apart, however, from the fact that no Greek theorist mentions this style of playing, the point is exactly one of those in which our own musical culture distorts our view of ancient practice. The explanation seems plausible to us, because it is just what we should attempt to do if these ancient pipes

[1] See pages 184–6.

were put into our hands today. But we know that this type of expression only dawned on Europe as an artistic possibility somewhere about the eighth century of our era.

The other explanation "alternate playing" is indeed more probable. An instrument with only a few holes was much restricted in the way of compass. By using another pipe of different length the player would obtain access to another segment of the "complete scale." It is difficult to see any possible advantage — beyond increased loudness — in pipes of equal length unless their finger-holes were differently spaced.

We may perhaps be allowed to offer a fourth suggestion, which, though grotesque from our own musical standpoint, is by no means improbable from that of the ancient Greeks. The player may have used the smaller pipe as a persistent *upper* pedal. In this case he would select the right note — probably the tonic or "middle" as the Greeks called it — and then sustain it above the melody, which he played on the longer pipe. In fact, he would be doing exactly what we hear done in certain parts of the Orthodox Greek Church music today. There is a bas-relief in the British Museum which supports this view. It contains, among other figures, that of a double-pipe player. The hands are evidently studied with the greatest care. That which is playing the larger pipe is modelled as if in the act of fingering the holes; while the other is "clutched down" over the holes of the smaller pipe. One is forced to admit that, if Greek sculptors meant Greek marble to speak, this special marble is saying "tune in the bass and held-note in the treble." [1]

The method of playing the double-pipe can be observed in the Cypriote statue, which has been reproduced as the frontispiece to this volume. The bewigged figure shows clear traces of Egyptian influence and belongs to the period 650–550 B.C. Though the stone-carving is rough and the

---

[1] For "instrumental conversation" see Westphal, Aristoxenus in Plutarch (page 16, line 1). Problem XIX has an allusion to simultaneous playing of two instrumental parts, the lower of which had the melody, the upper the accompaniment. (Willis, *The Aristoxenian Theory of Rhythm*, pages 19 and 20.)

inspiration as un-Hellenic as it well can be, it presents all the recognized peculiarities of the Greek player with a startling distinctness.

The twin-pipes in this case are obviously hollow reeds; though that tells us nothing as to the method of tone-production. At the top of the pipes are the "swellings" of which we have spoken, and the pipes themselves are held in the player's mouth by means of the usual bandage or *phorbeia*.[1] The object of this bandage is not clearly known. The common explanation is that it was used to compress the cheeks. If this were so, it must mean that the cheeks were *puffed out against it.* And one may prove this for one-self with a folded handkerchief and any small tube such as an empty (tobacco) pipe. All modern wind-instruments are played in precisely the opposite way — with compressed cheeks. A second explanation makes the bandage merely *a support* for the pipes. This is more likely, though no representation ever shows a player fingering with both hands on one pipe while the other dangles from the phorbeia. However, without pressing that point, one can understand the utility of such an arrangement.

The puzzle is to know exactly what was on the hidden side of the bandage. If there were two reeds, the bandage would prevent the player passing from one to the other. If there was only one, then both pipes must have sounded all the time the player was blowing.

Before leaving this general discussion of the aulos we may sum up in a few sentences, without antiquarian detail, what is known to us of its history from the descriptions of Greek writers and from specimens in our museums. The aulos originally had a cylindrical bore and 3 or 4 holes. These were increased so that in the fifth century the three then-existing modes (the *Dorian, Phrygian,* and *Lydian*) could be played on one pair of pipes. In our language this means a compass of a tenth. The compass was further extended, in some instruments at any rate, by an apparatus of sliding metal bands bored with holes that could be aligned at

[1] Φορβεία. Lat. *capistrum.*

pleasure with the holes in the pipe itself. This reads well enough on paper. But after handling such an instrument one is faced by the problem as to what advantage two aligned holes could possibly have over one hole. The finger had to do the stopping in either case. The turning of the bands was merely an awkward and uncertain substitute for the finger. But it is just possible that the bands were used to throw some one or other of the holes out of action during a complete piece or a portion of a piece. The band that was bored with the B-flat and B-natural holes was an undoubted melodic convenience. The player could use either note at discretion. And if he needed both he probably had plenty of time in which to make the change. He "saw it coming"; just as the orchestral players saw the flats and sharps coming in the early symphonic days.

Some pipes were cross-blown like our modern flutes, but with a reed inserted in the pipe. Originally the aulos is said to have had a double-reed. This is a philological guess founded on the word [1] used to describe the reed. Later it may have been a single-reed. The method of blowing, whether direct or indirect, is quite uncertain, as explained above. The longest compass of a pair of auloi was from

This, of course, presumes the employment of harmonics. There is no difficulty on this point as the bore was narrow and there was a "speaker."

Of the simple pipes ancient writers enumerate:

1. The *Monaulos* (single-pipe).
2. The *Plagiaulos* (sideways-pipe).
3. The *Syrinx Monokalamos* (single-reed syrinx).

Of double-pipes:

1. The *Partheneioi* (maidens').
2. The *Paidikoi* (boys').

---

[1] Ζεῦγος (zeugŏs), a couple.

3. The *Kitharisterioi* (to accompany the lyre).
4. The *Teleioi* or *Puthikoi* (perfect or Pythian).
5. The *Huperteleioi* or *Andreioi* (lower than the perfect, *i.e.* bass, or mens').

Of these the double pipes were the great professional instruments used at the Delphic contests.

The Greeks had two types of lyre. The first — already described on page 21 — they probably acquired from Asia Minor or Egypt. They regarded it as a small, handy, and somewhat informal instrument, more particularly fitted for the accompaniment of drinking songs and love-ditties by amateurs. It went by the name of "the tortoise" (*chelus*), but the word *lura* was used impartially for both kinds of instrument.

The illustration (see page 48a, Plate XI) shows Apollo and Artemis standing one on either side of an altar. The chelus in the god's hands has the two chief features of the Semitic type of lyre — the body formed from the empty tortoise shell, and the upward-curving horns joined by the cross-bar near the top. The seven strings are stretched from the tailpiece to seven pegs (very clearly depicted) lying in their line of tension.[1] A plectrum is being used to pluck the strings. As in many Greek vases, statues, and bas-reliefs, the left-hand is so portrayed as to lead almost irresistibly to the conclusion that it is being used either to pluck or to "stop" the strings. But this is only a convention. In the present case, it is obvious that the hand would be needed to support the lyre. The vase from which this photograph is taken is Athenian, of about the date 500 B.C. The awkward foreshortening in the figures is of course due to the curve in the pottery.

The second type of lyre was known as *kithara* or *phorminx*. This, their full-dress national instrument, they may be said to have invented and perfected themselves. Used only by professional players, it varied strikingly in size. It began with only four strings and ended with eighteen. The main

[1] See page 39.

features, however, were always the same.   First there was
a broad wooden sound-chest. The "block" was not built
into the body of the instrument (as in our modern violins)
but was glued or pinned to the upper half of the sound-
chest at its lower end.[1] In this respect, it resembled the
bridges of the mediæval lutes and was therefore, like them,
incapable of supporting any great tension.   From the sound-
chest on either side sprang two pillars in the ample and
exquisite curve so often portrayed in Greek sculpture. Between these pillars at about two-thirds of the total height of
the instrument ran the cross-bar, and it was from this cross-
bar to the bridge that the gut strings were vertically strung.

A row of knobs is almost always depicted on the cross-bar.
These were the attachments for the strings, but there is no
painting sufficiently detailed to show whether each knob
was used in this type of lyre as a tuning peg or not. One
would think that this must have been the case. On the
other hand, if the knobs actually were turn-pegs they must
have passed through the cross-bar in line with the strings.
From the standpoint of our modern practice this would
mean a position of maximum inefficiency: all string-pegs
are made nowadays to lie at right-angles with the line of
tension. The ends of the cross-bar outside the pillars are
often drawn with ornamental heads which, to our modern
eyes, look suspiciously like thumb-and-finger pieces; but
the musical difficulties in regarding them as such are overwhelming.

The vase selected to illustrate this type of lyre is the same
as the former in place, date, and subject — Attic; about
500 B.C.; Apollo and Artemis, this time performing a
libation at an altar. The god crowned with his chaplet
stands ready to receive the libation and holds his kithara
in his left-hand. All the details described above can be
clearly seen in this illustration; and the very different shape
of the instrument may be compared profitably with that on
the other vase.

----

[1] It was originally nothing but a strip of reed and always retained the
name dŏnax or kalamŏs (δόναξ, κάλαμος ὑπολύριος).

PLATE XI.   APOLLO AND ARTEMIS BEFORE AN ALTAR

PLATE XII. APOLLO AND ARTEMIS PERFORMING A LIBATION

In its fully developed form the kithara was a big, imposing instrument. Its weight necessitated the use of a cord or ribbon. The player held the instrument firmly against his chest and twanged the strings one at a time with a plectrum which he held in his right-hand. It is generally stated that the fingers of the left-hand also were used for plucking the strings. This is, however, doubtful.[1] Apart from the musical differences implied and from the fact that chord-playing was unknown, the left-hand must have been required mainly to support and steady the instrument. It is *possible* that the fingers of the left-hand were occasionally used for lightly stopping the strings so as to produce one or more harmonics. But we have no certain knowledge on this point.

The original four strings of the kithara were probably tuned to some such notes as

At any rate it is fairly certain that they were not tuned to four *consecutive* notes of a scale. In the course of time the number of strings was continually increased, and the chief milestone on this road bears the name of Terpander. He first gave the instrument its classical complement of seven. It is scarcely possible to mention *any* number as the standard-stringing of the kithara. Four, seven, and ten are usually specified, but the instrument eventually had eighteen. However, as the Greek diatonic tone-system was intimately bound up with the kithara-tuning, and as this tone-system could be fully exhibited in a fifteen-stringed kithara, that number may be taken as typical of the developed instrument.

[1] The passage in Cicero (Verr. 2, 1, 20) about the citharista of Aspendos has no meaning unless we presume that players did not normally employ their left-hands for plucking the strings.

THE GREEK TONE-SYSTEM

In attempting a brief description of the Greek tone-system one must, of course, use modern musical expressions and notation. The reader should, however, be warned that in most cases these do not represent the actual sounds which were played or heard by the Greeks. In diatonic scales they are quite near enough to serve as guides to the intelligence. But if we wished for complete accuracy we should have to invent a series of symbols each representing a note of a certain definite number of vibrations.

The Greek tone-system was based on the *tetrachord,* a word which simply means *four strings.* To a Greek the essential parts of the tetrachord were the top and bottom strings. These made a perfect fourth with each other and were known by the suggestive name of *standing notes.*[1]

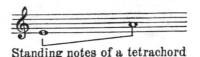

Standing notes of a tetrachord

The notes between were known as *movable-notes.*[2] We shall see later that, while the standing-notes never varied, there was considerable freedom of choice in the movable-notes.

The Greeks always held fast to this root-idea of tetrachords and, when their artistic development compelled them to lengthen their scale beyond a fourth, they did it by placing two or more tetrachords on top of each other. They had two main ways of doing this. Either they dovetailed the tetrachords thus:

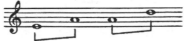

or they laid them out in a straight line thus:

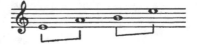

[1] Φθόγγοι ἑστῶτες (phthŏngoi hĕstŏtĕs).
[2] Φθόγγοι κινούμενοι (phthŏngoi kinoumĕnoi).

The first was known as the method of the *join;* [1] the second as that of the *break.* [2] Both methods could be and were used at different points in a long scale.

The space between the outside-notes of any tetrachord could be filled up in three different ways, and this gave the Greeks their three kinds of scale, the *diatonic*, the *chromatic*, and the *enharmonic*.

THE DIATONIC KIND

From our modern standpoint this is the most important kind of scale. It was the basis of the mediæval tone-systems and, in a modified form, of our own tempered scales, diatonic and chromatic. In this kind the Greeks filled up the space between the standing-notes of the tetrachord with what we may roughly call the white-notes of the pianoforte keyboard:

Then, by means of the two methods described above, they piled tetrachord on tetrachord and eventually attained what was known as the *complete system* of four tetrachords with an additional note at the bottom.

This gives the theoretical formation of the diatonic scale, but it will be noticed that the second and fourth are built up by the *joining* method. Theoretically the note E occurs twice in each octave. In practice, however, only one string was necessary to play this note wherever it occurred. Therefore by cutting out the two redundant E's from the theoretical

---

[1] Συναφή (sunaphē).
[2] Διάζευξις (diazeuxis).

seventeen-note scale we get the *complete system* a to a″ playable on the fifteen-stringed kithara.[1]

There are technical Greek names for the four tetrachords as well as for all the 15 strings of the kithara. These names were taken either from the finger-technique of the instrument, or from the position occupied by each note in its tetrachord, or in the *complete system*. Only one need be given here, the word *mĕsē* (middle string) which was naturally applied to the note

and practically stands for our word *tonic*. It may be added that, owing to the position in which the kithara was held, the lowest-sounding note was called *uppermost*[2] and the highest-sounding *lowest*.[3]

THE GREEK MODES

It must not be supposed that the Greeks invented the above elaborate diatonic scale *and then* made it the basis of their instrumental music. Indeed they approached the matter from exactly the opposite standpoint and viewed the *complete system* only as a summary of their diatonic theory rarely required in practice. They began with the creation of the octave-scales called *modes*.[4] It could not escape their attention that, in filling up the space between the outside-strings of the tetrachord diatonically, they had to use one half-tone and two whole-tones. The half-tone had therefore to fall in one of three places with regard to the bottom string — either first, second, or third.

---

[1] Σύστημα τέλειον (sustēma tĕleion).
[2] Ὑπάτη (hupatē).
[3] Νήτη (nētē).
[4] Τρόποι (trŏpoi) or Ἁρμονίαι (harmŏniai).

If it fell first they called it a *Dorian* tetrachord:

If it fell second they called it a *Phrygian* tetrachord:

If it fell third they called it a *Lydian* tetrachord:

(The half-tone in each case is marked with a slur.)

They then proceeded to form a complete scale from each of these tetrachords; and their method in each case was to place two tetrachords of the same kind, one on top of the other with a *break* between. These were the three oldest Greek modes — the *Dorian*, the *Phrygian*, and the *Lydian*. As an example, the *Dorian* mode was built up thus:

Lower Dorian tetrachord   Upper Dorian tetrachord

Break

No other arrangement of the half-tone was of course possible in a tetrachord. Nevertheless, at a somewhat later date, they formed a fourth mode of a slightly different and less regular character. Of this mode — the *Mixolydian* — no wholly satisfactory explanation has yet been given, though the Greek theorists tried in various ways to justify its existence. We need not concern ourselves with these discussions, but it is worth noting that, without the use of a harmonic, none of these modes can have been playable in its entirety on the old seven-stringed kithara of Terpander.[1]

The above four modes may be viewed for the sake of con-

---

[1] The *names* for these modes were formed by using the suffix *isti;* thus, δωριστί (dōristi), λυδιστί (ludisti), and so on.

venience simply as octave-lengths of notes cut out of the *complete system.* The effect of this method of tetrachord-building was to leave the Greeks with four diatonic scales whose lowest notes were

And these four scales differed among themselves originally both in pitch and in their arrangement of tones and half-tones. Furthermore each mode may be looked upon as divided into two portions — a perfect fourth at the bottom and a perfect fifth at the top.

In addition to the four modes already described there were four *subordinate modes.* They were formed, not by transposing the three original modes so that their arrangements of tones and half-tones remained the same, but by rearranging the positions of the two portions mentioned above. The upper portion (the fifth) was theoretically placed below the lower portion (the fourth). These three subordinate modes were attached one to each of the three original modes and were distinguished by the prefix *hypo*, that is *underneath.*[1] It is obvious that there could not be any hypo-mode to the *Mixolydian* as its scale would be merely e to d', a reduplication of the *Dorian.* In fact, as there are only seven diatonic notes to the scale, there could be only seven modes differing in their internal organization. See next page.

It must not be imagined that the Greeks viewed these seven octave-lengths as we should. To us the lowest note of any scale is the tonic: to them it was merely an accident if this happened and, as a fact, it only occurred in one case.

---

[1] The reverse process also was practised, and the modes so formed were known as hyper-modes. More important are the five scales which they called *high* or *stretched* (σύντονο-, suntŏnŏ-) scales. These were obtained by transposing five of the modes up and so forming scales of f'—f", retaining the original arrangement of tones and semitones by means of flats. The most used of these five were the high-Lydian, high-Phrygian, and high-Dorian. They even had three other *low* transpositions (e'—e") formed similarly with sharps. Neither of these two series was much favored by the theorists, but those we have named were in actual use. The preliminary "setting" of any particular scale on the kithara cannot have been a matter of any great difficulty.

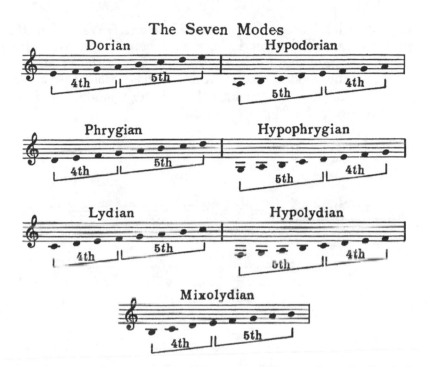

The Seven Modes

Their method was quite different. They referred all their modes to their *complete system*, which had

as the *mĕsē* or tonic. All their modes therefore had that note as tonic; and this had the further effect of giving all their diatonic music the general character of our white-note scale of A-minor.

Now we have good authority for believing that the tonic was somehow or other always forced to the front or dwelt upon in Greek music. In that sense it gave the pitch to the mode. The pitch indeed was not an absolute-pitch but a tonic-pitch. Therefore, in order to arrive at the pitch of the various modes, we have only to set them down where the order of their intervals will fit accurately into that of the *complete system*. We shall then see where the tonic falls in each case. This is easily done. We write the *mĕsē* as a semibreve, and the reader can be left to notice *where* that note occurs in each mode and so ascertain the pitch of the mode. It will be observed that the lowest series of sung notes is actually the "highest mode," and the highest series the "lowest mode."

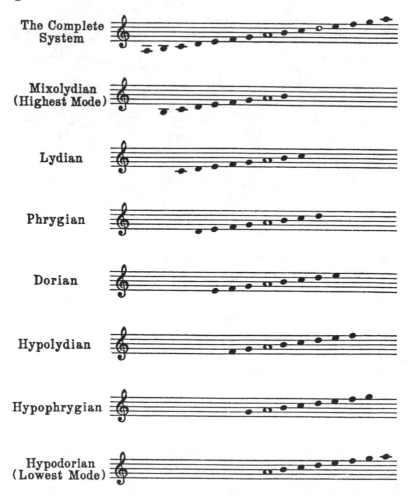

This pitch-relationship of the modes with each other is of importance when we come to consider the ethical value which the Greeks attached to their scales. The gradual sinking of pitch from *Mixolydian* to *Hypodorian* can also be conveniently shown if we make all the modes arbitrarily begin from the same lowest note. The order of intervals in each mode remains unaltered.

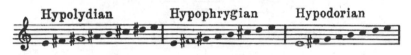

Finally we must mention that at a comparatively late period (B.C.) two other modes — the *Æolian* and the *Iastian* — were introduced. These, however, were only repetitions of the *Phrygian* and *Dorian* modes at a higher pitch, and as such they preserved the same arrangement of tones and semitones.

THE CHROMATIC KIND

All the above modes could be and were transposed in our ordinary sense of the word. Theoretically the diatonic system of the Greeks was, like the diatonic mechanism of the modern harp, capable of being flattened or sharpened by one semitone throughout. But it is very evident that any wide use of this extension was practically forbidden by their simplicity of taste, and also perhaps by the mechanical inefficiency of their instruments. However, it is quite certain that they made occasional use of chromatic notes for purposes of melody and modulation. Their attempts to do this were handicapped, as we have said, in two different ways, one practical and one theoretical. In the first place the kithara was not a chromatic instrument. For instance, if a B-flat was wanted, the B-natural string had to be *set* to that note. Again, the Greeks were never able to rise beyond their root-idea of the tetrachord. They regarded it as the immovable foundation of their system. They could not

face the conception of a musical system unfettered by this
constant restriction. The perfect fourth was, so to speak,
the skeleton. Break that, and the whole body fell to pieces.
Only the notes between the outside-strings of the tetrachord
could safely be tampered with. Thus, in attempting the
impossible task of combining the chromatic with the diatonic, they produced tetrachords of this pattern:

and scales of this sort:

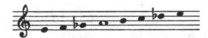

The production of these extraordinary scales was not the
result of mental timidity on their part but rather of what
seems to us a barren and misapplied inquisitiveness. There
is, however, no doubt that, in ancient Greece, the chromatic
system was a living artistic reality. Looked at from our
standpoint its scales are the most puzzling feature in Greek
art. They have neither the directness of the diatonic scales
nor the subtlety of the enharmonic.

The only satisfactory clue to their artistic value is to be
found in the more exotic types of the Indian *rāgs* mentioned
on page 25. These resume for us in the modern world the
practice of the ancient. They give us the magic key with
which to re-open the door of *melodic variety* so long closed
and barred to us by our *harmonic* preoccupations. The wonderful color which these scale-lengths give to the music
sung in them must be heard to be appreciated. A *rāg* of
this sort

in which the D-flat is the predominant note and the E-natural
is used only as a light passing-note makes our modern major
and minor modes sound almost colorless. Indeed, the uni-

form greyish tint of the two modern modes would be unbearable without the added color of harmony. The two go
hand in hand. The simplicity and sameness of the former
call for the variety of the latter. And the call is recip-
rocal. For modern harmony could not exist in the presence of complete modal, and especially *chromatic* modal,
liberty. Even the minor mode is accompanied only with
difficulty. In fact, the two things, chromatic modal freedom
of melody and harmonic accompaniment, are incompatible,
except in so far as the former is based on the latter — a
procedure impossible in ancient times and always doubtful
artistically.

THE ENHARMONIC KIND

The enharmonic system of the Greeks, though much
further removed from our artistic practice, is more definitely
organized and more easily understood than their chromatic
system. Its essence was, that each of the seven original
notes of the scale was followed by two supplementary notes.
These made with each other smaller intervals than any now
used on our modern keyed instruments. Such intervals
as the $\frac{1}{4}$-tone, the $\frac{1}{3}$-tone, and the $\frac{3}{8}$-tone were in common
use. They were perfectly comprehensible to the Greeks,
and would be so to us but for our lack of practice in listening
to them.

We cannot of course set such intervals down in our modern
musical notation. If we wished to do so we should have to
invent new symbols. We might, for instance, call the two
enharmonic notes which lie between f and g "f_1 and f_2".
The scale would then run f—f_1—f_2—g. The Greeks called
each of these groups of enharmonic notes *the puknŏn*, that
is to say, *the close-together*.

Now, though it is plain that there were twenty-two notes
available in each octave (inclusive of the top octave-note),
it must be understood that no octave-scale so constructed
was ever employed. The octave-scale, whether diatonic,
chromatic, or enharmonic, always consisted of eight notes
and no more. Therefore the employment of the *enharmonic*

kind in any tetrachord simply resulted in a group of *close-together* notes followed by a wide gap. It may be added that, though this kind of scale has practically disappeared in modern European music, it had great importance to the Greeks both theoretically and in the art of singing.[1]

Before leaving this subject the reader must be reminded that our knowledge of the Greek tone-system comes chiefly from the Greek theorists. Scarcely any music and almost no instruments have survived. Very little can be gathered from either of these sources. We have therefore to rely on the philosophers, most of whom were absorbed in explaining a musical system whose historical growth they had no means of investigating. We are thus liable to take a view of Greek musical practice which is far too bookish and, as it were, stereotyped. For instance, the pentatonic (or Chinese) scale can be attained philosophically by a cycle of ascending fifths thus, C–G–d–a–e'. But the Argive goat-herd who first made a pentatonic *Pan's pipe* knew nothing of this. He attained it by means of a bunch of river-reeds, a knife, and a measurement on his knuckle-joint.

Similarly with the more complex matter of the scale-systems. All the elaborate Greek treatises on this subject are nothing but desperately clever justifications of an already existing music. It is much more than probable that the diatonic modes were merely reed-pipe scales. Their variety and irregularity were due to original inequalities in the spacing of the holes.[2] In some cases these irregularities may actually have been *botanical*. And it is quite certain that in all three kinds of music — the diatonic, the chromatic, and the enharmonic — both singers and listeners disliked the artificial, philosophically correct music, and preferred an approximation to the old, subtle reed-pipe scales.

[1] For full details see Torr's *On the Interpretation of Greek Music*. The complete list of scales is given on page 18.
[2] See pages 8 and 9.

NOTATION

It is quite plain that any music which expressed itself in terms of the system just described must have had two characteristics, simplicity and subtlety. The limits were narrow, but the possible variations within those limits manifold. For this system the Greeks had a notation which would be complex and unpractical for our purposes, but yet was quite sufficient as a record and a reminder for their musicians. Very little music in this notation has survived, and we are therefore not always clear as to the origin and meaning of the signs which it employs. There are, however, certain well-understood facts.

The Greeks had two notations, one for singers, the other for instrumentalists. The latter was the more ancient. In the song-notation they employed an early form of their own Ionic alphabet: in the kithara-notation they used the first fourteen letters of a still older alphabet which was chiefly Argive. In both cases they represented musical sounds mainly by means of letters.

Now we use letters to express the sounds of our scale; but our letter-sequence a—b—o d c f—g has been called into existence solely to symbolize a seven-note scale. The Greek letter-sequences were designed to symbolize a two-octave-scale. In other words, where we attach consecutive letters to consecutive notes the Greeks attached them to consecutive octaves. For example, their consecutive letters D and E (Δ and E) were attached to the two octave-notes

and their consecutive letters M and N (these two capitals are the same in Greek) to

At first sight this may appear strange and awkward. But we must not overlook the fact that, besides this *notation,* the Greeks had a complete *general nomenclature*[1] for their *complete-scale-system.* This they always employed, just as modern musicians use the words "dominant," "subdominant" and so on. The Greek nomenclature, however, had the great advantage of a distinguishing term for every note in a fifteen-degree scale.

The notation described above can scarcely be called either simple or direct. It seems to have been designed for an already existing scale of two octaves. Greek singers, however, had a constant leaning towards the *enharmonic* in practice. The philosophers indeed objected to it on high grounds of morals and mathematics, but apparently without much effect. Consequently we find that, from the very first, the notation was specially directed towards this end.

The modifications which were introduced were mainly distortions, amputations, and displacements of the alphabet. In other words, a letter was taken; a piece was chopped out of it here and there; it was turned upside-down or right-about-face; and so it could be made to do duty two or three times. The result was a curiously jumbled system of notation which can never have been in use for purposes of quick sight-reading. Nevertheless, as we have already said, it probably served its end as a record and a reminder.

It is unnecessary to detail this complicated system here, but, to illustrate the Greek method of "displacing" a letter, we shall give a single example. The note

was, as we have mentioned, represented by the letter E. If the composer wished to write the *close-together* series of notes c''—$c\frac{1}{4}''$—c''-sharp, he employed this E three times, the first written normally, the second lying on its back, the third turned completely round, E ɯ Ǝ.

---

[1] Already mentioned on page 52. The actual Greek names have not been given, as they would only cause confusion in the reader's mind.

We may add that this enharmonic notation was so dear to the Greeks that they actually substituted it for the diatonic wherever possible. For instance, they preferred to write the four diatonic notes b—c'—d'—e' as b—b-sharp—d'—e'. Nor was this a mere convention. Everything goes to show that the Greek singer loved nothing better than a flattening of his diatonic *standing-notes*.

THE "MORAL VALUE" OF GREEK MUSIC

We now come to a very difficult matter in connection with Greek music. Strange as it may seem the Greek writers were all agreed that music had a serious *moral value*. They did not say vaguely, as we do, that music was a beautiful thing and had an ennobling effect on the human mind. On the contrary they said that, according to the way in which it was written, it was actually good or bad; that it had a definitely good or bad influence on the development of personal character; and that therefore the musical means employed was a matter of the most lively concern to educationists and statesmen.

This moral character, which they regarded as inherent in the art, was called the *ēthŏs* of music; its value to society in general was known as its *ethical* value. Philosophers differed in explaining why there was an *ēthŏs* in music; they differed also in discussing its practical application: but none of them ever dreamed of disputing its existence.

Now it is quite plain that all modern Europeans and Americans would agree that "good music" — that is, music which is the honest expression of life viewed through the personality of a great composer — is better than "bad music" which is just the opposite. But this was not the Greek attitude at all. Their constant subject of discussion was whether this mode or that mode was better suited for inculcating this or that form of moral excellence. In modern musical terms the ancient question might be put somewhat as follows: — We wish to represent a brave man battling against adversity. Now, which is the better key for enforcing the idea of courage, E-minor or C-major?

Let us examine this point. If we put our prepossessions on one side and admit that the question calls for a serious answer, we must agree that, whichever key we favor, our preference can only be supported on one of two grounds. The keys named differ only (1) in pitch, (2) in the arrangement of their tones and semitones. We must therefore justify our choice in one of two ways.

(1) We may say that a melody in the chosen key will, on the whole, lie at a higher (or lower) level of pitch than a melody in the rejected key; and that the difference of pitch makes the chosen key the better medium for the expression of manly courage.

(2) On the other hand we may say that pitch has nothing to do with courage or any other form of virtue; that the essential difference between the two keys is the difference between major and minor; that the varying moral values of scales are to be found solely in the varying arrangements of tones and semitones; and that therefore, whatever the pitch, we select the major (or minor) as the proper medium for exhibiting the idea of personal bravery.

Nobody denies that the Greeks must have answered the question in one of these two ways. The only doubt has been "in which?" Here our views were for long distorted by the fact that Greek musical practice was always examined through the lens of the middle-ages. It was known that mediæval priests and musicians consciously used *their* modes to express differences of feeling by means of differences in the order of the intervals. Scholars therefore jumped to the conclusion that the Greek mind worked in the same way. In fact, as recently as thirty years ago, it was held that the Greeks would have answered the question in the second (or mediæval) way. This was the orthodox German view.

However, since then, an English scholar has clearly shown that — whatever the mediæval prejudices in the matter may have been — every known reference to the question in Greek literature proves that the Greek himself would have made his answer depend solely on the pitch of the modes at his disposal. This is not the place to present the evidence or to go behind the whole difficult problem and ask *why* the Greeks associated a different *ēthŏs* with a difference of pitch. It is enough to say that the evidence for this association is historically cumulative and overwhelming.

But we must repeat here that the "pitch" was a "tonic-pitch" and not a "scale-pitch" in our sense of the words. It prescribed automatically the chief melodic feature of the song and its vertical place in the performance. Its effect on the arrangement of tones and semitones was only incidental and was so regarded by the Greeks.

It need scarcely be said that the whole of Greek music is intimately bound up with the *sung poetry* which was popular in Greece from the remotest times. These chanted poems are mentioned even by Homer. Their history branches out along two lines — the dramatic and the non-dramatic. But both forms were just as clearly *musical* as *poetic*.

On the dramatic side they began with the singing of the *dithyramb*, a loud choral-song chanted to a circular dance in honor of the wine-god Dionysus. Starting from that, the leading-singer improvised a narrative, and the improvisation in time developed into *tragedy*. Similarly, from the *phallic* processions of the countryside and the coarse jestings of the vine-dressers as they carted their barrels into the villages, came *comedy*.

Both these developments were accompanied by a remarkable extension and specialization of the lyrical elements to meet the demands of the Greek theatre. The most important of these lyrical forms were the *parŏdŏs*, or choral song of entry into the theatre; the various *stasima*, or "songs between the acts" as we should say; the *kŏmmoi*, or lyrical dialogues between the chorus and the actors; the *mŏnŏdiai*, or solo-songs; and (in comedy) the *parabasis*, an elaborate half-way-house go-as-you-please mixture of poetry and patter.[1]

On the non-dramatic side these lyrics were either *hymns* to the gods or purely secular songs — *thanksgivings* for harvest, *pæans* of victory, *marriage-chants*, and *funeral-dirges*. An

---

[1] The patter was known as "the choker" (πνῖγος).

intermediate sort, half-secular and half-sacred, was the rustic lament for *Linos*.

From these primitive types sprang the vast body of lyric poetry which, in the three centuries that lie between Terpander and Bacchylides, was the chief gift of Greece to mankind. These lyrical forms of course never remained stationary. They were altered and adapted by each generation to suit its own ideals. But among them we can distinguish as clearly-marked types, the *scŏlia*, or light social lyrics sung in turn by the guests at table; the *dithyrambs* which we have already mentioned; the *iambs*, originally sung in praise of the earth-mother Demeter, but afterwards modified into a brightly supercilious and familiar style of poem; the *prosodia* and *parthenia*, which were processionals for men or girls; and finally the *nŏmoi* and the *elegies*.

The word *nŏmŏs* [1] originally meant simply a "tune." But from very early times it had become partially restricted almost to our sense of *plain-song*. It was used specifically of the liturgical chant played and sung by a single priest. Now, the Greeks always divided these chants rigidly into *kitharedic nomoi* (tunes with kithara-accompaniment) and *auletic nomoi* (tunes with aulos-accompaniment). And it is suggestive that their own half-legendary history of these tunes points in both cases to an Asiatic origin for their music.

The *kitharedic nomoi* were traditionally believed to have been formulated somewhere about the end of the eighth century B.C. by Terpander, the poet-musician who was supposed to have increased the strings of the lyre to seven. He was said to have come from Lesbos, an island intimately associated with the Orphic legends, and the natural stepping-stone between Asia Minor and Greece.

The traditions connected with the *auletic nomoi* are still more curious, as the Greeks themselves were unanimous in ascribing their introduction to a musician called Olympus who came from Phrygia. They were quite conscious of the

---

[1] Νόμος. On the secular side the nomos developed into a brilliant species of lyric in which, from the fifth century onwards, the musical portion seems to have somewhat overshadowed the poetical.

fact that these pipe-tunes were a semi-foreign form of art. Both the *iamb* and the *elegy* — the latter a highly personal composition of sentiments and moods indispensable at social gatherings — were accompanied by the aulos. That was the regular practice. And it is interesting to link up our knowledge of the actual westward-spread of music with the fact that the Greek word for elegy (*ĕlĕgos*)[1] is Asiatic and originally meant nothing but a *reed-pipe*.

It is plain that the stories of the casting up of Orpheus's head on the shores of Lesbos and of the invention of the *nomoi* are separate statements of the one fact that Greek music came from Asia. The poetical minds of the earliest Greeks threw round this fact the soft veil of the Orphic legend, while the more prosaic minds of a later age called for the names of two definite founder-musicians.

As the foregoing study has occupied considerable space, we shall now merely add a few words on the Greek music itself. So far very little has been found, and *that* has been a disappointment to professional musicians. But to those who had studied the probabilities at all closely it came as something natural and inevitable under the conditions.

We had always known that Greek music and poetry were essentially *one*. The rhythm of the former was founded on that of the latter. The poetical *foot* corresponded to our modern *bar*. But we must not press that analogy too closely. Our minds have had hammered into them for centuries the heavy thump of regularly recurring beats and, however complex and subtle the rhythmical structure we may build up on that basis, the solid bed-rock remains underneath.

The Greeks had no such prepossessions. All they asked of music was that it should reinforce by means of pitch the highly elastic prosody of their solos and choruses. These were the conditions; and under them probably nothing that we should consider "fine melody" can ever have been written. The diggers may one day bring to light some simple religious plain-song which we can accept as we accept the

---

[1] Ελεγος.

Chinese Hymn given above. But the greater part of the Greek music — especially the theatrical music — must have consisted merely of a long, vague, tortuous, disjointed sort of *arioso*.

To us it would be unendurable. We should be exasperated by a constant rhythmical change and variety which we were unable to appreciate. There would be a continual and irritating switch-over of the music from two-beat to three-beat, four-beat, and even five-beat rhythms. And most of these rhythms would keep on intruding as "single bars" (to use our modern expression) into the other's playground. The direct musical expression which we should be always looking for was never intended or conceived by the Greek artist. He was a "musician" only in the sense that he served the muses. He probably called himself simply *poïētēs* — the *wright* or *maker*. Let us remember that the things which he wrought made Athens the most illustrious city in the world.

CHAPTER 4

Rome and The Dark Ages

THE reader must have noticed that, in the last two chapters, the fourth method of study mentioned on page 10 has been ignored: we have given practically no composers' names. In the case of the Egyptian and Asiatic nations none is known: in the case of Greece the names of the composers are mainly those of the poets. It is true that we know of a few men who — unlike Pindar, Alcæus, and Sappho — were composers.[1] These men actually composed tunes, some of which received names like our own hymn tunes, and were as well known to the ancient world as "God save the King" is to the modern. Many of these tunes — or *nŏmoi* as they called them — remained, so to speak, in the repertoire. A poet, even a great poet like Pindar, would write poetry "to the air of" so and so, just as Burns did.

We can see here how simple and impersonal these melodies must have been. The poet probably asked only for a meter that suited his purpose and a mode whose tonic-pitch corresponded with the *ēthŏs* of his literary idea. This is quite in the Greek character, and we must not confuse it by a false modern analogy. If Tennyson had produced a poem and had directed that it should be sung to the music of Schubert's *Erl-king,* we should consider it almost an outrage; because Schubert's music is fiercely directed solely to one end — the illustration of Goethe's poem. But nothing of this sort existed in the ancient world. Even the force of Christianity took many years to assert itself in this direction. Some few hymns and chants, it is true, were grouped round

---

[1] Phrynis, Clonas, Archilochus, Thaletes, Tisias surnamed *Setter-up-of-choruses* (Stesichorus), Timotheus, Kinesias, Philoxenus, and a few more.

the names of celebrated churchmen of the first 500 years
A.D., but even in these cases it is certain that they did not
actually write the music. Indeed, it is not till the second
millennium of our era that we can fairly name a composer, in
our modern sense of the word.

In Athens of 450 B.C. no such thing was possible. And
here we must remember two points. In the first place,
though the Greeks *did* very well in art, they *talked* very much
better. We can never be quite sure how far the nimble
minds of their philosophers were "hanging in the air" like
Socrates in his basket. In painting we *know* that, while
their philosophers were giving perfect expression to the
fundamental laws of perspective, their greatest artists were
painting pictures which, in this respect, would disgrace a
beginner at a modern art-school.[1] This reflection gives us
some qualms when reading the elaborate ancient treatises
on music.

The second point to be remembered is that Athens of 450
B.C. is by no means the whole of the ancient world. Athens
herself early passed into political slavery; and the streaming
baton-torch which she had lit was handed on to other
runners. Of these the strongest were Rome, who took over
the Athenian art as a lawful prize of war, and Alexandria,
who was at once the political vassal of Rome and the in-
tellectual descendant of Athens and ancient Egypt. These
two cities, and especially the former, are the two natural-
bridges by which we pass from the ancient world to the
modern, from paganism to Christianity.

Rome probably *invented* little. From the southern and
eastern nations, whom she could conquer only physically,
she *commandeered* both art and literature. The spoils she
turned over at home with a heavy hand and then — to her
credit be it said — passed on a portion to her more barbarous
subjects in the north and west. Thus she was for about a
thousand years the live-center that received and distributed
the current of civilization.

[1] See the account of Agatharcus, Democritus, and Anaxagoras in Vitruvius (lib. VII).

From the Greeks she took their tone-system and, as far as we know, made no advance on it, practical or speculative. The Greek and (neo-) Egyptian instruments she borrowed in the same way, always showing a true Latin leaning towards the showy and imposing.

The *kithara* in its most complex form was in common use in the early days of the Empire. It was probably on this instrument that Nero "fiddled," if he did so, "while Rome burned." More interesting than this, we learn from a sculpture of Hadrian's time (117–138 A.D.) of the existence in Rome of a true plucked *lute* or *pandoura,* — an instrument with a long neck, two or three strings, and a vaulted resonating body.

All the Greek wood-wind reappeared in the Rome of the Cæsars under the generic names of *tibiæ* and *fistulæ.* At this time they may have received some technical improvements. Indeed, we find Horace, in his favorite character of the old-fashioned Roman gentleman, complaining bitterly of the improved key-mechanism of the aulos.[1]

But Horace's complaint was not likely to effect much in the noisy days of Augustus. Indeed, the tendency was all the other way. The Roman brass in especial was elaborated and standardized as befitted a great military power. Their three chief instruments were the straight infantry-trumpet, which they called *tuba;* the *lituus,*[2] a J-shaped instrument something like the ritual-trumpet of the Hebrews in appearance and corresponding roughly to our primitive hunting horn;[3] and the *buccina,*[4] a long brass-bass which, through the mediæval buysine, was the ancestor of the sackbut and the trombone. The buccina is vividly por-

---

[1] In the *Ars Poetica.* The improvements are the metal bands described on page 45. Horace's complaint, still heard by each new generation of musicians, was not new even in his far-off day. Centuries before his time Aristophanes was regretting the loss of the simple vocal style of his youth (*Clouds,* 961 *et seq.*) Doubtless the first cave-man that ever made a reed squeak was told by the local cognoscenti that he was spoiling everything with his modern improvements.

[2] So called from its resemblance to the augur's official wand.

[3] The word *cornu* (= horn) was in common use. *Tuba* seems to have been used somewhat generically, as we use the word "brass."

[4] Connected with *bucca,* the cheek. The German word for trombone, posaune (Old German buzaun or busaun), is derived from buccina.

trayed in the sculptures on Trajan's column, and three actual specimens have been found. They are imposing instruments some twelve feet long and curved almost into a complete circle. An ornamental "stay" kept the tube rigid. As with all the Roman brass the player used a cup-mouthpiece. He put his left-hand close up to this mouthpiece and the right on the "stay" just as a modern trombone-player does. The whole instrument passed round his body on the right and the bell pointed over his left shoulder. In fact, the instrument was carried exactly like a modern circular-bass or helicon. Its fundamental note and harmonic series was G. A specimen of the lituus, dug up at Cervetri in 1827 and now preserved in the Vatican, was found to be pitched in g, one octave above the buccina.

The only two points which we need mention in connection with this family of brass-instruments are (1) that they certainly did not play in harmony except by accident; and (2) that, owing to the invariable way in which sculptors and painters represent the brass-players *with puffed cheeks*, there is some doubt as to whether they could have produced as many harmonics as our modern players would from the same length of tube. This practically means that each man would have at his command not more than three or four brassy notes. We need scarcely add that the Romans had all sorts of percussion instruments for military and other purposes. In particular they used the *tambourine*, or "light drum" as they called it, and a "bronze drum," which was a military improvement on the small gourd-drums of the Arabians.

But the instrument which interests us most as bridging the gulf between the pagan and Christian worlds is none of these. It is the *organ*. Until quite recently its existence and employment in Imperial Rome were matters rather of faith than of knowledge. It was a case of "believing what you know can't be true." The evidence on behalf of its existence could be put into three sentences. Philo of Alexandria, writing about 200 B.C., credits Ctesibius the engineer with the invention of an instrument which he calls *water-aulos* (hydraulus). Then Vitruvius, who wrote on

architecture in Augustus's day, describes the same instrument. Finally, we have an account of a similar but
perhaps more primitive instrument written shortly after
by Hero of Alexandria.

This was the evidence: and, though it was plain enough,
until about 100 years ago musicians refused to believe that
the organ could have had any definite existence in those
days except as a rare scientific toy. But since then a great
many facts have been brought to light by the antiquarians,
and the best opinion now is that the instrument had already
undergone considerable development and must have been
fairly well known in the first centuries of our era.

If the reader will turn back to page 41 he will see a description of the *syrinx* (or Pan's pipes), an instrument which
almost alone has remained unaltered to our own day. It
was in the attempt to play the syrinx mechanically that the
ancients invented the organ. The idea was to get rid of the
direct blowing by the mouth and substitute an air-reservoir
such as that of the bagpipe. This was comparatively easy:
it only involved one discovery in acoustics, and we know
that this discovery had been made long before. Normally,
in making a syrinx, each reed was cut off just underneath
the "knot"; and this "knot" acted as a "stopper" for the
pipe. The player blew hard against the open rim at the
other end. But it had long ago been found out that the
reed could be cut off some distance below the knot; a vertical
hole bored through the knot itself; and a "lip" cut in the
reed just above the knot. If this were done and the two
edges of the lip carefully turned inwards, one had a musical
instrument ready to hand. The part of the reed below the
knot could be tapered and fitted to a hole in a wooden box (the
wind-chest). Of course, if a row of reeds were so fitted,
the resulting instrument — a primitive *organ* — needed
blowing. And this, in all probability, was done originally
by a bellows, whose supply tube was in the player's mouth.
The arrangement for cutting off or supplying wind from
the box to any particular pipe was a matter of carpentering.
But we must credit the Roman or Alexandrine carpenter

with having solved this problem by means of the only two inventions that have ever been considered feasible by organ-builders: first, the small "sliders" which the organist could pull out as one pulls out the sliding lid of a box; and, second, the "balanced keys" which have been used ever since to actuate the "sliders."

The first demand for improvement lay in the direction of getting rid of the blower and substituting some mechanical arrangement which would supply air and keep it under pressure. This problem was solved in other places besides Alexandria and Rome; but the Græco-Roman solution, as described by Hero and Vitruvius, remained a mystery till the finding of an actual pottery model of a hydraulus. This big antiquarian haul was made in 1885 on the ruins of ancient Carthage, and the model is signed by a potter called Possessoris who lived about 100 A.D. From it an English scholar has constructed a half-scale copy of the original instrument.

The main points of the hydraulus may be summed up as follows. The water — in two containers, one on each side of the instrument — was driven up by a pair of air-pumps till its weight could act just like the lead-weights in a modern organ; that is to say, for exerting a continuous pressure on the wind-chest. There were three rows of pipes and a single manual. Balanced keys were provided. The depression of any one of these pulled a slider and so admitted the wind into the pipe. When the finger was taken off the key a gut-and-horn spring pulled the slider back and cut off the wind from its particular pipe. The height of the whole instrument was about 10 ft. and the width $4\frac{1}{2}$ ft. It corresponds in every detail with the written descriptions which had so puzzled musicians. Ctesibius cannot be said to have "invented" this instrument, though as a practical engineer he may have improved the hydraulic apparatus. The scale of the instrument from which the Possessoris model was made probably consisted of the following nineteen notes:

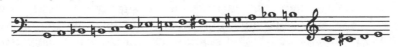

We must not suppose that all Roman organs were blown by this mechanism. Water is the one deadly foe of all musical instruments, and we know as a fact that the Romans possessed purely pneumatic organs. We must, therefore, not exaggerate the importance of this special musical detail simply because two classical accounts of it happen to have survived.

The organ, as we have described it above, remained in constant use during the early centuries of our era. Many such instruments were made in a small portable form for theatres, arenas, and places of public amusement. In fact, it was this very association with the coarse license of the circus that hindered its adoption by the early Christians. No great development, however, was possible till it had struggled into Christian recognition. It is indeed a strange reflection, that the instrument whose deep tones have most often been called on to praise the name of Christ may have been heard by the first Christian martyrs in their dying agonies.

In the eastern empire we hear of the continued existence of the organ only rarely — but quite often enough to convince us that it had not disappeared. In the fourth century we have a description of one that belonged to Julian the Apostate; in the eighth we are told of another that was sent to Pepin as a present from Constantine Copronymus and there are some few other allusions, literary and pictorial. But we have to turn to the west for the true development of the organ in the dark ages. In those days a monk or bishop who wished to stand well with society could not take up essay-writing or social-welfare: what he *could* do was to lay hands on all the available timber, metal, and leather, and start organ-building.

We hear of the results in such organs as those of St. Dunstan at Malmesbury, of St. Alphege at Winchester (tenth century), and later (in the twelfth and thirteenth centuries) at Cologne, Erfurt, and Halberstadt. The accounts almost frighten us. In those times, before the invention of the lever and long before the English invention of horizontal reservoirs and feeders, a man was wanted to every bellows or at least to every two bellows. The Win-chester organ had four hundred bronze pipes and two manuals of twenty keys. Each of these keys — fit in size for the hand of a giant — was lettered with its note-name and, when struck, gave the wind to ten huge diapasons tuned in octaves or perhaps in octaves and fifths.

What a picture of dark relentless mediævalism this mere catalogue summons up for us! Surely the world can never have known such a strange holiday as Winchester knew every time its organ was played one thousand years ago. We can imagine the organists — all men picked for their physique — darting madly to and fro at the keyboard, screwed up to the excitement of smiting the right key at the right moment, and attacking it with all the force of their bodies gathered into their thickly gloved hands; the toiling, moiling crowd of blowers behind, treading away for dear life to keep the wind-chest full; the frightful din of the heavy timber mechanism, creaking and groaning like a four-decker in a heavy sea; above all the diabolical blare as the wind suddenly poured into the huge metal diapasons and let loose their appalling series of empty stony fifths; while in the church the congregation cowered with a terrible astonishment, wondering perhaps whether, before the next Christmas or Easter came round, the Danes would not have put their long swords over the organ-men and claimed the instrument for their own. We have nothing like this in modern life; nothing to put the fear of the devil into us. Perhaps it is as well.

Not very much is known as to how these archaic monsters developed into the fine church-organs of the early seventeenth century. But a few words may be spared for a summary of the later history of the organ. As we have seen, balanced keys had always existed, especially in the smaller sorts of organ. However, their use was by no means general. The probability is that they were re-discovered in the middle ages. The very first keyboard of which we know anything was that at Magdeburg. It dated from the eleventh century and had sixteen keys, each three inches broad.

Mosaic portraying an organ and horn players (138-177).

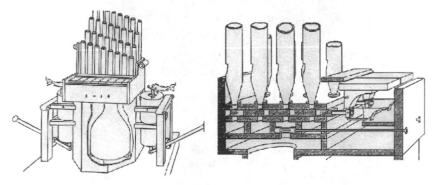

Het orgel

Plate XIII. Organ

PLATE XIV.   HURDY-GURDY

The nearer landmarks in the history of the organ are the invention of pedals and the re-introduction of reed-pipes, both in the fifteenth century; the treatment of the softest manual as an "echo organ" and its supersession by the "swell" first used in an organ built by the Jordans for St. Magnus's, London Bridge, in 1712; the invention of "composition pedals" controlling chosen groups of stops, due to Bishop, the English organ-builder, about 1850; the invention of the penumatic action and the introduction of Willis's many improvements in the nineteenth century; and finally the twentieth century alterations which practically supply electricity everywhere except to the organist's fingers.

The only other instruments which made their appearance during the first millennium of our era were the *organistrum* and the *fiddle;* the one, the ancestor of nothing but the despised *hurdy-gurdy;* the other, the forerunner of the *violin family.*

The organistrum was a *mechanically bowed* instrument. It consisted of three heavy gut strings laid parallel to each other in the arc of a circle over a sound-chest. A wheel of wood, faced perhaps with leather and well rosined, pressed against all three strings at the same time and was turned by a crank. A series of movable wooden bridges was used to "stop" the strings simultaneously, and these bridges were controlled by means of wooden pin-heads, which projected outside the instrument. The organistrum was portable and could be placed on the knees of two seated players. As will be explained later, its obvious use was to play the octaves and fifths which made up the style called *organum*.[1]

We cannot give an illustration of an organistrum, for no specimens of that instrument are in existence. But, as a makeshift and in order to show the type to which it belonged, we shall include a picture of its descendant, the hurdy-gurdy. This instrument is still common in Europe. It is heard fairly frequently even in the streets of London. Observe its chief points in the illustration (p.76b). The wheel is

[1] The description is by Odo of Cluny; there are also illustrations of this instrument extant.

inside the wheel-box (decorated with a double white line). On the extreme left is the crank-handle that turns the wheel. The low outside strings that pass through the wheel-box are the drones. Only one of these is in its place in the photograph — that on the side nearest the observer. These strings — usually tuned in fifths — are of course not "stopped." The upper string running from the tailpiece (on the left) to the peg-head (on the right) is the one on which the tune is played. Often there are two of these. The little wooden "stopping" pins — seen in a row at the top of the illustration — were originally *pulled* against the string, but are now *pushed* by means of wooden finger-pieces on either side. The musical effect of the instrument is — within its limits — by no means uninteresting. We may add that the present photograph is taken from a nineteenth century hurdy-gurdy of French make.[1]

We have already said something with regard to the first introduction, possibly from Arabia, of the fiddle family — the true bowed ancestors of our modern strings. As we shall take this point up later, we need only mention that the earliest form of the instrument was a pear-shaped *rebec*, *gigue*, or *lyra* (as it is still called in Greece). This instrument, sometimes called *ribibe*, *rubybe*, and *rubible*, can have had only a very small compass, but it enjoyed great popularity down to and even after Chaucer's day.

> In twenty manere koude he trippe and daunce
> And pleyen songes on a small rubible.[2]

Its successors were the oval *Troubadour fidel* and the big *Minnesinger fiddle*, themselves the ancestors of the great *viol* group which held in the fifteenth, sixteenth, and seventeenth centuries the same position as that held in our own day by the *violin* family.

After this rapid glance at the instruments of the dark ages,

---

[1] The hurdy-gurdy has been favored with many different names. In France it is known as *Vielle à manivelle*, *Symphonie-* or *Chyfonie-à-roue;* in Germany as *Leier* combined with some such word as *Dreh*, *Bauern*, *Rad*, *Bettler*, or *Deutsche;* in Italy as *Lira Tedesca*, *Lira Rustica*, or *Lira Pagana*. Schubert's "*Leiermann*" is of course supposed to be playing this instrument.
[2] *Miller's Tale* (1386).

we must turn our eyes back to observe what little can be clearly seen of the earliest Christian chanting. It is there that we find the spring from which flowed the broad stream of mediæval church music. In the first century of its existence the Christian church had to oppose and overcome, not only the decaying worship of the heathen gods, but also the much more dangerous cult of the eastern god Mithras. In doing this its adherents undoubtedly allied themselves with the Jews, and drew on Jewish art for something, at any rate, of their services. This was only natural. But, besides the Jewish Temple Songs, they incorporated and transformed many heathen tunes, both Greek and Latin. How far this process went we have no means of judging: nor do we know whether these melodies were mainly religious or secular.

From the earliest times the *Sanctus, Magnificat, Benedictus,* and *Nunc Dimittis* were sung to the simple melodies whose origin we have suggested above. And from the earliest times we hear of those vocal abuses which seem always to infect the art whenever singers are allowed to control performance. In Rome these took the form of certain loud improvisations in the Hallelujahs. At this distance of time we can only dimly guess what was their scandalous effect. However, these and other abuses in the service were checked at various times between the fourth and seventh centuries; and the two chief reformations are grouped round the names of Saints Ambrose and Gregory. But it must be remembered that, though both these men reformed and purified the church-ritual and paid great attention to the musical portion of the service, neither can be said to have written any music in the sense that Palestrina wrote the *Missa Brevis.*

St. Ambrose, Bishop of Milan (340–97), was partly guided in his reformation by the success of St. Hilary of Poitiers and of the Arian system of psalmody. He has left us a number of simple hymns all written in eight 4-line stanzas and in the rhythm called Iambic ($\smile -$) tetrameter (4-measure). Among these are the *Deus creator, Æterne rerum, Jam surgit hora tertia,* and the Christmas hymn *Veni re-*

demptor. Besides this purely musical work he compiled an Antiphonary [1] which has now been superseded by that of Gregory. The *Te Deum* usually called after him *Ambrosian* dates from his day. He probably authorized its use, but it is very unlikely that he actually composed the music. Ambrose's efforts were mainly directed to a checking of the musical license common in his time and to the introduction of a sweeter, simpler, and more devout style of performance.

St. Gregory (540–604) was not only "Great" by surname but by his reformations both in church ritual and music. The missal in those days and down to the eighth century was known as a *sacramentary;* and it was the sacramentary of Pope Gelasius I that Gregory issued in a simplified form, thus laying the foundation of the modèrn Roman missal. He also fixed for all time the method of performing the antiphons and psalms. Here a word of explanation is necessary.

"Antiphon" — from which comes our word *anthem* — originally meant the breaking up of a long psalm or other musical work into passages of about equal length which were sung alternately by the two halves of the choir. This simple method of dividing the psalms is of course still matter of daily routine in our churches and cathedrals. The *decani* sing one verse, the *cantoris* the next. It relieves the voices of the choristers and lightens the musical effect. But in very early days the word *antiphon* became specialized to a single sentence which was interpolated by one half of the choir after every verse of a psalm sung by the other half. The method of performing these antiphons varied greatly, and there seems to have been a good deal of confusion and discrepancy as between one church and another; till Gregory fixed the form by treating the psalm as a single verse (so to speak) and ordaining the practice which has now been constant for 1300 years.

$$\left\{ \begin{array}{l} \text{The Antiphon} \\ \text{The Psalm with its Gloria} \\ \text{The Antiphon.} \end{array} \right.$$

[1] The old name for *gradual.*

In addition to this and other non-musical changes in the service Gregory's name is traditionally associated with the rubric that enjoins the chanting of the Hallelujah after the *gradual* at other times besides Easter; the compilation of the antiphonary still in use in the Roman Catholic Church; and the foundation of the *schola cantorum* at Rome.

But to the general reader the chief interest of Gregory's name is in connection with the *Gregorian Chant*. This must be discussed.

We need not point out that all language depends for its intelligibility on two elements, quantity and accent. But it needs a moment's thought to see that in all ages all poets have paid a mixed regard to these two principles. This dual homage has been well called the *architectonic* of poetry. Its existence is just as plain in the verse of Vergil as in that of Milton. But underneath this *architectonic* we find that one or other of the two principles which we have mentioned lies as the main strengthening and straightening rule of the verse. It may be likened to an electrically-charged rod, which is continually guiding the path of the meter.

Now, as we have said, both ancient and modern poetry include the two elements of quantity and accent; but the guiding principle underneath differs. In the case of the ancient poetry it is *quantity at fixed intervals:* in the case of the modern it is *accent at fixed intervals.* Gregory lived just at the time when the quantitative was breaking down and giving place to the accentual. Neither principle could be said to be in possession of the field. A Roman of his time probably regarded poetry as much from one standpoint as from the other. Hence came great confusion when music had to be provided for words. One need only take a passage from any first-class poet and see how very different would be two settings of it; the first designed to illustrate the quantity, the second the accent. And this holds good even in English, where the syllables of greatest quantity are also generally the syllables of greatest accent.

Gregory's problem, then, was to make his music a satisfactory vehicle for the singing of the psalms in Latin. These, be it noted, were poetical prose; but they were liable to be sung according to accent or according to quantity. He solved the problem by a totally new method of expression, adapting to Roman purposes the sweeping delivery which had been used for centuries in the Hebrew Temples. In effect he issued or authorized a series of simple musical tones, in a sort of *free recitative*. This was the *Gregorian Chant*, a method designed to give the utmost rhetorical freedom and the vividness of a new kind of speech.

The tones were arranged so that often many Latin words were uttered on a single note, while others of greater importance had special notes allotted to them. Often too the same musical basis could be arranged for the delivery of two different sets of words. Where the music actually came from we do not know. Its supposed sources we have already hinted at. The chants were prepared for use in a masterly manner with a single eye on the one object, the lively and impressive utterance of the choir. We must not judge Gregory's music by the dull and lifeless perversion of his intentions which we generally hear at the present day.

Finally it should be mentioned that, in the smaller field of setting verse to music, Gregory adopted a precisely opposite style — a style which has influenced the setting of all metrical hymns from his day to ours. In the majority of cases the hymns which he was called on to edit or authorize were accentual hymns like our own. But, whether they were governed by this principle or by the principle of quantity, he caused the verse to be set simply, on the main system of a syllable to a note or at least to a beat (in the modern sense of the word). There was a direct intention to avoid rhetoric, and in this respect the hymns of Gregory's day must have sounded very much like those of our own.

The only other early church forms that need detain us are the *sequences* and the *proses*. These can be dealt with in a few sentences. We have already mentioned the vocal improvisations that were found in the first services of the church. After they had become almost a scandal, an effort was made, not to oust them, but to legalize them by pinning

down their wild phrases to the four syllables of the Hallelujah. When so distributed these vocal phrases were known
as the *sequences* (sequentia) of the graduals. Naturally,
with no better guide than the four syllables Hal-le-lu-jah,
there was great difficulty in memorizing and performing
these long amorphous passages. An attempt was therefore
made to assist the singers by fitting sacred prose texts under
the music. With these attempts are especially associated
the names of Notker (or Notger) Balbulus in the ninth
century and of the monks who directed the celebrated
singing-school at St. Gall. The Latin texts were commonly
called *proses* (prosae) and of these Notker has left about
forty specimens.

It cannot be said, however, that this primitive form was
ever particularly successful. It involved the mathematical
difficulty of adding two to three and making the answer
four. The text had to be taken from the Bible and was
therefore rigid. In other words, the trouble was to find a
text which would exactly last out a phrase of music already
composed.

Consequently we find that in a short time the attempt was
given up in favor of a more rational treatment. The prose
sentences were retained, but almost the whole of the vocal
part was abandoned. The remaining portion was used as
a basis on which to build an artistic chant-setting of the
words. As the treatment of these proses grew more cunning
and the touch of their authors became firmer, a new style of
choral music came into existence. The words themselves
began to be put into rhymed accentual meter — though even
then they never lost their conventional name of *prosae*.
Many great churchmen wrote such rhymed sequences and
proses during the first 1500 years of Christianity. Of these
the best known are the *Stabat Mater* and the *Dies Irae*.

ANCIENT LUTE

ANCIENT LUTE

LUTE

PLATE XV.   ANCIENT MUSICAL INSTRUMENTS

LYRE

LYRE

PLATE XVI.   ROMAN MUSICAL INSTRUMENTS

LYRE

LYRE

PLATE XVII.   ROMAN MUSICAL INSTRUMENTS

CHAPTER 5

Part II - The Medieval Period

Scales and Notes

IF we take a general survey of the history of art, one striking fact jumps into view. It is that modern music differs *in its essence* from ancient. This is not so in poetry, in painting, in sculpture, or in architecture. In all of these the modern artist is generally working in the same materials and facing somewhat the same problems as the ancient artist. In quality, quantity, and method of presentation, his work may be different; but practically all the forms in which he works were invented, developed, and sometimes even perfected before the time of Christ. Even in the domestic and manufacturing crafts most of the great simple inventions, such as the wheel, were made so long ago that the record has been lost. This general statement, though liable to some allowance in detail, is beyond reasonable doubt.

Now in music this is not so. From the time of the caveman to about King Alfred's day music was always "one-line melody." Then came a great discovery — the discovery of part-singing. It is no exaggeration to call this the most important invention of the last 2000 years; for it betokens the existence of a new and hitherto unsuspected human faculty. Naturally in all ages the *accidental* coincidence of voices singing or shouting must have been common. But there was nothing *a priori* to show that these haphazard intersections of speech could be made the basis of a new and complex art-form. To a Roman of the fourth century A.D. such an idea would have appeared to be a fantastic dream. What should *we* say if we were told that in 3000 A.D. there would be a great art based, let us suppose, on the combinations of perfumes?

The reader should endeavour to grasp the fundamental importance of this discovery. All the great musical reformations such as those of the Monodists, of Gluck, and of Wagner, are incomparably smaller when viewed on the wide field of human history. These reformations, it is true, were the work of men whose names we know. The discovery of plural-melody, on the other hand, was not made by one man — not even by any single group of workers. It required the slow effort of many nameless men and probably a desperation of painful thought.

However that may be, we can give a rough date to its first appearance in the chronicles of music. And this date — 900 A.D. — serves to mark off the period of greatest darkness from the second period, when Europe was struggling towards the light.

In other words, from about 900 to 1400 men were trying to fathom the depths of this invention, to extend its boundaries, to amplify its possibilities. It was a time of doubt, confusion, and disappointment. New ideas were born, only to be abandoned almost before they were swaddled. The men themselves who begat these strange dream-children are shadowy monkish figures, scarcely more than names. Some not even that; for their existence hangs on the thin vicarious thread of others' names with the ghostly prefix "pseudo." This then was the period. But let us hasten to add that, after all the infinite turmoil in semi-darkness, came the dawn. The sun shone and the first composer — John Dunstable — stepped out into its glory.

Now we need scarcely say that between the days of Periclean Athens and those of Plantagenet London many changes were made in music. Dunstable inherited a very different musical estate from that of Pindar; and the former's estate has been so much developed since his day that he would not recognize his own park-gates.

Let us gauge the width of the musical gulf that lies between us and ancient Greece by a simple comparison. When Pindar wrote the first two words of his Pythian Ode

"Chrusea phorminx," [1] he composed or selected music, and set it down as follows:

ⵡⵡⲅ ⲑⲓ

Today that looks somewhat strange as a piece of music. Let us jump the 2500 years that separate us from him and set it down in our own way:

Χρυ-σέ-α   φόρ-μιγξ

Now though this looks excessively natural to us it would look excessively unnatural to Pindar.   He would probably guess that the five upright scratches, all weighted with little black blobs, somehow represented the five syllables of his "golden lyre."   But he would have to ask us (1) what we meant by those three barbarous lattice-work signs in the left-hand top corner;   why we arranged everything on five parallel lines instead of fifteen, say, as would appear much more natural to him;   (2) why we began with the long looped thing and the letter C;   why we drew a vertical line before the second syllable of "phorminx";   and finally (3) if we told him that we did not consider this a complete musical composition at all but only the tune of a composition, his criticism on our sanity would probably take the form of a frightened glance towards the door.

Now the object of this chapter and the next is to answer Pindar's three questions in a simple and broad way.   We shall therefore, in the present chapter, take the two subjects of *tone-systems* and *notation* and shall treat them in turn from early Christian times down to our own day.   The two topics cannot be altogether separated.   They intersect. But in the main we shall be able to keep them apart.   The third subject, which practically means the development of the art of composition, we shall reserve for the next chapter. There we shall begin where we left it at the end of the dark-

[1] Χρυσέα φόρμιγξ, golden lyre.

est period — 900 A.D. — and show what happened between then and the advent of Dunstable, Josquin des Près, and others in the fifteenth century. The later history of the subject will of course be treated as it comes up for discussion under the names of the various great composers.

MEDIÆVAL AND MODERN TONE SYSTEMS

From the earliest times the Christian church showed a healthy dislike of the Greek chromatic and enharmonic scales. And in doing this it was unconsciously giving effect to the soundest precepts of pagan philosophy. The diatonic scale which it enforced had, as its bottom note, the low "a" which we mentioned on page 51 as the *additional note* of the Greek *complete system*. This scale was not the white-note scale on the pianoforte a—a', but the white-note scale c'—c''. It was what we should now call major, not minor. But it was lettered with the first seven letters of the Greek alphabet α—β—γ—δ—ε—ζ—η (a—b—g—d—ĕ—z—ē). Later on, as we shall see, it was transposed up a major second in eastern Europe and down a minor third in the west.

We need not remind the reader that the Roman empire became split up into two halves — the Eastern having its capital at Byzantium (Constantinople), and the Western remaining at Rome. A similar division was made in the church; and the government, ritual, and music of the two still remain distinct.[1]

The Byzantine church clung to the original Greek lettering, and these letters in process of time became distorted into a series of signs (*maturiai*) which are still prefixed to the chants as indications of the modes in which they are to be sung. The rest of the notation became, like that of the western neumes,[2] unbelievably complex; but the modal

[1] The word "Byzantine" is used throughout this chapter in order to avoid confusing the word "Greek" in its meaning of "Greek church" with the same word in its meaning of "Ancient (pagan) Greek." "Byzantine" is of course just as accurate in the period under discussion, but the reader must understand it in the sense of "Greek (christian) church."

[2] See pages 99–101.

system itself, after passing through a stage in which there were four chief or "master" modes each attended by its subsidiary mode a fifth lower, eventually settled down into the form which it still possesses — a series of four chief or "master" modes and four subordinate modes a perfect fourth lower.[1] The *marturiai* of the older modal-forms are still prefixed, with desperate ecclesiastical inaccuracy, to the newer modes. The subordinate modes must be looked on as corresponding to the ancient hypo-modes of the Greeks. Their name, however, both in the east and in the west, was altered to *plagal*.

The Byzantine Church Modes

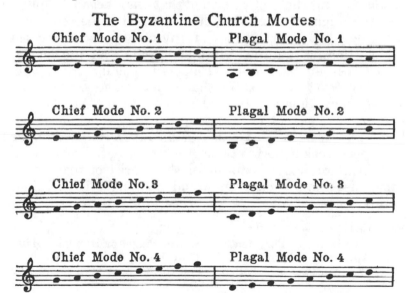

In the west the Roman church received and studied this system without any great comprehension.[2] For the scarcity of books and the difficulty of communication were great in those days. The Byzantines themselves had intended it to represent in some measure the ancient Greek modal-system. The western church, however, adopted it as if it had been the private invention of the Bishop of Con-

[1] Called ἦχος κύριος, α′, β′, γ′, δ′; and ἦχος πλάγιος, α′, β′, γ′, δ′.
[2] Boethius (sixth century), Alcuin (eighth century).

stantinople and his choristers. The names alone they changed. Instead of "chief" or "master" mode they used the word "authentic." They kept the word "plagal" but, in place of their own ordinals (*primus, secundus,* etc.) they transliterated the Greek ordinals into Latin. So that they had

Authentus protus, deuterus, tritus, tetartus

followed by

Plagius protus, deuterus, tritus, tetartus.

It was not till the tenth century that they began to inquire into the origin of these church-modes and to become aware that they had a history. Unfortunately in studying that history they were misled [1] into supposing that the four ancient Greek modes, *Dorian, Phrygian, Lydian, Mixolydian,* each lay *below* the next in that order. The *Dorian* came lowest, they thought, then the *Phrygian* one step higher; and so on. On that false assumption they took the Byzantine *Chief Mode No. 1* (d'—d''), named it *Dorian* and applied the other Greek names to their own *ascending* series of modes. So that, if we had asked a monkish theorist of that time to name his church-modes he would no longer have said (in Latin) *Authentic No. 1, Plagal No. 1,* and so on; but

First Authentic or Dorian	First Plagal or Hypodorian
Second Authentic or Phrygian	Second Plagal or Hypophrygian
Third Authentic or Lydian	Third Plagal or Hypolydian
Fourth Authentic or Mixolydian	Fourth Plagal or Hypomixolydian

In fact, he would have been *saying* almost exactly what a Greek musician would have said 1300 years earlier. But he would have been *meaning* something totally different. In order to make this musical difference quite clear we subjoin a complete list of the two series of modes. It will repay the reader's diligent study.

---

[1] By Ptolemy. But his statement was true as he meant it of the *mĕsē* of each scale when transposed. Turn to page 57 and read the four chief *mĕsē's* (the semibreves) in this order — *Dorian, Phrygian, Lydian, Mixolydian.*

Ancient Greek Modes

Dorian

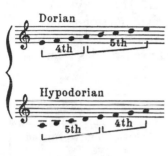

Hypodorian

Phrygian

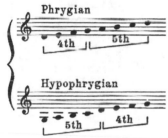

Hypophrygian

Lydian

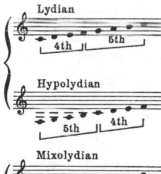

Hypolydian

Mixolydian

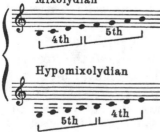

Hypomixolydian

Mediaeval Church Modes

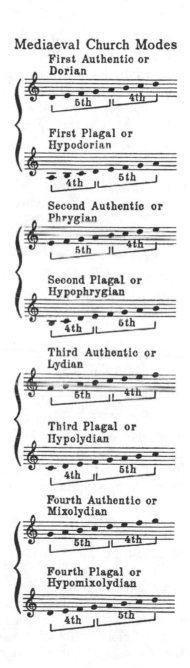

First Authentic or
Dorian

First Plagal or
Hypodorian

Second Authentic or
Phrygian

Second Plagal or
Hypophrygian

Third Authentic or
Lydian

Third Plagal or
Hypolydian

Fourth Authentic or
Mixolydian

Fourth Plagal or
Hypomixolydian

It will be remembered that on page 54 we explained the method by which the Greeks formed their hypo-modes. The original mode was made up of two portions, a fourth below and a fifth above; and these were reversed to form the hypo-mode. Now the mediæval church-modes were organized in just the opposite way.

MODE	GREEK	MEDIÆVAL
Original	Fourth below, fifth above	Fifth below, fourth above
Hypo- (or plagal)	Fifth below, fourth above	Fourth below, fifth above

Compare, for instance, the Greek *Phrygian* with the Mediæval *Dorian*. The notes of the one are the notes of the other. They appear to be identical. But are they so? Certainly not. We have only to put them side by side to see their radical difference.

A similar comparison can be made even between modes of the same period; for example, the first Authentic and the fourth Plagal. In effect all the ancient principal modes have changed places with their subordinate modes; and this quite apart from the fact that their names (*Dorian, Phrygian*, etc.) have been altered. This new disposition of the fourth and the fifth had a profound influence on all composition down to the end of the sixteenth century.

Before leaving the subject we must draw the reader's attention to one important point. The mediæval musicians had at their command eight modes without key-signature as we should say. But from the times of ancient Greece the introduction of a B-flat had been recognized. This put at the disposal of church musicians a new series of eight transposed modes, each of which by adopting what we should call "a key-signature of one flat" retained at its new pitch its old arrangement of intervals. A single example will make this plain.

Mediaeval Dorian   Mediaeval Dorian (transposed)

The church frowned on any further license than this one B-flat. And it was able to translate its frowns into effective penalties. But there were the singers to be considered. Their cry was all for smooth voice-parts in the best possible register. Hence came the ingenious system of "little clefs" (*chiavette*). This system we shall explain later,[1] but we may mention here that its effect was to leave the written notes unaltered while changing the actual pitch of the sounds. By this plan the Pope was satisfied and the singers had their own way.

The modes and scales which we have described above remained sufficient for all music down to the end of the sixteenth century; and sufficient in the sense that they gave great composers the opportunity of making a music that was different from, but hardly inferior to, our own. But even the Gregorian Chant had permitted the discreet use of the B-flat, not only for the purpose just mentioned but in order to secure smooth movement of individual voice-parts. Furthermore its artistic effect as a means of expression was very great. And this is known to all who have heard pure modal part-singing.

The b was therefore written in two ways, either as a *soft* or *round* b (♭) or as a *hard* or *square* b (♮).[2] And this, in a word, is the origin of our ♭ and ♮. We shall have more to

---

[1] See page 109. A similar sort of "artistic cant" is used even today in the key-signatures of some orchestral brass instruments. Those composers who are the special inheritors of the "glorious classic past" like to put on paper only those notes which could have been played before the invention of pistons. But they would be horrified if the players took them at their word and abandoned their chromatic horns and trumpets.

[2] b *molle, rotundum;* b *durum, quadrum.*

say about this when we deal with Guido's system of *hexachords*.[1]

But soon a very natural process of analogy began to work in the mediæval musical mind. Let us take the two *Dorian* scales printed above — the scale in its original and in its transposed form. "If," said the composer, "I am to be allowed to flatten my sixth note (B) just where it is so awkward to sing as a semitone below the C, why should I not be granted the same liberty in my transposed mode, and allowed to flatten my sixth note *there*, my E?" To this there was really no answer unless one was willing to fall back on theology. And in practice the composer did what he claimed to be allowed to do. He even pushed the analogy further on some rare occasions and used an A-flat as well. But before this analogy could be carried to its logical limits the whole modal system had been thrown on the dust-heap. We may take it as a general rule of modal composition that a transposition of a transposition was forbidden as indecent; and that all music which required anything beyond a B-flat, an F-sharp, or a C-sharp was *musica ficta* — a term that almost represented to the mediæval mind the idea of *faked music*.

The last step in the history of the modes occurred so late that it is difficult to class it as a legitimate development. It is more in the nature of a scientific afterthought that gave recognition to an already existing practice. A change was coming over the minds of musicians. They saw — as we still see — that the modes were the ideal vehicles for certain kinds of expression. But composers were beginning to call for a more stringent harmonic organization. At the cadences (or ends) of their movements especially they felt the need of what we should call a subdominant-dominant-tonic progression. In the path of this ideal stood the frightful inequalities of their modes. In the *Dorian* they had normally no B-flat or C-sharp; in the *Lydian* no B-flat; in the *Mixolydian* no F-sharp; while in the *Phrygian* they had to be contented with a "sixth" on F followed by an E-major chord.

[1] See page 107.

About the end of the sixteenth century this groping out towards modern harmony became so noticeable that musical theorists[1] — unable to foresee the course of history and anxious to provide technical justification for the composers of their day — invented two new modes with their plagals. These were the *Ionian* and the *Æolian*, practically our *major* and *minor* modes.

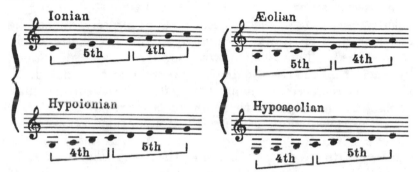

The investigation of the new major scale and its possibilities was the work of Zarlino, the sixteenth century Venetian organist. He established two facts. The first was that the modality of the scale depended chiefly on the quality of its third note. In everyday language this merely states the difference between two scales of C to c; one with an E-natural, the other with an E-flat. Zarlino's second discovery was that you can arrive at a major third in two different ways. You can tune it in its theoretically correct proportion of five to four, direct from its fundamental, thus:

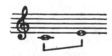

or you can come at it by a series of perfectly tuned fifths, thus:

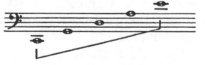

---

[1] Glareanus, for instance.

And he demonstrated that the two E's so reached are not the same note. The former is about $\frac{1}{10}$ of a tone lower.

The idea of getting rid of all the small differences in the chromatic scale had been in the minds of musicians since the beginning of the sixteenth century. And the plan was to divide the whole octave into *12 equal semitones*. This was of great advantage to the keyed instruments. For the composer it amounted to this: that, instead of having at his disposal a few selected keys all accurately tuned, he had access to all the keys, slightly — but not distressingly — mistuned. This system was supported and developed by such thinkers as Neidhardt, Werckmeister, and J. S. Bach. It received the name of *equal temperament* and may be said to have opened the door to modern harmony.

In the seventeenth century the foundations of practical modern harmony were laid. But it was left for the eighteenth to produce an original theorist. This was J. P. Rameau,[1] who enunciated the theories of the inversion of chords and of the multiple character of single notes. In effect Rameau saw that chords of the sixth or 6–4 were merely new positions of the 5–3. His scheme was to cut up everything into yard and half-yard lengths; to docket and card-catalogue the composer's implements; to "mark everything in plain figures"; and especially to see that the theoretical shopkeeper's lights made a comfortable glow on the practical pavement outside. By this means he undoubtedly led the musicians of his time along the safe flat footway for which they were searching. He was able to point out the safety of the road which he himself had made, and to give them, at any rate, the chance of holding their heads up, without danger to their feet. It has been recently questioned whether a rougher road then would not have led to higher places now.

The other subject which Rameau investigated lies somewhat farther outside the realm of musical development. Nor has it afflicted the sad minds of composers so greatly. He showed that the major triad could be explained *from*

[1] *Traité d'Harmonie*, published 1722.

nature; that a stretched string or a brass tube could be made to give the overtones which we now call the "harmonic series"; and that the latter theory[1] could be specially directed towards the explanation of the harmony of his day. Musicians at the time may be said totally to have ignored this theory as a working contribution to their profession. At the same time they were most unanimous in their delight at finding that their own humble exertions have been in a manner anticipated and justified by the Creator. Consequently they heard with disappointment that nature had apparently got no further than the major triad — a point which they reached and quitted some 300 years before. However, to them this was not a practical matter. They shut their ears to all the other sound-combinations of nature and kept writing their music; eventually conscientious enough examiners arose to show a more complete view of the harmonics found in nature.

MEDIÆVAL AND MODERN NOTATIONS

As this subject is somewhat technical and liable to cause confusion in the reader's mind, we shall begin its study with a table of rough descriptions and dates. See next page.

We have already mentioned that the earliest Byzantines, perhaps copying the ancient Greeks, used a pure letter notation a—β—γ etc. for their diatonic scale. We have no exact knowledge as to when this was first adopted, but it is supposed to date at least from Christianity. It seems to have been transplanted to the west somewhere about the tenth century in the form of an ABCDEFG series, but never to have taken root there.

However, it was impossible to keep choirs singing by rote only. A notation was one of the first necessities of the church. There may have been a time when the services

---

[1] Afterwards studied by Tartini (1692–1770) in its particular bearing on the multiple character of single notes. In the nineteenth century it was greatly extended and developed by Helmholtz.

Name	Description	Date
Letter Notation	The representation of sounds by means of written letters.	Ancient Greek. Early Byzantine. Western Europe, tentatively about tenth century. (See also *Tablatures.*)
Neumes	Vague signs of pitch written above the text in the church service-books.	Byzantine, but more particularly in the Roman church from about sixth to tenth century. Lingered on till fourteenth century.
Black Notation	The black notes (long, square, or diamond-shaped) which were the developed forms of the neumes when placed on the staff.	Came in during the twelfth century.
White Notation	Our present notation, a modification of the black.	Came in during the fourteenth century.
Tablatures	A system of instrumental lettering or figuring which represented sounds mainly by the technique of the instrument.	Fifteenth to seventeenth century (lute). Lingered on into eighteenth. Reappeared in twentieth, mainly for guitarists.

Figured Bass is not a distinct notation, but rather a special short-hand applied to an existing notation.

Tonic Sol Fa (and its various allied systems) are " mechanical sub-stitutes " for our present notation. They refer the intervals of the scale not to pitch, but to key.

were so simple and infrequent that one man could memorize the music, teach it to the choir, and pass it on to his successor. All that he would need would be the text of the services and a strong memory. But these days ended so long ago that we are not even sure that they ever existed. It

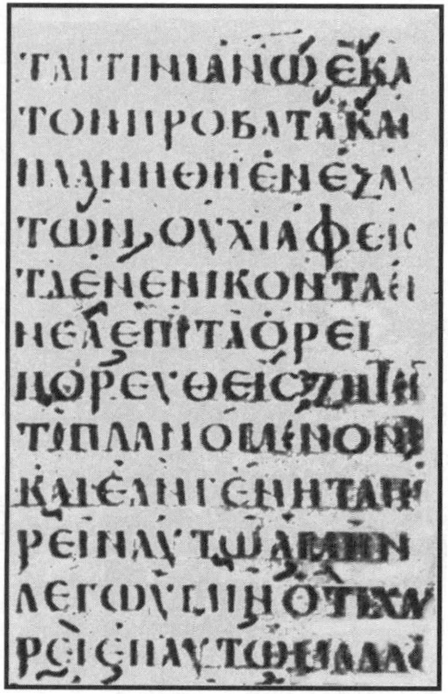

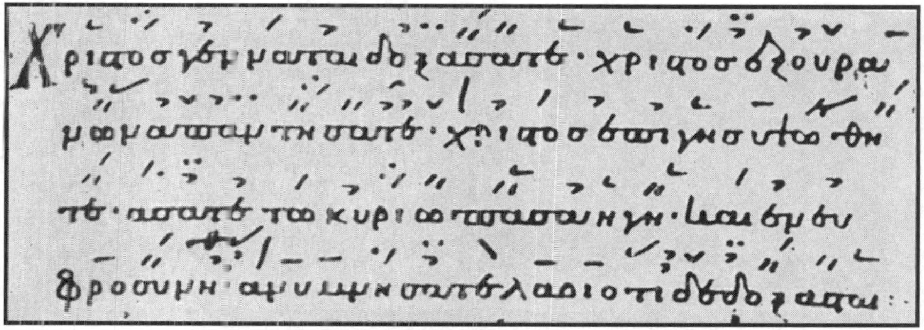

Fig. 2. Middle

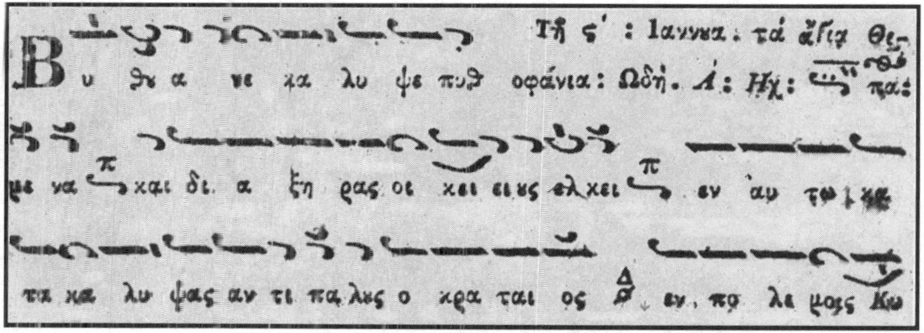

Fig. 3. Modern

Fig. 1. Early

Plate XVIII. Byzantine Notation

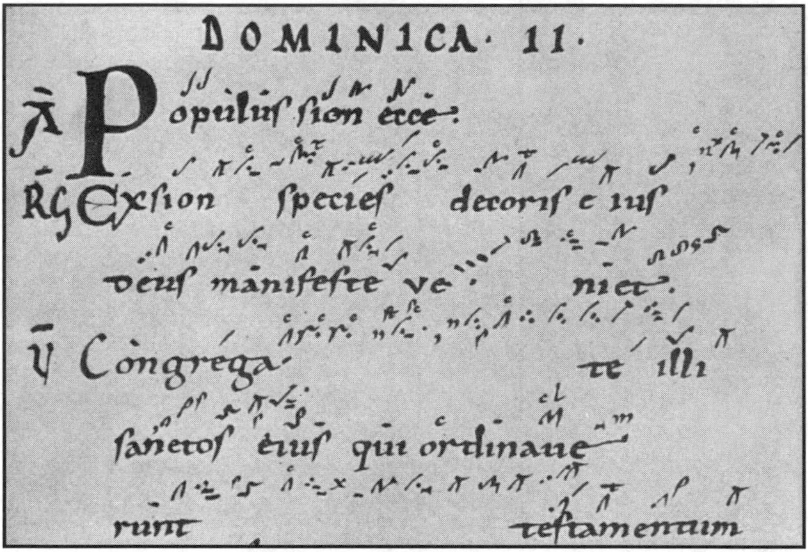

Fig. 1. St. Gall

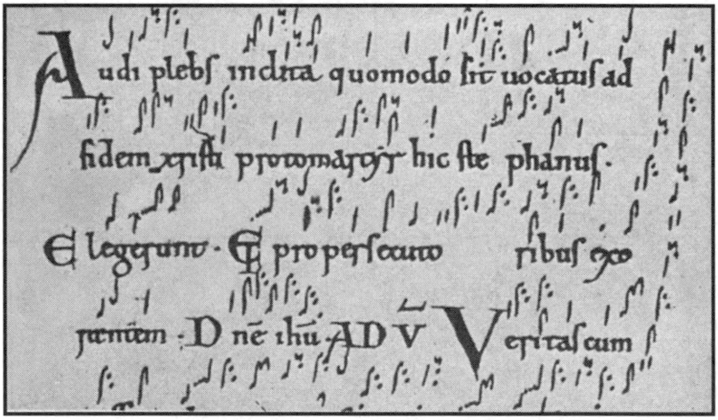

Fig. 2. Anglo-Saxon

Plate XIX. The Neumes

soon became essential that the cantor should have an *aide-memoire*. And the system that supplied this deficiency was called the Neumes.[1]

The first suggestion of such a system appeared in the Byzantine church. From this the Roman church took its cue and developed the system which we are about to describe. The Byzantine system itself is somewhat outside the line of our present study; but as it gave the original hint for the western notation, we shall devote a few words to the subject.

The Byzantine notation divides itself into three types — the *early, middle,* and *modern*.[2] (1) The *early* consists of a series of simple signs written above the text. Most of them are rectangular and appear to have been used rather as marks of accent than of pitch. But they have been disused for so long that their interpretation is now mere matter of guesswork. (See Plate XVIII, fig. 1.) (2) The *middle*, which came into use between the eleventh and thirteenth centuries, is an extension of the rectangular system mixed with the curved neumes whose meaning we shall explain in the next paragraph. (See Plate XVIII, fig. 2.) (3) In the *modern*,[3] which is still used by the Greek church, the rectangular element has disappeared, and we have an elaborated system of curved signs representing rhythms, the rise and fall of the voice, and the traditional church ornamentations. (See Plate XVIII, fig. 3.)

Very early in its history the idea of a neume-notation passed to Rome. In its essence the notation consisted of a series of tiny signs written above the Latin text. At least twenty-eight varieties of these signs are known to have existed. They included up-strokes, down-strokes, sideways-

---

[1] Probably = νεύματα (nods or signs). Others say that the word comes from πνεῦμα, the Holy Spirit. But antiquarians who have to wrestle with the intricacies of the subject assign it a precisely opposite origin.

[2] The first two are known to scholars as the *ecphonetic* and the *hagiopolite* (or *Constantinopolitan*). The *early* example given on Plate X is from an uncial MS. of the seventh and eighth century in the convent of St. Panteleemon on Mt. Athos. N. B. Plates XVIII/XX/XXI and fig. 2 of Plate XIX are abbreviated and rearranged from Thibaut's *Origine*.

[3] This notation has before now figured in a library catalogue as "Greek interlined with Turkish."

strokes, flat-strokes, dots, crosses, pothooks, hangers, and "curleywigs" of all kinds. The force of these signs undoubtedly depended in the first instance on their actual shape. The upward dash to the right called *virga* (something like a raised golf-stick) would mean "sing a higher note on this syllable"; the flattish sign called *jacens* (something like a hockey-stick on the ground) would mean "stay where you are for this syllable"; the curly sign called *quilisma* (something like an ordinary schoolboy's picture of a snake) would mean "backwards and forwards here"; and so on. These and many other more elaborate forms can be seen on Plate XIX, fig. 1.

But all this was very vague and could be of no use except as a mnemonic to an experienced cantor. So an additional definiteness was attempted and partially obtained by placing each neume nearer to or farther from its syllable according as its pitch was lower or higher.

The neumes are difficult to read. Unless we have the early church-transcriptions before us to act as a guide, they are often quite unintelligible. Handwritings varied very much. And we must remember that the monks, who wrote out the neumes, already knew their meaning and only needed them as a guide to their memory. A modern chorus singer might reconstitute these conditions for himself if, before an oratorio performance, he found that programme-books were to be substituted for vocal-scores and that he had an hour or two in which to make a dot-and-dash mnemonic in his copy.

On the opposite page we give two examples of the neumes as they appeared before the musical staff was invented. The first is from the St. Gall antiphonary which was itself a copy (made for Charlemagne by Pope Hadrian I in 790) from the original antiphonary of St. Gregory (590). The second is from an Anglo-Saxon manuscript of about 1150. There is therefore the same distance of time between these two as between us and Chaucer. This may profitably be kept in mind as showing that the neume-system was by no means an experiment easily made and soon discarded. With all its imperfections it had to serve church purposes for many centuries. To us its great interest lies in the fact that the neume-forms were the actual parents of our note-forms. We shall have something to say on that subject later.

Meanwhile the reader may get a hint by comparing the two specimens on Plate XIX. If he will examine any of the long groups of neumes in the earlier one (fig. 1), he will see that they are all conventional mnemonics and nothing more. They bear little resemblance to our present note-forms (though it would be quite possible to point out some connection). In the later example (fig. 2) the signs have become more stereotyped to definite musical purposes. Their meaning has not been much altered, but they have lost a good deal of the "dot-and-dash" character of the earlier example. The thickening of some of the heads suggests our own note-forms. There are little groupings which with some trimming and filling-out might be comfortably placed on a staff. This suggests the future. But it must be understood that to the writer of this manuscript it is a future and not a present.

Naturally a notation like the above was the subject of constant complaint. Its inherent vagueness and the varieties in handwriting made any approach to certainty impossible. The same set of neumes could be read and taught by two different cantors as two totally distinct series of notes. Something had to be done about it.

We find that a good deal was done. For everybody now started inventing a musical notation. It became a sort of fashionable amusement in monkish circles; and a frightful confusion reigned in the minds of musicians. However, like the inventions in our own Patent Office, many of these were evidences rather of mental activity than of any solid practical advance. Most of them sank before they had got well into the water; but one came to the surface and swam to land, there to become the ancestor of our modern notation. But before we describe how it managed to come into home-waters we shall just mention three of the inventions that went to the bottom.

1. *Pseudo-Hucbald* (ninth century?). A perversion of an ancient Greek procedure. The essence was the selection of arbitrary signs for the "finals" (tonics) of the four Authentic

Modes and the use of these signs in varied positions to represent ascending fourths and fifths.

2. *Odo of Cluny* (tenth century). This notation was an application to the organ and other instruments of the old Byzantine letter-notation and was probably based also on the fact that at this time all organ-keys were lettered. In effect it suggested a letter-notation for the twenty-one notes that lie between low G and the d″, two octaves and a fifth above (B-flat and B-natural in each of the two upper octaves). Its great interest to us is that it shows the round b (♭) used for B-flat, and the square b (♮) used for B-natural.

It will be seen that the Greek capital letter Γ (G) was used for the bottom note. In the top fifth there was a choice of notation. Originally Greek minuscules or small letters (*a, β*, etc.) were used, and two "square b's" were written one under the other to distinguish this note from its lower octave. But in time this hint was applied to the whole top fifth. Each letter was then doubled, but the ordinary Latin minuscules were retained. In this form the notation with its modern musical equivalent was as follows:

3. *Hermann Count Vehringen*[1] (eleventh century). A complicated letter-system which, like the modern Tonic Sol Fa, had the fatal defect of leaving the actual pitch uncertain.

Among other efforts of this time was one of Hucbald the Flemish monk and theorist of the tenth century. He hit on the idea of plotting out the Latin text on 6 parallel lines each of which was marked at its beginning "t" (tone) or

[1] Known as Hermannus Contractus.

"s" (semitone) to show its pitch-distance from the next highest line. This was in some ways a clever notion, and an attempt was made about the same time to increase its utility by adding the neumes to the words.

But it was reserved for the keen mind of Guido d'Arezzo (990–1050) to see that the spaces were as important as the lines, and that the neumes were of more importance than the text. Already, in the tenth century, there had been a great stride forward. An unknown genius — to whom a monument should have been put up long ago — saw the fundamental necessity of the case — *a horizontal straight line representing one fixed note.* This line he drew in red above the Latin text and he called it the F-line.

(Red)

E F G

Guido seized on this line and gave it relative rank both with other lines and with the intervening spaces. A second (yellow) line was added above for C.

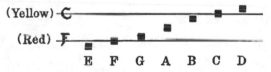

E F G A B C D

And later still two black lines one on either side of the red.[1]

C D E F G A B C D

All this did not come in a day. But the minds of men were now becoming accustomed to the idea of pinning down one pitch to one horizontal line. Also the *clef* was on its way.

The three musical examples which we have just printed are of course only *plans* or *diagrams* of Guido's invention. In his day these square black notes had not come into existence. His innovations were first the straight line or lines representing pitch, and then (equally important) the idea of

[1] The order varied somewhat.

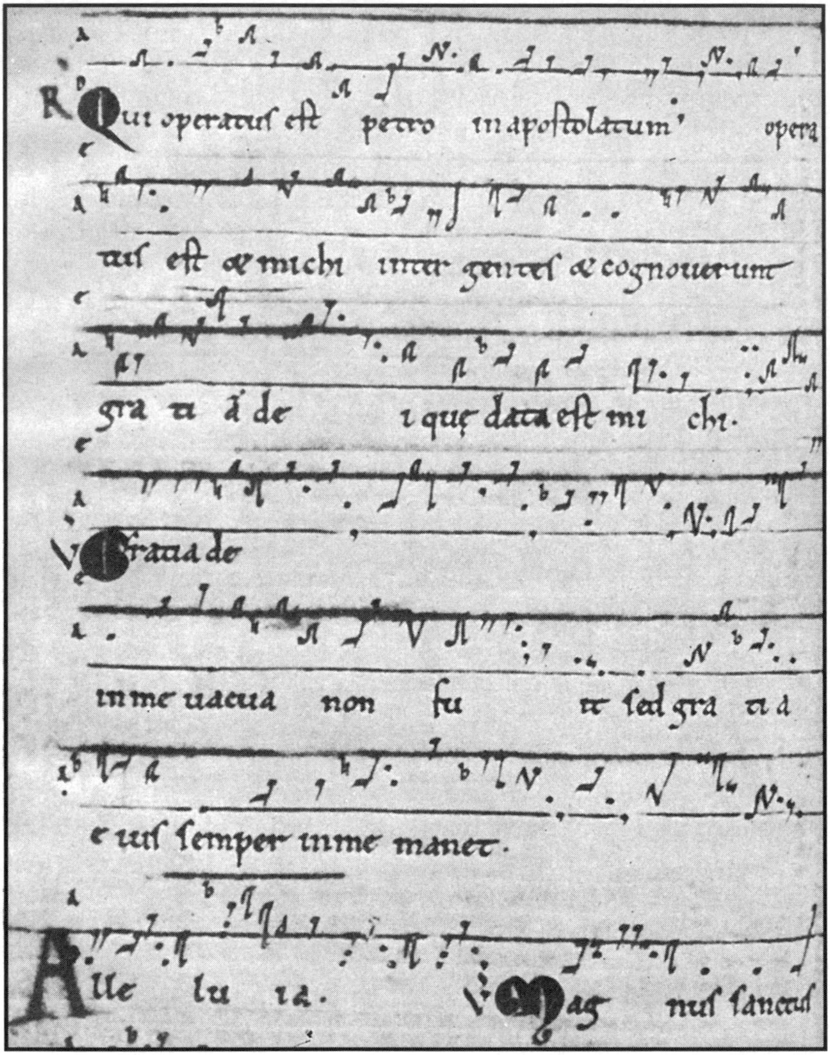

PLATE XX. SETTLEMENT OF THE NEUMES ON THE LINES

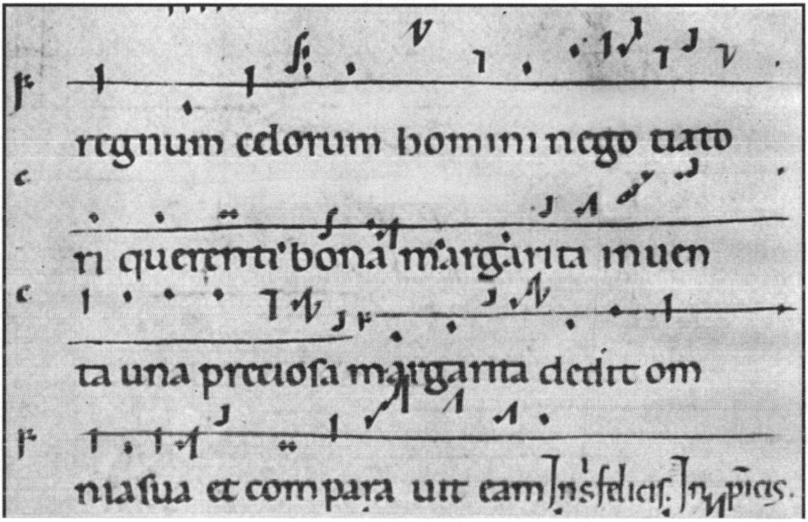

FIG. 1

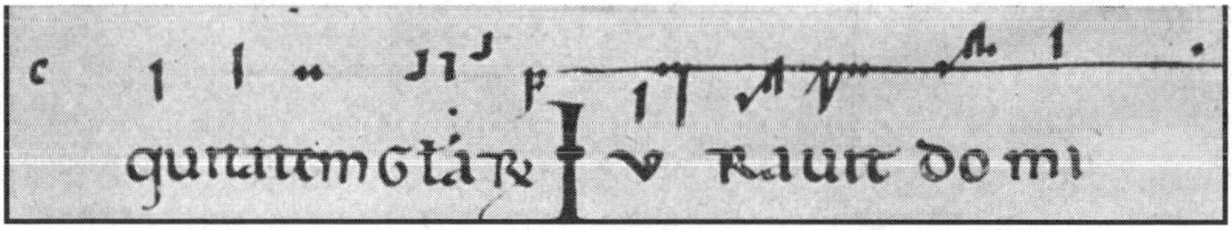

FIG. 2

PLATE XXI. COLORED LINES WITH NEUMES

writing the neumes so that they fell actually on a line or in a space. Certain types of these neumes were already fairly well fitted for such a purpose. And Guido saw that if he regulated them and placed them on the staff, all the old uncertainty would disappear, and the singers would know precisely what sounds were represented.

He did not start out with a brand-new scheme of substituting "notes" for "neumes." He kept the latter. But he thickened their heads, regularized their shapes, and dropped many that were redundant. All these points and some others can be seen in the illustration on the opposite page (Plate XX).[1] It shows the neumes just settling on to the lines. Both the text and the neumes are there (as in Plate XIX), but the latter have become *tied down* to the horizontal lines and spaces that now separate each row of text from the next. The F-line, being red in the original, comes out a strong black in the photograph. The C-line is yellowish-green and is therefore fainter. But the reader will easily make out the clef-letter "C" which is at the left-hand side of each yellow line.

A great deal might be said about this specimen of early notation, as it shows practically all the neume-forms that afterwards developed into the notes and note-groupings[2] of the church-musicians. But we must content ourselves with drawing attention to three particular neume-types, each of which had a future.[3] These three types (which are all to be found in the illustration) are: first, the little rod with the thickened upper end. This became the *longa* (or long) ¶ of the black notation. Second, the squarish dot which turned into the *brevis* (or breve) ■. And third, the sign something like a manuscript capital A, written sprawlingly and without the cross-bar. This became the three-note group:

---

[1] From the *troparium* of St. Evroult (twelfth century).
[2] The *ligatures* were the ancient compound signs developed directly from the neumes to represent groups of notes usually not all of one time-value.
[3] Known as *virga*, *punctum*, and *torculus*.

The last illustration has been given mainly to show the neume-forms, not the colored lines, though the latter are incidental to it. We shall therefore add a second illustration (Plate XXI, fig. 1) which, although much later in date [1] than the invention of these lines, presents them very clearly. The clef-letters "F" and "C" are in the left-hand margin. Half-way through the third row of text the red-line changes its level, and the "F" is written at the break as a help to the eye. The necessity for this double guide enables us to appreciate the difficulty which singers undoubtedly had in fixing their attention on this rigid line. The second figure in the illustration is rather an instance of economy than of artistic difficulty. It is a photograph of the bottom row of text and music taken from the same manuscript page as fig. 1. The line in this case begins as a C-line (yellow) and changes in the middle to an F-line (red). As is usual, the clef-letter "F" is written-in carefully at the change — just before the capital "I" in the text.

We have now studied the first beginnings of the *musical staff*. It need scarcely be said that the invention was primarily caused by the necessities of the new art then springing up — plural-melody. The fact that Pindar had no such notation at his command is proof as good as any other that he knew nothing about part-singing. The invention itself provides the musician with a *picture* in which relative pitch is shown by means of relative height on a horizontal scaffolding (the staff).

The reader cannot fail to notice that a musical staff of this time differed from ours in that all its intervals were fixed. For instance, the spaces below F and C were normally *semitones*. There were, strictly speaking, no key-signatures and no accidentals. These had to be provided.

Guido set the ball rolling in this direction. As we have already explained, the Greeks had descriptive names for each note in their *complete system*. When they wished to mention the note g' (the seventh upwards from the *additional note*) they said *lichanos meson* which simply means *forefinger*,

---

[1] Lombard, sixteenth century.

middle (tetrachord). Guido found a similar nomenclature. He had already begun classifying his six-note scales into *natural, soft,* and *hard,* according as the semitone fell below f′, b′-flat, or c″.

THE GUIDONIAN HEXACHORDS

And, as a guide for the memory of his pupils, he had taken certain syllables from the *Hymn to St. John;* each half-line of which in the original plain-song began on an ascending degree of the scale c′—d′—e′—f′—g′—a′.

UT queant laxis	**RE**sonare fibris
MIra tuorum	**FA**muli gestorum
SOLve polluti	**LA**bii reatum
	Sancte Johannes

These syllables were not only used as *names* in speaking of the notes, but as *words* on which to sing any of the six-note groups.[1] Hence — as the semitone always fell between the third and fourth notes, and the words MI–FA always fell on those semitones — the expression MI–FA gradually acquired the meaning of "the semitone interval."

However, it was very soon observed that when a B-flat was wanted throughout a piece the pitch-sign (C) at the beginning of the staff was insufficient and, to their minds, inaccurate; for the MI–FA no longer occurred there. So a round (or soft) b was placed at the left-hand side of the staff thus ♭; and if it had to be contradicted later it was not contradicted by putting in the true signature (C) but by a square (or hard) b thus ♮. Here we have the origin of our modern ♭ and ♮. The idea was afterwards extended, first to the

---

[1] Much the same thing happened in the Byzantine church. The first seven letters of the alphabet (each representing a chief mode and its plagal) were thrown into a sentence, out of which the consonants were afterwards dug and used to indicate the pitch and key of the chants. The reader will see some of these consonants on Plate XIX, fig. 3.

note E, then to the note A, and gradually the sign acquired the conventional meaning of "a semitone lower."

The ♯ came much later. Its use was perhaps stereotyped by Josquin des Près towards the end of the fifteenth century. Its origin has been the subject of discussion, but the probability is that, like the ♮, it sprang from the old b-durum ♭. The two signs ♭ and ♯ were for long used without distinction as meaning "raised a semitone." However, with the rise of instrumental music in the seventeenth century, the modern difference between the two becomes apparent. The other two signs ♭♭ and × are recent conveniences intended to keep pace with the modern system of chromatic harmony and to justify its conventions.

It need scarcely be said that the existence of the three signs ♭ – ♮ – ♯ does not imply the existence of key-signatures in our sense of the word. These came at a very much later period. In fact it is not till about Bach's day that we find them in their present cut-and-dried form.

We have already mentioned the *chiavette* and their use. A few further words of explanation may now be added. Ledger lines were unknown till the sixteenth century. It was therefore necessary to keep the voice-parts on the staff, however high (or low) the actual sounds might be. And this end was attained by the simple expedient of altering the clef. When this was done originally — perhaps in the middle of a movement — the colored line (C or F) was bent into the new position. A little later a small guiding mark, called the *custos* or guardian, was placed on the staff to direct the singer's attention to the new clef line. The movable clefs themselves were called *chiavette*. It is easy to see how they worked. Let us make a modern (and wholly fanciful) supposition. Imagine that we had to indicate "top E" for a bass-singer by using the F-clef *and no ledger lines*. Obviously all that we have to do is to place the clef on the bottom line but one thus:

Now this was exactly the plan adopted. The clef was lowered for the higher registers and raised for the lower. Hence came the old rule "the higher (or lower) the clef, the lower (or higher) the pitch."

Now it was just when the F- and C-clefs were becoming established that the ecclesiastical objections to E-flats, A-flats, and C-sharps began to be heard. Protest was out of the question, so musicians used the clefs to outwit the church. We may show what they did by another modern supposition. We wish to make a soprano transpose a passage from C-major to E-major. *But we must not use any sharps.* All we have to do is to place the treble-clef on the third line instead of the second, and to pass the word that the order of the intervals is governed by the clef alone and therefore remains unaltered.

Instead of our original [music notation] we write [music notation]

This is precisely what the medieval composers did. The performers sang the notes as if in the original clef (in this case G on the second line) but they were guided as to the key by the transposed clef (G on the third line). In this way the singers were made happy and the ecclesiastical proprieties were observed.

The clefs that were used with this object in the fifteenth and sixteenth centuries were known as transposed clefs (*chiavette transportate*). Only the C- and F-clefs were employed for this purpose; three (the "high chiavette") for upward transpositions, and four (the "low chiavette") for downward transpositions. But the reader must notice the essential difference between the first-named *chiavette* and the *chiavette transportate*. In the former the only object was a mechanical one — to allow the voices to use their various registers without leaving the staff. Hence came the maxim "the higher (or lower) the clef, the lower (or higher) the pitch." In the latter the object was to use a new key without appearing to do so. Both the notes and the clef were therefore moved up (or down). So that now the rule was reversed and became "the higher (or lower) the clef, the higher (or lower) the pitch." A glance at the two modern suppositions above will make the logic of this change perfectly clear.

The G-clef — the last to arrive — came in timidly in the thirteenth century. But it was scarcely used at all for vocal music. Indeed so intimately did the medieval mind mix up the two ideas of clef-signature (pitch) and key-signature (the place where the semitone interval MI–FA came) that for years it was customary to contradict a ghostly F-sharp which was supposed to show its head whenever this clef was used. It was not until the introduction of the violin in the seventeenth century that the G-clef began to assert something of its modern supremacy. The shapes of the three clef-letters F, C, and G have gone through many vicissitudes. Here are some of the forms which are recognized in written and printed music.[1]

F Clef:

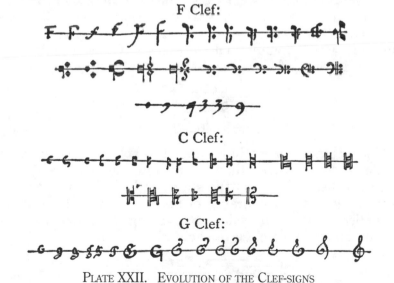

C Clef:

G Clef:

PLATE XXII. EVOLUTION OF THE CLEF-SIGNS

No other letters have ever been used as clef-signs. But these three have become domiciled in certain positions as

[1] From Riemann.

the recognized inhabitants of the staff. Two of them (the Bass and Baritone) are F-clefs; four (the Tenor, Alto, Mezzo-soprano, and Soprano) are C-clefs; while the remaining one is the G (treble or violin) clef. At the present day the Baritone, Mezzo-soprano, and Soprano are completely obsolete. Here is the list: the obsolete clefs are placed in brackets.

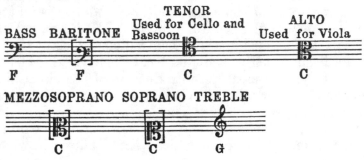

To this list, perhaps, may be added the publishers' double G-clef which is used mainly to show that a tenor is not a soprano. The clef is scarcely necessary; as conventions of this sort without additional clef-signs have been matters of routine in the orchestra for many years.

G (one octave lower)

The neumes, as we have already explained, were rough guides *to pitch.* They had no definite time-values. After they had been placed on the staff and had begun to assume something of the appearance of notes, an attempt was made to indicate their time-values by writing the notes attached to any one syllable close to each other; thus:

This was somewhat vague; and, though the new *measured music* did not differ widely from the old *plain song,*[1] it was

---

[1] *Musica mensurata* and *musica plana* (or *cantus planus*).

felt to be insufficient. Musicians had recourse to desperate expedients in order to secure some freedom and exactness in their part-writing.

Let us see what the position was. By the end of the thirteenth century the neumes had been stereotyped into five signs (the *black notation*) each of which, from the *maxim* downwards, had a nominal value of twice the next lower.

⌐   Maxim (*maxima* = greatest)

◣   Long (*longa* = long)

■   Breve (*brevis* = short)

◆   Semibreve (*semibrevis* = half-short)

⊥   Minim (*minima* = least)

Of these the breve ■ was taken as the standard of value.[1] But, though this was simple enough, it must be remembered that they had no bars or bar-lines. Ideas of measurement were only just dawning on them ; and they were much hampered in their minds by the constant reflection that the Holy Trinity contained three persons, and that therefore anything worth doing must have a "3" in it. They said:

When ■ = ◆◆◆, it is *perfect time*.
When ■ = ◆◆ , it is *imperfect time*.

But a nice question then arose. How were these different values to be indicated for the performers? How were the singers to know *when* the breve was supposed to have three, and when two, semibreves? The composers' predicament was very much what ours would be if, every time we went into a shop, we had to make a *preliminary bargain* with the shopkeeper as to how many cents there were in a quarter and how many quarters in a dollar.

---

[1] Franco of Cologne (eleventh century). It was called simply *time* (tempus).

However, a way had to be found out of this difficulty; and they found it by means of a system which they called *prolation*. They said :

The circle ◯ is perfect like the Holy Trinity.   It shall represent 3 beats (*perfect time*).

Half the circle ◖ is imperfect unlike the Holy Trinity. It shall represent 2 beats (*imperfect time*).

When ♦ = ♩♩♩ we will call it the *greater prolation*.
When ♦ = ♩♩ we will call it the *lesser prolation*.

We will put a dot in the circle or half-circle to represent the *greater prolation*.

The result of all this scheming was that they had *four prolations*, each of which was (to resume our analogy) merely a preliminary bargain with the performers as to the relative time-values of their notes.[1]   Here are the four, with their meanings.

Sign	Name	Meaning	Modern Equivalent (in a lower unit)
⊙	Perfect time. Greater prolation.	■ = ♦ ♦ ♦ and ♦ = ♩ ♩ ♩	$\frac{9}{8}$
◯	Perfect time. Lesser prolation.	■ = ♦ ♦ ♦ and ♦ = ♩ ♩	$\frac{3}{4}$
◖·	Imperfect time. Greater prolation.	■ = ♦ ♦ and ♦ = ♩ ♩ ♩	$\frac{6}{8}$
◖	Imperfect time. Lesser prolation.	■ = ♦ ♦ and ♦ = ♩ ♩	$\frac{2}{4}$

By the fifteenth century people were no longer counting in breves (one "long" to the bar, as we should say), but in semibreves (one breve to the bar).   And it became necessary to mark this change from *alla longa* to *alla breve* by a change in the notation.   The simplest possible plan was adopted, that of drawing a vertical line through each of the four prolation marks given above; and this practically produced the C and ¢ which we still use as time-signs.

φ φ ¢ ¢

[1] See page 113.

The only further step in the notation was the change from black to white. The origin of this was the difficulty which the thirteenth century singers had in performing passages which were, in our words, contrary to the general time-signature of the piece — twos against threes and threes against twos. To mark these passages the monks left the notes in black outline and then colored them red. Ease of writing and the gradual acquirement of a surer sense of time-values soon abolished the latter half of the process. By the beginning of the fifteenth century the new *white notation* was established as follows:

⊢	Maxim
⊢	Long
⊔	Breve
◊	Semibreve
⟨	Minim

As music became more elaborate, and instrumental figures were developed, there was a continual cry for notes of smaller value. The minim was first split up into two half-minims. The old shape was retained for the new note, but it was given a crutch or hook ♭ . This half-minim or crotchet (*crocheta* [1] = minim with ◊ the crutch) was soon replaced by a note in appearance just like the old black minim ↓ and (though it has always retained its original name crotchet in England) the actual crutches have been appropriated to its family of descendants the quaver, semiquaver, and demisemiquaver:

♪ ♪ ♪

[1] The Latin word *crocheta* was afterwards passed on to the one-crutched black note; and it still retains that name (*croche* = quaver) in France. America, following Germany, has a strictly mathematical nomenclature for the musical time-values — "whole note," "half note," etc. But besides the historical loss involved, this has the further disadvantage that, for the smallest notes, one has to use numerals — already so much employed in

We scarcely need to point out that all our modern note-signs are multiples of two. But there is one sign which we have not yet mentioned — the *dot.* This is nothing but a dwarfish descendant of the circle which represented "perfect time." It is a miniature black circle, so small that it is no longer worth drawing as one. If we ask what is the effect of the modern dot, we are invariably told that it "adds one-half to the original value of the note after which it is placed." That is quite correct. But this effect is only an incident in the dot's benevolent activities. The true answer to the question is that "it turns the note into a multiple of 3" — or, as the monks would have put it, "it makes the note *perfect.*"

We have now completed our sketch of the evolution of notation; but we think it well to summarize for the reader the earlier and less familiar steps in the process. This can best be done pictorially. The changes through which the church notation has passed are therefore shown in tabloid form on the opposite page (Plate XXIII). All the examples in this illustration are drawn from well-known cathedrals and abbeys, English and continental. Furthermore, the same musical phrase is presented in all of them. It may be studied in its neumatic form pure and simple; then in the form of neumes on lines; and so, through the black and the white notations, to the comparatively modern square Roman notation.[1]

Before concluding this chapter we must say a word about the *Tablatures* mentioned on page 100. But, as these have now disappeared from all professional applications, we shall merely indicate their general character. Tablatures were used for the organ, the lutes, and for some of the wood-wind, such as the flutes and recorders.

The organ-tablatures were elaborated letter-notations; of which an early example has already been given. Various signs were used to indicate time-values, and this system

technical musical parlance. It is to be noted that the American system is inferior to the German. For a German word such as ach*tel* actually means eighth-*part*; while the Americans merely use the ordinals "eighth" and "sixteenth" in a restricted and slightly unnatural manner.

[1] Re-arranged and much compressed from Lambillotte.

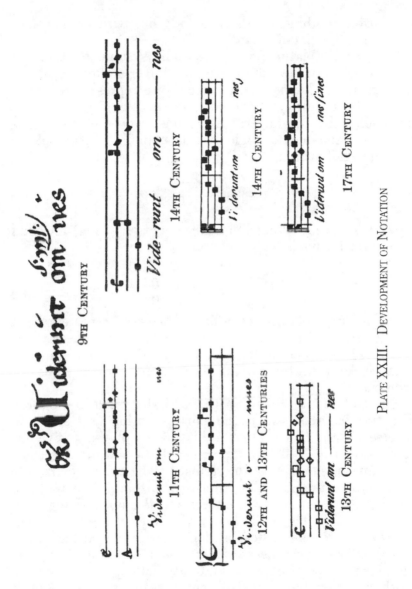

PLATE XXIII. DEVELOPMENT OF NOTATION

was often combined with a melody-line written in black notation on a five-line staff.

The other tablatures were essentially systems of recording the music by means of the actual finger-technique of the instrument. That is to say, notes were represented by the "fret" (on the lute) or the hole (in the pipe) which was to be touched by the finger. A violinist would easily appreciate the fundamental logic of this plan if, in place of his five-line staff, thus:

he were reduced to four lines (one for each string) and had to rely for his notes on the figures

    2 3
    1 3
    0 2
    0 1

In the lute-tablatures each line of the staff represented an actual string of the instrument. Letters (or figures) were then used to represent an ascending semitonic scale on each string. As with the organ, there were various signs for showing time-values.

The Italian lute-tablature used a six-line staff and figures. The top-line represented the bottom string and so on in reverse order. The French tablature employed a five-line staff, letters instead of numbers, and the lines in the same order upwards as that of the strings. The two systems were afterwards combined. The German lute-tablature was still worse; for it employed numbers for the open strings and letters running diagonally across the frets of the instrument for the semitones — a fearful depth of misplaced ingenuity.

Tablatures never became *stereotyped*. To the last they remained things of personal and national caprice. Founded as they were on an essentially cumbersome and unworkable idea they could not hope to survive. Constitutionally they were all *dropsical* and, though they lingered on into the eighteenth century, the doctors of music always knew they were past praying for.

CHAPTER 6

The Less Dark Ages

IN the last chapter we laid some stress on the invention of plural-melody as being fundamental in its importance. It occurred somewhere towards the end of the first millenium of our era; and the date chosen — 900 A.D. — may fairly be called the great dividing line in the history of music. At present the full meaning of this development to the human race has not been adequately studied : nor have we space for any such discussion here. But the purely musical side of the change has received attention both in Germany and England.

We may say at once that, if the reader puts the difficult question *why* men should have been content with simple melody from their time of savagery down through all the brilliant pre-Christian civilizations to the days of King Alfred, and *why then* they should suddenly have felt this immense craving for a new musical experience, we can only say that we have no answer worth giving. A good deal of academic hot air has been blown off in the attempt to answer this question. Learned persons say that "the Greeks already understood the art of magadizing." That is so. But it does not answer our question. It only tells us that they knew the difference between groups of boys and men singing the same tune separately or in octaves together; and that they allowed the latter as an extension of the former. But people have always done this either with voices or stringed instruments. Still less satisfactory is the suggestion that the new art sprang somehow from an analogy with the "drones" of the bagpipes and the mediæval hurdy-gurdy. For, if that were so, we should expect the earliest forms of harmony to consist of tunes with pedal basses. And this they certainly are not.

ORGANUM (OLD STYLE) 900

What then was this new and inexplicable craving of the harassed generations that lived between 800 and 900? In a few words it was the desire, when they heard a tune, to sing or play that tune simultaneously at a different part of the octave. If we had that craving at the present day it would impel us irresistibly when we heard

God save our gra-cious King

to sing or play it at the same time a fourth or a fifth lower; so that the effect would be

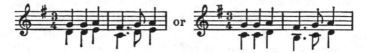

We first hear of this movement in the ninth century as having come among the Franks from Rome. The music which was so produced was called *organum*, and its technique was known as *the art of organum* or *of organizing*. In the tenth century Hucbald, the Flemish monk, wrote a work called *Musica Enchiriadis* [1] in which this new art appears as something already studied and partly systematized. He speaks of it as being a matter of regular church practice and gives it also a second name — *diaphony*.

The rules for making this diaphony or organum were very simple. The original plain-song was called the *principal voice* (P. V.).

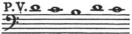

To this might be added a second part — the *organal voice* (O. V.) [2] a fifth lower:

---

[1] The authorship has been questioned.
[2] *Vox principalis* and *vox organalis*. In the chapters devoted to mediæval music, English has, wherever possible, been substituted for Latin.

Furthermore, the O. V. could be doubled in the octave above and the P. V. in the octave below; so that the total effect would be

Finally, the whole of this process could be carried out at the fourth instead of the fifth below.   So that a fragment of plain-song such as this

became

By this plan our original tune of *God save the King* would stand so:

Only one prohibition existed in the earliest days of organum.   The O. V. was not allowed to go below

This may have been due to the fear of mixing with an upper scale (having B-natural) a lower transposed scale (having B-flat). Or it may have been caused simply by the fact that the organ played the O. V. and, on that instrument as constructed in the tenth century, no lower note was possible.

If the latter supposition is true, it gives us a clue to the intense mental satisfaction which must have been felt in these primitive fourths, fifths, and octaves. For at that time the mind dwelt only on the pure consonance of each individual note as it was sung against its organ accompaniment. The singer was conscious that he was singing a tune; but, at each step, he took for the first time in history a daring and unexampled look vertically downwards. The joy that he had, came from an unparalleled artistic courage. His results have often been made the subject of idle jest and comparison. But we must view this matter from the standpoint, not of today, but of 700. And if we do so with candor, we shall probably revise in some degree our hasty generalization, the *dark* ages; and view this special age as that of the *dawn*.

As we have described it above, the organum was theoretically (and at first practically) a matter of similar motion and nothing else. If the plain-song stood still, the organal part stood still, too; if it went up or down, the organal followed it up or down.

Except for the one restriction mentioned above, it was a series of *parallelisms* between two versions of the same tune. But this archaic type of organum soon became more a text-book affair than a practical routine. The very fact that sometimes the O. V. *had* to stand still while the P. V. went on, at once introduced the idea of oblique motion. In addition to

we get

The tendency towards freedom of movement was, of course, always more in favor of the organal than of the principal voice. The latter was, and remained for centuries, the bony skeleton of the musical body. Or perhaps it would be more correct to describe it in these early years as the framework within the sculptor's clay — a thing whose rough outlines were put there to be followed and whose removal meant the collapse of the whole model. But it is quite apparent that, by the first half of the eleventh century, musicians were beginning to use their ears. They were beginning to see in their organum a plastic something which could be gingerly handled and molded, touched here and retouched there, so as to produce new and pleasant sensations. It perhaps meant more than they had originally suspected. Accordingly we find Guido d'Arezzo discussing the best practical ways of treating the archaic organum.[1] He was no great innovator in this field. But he summed up the possibilities of what has been called the *old-style organum;* that is to say, the organum first of similar and then of similar-plus-oblique motion. The single example of his method which we give[2] should be compared with the examples of the oldest organum on pages 120–21.

Ve - ni ad do-cen-dum nos vi - - am pru-den-ti- æ

ORGANUM (NEW STYLE) 1050

As we have already shown in the previous chapter, Guido left the world a good deal richer at his death than he found it. He fixed the notation and invented the art of solmization. But, as far as the texture of the music went, he looked rather backwards than forwards. The new organum began about the time of his death in 1050. During the next 100 years the

[1] *Micrologus*, written between 1000 and 1050.
[2] Quoted from *The Oxford History of Music*, vol. 1.

cry was all for contrary motion. Undoubtedly, towards the end of the former period, singers must have occasionally noticed the happy effect produced by two voices moving in opposite directions. Especially at the ends of the chants — in what they called the *occurse*[1] — one voice would naturally move to meet the other. And a singer who had sung such endings year after year would be tempted to a similar enterprise elsewhere. At any rate, we find as the characteristic development of the *new-style organum* that the musician has added to his armory the third possible form of movement, and has now not only

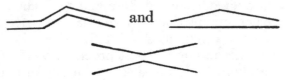

but also

John Cotton, writing at the beginning of the twelfth century, demands this sort of variety throughout the whole of the chant; and the Milanese treatise which gives rules *for making organum*[2] supports this appeal. Such devices as the momentary crossing of parts and — more important — the setting of two or three notes of the organal voice against one long note of the principal begin to appear. In fact, if we compare the following piece of organum with the specimens given earlier we shall see how great has been the advance. No, if we can rid our minds of our inherited prepossessions against fourths, we shall be forced to call this twelfth century composition an intelligent bit of counterpoint.[3]

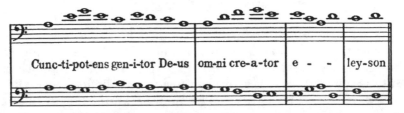

---

[1] Lat. *occursus*, a running together. See the last two notes of the example on page 123.

[2] *Ad organum faciendum*, twelfth century.

[3] Quoted from *The Oxford History of Music*, vol. 1.

DISCANT (1150)

(MEASURED MUSIC. TRIPLE TIME)

The example just given is about as satisfactory as any we may expect to find under the rigorous conditions of diaphony—that is to say, a note-against-note musical commentary on the plain-song. It is to be observed that the movement of the upper part is dictated solely by that of the lower. Except at the two ends of a piece no *harmonic* prevision can be said to exist. Concords and discords, though used in about the proportion of 2 to 1, seem to be scattered haphazard without any consciousness of their very different values. Finally — and this is the most important point — the music has *no measure*. It must have been sung in the free and constantly varying rhythms of the Latin text.

Somewhere about the year 1150 attempts began to be made to introduce measure. We know of these attempts chiefly from two anonymous treatises, one of that date, and one later;[1] from a celebrated work attributed to Franco of Cologne; and from others by two Englishmen, John Garland and Walter Odington.[2] This new music we now call *measured music*, but it is worth noting that its own godfathers preferred for it the name *measurable music* (musica mensurabilis). A second and shorter name — *discant*[3] — was also employed. And, as Franco's treatise, *Ars Cantus Mensurabilis*, is intimately associated with the whole movement, the years from about 1150 to 1300 are often known as "The Franconian Period of Discant."

So far for names and facts. Let us now go back to the human side of the matter. We have just said that attempts were made "to introduce measure." But the problem as it presented itself to the men of that date was somewhat different. They had had 250 years of the old note-against-note organum and they were tired of its sameness. They

[1] The *Discantus Positio Vulgaris* and the *Anonymus* of the British Museum.

[2] *De Musica Mensurabili Positio* and *De Speculatione Musicae*.

[3] Dis-cantus is merely a Latin translation of the Greek δια-φωνία (diaphōnia) = discord.

craved for some sort of variety, but they had no means of obtaining it. The leather of the old organum had been stretched to its limits. No more could be done with the music. So they turned *to the words*.

Now the words, as we have already said, were sung mainly according to the spoken rhythm. The only way therefore to secure variety from them was to take two sets of words differing in rhythm and to make them fit as a piece of two-part counterpoint. But in order to do this it was necessary to find some unit of time to which both sets of words could be referred. The result was that, in going out after the oyster *simultaneous verbal rhythms*, they found the pearl *musical measure*.

There has been some discussion as to why they adopted *triple* time as the ground-rhythm on which all their verbal combinations should be made to march; and the question has been asked whether they really could have made their choice — as has been generally understood — on religious grounds. It has been urged that they would undoubtedly have been wiser to start with *duple* time. The change to triple would have been easier; progress more speedy. Fur-thermore the genteel school of modern criticism, ignorant of the ingenuous depths of the medieval religious mind, has transferred to that mind its own comfortable middle-class ideal of "keep religion for Sunday." But we must remark first of all that the early composers could have no prevision on the musical side of the question. They were as helpless as a Wiltshire laborer would be today if he were asked for a plan by which to reconcile "The curfew tolls the knell of part-ing day" with "When the hounds of spring are on winter's traces." Faced with the same problem as that of the twelfth century the modern musician would have to make an arbitrary choice. The ancient musician went to his religion for help. Nothing was more natural. And, as he himself referred his procedure to the Holy Trinity, it is a waste of time to seek any other origin.

However that may be, it should be understood that from now till about 1300 there is no music but triple-time music.

The only two ways of splitting up the fundamental measure are into three equal or two unequal parts.

And the whole preoccupation of the musician from 1100 to 1250 consists in finding two sets of triple rhythms which can contain his words and at the same time be laid parallel to each other. In their simplest states these rhythmic-molds were no more than constant repetitions, such as

But, as this system of metrical combination became more studied, its bounds were extended to include what we should now call phrases of a greater length than one bar in either part. This extension, if pushed to its logical conclusion, would undoubtedly have produced most ridiculous results. But towards the end of the period men's minds began to turn very decidedly from the *metrical* to the *mensural*. The worst absurdities of the system were therefore never put in practice. However, even without these, the music of the period rarely strayed far above the mud-and-water line of a desolate dulness.

In the texture of the music we have to note some improvements. And these — historians seem to be agreed — give us our first example of the general effect of English music on that of other nations. As far as this rather obscure subject can be understood there seems to have been in the twelfth century a school of English popular singing that was ahead of contemporary church music somewhat in the same way that the man who wrote *Sumer is icumen in* was ahead of his own theorists in the next century. These Welsh and west-country singers, we learn from the writer Gerald,[1] sang in thirds and sixths — a musical procedure unknown till these days.

The light brilliance of this style must have been as amazing as it was unexpected. It had an immediate effect on the continental musicians. Major and minor thirds begin to be sung in the church discant; and even the sixth — hitherto regarded much as a sixteenth century contrapuntist regarded a sharp seventh or a B-natural against an F — began to put in a timid appearance when well supported on either side by the more decorous fifths and octaves. We may add that it was probably a continuation of this popular school of English singing that produced in the fourteenth century the musical system known as *faburden*. At any rate we find at the end of the twelfth century that, though the stricter theorists still regarded consecutive perfect intervals (fourths and fifths) as infinitely preferable to consecutive imperfect intervals (thirds and sixths), the third had become so well established that modern-looking voice parts such as the following were possible. A comparison between them and the earlier specimens already given will show how great has been the advance. But we must remember that we are 300 years from the time of Hucbald and 150 from that of Guido d'Arezzo.

At this time the organal voice had, after some hesitation, become finally fixed in its position above the plain-song. In the writing of these two parts the musician's harmonic stand-by was still alternate fifths and octaves. But he was beginning to use a significant cunning in treating his upper part. As this part had to move or "discant" on the longer notes underneath, its unaccented beats were used sometimes (1) in

[1] Giraldus Cambrensis (1146–1220).

arpeggio, sometimes (2) as passing-notes, and sometimes even (3) as changing-notes.

We must now say a few words with regard to the musical forms that were in use during the period of discant. Of these, four may be mentioned, the *Free Organum*,[1] the *Conductus*, the *Rondel* (or *rota*), and the *Motet;* of which the last alone survived.

THE FREE ORGANUM

The free organum is characteristic of the oldest style of discant. It is usually in two parts, though triple and quadruple examples are to be found. In this form the tenor always sings the long notes of the lower part and often stops singing till a convenient and concordant opportunity occurs for his reëntry. Meanwhile the upper part *discants* in a manner that justifies the colloquial use of the word. In a single specimen quoted by Wooldridge the first three notes of the tenor have seventy-eight discant notes above them — not counting the added ornaments. In the three- and four-part compositions the upper voices are of course not nearly so free, but even here the main characteristic is the enormous length and weight of the tenor notes.

THE CONDUCTUS

The conductus was a two-part (sometimes three-part) composition in which the lowest voice (the tenor) sang a purely metrical part of the sort described on page 127. The tune of this might be invented or it might be borrowed from any popular folk-song. The treatment varied from a rigid mathematical simplicity in which the voice-parts seem to have been laid off with a foot-rule, to an amazing melodic

[1] *Organum purum* or *organum proprie sumptum.*

freedom in which the wild sweeping phrases of the discanting-part are only just held down to earth by the long solid notes of the tenor. The musical devices used were a primitive sort of sequence and imitation, and a cruel medieval stratagem called the *hocket*.[1] This last was a plan by which a part of this sort

was cut up between two voices, so that one sang the odd-numbered notes and the other the even. This seems mechanical enough. But from the many indignant protests of the church authorities that have come down to us there is little doubt that the "hocketting" was often not far short of scandalous. It is a little difficult at the present day fully to understand the depths of degradation to which the singers continually dragged the divine service. We shall have occasion to refer to this again under the heading " Faburden and Gymel " (page 138). There seems, however, to be very little doubt that the vile practices against which churchmen exclaimed were not merely musical ornaments and elaborations, but things of a much more disreputable nature. It is perhaps as well not to inquire too closely what they were. But the *hocket* was clearly the worst offender. Uncomfortable vocal stoppages are indeed characteristic of this period. Examples can be found of thirty-bar phrases set to a single syllable, and yet with two or three separate silent bars in the middle. The conductus at its best was sometimes a simple unaffected composition in which we find the new devices used side by side with the old. These latter — the glaring consecutive octaves and fifths — were of course perceived in those days merely as passages in the good ancient solid style. In the following well-known conductus, *Quen of Evene*, the tenor has a range of a fifth while the discant has no more than a fourth. Despite its one or two awkward places it undoubtedly reaches a certain level of pleasant smoothness.[2]

[1] Probably = hiccough.
[2] From the Arundel MSS. in the British Museum.

Quen of Evene

THE RONDEL (OR ROTA)

Theoretically the rondel was a three-part song, each of whose phrases was sung through thrice. At every repetition the singers changed parts. Thus, with mixed voices, the effect would be a sort of triple counterpoint. This was the theory.[1] But, if ever it was put into practice the results have disappeared. The rondeaux of Adam de la Hale [2] (1230–88) are merely three-part compositions with a certain amount of repetition founded on the rondeau-form of their poems. In character they would all sound something like a modern "round" if, in the latter, all the singers began together.

The true rondel type is better shown in the two interchanging parts that make up the *pes* of *Sumer is icumen in.* This celebrated piece — the theme of honorable pride to every Englishman — was probably written in the abbey of Reading (Berkshire) by a monk, one John of Fornsete (in Norfolk). Its date is certainly between 1200 and 1250. It exists in a single manuscript in the British Museum [3] and is there specifically called a *rota* (wheel or round). The notation is on a six-line staff with the C-clef on the fourth line and a B-flat in the signature. Exact instructions are given in Latin for its performance. The work is for six voices. The four upper voices — tenors — sing the melody in strict canon. The first one leads off, and when it arrives at "the first note after the cross" the second voice enters, and so on with the others.[4] Meanwhile each of the two lower voices hunts the other's trail through the rondel-like passage that makes up the *pes* or "foot."

This extraordinary work is a never-ending wonder. Technically it is at least two centuries ahead of its time. Its firm outlines were drawn by a master with a great knowledge of effect and with a complete command of the means by which to secure it. The smoothness and richness of its harmony are practically what we look for in vocal writing at the present

[1] Walter Odington is the authority.
[2] Known as The Humpback of Arras.
[3] MSS. Harl. 798.
[4] Ad primam notam post crucem incohat alius et sic de ceteris.

day. In fact, no greater tribute has ever been paid to it than the remark of a recent scholar that its "frequent use of consecutive fifths and octaves, in strict accordance with thirteenth century principles, has to our ears all the effect of a series of grammatical blunders, so sharply does it contrast with the smooth counterpoint of the rest." [1]

The question has been asked over and over again "How came it to be written?" But no answer at all satisfactory has ever been forthcoming. The present writer confesses that it is the same marvel to him as if he were assured that the sonnet "When to the sessions of sweet silent thought" had been found in Chaucer's handwriting.

Sumer is icumen in has been printed many times before in many different forms. But it cannot be shown too often. We shall therefore include it here, placing above it four bars of music which a professional theorist and composer *of fifty years later* recommended to his readers as the correct way to write a rondel. See page 133.

THE MOTET

The Motet was generally a three-part composition founded on some portion of the church service. In making it, the musician selected for his tenor-part either a fragment of plainsong or less commonly a secular tune. This he turned from unmeasured into measured (triple time) music. Almost always its length was insufficient for his purposes. He was therefore confronted with the necessity of adopting not only a rhythm, but a method of laying out that rhythm and a system of repetition.

His choice in these matters was guided partly by chance it would seem, partly by his own taste, and partly by an elaborate system of medieval musical carpentering called the *ordines*. These ordines gave him fixed patterns to which he could work. But it must be remembered that, as he had only the narrowest range of rhythms from which to choose — practically those given on page 127 — the disposal of the com-

[1] D. F. Tovey.

plete phrase over a number of bars was wholly arbitrary. In modern language it came to this, that after he had selected his rhythm he had the option of putting in rests of a constant value at certain fixed intervals in his composition. Twenty or thirty of these rhythm-schemes were in use. The following may be quoted as examples:

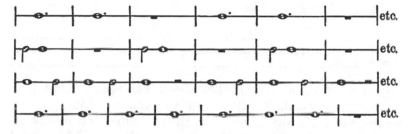

This mathematical laying-out of the tenor-part of course controlled the whole composition of the motet. To us it seems highly mechanical; but it did good no doubt in that it forced musicians to contemplate their rhythms in groups-of-bars, as we should say. Probably the most awkward schemes were little used. But there are actual motets in existence throughout the whole of which the tenor sings three single notes, one in each of three successive bars, and then pauses for the fourth bar. At its best the system gives us long-note tenor-parts such as this, from the motet *Alle psallite cum luya.*

In the above example the upper parts do not follow this rhythmic scheme at all. As a rule, the *discant* was somewhat pinned to the tenor phrases while the *triplum* wandered vaguely on without much reference to either. But occasionally there seems to have been an attempt to make two tenor phrases equal to one in the other parts. So that the rhythmic scheme was like this:

Triplum ———————————— ————————————
Discant ———————————— ————————————
Tenor ———— ———— ———— ————

It has been questioned whether these tenor-parts were actually sung to words or not. In the manuscripts there is generally to be found a Latin tag taken from the words of the plain-song from which the tune was originally borrowed. This varies in length from a single syllable to two complete words. And it has been asked whether the object of this tag was not to remind the singer of the plain-song words so that he could supply them from memory in the motet. The question has been answered both ways, but the best opinion is that the singer merely vocalized. If he had only one syllable he used that syllable throughout. With two he probably vocalized on the first syllable and used the second for his final note; and so, appropriately to the plain-song, with his three syllables.

DUPLE TIME

Towards the end of the thirteenth century church musicians seem suddenly to have realized that the world would go mad if it had any more 3–2 rhythm. There was a violent wrench and snap; followed by a period of expansion and confusion which — as far as the church was concerned — was ended by a decree of the Pope in 1322. From that year we date the introduction of *faburden*. These three sentences give us the main outlines of musical history from about 1280–1400.

No technical reasons have ever been suggested for the sudden introduction of duple time. However, we shall probably be not far wrong if we regard its appearance as a natural but long-delayed protest against the restriction of human rights.

But here let the reader pause to consider what a frightfully disturbing element this new rhythm was. No uninvited guest at a feast ever caused such trouble. Imagine the feelings of an elderly musician in 1280, who after being suckled, baptized, and nursed to 3–2 music and after spending his whole life on the supposition, — not that music *could be* written in 3–2 but that music *was* 3–2, — suddenly found from his juniors that it *might be* in duple time. The ground was wiped from under his feet. Our modern innovators who insist that the triad of C-major should include a D-flat and an F-sharp would be almost harmless beside these mediæval revolutionaries.

But, whatever the opposition, the poisonous 2–2 wriggled in somehow. The elder men probably refused to handle the viper at all. But the modernists of the day not only handled it but managed to pack its curves safely into the family musical-box. In other words, at this time began the series of experiments in reconciling twos with threes which are generally associated with the name of Philippe de Vitry. We have already referred to this system of *prolation* in a former chapter. It was nothing but a new form of notation forced on musicians by the sudden intrusion of the hobgoblin 2–2 at the feast of the aged king 3–2.

Of course, with this grand shifting of the foundations there came many smaller changes in the house-musical. Consecutive perfect intervals were buried: their ghosts exorcised. And in their room sat the pleasant smiling figures of the twin-thirds and sixths — young then, but ever since welcome visitors. The old metrical formulas with their stencilled patterns were banished to the second-best parlor on their way to the attic and the dust-heap. And when these had disappeared men began to take heart; to control their voice-parts instead of being controlled by them; to devise little contrapuntal phrases which were happy in themselves and made happy friends with the other parts. Stupid endings that only made people say "well?" went out of fashion.

Once and for all musicians found out that if the two parts met so

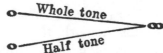

everybody would be satisfied. Great things were stirring. Attractive F-sharps, C-sharps, and B-flats walked almost openly in the streets. The professors of *musica ficta* even permitted G-sharps to come forth when respectably supported on either side.

In France the troubadours and trouvères with Machaut at their head sang *rondeaux, chansons, ballades,* and snapped their white fingers at their inky-fingered brethren; while the latter snapped their fingers back and stole their best things from them. In Italy they woke up, dressed, and ate their breakfasts *in canon.* One who could not do this probably wished himself back in the days of Hucbald. They had songs of the chase, songs of the street, songs of the early-morning market, and always ballads of the lover sick to death. The *madrigal* came in. Not our madrigal — that is to say, the madrigal of Elizabeth's time — but a pleasant part-song where the same music served for two or three stanzas and was separated from the next section by a little bridge-stanza called the *ritornello.*

FABURDEN AND GYMEL (1322)

But the question may be asked "what was the church doing all this time?" Well, apparently, the church was doing very badly. When the world turned topsy-turvy and people first realized that music was not carpentering in 3-inch lengths, a sort of licentious orgy of music set in. It is difficult to explain with reverence just what happened. But if the reader wishes a modern analogy with the state of church music at that time, he may imagine one of our church composers taking for his bass an Anglican chant and spreading it out so that each note occupied three or four bars ; then for his treble using *Take a pair of sparkling eyes* (allegro molto) ; and for his alto part fitting in as much as he could of *Tipperary* or *Onward Christian Soldiers*, or both.   What the church service sounded like under these conditions can be better imagined than described.   It *has* been described by contemporary sufferers, and if half of what they say is true it must have been like rag-time gone mad.

However, the Pope[1] held up his little finger at Avignon in 1322, and the tumult ceased.   In effect his decree said "The old tunes are best.   Don't try to write new.   Also don't *hide* the old with hocketting and discanting.   Go back to plain-song.   For great occasions you may add consecutive fourths, fifths, and octaves" — *he was thinking of Hucbald* — "but the plain-song must be heard if it is to do good to the singers and congregation."   And back they went to plain-song.

It is a curious reflection that in all the crises that arose between the musicians and the church authorities the music-men were always wrong and the churchmen always right. It is a still more curious reflection that we are asked to believe that the musicians always outwitted the authorities by worthless technical pretences.   In the present case an odd thing occurred.   When the Pope said "go back to plain-song, plus fourths, fifths, and octaves for great occasions" he clearly enjoined unison-singing on ordinary days and the old-style *organum* for festivals.   What we are told the musicians did, is this.   They said "here is something that *looks* ancient and severe.   There can be no objection to this.

Now let us make our first tenors sing the bottom part (the bass) in their best register — an octave higher that is to say.

[1] John XXII.

We shall then have something that· *sounds* really light and modern and interesting."

There is a psychological difficulty here. If this rearrangement into a series of thirds and sixths really did sound brilliant and modern to them — and we have every reason to believe that it did, in a way hard to understand at the present day — how is it that the church authorities did not notice it? Are we to suppose that they were content to compromise the matter? To allow the singers their effective modern style of singing the plain-song provided they kept to its long notes and attempted no *discant* or *floreation?*

It would seem so. At any rate, this system of *faburden*,[1] as it was called, came in as a recognized church-practice after the papal decree. With it was joined a subsidiary system called *gymel*.[2] Very little is known about this, but, like faburden, it appears to have been a plan for inverting intervals. In this case it was concerned with the doctoring of consecutive thirds into sixths. The upper singer read the lower part, but transposed it up an octave. So that a succession of thirds

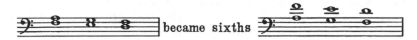

Nothing very accurate is known as to the first history of faburden. But it was in existence as a secular practice long before it was received into the bosom of the church. The German doctors say that its home was England. The English doctors reply that it has left no written trace of its residence there. This would be conclusive but for the fact that scarcely *any* written music of that time is now in existence. Possibly its invention should be credited neither to England, France, nor Italy. Nothing could be more natural — almost inevitable — than its occasional use in any country for

---

[1] Faulx Bourdon, falsobordone. [2] Probably = *couple*.

two or three notes in the accompaniment of the plain-song. The English may have seized on it as a new, light, and effective method of extemporizing, and may have made it more particularly their own.

It required the minimum of mental exertion from the singers. Its results were *certain*. Three-part singing from a one-part service book must have often produced sadly undevotional music.[1] Nothing of this sort was possible with faburden. The two lower voices (*contratenor* and *tenor*) had merely to watch the plain-song and sing it a fifth and a third higher respectively. The leading tenor (*supranus*) was even better off; for he had to sing the plain-song itself just where a leading tenor always wants to sing — in his top octave. Finally, there can be no doubt that towards the end of the fourteenth and the beginning of the fifteenth century Englishmen took a very prominent and active part in the development of counterpoint. Lionel Power, Chilston,[2] Simon Tunsted, and William the Monk,[3] all wrote treatises on the subject. The last-named was — like John Hothby a little later — a resident in Italy.

As we have now come within sight of the fifteenth century we may pause for a moment to look both backwards and forwards. Six centuries lie behind us. And in them music has developed — through the various forms of organum, discant, and so on — from simple melody to a fairly complex form of three-part and even four-part vocal composition. It is still stiff and ungainly. Even the best tune is liable to be spoilt at this time by harsh, empty, and awkward harmonies. But these are only the footprints of an old and dying past. They are already being more and more obliterated by the constant tread of feet moving forward. As we stand on the dividing line (1400) we can see that all these feet are hurry-

[1] This sort of singing was known as "counterpoint over the book" (*contrapunctus supra librum*). It was the usual method of church performance. In fact, the word *sight* continued in use down to the seventeenth century in the sense of "interval from the plain-song."

[2] The MS. was at Waltham Abbey in the middle of the sixteenth century. It then passed into the hands of Tallis, who was organist there, and from him to Morley. It is now in the British Museum.

[3] Guilelmus Monachus.

ing into a New World, whose possible existence dawned on Europe about a hundred years before Columbus sailed.

But, for the first time in history, we begin to notice that, though all the makers of music are journeying towards the same spot, they go by different paths. In other words, they are not merely musicians, but *composers of this or that country*. This distinction is fairly strong even between 1400 and 1450. It becomes increasingly stronger as the years go by, and in time stands out as the great controlling factor in music.

The chief names which are associated with the national movements of the fifteenth century are first John Dunstable, then Guillaume Dufay, and then Josquin des Près. The last-named composer, both from his musical work and from the date of his life (1445–1521), may be looked on as the bridge which carries us over into the sixteenth century, the "golden age," as it has been called, of vocal composition. In that century it would be easy to make a long list of names, but as guides to the memory one may mention Goudimel, Orlando di Lasso, Vittoria, Wilbye, and Palestrina.

The reader has by now gained some acquaintance both with the technical terms used by the monkish theorists and with the names of the chief composers of the fifteenth and sixteenth centuries which are to be treated in the next two chapters. In order, therefore, to fix the succession of events in his mind we shall subjoin a very simple *conspectus* of the whole 800 years; merely adding that the dates are in some cases only approximate, and that the fewest possible names and facts have been included.

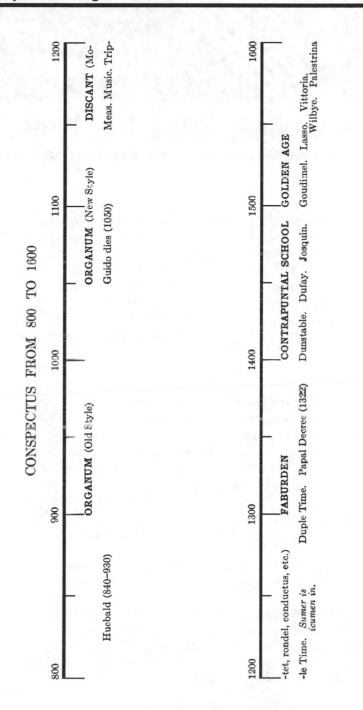

CONSPECTUS FROM 800 TO 1600

ORGANUM (Old Style)

Hucbald (840–930)

ORGANUM (New Style)

Guido dies (1050)

DISCANT (Mo-

Meas. Music. Trip-

-tet, rondel, conductus, etc.)

-le Time. *Sumer is icumen in.*

FABURDEN

Duple Time. Papal Decree (1322)

CONTRAPUNTAL SCHOOL

Dunstable. Dufay. Josquin.

GOLDEN AGE

Goudimel. Lasso. Vittoria.
Wilbye. Palestrina

800   900   1000   1100   1200

1200   1300   1400   1500   1600

CHAPTER 7

Dunstable. Dufay. Des Pres.

In the year 1400 England had just passed through a century of foreign warfare. At home pestilence, famine, and the boundless rapacity of the clergy had eaten deep into her life. A generation had grown up, had stood even in the high places of the king, and had found that neither days nor works availed them in their struggle towards the light. On all of them lay the heavy hand of the past. Bitter dreams and the slow-burning embers of an unappeasable yearning were the only things left to them.

The men of this time show a child-like depth of tenderness, an unconscious poetry which they seem scarcely able to utter. They stumble on their ideals in the dark. Standing at the birth of a great movement they are forever haunted by the strange sounds whose beauty they cannot fathom. The chanting voices in the minster reëcho through all their dreams. And, as the sound goes up to heaven, it mingles in a floating cloud with the longings and desires of the worshippers below. The poor wanderer on the Malvern Hills — "wery of this worlde" — with his vision of the glories of Palm Sunday has rekindled for us the flame of this yearning.

> Of gerlis and of *gloria laus* gretly me dremed
> And how *osanna* by orgonye olde folke songen.

Not less serious, though perhaps more simple, is the picture of the widow's little son — the "litel clergeon" — sitting in the choir-school over his primer, and edging inch by inch nearer to the open door, all ears to catch another note or two of the *Alma Redemptoris*.

> This litel child, his litel book lerninge,
> As he sat in the scole at his prymer,
> He *Alma redemptoris* herde singe,
> As children lerned hir antiphoner;
> And, as he dorste, he drough him ner and ner,
> And herkned ay the wordes and the note,
> Til he the firste vers coude al by rote.

And if we wish to place between these two pictures a third which shall tell us what was the music of the young and care-free, we need only peep in at the Clerk of Oxenford's room and hear how he sweetens his studies in Aristotle.

> And all above there lay a gay sawtrye
> On which he made a-nightes melodye,
> So swetely that al the chambur rang,
> And *Angelus ad virginem* he sang.

Alma redemptoris mater — Angelus ad virginem — Osanna in excelsis. These three may well be kept in mind. For they must often have been heard by the men of whom we are about to speak. And where so little is known and so much has to be surmised, any key, even the smallest, is worth trying. It may unlock for us some shuttered casement high up above the world of facts and figures. And from there perhaps we may catch a glimpse of the strange lands whose bare winter these very men changed to spring.

In this and the next chapter we are about to describe the music of the contrapuntal school (fifteenth century) and of the "golden age" (sixteenth century); and as this description must involve us in a maze of names we think it well that the reader should have before him a bare outline of the course which musical history took in those centuries. To furnish this is comparatively a simple matter.

FIFTEENTH CENTURY

The contrapuntal school began in England with the invention of composition by Dunstable. But neither he nor his many English associates founded a permanent school *in*

England. On the other hand, their influence abroad was very great.

In particular the Netherlanders (Flemings) seized the torch which Dunstable had kindled and before long had it well alight in the hands of Dufay. This man's pupils and followers (Busnois, Obrecht, etc.) labored hard at the knotty contrapuntal problems of music at the same time that these problems were being attacked in Paris by Okeghem. The torch was still alight. And very soon it was blazing in the grasp of Josquin des Près, the great Flemish contrapuntist, who takes us over into the "golden age."

SIXTEENTH CENTURY

The whole of Europe may be said to have profited by the results of the Flemish labors. The Flemish school itself continued (Arcadelt, Clemens, Lasso); and there were schools in France (Certon, Goudimel); and Spain (Morales, Vittoria); with various offshoots from the earlier Flemish schools such as that of Venice (Da Rore, Zarlino, Croce, Gabrieli).

But it is to England and to Rome that we have to look for that perfecting of the art of vocal counterpoint which gives this century its title of "golden." Both places produced great schools of secular and of church music. To England the torch had, in a way, come back after long waiting. The men there held it aloft so that its rays still illumine the pathway of art. Chief of these were Tallis, Gibbons, Morley, Byrd, and Wilbye. In Italy they were Luca Marenzio and — greatest of all — Palestrina.

Let us now return to the point and place where we left our story — England in 1400. We may note that in English musical history there has always been a certain want of continuity. The national character, violently bent on exteriorizing its energies abroad, has once or twice produced single great musicians or groups of great musicians. But these masters seem to have made their appearance in spite of, not in consequence of, the national character. There was such a group at the beginning of the fifteenth century; a similar group — the madrigalists and church composers of the sixteenth century; then Purcell in the seventeenth — a solitary genius born out of his time; then nothing till the renaissance in 1870.

It would be pleasant for an English historian if he could point to *Sumer is icumen in* and hail its author as Dunstable's artistic godfather. But the plain fact is that there is not one line of music in existence to show that the culture represented by the former is at one end of a line that leads to the latter. They are isolated points. And probably if Dunstable could have seen the Reading *rota* he would have been as much astonished by it as Mr. William Chappell was.

In the centuries that lie between Hastings and Agincourt we have very little knowledge of the musical life that existed in England. But what we have is significant. It is very nearly certain that *bowed* stringed instruments were invented there.[1] The same thing — with rather less probability — may be said of *keyed* stringed-instruments. For the rest — a few entries in the Royal Household Expenses of moneys paid to minstrels and to military trumpeters and drummers; a few illuminations in service-books; chapter-accounts for the building of organs; and the writings of the English theorists whom we have already mentioned. These are all we have.

But historians are agreed that the foundation of the Chapel Royal — that is to say, of a body of composer-singers — probably in Henry IV's reign had an immediate and widening influence on English music. The Chapel was undoubtedly in existence in Henry V's reign and indeed was in attendance on the King in France three years after Agincourt.[2] Henry VI, his successor, was an excellent composer who did not need to hide musical deficiencies under the cloak of majesty.

The music of this period has come down to us in several manuscripts.[3] It includes both secular and sacred composi-

[1] See pages 23, 24.
[2] The accounts are in existence. Among its members were Thorley, Wodehall, Dyolet, Laudewarnake, Wodeford, and Hesyll.
[3] St. Edmund's College at Old Hall near Ware (Herts) containing 138 compositions from 1430–80 (two by Henry VI) ; miscellaneous music in the

tions. Of the former we have the little round *Row the bote
Norman*, the catch *Tappster, Dryngker*, possibly the *Boar's
Head Carol*, and the great *Agincourt Song*. The last, as arranged for two solo voices and three-part chorus, has all
the characteristic harshness of the earlier portion of the century. The tune itself, however, is a wonderful thing, greatly
instinct with the medieval lust of battle. Its frantic cry
of thanks to God at the end is worth all the commentaries
on Agincourt that have ever been printed. Shakespeare
himself tells us less.

The Agincourt Song

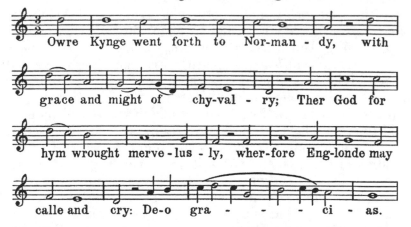

In the church music the chief point of technical interest is
the still complete dependence of the composer on some form
of *canto fermo*, that is to say, either plain-song or popular
melody. Given this, he seems to have made continuous and
increasingly successful efforts to get some sort of concord into
his accompanying parts.

This was almost wholly due to Dunstable. But it must be
understood that when he appears there is no sudden revolution in the method of handling the musical material such as

Selden, Douce, and Ashmole Collections (Bod. library, Oxford) ; and manuscripts at Modena, Bologna, and Vienna (removed from Trent). The
last group is our principal source of information for the music of Dunstable
and his school.

the monodists engineered in 1600. He does not throw the work of his predecessors to the winds and proclaim a new gospel. But for all that, we feel that his appearance is the entry of a master into the music-room — a master who sets the window open to the beautiful world outside, and *"sumer is icumen in."*

Of the external events in his life we know almost nothing. We do not know where or when he was born, or, with any precision, where he lived. He was buried in London (St. Stephen's, Walbrook) in 1453, but his grave was destroyed by the Great Fire two centuries later. Two epitaphs exist praising him as a musician *and astronomer*. However, we do know without a shadow of doubt that his continental contemporaries recognized him as their model and master.[1] His memory, more than that of any other composer, has been the sport of careless historians. Alternately forgotten and rediscovered by every generation, he was at last disinterred and canonized by a Dutch historian who thought that he must be St. Dunstan under an alias — much as one might confuse Brahms with Brahma. A later historian robbed him of his credit as the first composer by making a mistake in the date of Dufay's career; and this error, once set going, haunted the text-books for forty years. Even today, just when the whole world was settling down to believe that he was what his contemporaries knew him to be — the inventor of composition and an Englishman — the most distinguished of German musicologists casually refers to him in print as "the Scotchman." Probably in a few hundred years they will be arguing as to whether he was pre- or post-Christian, and saying that he was born in Belfast.

From what we have said above, it will be apparent that of all the figures of this time Dunstable's is the greatest and the most shadowy. Scarcely more solid are the shapes that have gathered round his — associates — friends perhaps — men

[1] The French poet Martin le Franc does homage to him as the model of the French school; Tinctoris, the Flemish historian, mentions him three times; John Hothby — writing probably as a resident in Florence or Ferrara speaks of him as "the distinguished Englishman" (*anglicus ille*); and there is a reference to him in a Spanish manuscript in the Escurial.

who lived, worked, and died, leaving behind them their best thoughts almost wholly to perish — Lionel Power, Benet, Forest, Stanley, Bedingham, Alain, Stove, Merkham, Morton, and Hothby.

One point, however, is clear. Some, at any rate, of these men lived and were honored abroad. We know that was so in the case of Hothby and probably also of Morton. So, from a consideration of the foreign tributes that came to Dunstable in his own century and of the fact that his works have almost all been preserved in manuscripts abroad, it has been suggested that the main part of his life must have been spent on the continent. This is more than probable; and it would account in part for the fact that, while his brilliant methods were causing a sensation in Europe generally, his own coevals at home were content placidly to follow the tradition of the elders. His influence indeed did come back to England, but it came through the Netherlands when he himself was forgotten — if he had ever really been known in his own country.

It is difficult to say exactly how many of Dunstable's works are in existence. From English sources very few have been obtained. But on this point we must not forget the wholesale burnings of cathedral libraries at the reformation. Since 1847, however, a considerable number have been copied from foreign manuscripts. One of these (at Modena) yielded thirty-one. It is characteristic of English contempt for their own artists that one-tenth the price of a thoroughbred could never be spared for a complete edition of his works.

Dunstable's great claim to remembrance is the fact that he was the first man *to compose*. He was the first man to see that organum-rules and discant-rules and theoretical prohibitions might be made till the crack of doom; but that, so long as you allowed their *practice* to be the business of choir-men using their powers of extemporization or of memory in front of an imperfect service-book, so long would you have timid and ugly music.

Furthermore he made up his mind that, as far as in him lay,

his music was going to sound well. It was not enough for him that his voice-parts, on a paper examination, just "scraped through." He looked at his music as a whole. He organized it — in our sense, not Hucbald's. He grouped his voices. He preferred short singable phrases followed by a rest, just as Palestrina did later. He understood the lengthening or shortening of his tenor-parts by putting them into longer or shorter notes — *augmentation* and *diminution*, as we call it. But he understood this as an artist, not as a journeyman-carpenter.

By these and other methods he secured a charm and a fresh beauty of sound that were unknown till he took up the pen. Of course, we must not judge him by the finished perfection of Wilbye or Palestrina, both of whom, as a plain fact, owed him the same debt that Brahms owed to Haydn. What Giotto is to painting, Dunstable is to music. And to appreciate either we must bear in mind the stiffness and angularity of his predecessors.

Dunstable's work came as an artistic revelation to continental Europe. But every seed dropped from the hand of the sower does not come as corn to the thresher's flail. At first there was only one country in Europe whose soil was rich enough and sufficiently undisturbed by the harrows of war to nourish this strange new plant.

The Netherlands contains within its borders two distinct types of country and of men. The one — the modern Dutch, as we call them — eminently fitted for service in the world, as sailors, explorers, colonizers, and as cultivators of all those arts that depend for their impulses on the external stimuli of the senses. The other — the Flemings — more reflective, not less active, but much less active externally, ready to turn their minds inwards and away from international conflict; consequently ill-suited for many types of worldly success, but capable of this one kind — *music*. It was in this soil that the seed, falling from Dunstable's hand, germinated.

Guillaume Dufay (?–1474) was a Fleming who after the fashion of his times took service in the papal choir. On returning to the Netherlands he held church appointments both at Mons and Bruges. But he is best remembered as Canon of Cambrai, where he lived and for whose church he wrote most of his music. There he became one of the great figures of his time, composing a large quantity of church-music — masses, antiphons, hymns, and magnificats. His work is perhaps more advanced than Dunstable's, but not greatly so. It may be said rather that the two were mental contemporaries. They faced the same problems, though Dunstable had given the earlier answer. Dufay searched for the same sweetness of expression, and his methodical mind tended towards the use of *canon;* not, as it was after-wards employed, to make the fabric of a movement from start to finish, but rather as a tentative device introduced here and there in the progress of a work. Furthermore, he is recog-nized as the first man to understand the essential elements of the *perfect cadence.*

In one respect his position is unique. He was probably the last musician in the world who still clung to the idea that his *canto fermo* — the bones of his movement — was still there only as a dry skeleton to be decently covered up by musical flesh and blood.

With his pupils and followers, the so-called "transitional school," Gilles Binchois (?–1460), Anthoine Busnois (?–1492), Philippe Caron (1420 ?– ?), Philippe Basiron (?– ?), Jean Regis (?– ?), and Jacob Obrecht (1430 ?–1500 ?), came the first dawning of the new idea ; that perhaps if the skeleton had a marrow, the rest of the body would have more chance of life. In addition to that, they improved his methods of canon along freely-moving lines, at the same time de-veloping little points of fugue, and embellishments of the cadence.

The great theorists who accompanied and explained the history of this age were Franchino Gafori (1451–1522), Johannes Tinctoris (1446–1511), and Sebastian Virdung (?– ?).

In Germany the Flemish influence produced for the moment less interesting results. But the fifteenth century German school has some important names ; such as Heinrich

Isaak (?–1517), Adam von Fulda (1450?–?), and Alexander Agricola (?–1522).

In France the tradition that had been established by Adam de la Hale and Machault continued without a break nearly to the middle of the fifteenth century. At this time the influence of the new movement began to make itself felt, and the banner of advance, which had been unfurled by Dunstable and carried forward by Dufay, passed into the keeping of Johannes Okeghem (c. 1430–1513).

This man was a pupil either of Dufay or of Binchois and held the post of director of the Chapel Royal in Paris. As we see it now, his main contribution to music consisted in the fact that during his long career he devoted the energies of a very strong mind to weighing and assaying the metal in which he knew all musical craftsmen had to work. He thus rendered considerable services to his successors who were able to use his formulas without further experiment. But his own name — though it should be coupled with certain developments in the arts of primitive canon and fugue — has almost become interchangeable with the words "dry-as-dust." This is not altogether fair. It is true that much of his music appears to be constructed under self-imposed prohibitory conditions. But this stage in art is an absolute necessity to progress. And the resulting excesses, of which we shall say something presently, are less characteristic of him than of his successors.

At any rate the task that confronted his great successor Josquin des Près (1445–1521) was a much easier one. Okeghem had had to break in a colt rough and raw from the field : Josquin found it saddled and bridled, ready for its first lesson in the *haute école*. The name "first great composer" has been given him, and that title is perhaps justified if we notice that it is "first great composer" and not "first composer."

He was a pupil of Okeghem and had sung in the papal choir at Rome. Lucky in the time of his birth, when the great awakening was beginning in Italy, he was still more lucky in being able to find in the north a technique already tested and analyzed. He used this technique with an unparalleled ease; pushing it up to and even beyond its proper limits. But he did more than this. For he is the first composer to whom we can safely apply the adjective "personal."

The sound of Dunstable's music was infinitely better than that of any music before his day. But, beyond the fact that he probably regarded canon as appropriate only in certain circumstances, we feel that his text — that is to say, the subject which he was illustrating — was a matter of indifference to him. The music was all of one kind, and it had to fit the words. He was aware of no deeper problem.

But this was not so with Josquin. He began to see dimly that poetical words call for definite musical expression. And in searching for that expression he made many musical discoveries. He found first of all that, as music had to be sung, there *must be* clear musical phrases; and that these could not possibly be intelligible to his hearers unless they were based on a satisfactory harmonic scheme. If we examine any work of about fifty years before his time, we are constantly coming on senseless arbitrary discords which, in common language, "spoil the whole thing." The composers of these works were probably only too thankful to be able to keep their parts moving *somehow*. Josquin saw — as we see — that this "somehow" prohibited all musical logic. That is his great contribution to history.

Beyond this, Josquin is noted in a smaller way as being the first man regularly to adopt the unaccompanied canonic opening. Before his time composers had often begun their movements with a point of canon or imitation. But, in doing this, they acted like boys swimming a new toy-boat in a pond. They thought it as well to keep it on a string. In other words, they began their canon, but tied it to land by some simple unimportant accompanying-part. Josquin took his courage in his hands and left the string at home.

The most celebrated of Josquin's contemporaries were Pierre de la Rue (?–1518), who was a chorister in the Duke of Burgundy's chapel; Antoine Brumel (c. 1480–c. 1520), who served at the court of Ferrara and wrote the mass with the unsolved puzzle-title *De dringhs;* Gaspar van Weerbecke

(?–?), who held an appointment in the Sforza chapel at Milan; Matthäus Pipelare (?–?), Jean Ghiselin (c. 1440–?), and Loyset Compère (?–1518). Of all of them it may be said that they inherited the same estate as Josquin, and did very much less than he to improve it.

Josquin's pupils travelled far and wide. They were true descendants of their forbears in that they all looked to Italy as the commercial goal of their existence. We shall have something to say on this point in the next chapter. Meanwhile, we must note among them the most distinguished names — Jean Mouton (1475?–1522), singer-composer to both Louis XI and Francis I, and — like his master Josquin — Canon of St. Quentin; Eléazar Genet (better known as Carpentrasso, c. 1475–c. 1532), the aristocratic churchman of Avignon, at one time director of the Sistine Chapel at Rome; Antoine de Févin (1490?–1516?), the brother of Robert de Févin; Lhéritier; and François de Layolle, who had the uncomfortable honor of giving music lessons to Benvenuto Cellini.

The characteristic of this whole group is an aversion from the frightful mechanical ingenuities of Josquin and his fellow-workers. This aversion becomes more noticeable in the group of men that immediately succeeded them. And we may be thankful that it was so. For these men cleared away the choking masses of blind-weed that lay on the foot-hills leading upwards to the heights of Palestrina.

Let us explain what this blind-weed was. The reader is already aware that the foundation of music was, and always had been, the notes of the plain-song. Immemorial usage, the pressure of the church, and the course of musical development had combined to keep it so. But the plain-song itself never underwent any process of evolution. The music expanded under the heat of new energies, but the core inside remained cold and rigid. Meanwhile, men were trying every possible expedient to keep the two in contact while giving an appearance of novelty to the resulting art-work.

Hence came endless (and perhaps necessary) experiments in the art of lengthening and shortening the notes of the various parts so that they should fit together — fit together, that is to say, by the stop-watch. *How* they fitted or what was the musical effect of their unnatural union was quite another matter.

This idea, originally the result of a harmless curiosity, soon became a poison. And its virus infected and undermined the constitution of every fifteenth century musician. Unheard-of outrages were perpetrated. A tune in short notes would be put into long notes, into longer notes, into impossibly long notes. It would be combined with itself in shorter notes at the same pitch and simultaneously with itself in longer notes at a different pitch. It would be repeated on every degree of an ascending scale. A composer would take a fragment of plain-song or a well-known air such as *L'homme armé* and cause it to be sung in every portion of a long work. Often the secular tune which he chose had for his hearers only associations erotic or Bacchanalian. Yet it was permitted to masquerade through a work designed to deepen the sacredness of the vicarious sacrifice.

Then came Chinese puzzles. One found that by using three clefs and three time-signatures he could pack a fairly elaborate work into a one-line part. Another wrote out only five notes of his tenor-part and placed under it an enigmatical Latin tag. A composer, after burying himself in the country for a few weeks, would bring back a couple of square inches of paper and set his friends guessing. Full-scores were written, so to speak, on the thumb-nail.

Then came diabolical pleasantries. The notes were written out innocently enough and appeared to be firm ground to walk on; but a humorous Latin finger-post showed the unhappy singer that he was in a quagmire from which he could only escape by following its directions. One such finger-post said "look in the mirror" or "walk like a crab," meaning that the part was to be read backwards. Another said "turn night into day," that is, "sing the black notes as if they were white"; "don't stop shouting," that is, "neglect the rests throughout the part"; "he who is exalted shall be abased," that is, "go up where the music goes down and vice versa."

These and other deplorable extravagances seemed for some time likely to lead composers astray. From such consequences, however, the secular side of the art was saved by the healthy coöperation of the composers with the people — in other words, by the influence of folk-song. We shall explain how this happened in the next chapter. Meanwhile, we need only add that in the domain of church-music a similar spiritual cleansing took place.

It must not be imagined that the muddy stream of misplaced ingenuity dried up suddenly with Josquin's death. On the contrary, it continued to flow for many years. But it was not the main stream. And its impurities were only a fleck on the surface when it met the big tidal-wave that brought Palestrina's galleon up to her anchorage.

CHAPTER 8

The Golden Age

IN studying the history of the fifteenth century the reader must have been struck by one fact — that we have to chronicle almost continuously the residence of foreign musicians in Italy. The first to go there were possibly the English; but very soon there was scarcely an ecclesiastical, princely, or ducal establishment of the first rank that did not possess a Flemish *maestro*.[1] Two points call for explanation here. In the first place, why did the Flemings go to Italy to write music? And, in the second place, if the Italians were so much devoted to music, why did they not write their own?

The answer to the first of these questions is simple. We have already shown how ideally fitted was the national temperament of the Flemings for the cultivation of the art. Furthermore the country, except on the few occasions of foreign intrusion, was removed from the general activities of Europe. She was not attempting to sail the sea, to acquire colonies, or to dominate other races. She sat at home reflectively. Her sons naturally went for their life-work to those places which were wealthiest and best equipped for music. And it is noteworthy that most of them regarded Italy only as a sojourning-ground. After their work was done they returned to their homes in the Netherlands.

The second point is more difficult. Why did not the Italians write music in Italy? Let us try to find an answer for this. During the whole of the fifteenth century Italy was the scene of a five-cornered struggle for power. And the

---

[1] So tight was the grip of the Flemings on the national musical life that when Festa was appointed *maestro* at the Vatican he was actually the only Italian in Italy holding such a position.

five corners were Milan, Florence, Venice, Naples, and the Papacy. In 1494 two enemies appeared on her threshold — France and Spain. Into the long record of bloodshed, alliances, and cross-alliances that followed it is not necessary to enter here. Suffice it to say that the outcome of the whole bitter struggle was that by the middle of the century France had been driven out; Spain had subjugated and was ruling Italy. She continued to do so in one form or another till 1650.

The point of importance for us to note is that it was at the moment of Italy's subjugation that — for the first time — her music stood forth as all-important in European history. Up to then the whole country had been red-hot with fierce, determined, never-ending jealousies. Now the friction had come to an end. The temperature sank below fusing-point; and in consequence musical thinking became a possibility.[1]

It is with the music resulting from this profoundly changed national state that we have now to deal. And to do so, we must return to our historical study as we left it about the time of Josquin's death. As we have already said, the tendency towards a greater simplicity of style and a more purely agreeable and beautiful quality in musical composition becomes stronger the farther we advance into the sixteenth century.

But we cannot penetrate very far into that century before noticing one very striking change in the musical landscape. In a word, we have stepped out of the ecclesiastical centuries into a century that is both ecclesiastical and secular. Hitherto the church alone had said "yea" and "nay" to the musicians. Now for the first time we hear of another force — the people.

Of course, from the dawn of time the latter had always made little songs and dances for themselves. The mother sang her child to sleep, and the lover had a ballad for his lady. These things were, and are, and will be. The church too had always recognized the hold which simple melody has

[1] For a more detailed discussion of this subject, see the author's *Music and Nationalism* (Macmillan).

on the heart. More than once she had pressed these melodies into her service. But on her own conditions. The simple tune, with its pleasant human associations, was devoted to the service of an awful and revengeful God. Then it was elaborated into a mechanical travesty of itself. The divine words which in music are the sword of the spirit were utterly despised by musicians and became a thing of lead to be heavily dragged after the tune or thrown aside altogether.

But for all that, cradles were still rocked and women wooed. And for these and all the other satisfactory warm-blooded things in life there had to be a tune. From this source flowed the ever-changing but never-ending stream of folk-song. And it was at this spring that the musicians of the early sixteenth century took their first draught — if one may put it so — of humanity. It toned up their constitutions marvellously.

Besides finding out in a general way that humanity was not necessarily satanic, they began to learn, especially in Italy, that song meant the singing of *words*, not merely of notes. Then they began to stumble on the fact that people really enjoyed singing their little songs — *villanesche, frottole,* and so on. This made them uneasy. Music apparently was not mathematics. Also this sort of music was — they confessed to each other — much pleasanter than their own. So they began to imitate it; to write *canzoni, balletti,* and other pieces in a light and charming vein. Eventually, being very sensible people at heart, they determined to adopt the course which of all others is noblest for the musician: to take from their own people the living seed and after tending to render it back — a perfect flower — to the giver. And this is the history of the Madrigal.

We have already mentioned an old type of music that bore this name.[1] As a musical form it existed no longer, but it had survived as a poetical form. And it was on this foundation that the great secular school of the madrigal was built.

The first bricks were laid by the Flemings, Jacob Arcadelt (c. 1514–1570), Jacques Clémens [2] (?–c. 1558), Adrian Wil-

---

[1] See page 138.　　　[2] Commonly called Clemens non Papa.

laert (1480?–1562), and Philippe Verdelot (?–1567?). Compared with what had gone before, their work does not show a mechanical advance — for no such development of Josquin's ingenuities was humanly possible. But it does show a complete infusion of the new spirit in art. The night had passed away and the early Netherlanders were the morning of a day that was to blaze full of glory to England and Italy.

One great master both in the church and the madrigal style was produced by the Flemings — Orlando di Lasso. This man whose Flemish name was Roland Delattre was born in 1520 at Mons; studied his art in Sicily and Rome, where at first he wrote in a somewhat hard, mechanical style; visited England in the reign of Queen Mary, and probably learned a good deal there; and finally spent the greater part of his long life at Munich, where he died in 1594. He wrote an enormous quantity of music, and in his command of harmonic beauty is generally considered one of the world's supreme masters.

An interesting offshoot from this school is to be found in the group of Venetian madrigalists whose activity in northern and central Italy lasted right through the century. The impetus came from Willaert, the distinguished pupil of Mouton and Josquin des Près. He had settled in Venice and had introduced there the simple madrigal methods of the earlier Flemings.[1] On this stock was grafted the somewhat more ornate style of Costanzo Festa,[2] a Roman and the first Italian to write madrigals. The result of this "cross" was the Venetian school — a school which speedily abandoned the cautious methods of the early Netherlanders for a greater freedom of vocal outline. In their harmony the Venetians show a very decided leaning towards the modern.

The principal names in this school are the Fleming Cipriano da Rore (1516–1565) and Costanzo Porta (1530?–

---

[1] Willaert invented the double-choir while in Venice — a novelty that was speedily taken up by the other Venetian masters. It soon became popular all over Europe and was specially studied by the organist Sweelinck (1562–1621). The Roman and the Venetian differed fundamentally in the treatment of the eight-part chorus. The one looked at it through a telescope, the other through a not quite perfect pair of opera-glasses.
[2] Died 1545.

1601), both pupils of Willaert; Gioseffe Zarlino (1517–1590), Giovanni Croce (1557?–1609), Andrea Gabrieli (1510?–1586), and Giovanni Gabrieli (1557–1612). The compositions of the great Spanish school of the sixteenth century have always been recognized and held in memory by Europe. But it is only recently that the work of their immediate predecessors has come to light.[1] Between four and five hundred of these compositions of the late fifteenth and early sixteenth centuries are now known to students. Of the sixty-four composers' names which are attached to these works we may mention Cristobal Morales (1512–1553), Francisco Peñalosa, Bernardino Ribera, and Juan del Encina. But of course the special glory of the Spanish school is T. L. de Vittoria (1540?–1613), a man whose name has been thought worthy of a place beside that of Palestrina.

The French masters of this century are first of all a group of witty, brilliant writers, some of whom may have sat at table laughing with Rabelais. Their subjects are secular and in treating them they show that lightness and charm which are the perennial and happy gift of their race to mankind. Among others of this group the most celebrated are Clément Jannequin and Nicolas Gombert (c. 1495–1570). The latter was a pupil of Josquin and lived through the first half of the century. Though a Fleming by birth, he is characteristically French in his choice and treatment of subject.[2]

Among the strictly ecclesiastical composers we must single out for special mention Pierre Certon (?–1572), the director of the Sainte Chapelle at Paris and composer of much church music; and, in particular, Claude Goudimel. The last named musician was born at Besançon in 1505, and at the age of twenty went to Rome, where he had the somewhat awful privilege of teaching Palestrina counterpoint. He afterwards returned to France, changed his religion, and became the first and greatest French Protestant composer.

[1] In the Madrid manuscript known as the *Cancionera musical de los XV y XVI siglos.*

[2] There was also a Polish school of music which began in 1522 and was centered at Krakow.

He paid for his beliefs with his life; for he was killed as a Huguenot at Lyons in August, 1572.

We now have to say something of the two greatest schools of unaccompanied vocal composition — those of England and of Rome. But, before doing so, a few words must be spared for two widely differing topics — music-publishing and the sixteenth century modal system.

The earliest *English* printed song-book in existence is, we believe, the bass-part book published by Wynkyn de Worde in 1530 and now in the British Museum.[1] It is true that, in 1482, Caxton had published a work that needed music-printing.[2] But he had contented himself with printing an eight-line staff and leaving the notes to be filled in by hand. It was not till 1502, when Petrucci started issuing the works of the Flemish composers from Venice, that the real business of music-publishing began. It is scarcely necessary to dwell on the international importance of this new venture. Some of these books must have found their way into England — at any rate, into London. It is impossible to think otherwise when there was a king on the throne who bought up everything musical that came within his reach. In this way, probably, the English composers first learnt what the Flemish madrigalists were doing.

Now we come to the question of the modal-system. We have already given a list of the church-modes which were used in the sixteenth century. But a mere list does not go far in the direction of explaining their artistic value. To the sixteenth century composer the modal-system was as definite and necessary as our major and minor modal-system is to us in the twentieth. As definite a fact — but, one must add, quite different in its quality and much more elastic in the opportunities it offered him. The main difference between our methods and his is that all our melodic ideas are pivoted on certain arrangements or relationships *of harmony*.

But, except at the final close, the sixteenth century com-

---

[1] The collection consists of nine four-part and eleven three-part songs. The other part-books of this set have never come to light.
[2] Trevisa's translation of Higden's *Polychronicon*.

poser had no such restrictive preoccupation. He selected his mode, and that bound down each of his voice-parts to a definite scale-length. This, in its turn, produced a harmony differing from the harmony of any other mode according as its position in the *complete-system* [1] differed from the position of that other mode. The harmony grew naturally out of the mode. One might almost say that it required no effort on the part of the composer, except a preliminary effort of choice. If, to a modern listener, it appears vague and unsatisfactory at a first hearing, he must remember that he is probably judging it by inherited harmonic prejudices which are incompatible with modal thinking.

Before leaving this subject we must say a few explanatory words with regard to the "bad places" which are occasionally found in even the best madrigals. These "bad places" — such as the clashings of B-naturals against B-flats and of F-naturals against F-sharps — always look terrifying on paper and sometimes sound really awkward. We have already shown how the rules of *musica ficta* allowed certain notes to be flattened or sharpened for melodic purposes. This was permitted purely for the sake of vocal ease and smoothness. It was not only permitted, but encouraged and even enforced. The composer, wholly without harmonic preoccupation, clung to this regularization of his melody. For instance, the *Agincourt Song* given on page 148 has as an integral part of its modal beauty the note B-natural. But in treating this tune musically the fifteenth century composer did not hesitate to introduce a flat when the B occurred between C and A. He kept the rule and spoilt the tune.

This was the worst feature of the early *musica ficta* — a substitution of the mechanical for the artistic. But in the sixteenth century the boundaries of music were continually being pushed out farther and farther. Composers were now dealing with much more complex masses of sound. They often had a large number of voice-parts to combine, and they had many modes in which to write. Their technical difficulties were increasing; while the only possible

[1] See page 51.

solution of their difficulties — a sense of *key* — was still far off and involved the destruction of their whole musical system. They were compelled to think horizontally. They therefore adopted the old rules of horizontal composition. In general, the result was quite satisfactory. The composer used his discretion and avoided those vertical combinations which his experience taught him would be unpleasant in performance. But this could not be done always. The horizontal view of the matter — so much more congenial than the vertical at that time — would now and then triumph over the common weal of the combined parts. So that occasionally we get a "bad place" — one that is downright offensive to our ears. This may be due to the composer's carelessness or to his courage. In the former case a way out of the difficulty can usually be found by sharp eyes and brains. But, in the latter, the passage is generally past mending. It implies an attempt on the composer's part to say something which is outside the range of modal vocal counterpoint.

It is a little difficult to deal clearly with the Elizabethan [1] madrigalists in a small space. As is usual in England, individuality counts for more than school. There is also the disturbing factor of the reformation which affected different men in different ways. One almost needs to write separate biographies. But that again is impossible: the number of known composers is so great. We have to face the chance of some loss. For, as in turning the pages of a quite uninteresting Elizabethan book, we often come on a phrase, a verse, or a poem that the greatest of masters would gladly have signed, so in the Elizabethan music, we find among the least-known composers unexpected happinesses, sudden illuminations of the spirit, and a vivid air of personality which tells us that we are in the age of great poets and great men.

As we have said, it is not possible to divide these com-

---

[1] In its usual loose, but convenient, sense. The period runs from about Henry VIII to James I. But all the best madrigals were written within twenty-five years of each other.

posers into strict periods but, if we had to select representative names for three groups in roughly chronological order,
we should mention the following; always asking the reader
to remember that the whole movement culminated in the
publication of the *Triumphs of Oriana* (1601), a collection
of twenty-five madrigals by twenty-three great composers
designed to celebrate the peerless qualities of Queen Elizabeth.

THE ENGLISH SCHOOL

GROUP	PIVOT-DATE	NAMES
Early	1500	Robert Fayrfax (1460?–1529), John Taverner (?–1530?), Hugh Aston (?–1522?), Richard Davy (?), William Cornysche (?–1524).
Middle	1550	Christopher Tye (c. 1500–1585), Thomas Tallis (c. 1510–1585), Richard Edwardes (1523–66), Richard Farrant (?–1580), Robert Whyte (?–1574).
Late	1600	William Byrd (1542–1623), Thomas Morley (1557–1602?), John Dowland(1562–1628), John Bull (1563–1628), John Wilbye (1574–1638), Orlando Gibbons (1583–1625), Thomas Weelkes (?–1623), John Benet (?–1614), Thomas Bateson (?–1631), Peter Philipps (?–1633?).

With regard to the first group, the reader must remember
that most of its members were born while Dufay was still
alive and were strictly contemporary with Josquin des Près.
When that master died there was no music in Europe but
Flemish and English. The Italians had produced nothing
and the Germans almost nothing. As we have already said,
the spread of music-publishing probably brought to England
a knowledge of the Flemish achievements, and without much
delay the English musicians started a healthy rivalry.[1]

[1] The chief sources are the *Fayrfax Book* in the British Museum obtained
from the Yorkshire family of Fayrfax; Seven *Add.* and *Harl.* MSS. in

We have not space to examine all the individuals mentioned above. But, from the first group, we must select its most imposing figure — Robert Fayrfax, a Hertfordshire man, who was organist or precentor of St. Albans Abbey. To him particularly is due the credit of the great advance about 1500. Cornysche was in the employment of both Henry VII and Henry VIII; and to him the latter monarch entrusted the anxious duty of devising the pageants for The Field of the Cloth of Gold. A great deal of Taverner's music is still in existence, including a mass on the then popular theme of *Westron Wynde*. Aston's claim to immortality rests on the fact that he invented instrumental composition. While Davy — at one time organist of Magdalen College, Oxford — has an equal claim to remembrance as the writer of the first *Passion Music*.

By the middle of the century it may be said with justice that the Englishmen had mastered the Flemish methods and were surpassing the Flemings themselves, when the whole musical life of the nation was torn asunder by the reformation. The monasteries were dissolved; organs and part-books destroyed; singers and players dismissed; and the service itself underwent radical changes.

As with the rest of the nation so with the musicians; some accepted the new régime heartily, others clung stoutly to the Roman church, others again put their consciences in their pockets and accepted sulkily whatever changes the new secular force brought into their religious life.

the British Museum, and other MSS. at Lambeth, Caius Coll. Cambridge, and the Univ. Library, Cambridge; the *Sadler Part-Books* in the Bodleian; and the *Christ Church Part-Books*. In the MSS. the names of the same composers occur again and again. But, in order to show the extraordinary fertility of the period, we shall here print a list of the names that are found in the above MSS. It practically excludes the whole of the best and most prolific group — the last. Adams, Alcoke, Alwood, Appleby, Ap Rice, Ashwell, Aston, Avere. Banastir, Barker, Blithman, Bramston, Browne, Bullman, Byrd. Carleton, Causton, Cooper, Cornysche, Corsum. Davy. Edwardes, Endsdall. Farrant, Fayrfax, Ferynge, Franctyne. Hake, Hawte, Heath, Heywood, Hoskins, Hyllary. Johnson (2). Kinton, Knight. Ludford. Merbecke, More, Morley, Mundy (W. & J.). Newark. Okeland. Parsley, Pasche, Philipps, Preston, Prowett, Pygott. Redford. Sadler, Shelbye, Sheppard, Sheryngham, Stonings. Tallis, Taverner, Thorne, Tudor, Turges, Tye. Whitbroke, Whyte, Wilkinson, Williams, Winflate, Wright.

We have no time to detail any of these changes. But to men like Tye and Tallis — both in royal employment — they meant much. Tye himself was organist of Ely Cathedral and afterwards took holy orders. He was an earnest student of the Flemish school, and in early life wrote a mass (*Westron Wynde*) which shows clearly that he had learned easily all that it could teach him. Nor was he content with the student's lot. The work of his middle and later life is a record of continual artistic progress. His beautiful anthem *I will exalt thee* and his six-part mass *Euge Bone* are as masterly as anything that had been produced in the world up to that time.[1]

Tallis was about ten years his junior. He was an Oxford man, afterwards organist of Waltham Abbey, and then a member of the Chapel Royal. It is impossible here to do justice to his extraordinary powers. In middle life he produced a series of noble masterpieces among which we may note the *Forty-part Song*, the *Cantiones Sacrae*, and the motets *Audivi media nocte* and *O bone Jesu*. We need scarcely add that he set the prayers, responses, and so on for Archbishop Parker's psalter.

Byrd's name might with justice have been included in both the middle and later groups. For he served both Elizabeth and the first James in their Chapels Royal from 1569 onwards. He is, in a way, the central figure of the Elizabethan period; not only from his length of life, but from his variety of accomplishment. There were others greater than he in each department. But it is no mean thing to be able to shine at all in the brilliant light of Tallis, Bull, Dowland, and Wilbye. Byrd was a Romanist, heart and soul. His masses are his chief monument; but he wrote in all kinds, vocal and instrumental.[2] Technically his tendencies were towards the modern major and minor systems.[3]

---

[1] Tye and his son-in-law Whyte were the last composers to use *gymel*.

[2] Ferrabosco and he, with the titanic playfulness of the Elizabethans, each wrote forty canons on the plain-song *Miserere*.

[3] He uses both an F-sharp and a D-sharp for his dominant close in E-minor; treats the 7-5-3 chord as existing harmonically for melodic purposes; and even employs what we should call a chord of the 6-5-3.

Morley was a delightful madrigalist, an instrumental composer, and a theorist. His madrigals and *ballets* in particular are as fresh and exquisite now as the day they were written.

John Dowland, whose books of *Songes and Ayres* made him famous, was, like Bull, a "touring virtuoso." [1] The former in especial seems to have published music in at least eight continental cities — a surprising achievement for that time. His *ayres* are really charming tunes simply harmonized for four voices with accompaniment of lute and viol da gamba.

Gibbons lived at the extreme end of this period. But he belongs wholly to that period for, though he survived till 1625, he never attempted the monodic style. In his church music he had the good fortune to be able to write at court freely for what we should now call the "high church party" — an advantage which we must remember when comparing him with Tallis. To Englishmen his name calls up *The Silver Swan*, the *Service in F*, *Hosanna to the Son of David*, and *O clap your hands*, as surely as Milton's calls up *Paradise Lost*.

With the publication of the *Triumphs of Oriana*, English music reached its highest point — a point indeed so high that it is questionable whether any more lofty exists. The peak where Palestrina sits enthroned may perhaps be allowed. Though even there the Englishmen have some compensating altitudes in the way of vivid personality. But when two towering mountains exist in two widely separated lands, it is folly to attempt their measurement with the yard-stick. Their geological formations differ. At the foot of the one are olives and vines; at the foot of the other elms and oaks. Then, where the undergrowth ceases, the difference of atmosphere distorts our judgement. In the one case, it is calm and steely, revealing everything and hiding nothing; in the other case, it is laden with a pearly floating mist that is for ever drifting to and fro, troubling our vision.

We shall therefore attempt no comparison in this matter. But, as we have hitherto said nothing of the greatest and

[1] Henry Davey's expression.

noblest member of the English madrigal school — John Wilbye — and as he in a way sums up all its excellencies, we shall here add a few words on this subject, joining his name to the immortal *Oriana*.

John Wilbye was born at Diss in Norfolk and baptized there March 7, 1574. The name, which still survives at Diss, was a common one and probably originated from the little village of Wilby in Suffolk. His family was musical and of the yeoman class. The turning point in his youth was the marriage of Elizabeth (daughter of Sir Thomas Cornwallis of Brome Hall near Diss) to Sir Thomas Kytson, the owner of Hengrave Hall, Suffolk — the great Tudor house whose stately musical magnificence has been so often described.

There Wilbye passed the greater part of his pleasantly secluded life as a yeoman-musician in the service of Sir Thomas and Lady Kytson. From the inventories of furniture in "Wilbee's Chamber" at Hengrave he appears to have gradually increased in importance, and it is plain that he was a valued member of the family.

On the death of Lady Kytson he entered the household of Lady Rivers (Kytson's youngest daughter) and lived as a gentleman-musician at her residence, the Great Brick House at Colchester. Between him and Lady Rivers there appears to have been something more than a mere business relationship. And this partly explains the strong melancholy cast of his best music and the fact that he never married. During the last twenty-four years of his life he wrote (or at any rate published) nothing, and seems to have been absorbed in the management of his landed-property. He died in 1638 and was buried at Holy Trinity Church, Colchester. In his will he left his "best vyall" to the little Prince (Charles) of Wales,[1] thus forging a link with his great successor Purcell.

---

[1] Then only eight years old; afterwards Charles II. These details are taken from the *Proceedings of the Musical Association* (1914–15). The author wishes to make his sincere acknowledgments to Mr. Fellowes. Before his famous discoveries (published in the *Proceedings*) the life of Wilbye was almost a blank. Even the identity of the Hengrave Hall "Wilbee" with the great madrigalist was a mere matter of conjecture.

Wilbye published two sets of madrigals — one of thirty in 1598 (dedicated from Lady Kytson's house in Austin Friars to Lady Rivers's brother-in-law Sir Charles Cavendish), and the other of thirty-four in 1609 (dedicated to Sir Charles's niece Lady Arabella Stuart). In addition to these he contributed one madrigal ("The Lady Oriana") to the *Oriana* series. He also wrote two Latin *motets* and two others for Sir William Leighton's *Teares or Lamentacions* (1614), and three instrumental *fantasies*.

The quantity is small but the quality unsurpassed. In his power of vocal characterization, of dramatic color, and of musical word-painting Wilbye is easily the first man of his age. His lighter madrigals, such as *Sweet honey-sucking bees*, *Lady when I behold*, and *Flora gave me fairest flowers*, are models of facile delightful composition. But the real Wilbye is to be sought for in his bigger and more serious works. In these there is a spacious and noble sadness which is scarcely to be found in any other music. *Oft have I vowed*, *Happy, O happy*, and *Unkind, O stay thy flying* are fine examples of this exalted style.

Wilbye may be justly regarded as the head of a school of composition which "found itself" so to speak in the great publication of 1601.[1] We are not able to examine the *Triumphs of Oriana* in any detail. But we may point out that the works in that book have certain common characteristics. First of all they have an unapproachable perfection of form and expression. Next an elegant simplicity and charm that have never been attained by any other school before or since. And finally they have the variety (within the limits of a common aim) that marks them as the product of many minds all working in one direction. In other words they are the living monument of a true school of composition.

We have already mentioned the name of Hugh Aston as

[1] The names of the composers who contributed to the work were Morley, East, Norcome, Mundy, Benet, Hilton, Marson, Carleton, Tomkins, Cavendish, Cobbold, Farmer, Wilbye, Hunt, Weelkes, Milton (father of the poet), Kirbye, Jones, Lisley, Johnson, Gibbons, Bateson, Pilkington. The names of Dowland, Bull, Byrd, and Philipps do not appear. The two former were travelling; the two latter were strong Romanists and probably did not wish to contribute to the glory of protestant Elizabeth.

the inventor of instrumental composition. To that we must now add that all through this period there was the liveliest interest in that form of music. English composers and executants with their *fancies* — a type of music which they had recently invented — enjoyed a great reputation on the continent. Besides Bull, Dowland, and Byrd, there were many others of smaller reputation, such as Redford and Blithman. The instruments in greatest favor were the lutes, viols, and virginals. And for these, various collections were written or published from time to time. The most celebrated are *Lady Nevell's Booke* (now at Eridge Castle, Sussex) which has forty-two pieces by Byrd (including his *Battle*, the first known example of programme-music); and the *Fitzwilliam Virginal Book* sometimes miscalled *Queen Elizabeth's Virginal Book*. This volume contains two hundred and ninety-one pieces (including sixty-seven by Byrd, Mundy's *Faire Wether* and *A Cleare Day*, and Bull's elaborate *Variations*).

We now come to the Roman school of madrigalists and church composers. And here our task chronologically is a simpler one. Not only was there much less musical activity in Rome than in London but it was much less spread out, more definitely concentrated into a few powerful hands.[1] We have already mentioned the fact that Goudimel, the great Franco-Flemish musician lived for some time in Rome. He went there about the year 1535 and taught not only Palestrina but Animuccia and the two Nanini. These, with the brothers Anerio and Luca Marenzio, practically complete the list of composers.

We see here a striking difference between the English and the Italian schools. When the first edition of the *Triumphs of Oriana* appeared there were probably at least thirty men of genius in London, each of whom was capable of producing and most of whom actually did produce masterpieces. At the turn of the century the Italian monodists were proclaiming their new gospel. But these Englishmen — many of them comparatively young men — went on for years writing

[1] The total number of Elizabethan madrigals now in print is about 2000.

vital music of the old type, unconscious or contemptuous of the glad tidings.

In Italy some of the younger composers, such as Allegri, Cifra, and Valentini, continued to follow the old way. But these were not men of the caliber of Gibbons, Byrd, or Wilbye. The composers who may be considered Palestrina's direct artistic inheritors are all men much feebler mentally and spiritually than he. They do not bear the same relationship to him that Gibbons and Morley bear to Tye and Tallis. Luca Marenzio indeed was a great composer both ecclesiastical and madrigalian. But though he was about thirty-five years junior to Palestrina by birth he only outlived him five years; and his light pales in the blinding glare of the elder master.

It is true that the two pairs of brothers Nanini and Anerio rode in Palestrina's chariot. But, when Palestrina dropped the reins, it was at the top of a hill. The new drivers thought, no doubt, that there was a long stretch of level road in front of them. But certain cunning eyes in Italy saw even then that the grade was imperceptibly downhill and was likely to end in a quagmire. So the owners of those eyes took their courage in their hands and began to open a new road up a new hill, leaving the chariot to dawdle along like an elderly invalid who is only too glad to escape the traffic on a by-road.

We shall therefore only set down a few names as representative of the Roman school. And these the reader may bring into focus with his general historical knowledge by remembering that Palestrina's creative life corresponds roughly with the middle and later groups of the Elizabethan school, and that his great continental contemporaries are the Venetian, Giovanni Gabrieli, the Fleming, Orlando di Lasso, and the Spaniard, Vittoria. Palestrina's life and work, indeed, sums up the glories of the " golden age " more perfectly than that of any other composer. There are marked personal differences beween his maturest work and that of Luca Marenzio, Orlando di Lasso, and Vittoria. But, apart from this, their brilliance (great as it is) seems only to throw his greater figure into the more startling relief.

THE ROMAN SCHOOL

GROUP	NAMES
Early	Costanzo Festa (?–1545)
Middle	Palestrina (1526–94), Luca Marenzio (1560–99).
Late	G. M. Nanini (1540–1607), G. B. Nanini (?–1624), Felice Anerio (1560–1630), G. Francesco Anerio (1567–1620)

Giovanni Pierluigi Sante was, in the manner of those times, called "da Palestrina" after his birthplace.[1] He secured his first important appointment — that of "master of the boys"[2] — at St. Peter's in 1551. This was shortly afterwards exchanged for the higher post of music-director. In 1555 he entered the Sistine Chapel as chorister, but was dismissed as the result of an intrigue. His next positions were as director at the Lateran and at S. Maria Maggiore.

By this time he was well known in Rome as a composer, but he had by no means reached that unique European position which he afterwards attained. From Goudimel he had absorbed in his boyhood the Flemish traditions in their greatest severity and complexity.[3] He had also tested the worth of these traditions in his own work. But his strongly selective mind and his all-pervading good taste led him to use these traditions with judgment. He was a Roman to his inmost core. And in Rome the Papal choir had set up an ideal of soft magnificence which he alone was to realize.

In 1560 a profound impression had been made by his *Improperia*,[4] and this impression had been deepened in 1563 by his great six-part mass *Papae Marcelli*. The exterior facts in the church history of this time as they affected him are not very definitely known. It appears, on the one hand, that grievous abuses had been creeping into the church-service during the first half of the sixteenth century. These

[1] The date of his birth is not quite certain. If it was not 1526, it was probably either 1514 or 1515. [2] *Magister puerorum.*
[3] From 1540 to 1544. [4] Good Friday Lamentation.

abuses were somewhat of the same character as those which had provoked Pope John XXII's decree in 1322. Roughly, they may be described as superfluity of ornament, unnecessary complexity, and the employment of secular melody as the foundation of the mass.

On the other hand, the church was alarmed by the great success of the revivalist methods originated by Luther. We have no space to discuss these here, but in general they consisted of replacing the congregation where it had been in early Christian times, and in giving it an actual share in the musical service by means of rhymed hymns instead of Gregorian chants.

These secular methods were inspired not by any license of feeling but by a deeply devotional piety. The Roman church knew this just as well as Luther did; and it determined to set its house in order. The Council of Trent which sat from 1545 to 1563 had as one of the subjects for its consideration the best means to effect the desired reformation. The result of its discussions was that it recommended the noble style of Palestrina as the only one fitting for the service of God. But popular imagination has dramatized this recommendation into a request made to Palestrina for guidance. The tale then goes on that Palestrina produced three masses of which the *Papae Marcelli* was chief and that the authorities, struck by its sublimity, endorsed it as the permanent model for all music used in divine worship.[1]

One need not labor the point that artistic revolutions are not brought about in this way. Side by side with the scandalous singers and writers there must have been many composers and worshippers of deep earnestness who already felt that nothing less than the sublimity and dignity of Palestrina's music was adequate for the Roman service. The church recognized the existence of this force and was

[1] He succeeded Animuccia as music-director at St. Peter's in 1571. The latter musician is more especially famous as having been associated with Philip Neri the founder of the *Congregazione dell' Oratorio*. This society was formed in Florence about 1550 for purely religious purposes. Its musical services, however, contained the germ of a particular style of sacred performance to which the name *Oratorio* (literally "oratory" or "chapel of prayer") has ever since been given.

so fortunate as to be able to solve its own musical problems and at the same time to answer the Lutheran challenge by bringing into the field the greatest ecclesiastical composer of all time.

Palestrina's personal leaning as he grew in years was towards a certain added simplicity and severity of style; and this very natural tendency may in some degree have chimed in with the progress of events in the church. His musical activity was amazing. Besides madrigals and various settings of hymns, prayers, responses, and psalms, he produced ninety-three masses and one hundred and seventy-nine motets. Technically they show the limit of perfection to which human brains could bring the art of modal composition. No fortune of circumstance or brilliance of individual talent could have improved on them in the next century. One feels that the monodists must have appreciated this fact profoundly when they left his pleasant garden and took to their stubborn ploughing on the heathside.

In all the details of modal practice he was magisterial. In his association of the authentic with the plagal; his treatment of discords and cadences; his right admixture of conjunct with disjunct movement; his perfect method of evolving the harmonic from the melodic; he has remained without challenge the greatest master in the world. He inherited much. But, in dealing with his inheritance, he showed the sublimated taste and judgment that can only be expressed by the word *genius*. That is, by common consent, the verdict on him as a man and an artist.

We do not know if the spirits of departed singers ever leave their solemn troops and sweet societies to hear what new glory of singing has been since created on the earth. But if the spirit of John Dunstable could so have heard the *Æterna Christi Munera*, he would have recognized it as the music which he had often dreamed but never written.

CHAPTER 9

The Palace of Greenwich
January 26, 1595

Tudor Instruments

THERE is an old story of an Arabian enchanter who owned
a curious finger-ring. To all appearances this ring was
just like any other ring — a plain circle of gold. But it
had one particular virtue. Its wearer — after turning it
on his finger — became possessed of a free and instantaneous
pass-ticket to both space and time. However, like other
tickets, this special "pass" was only issued under certain
stringent regulations and by-laws. Its owner could be
where he liked in any of the three places Asia, Africa, or
Europe : he could also be *when* he liked in any of the three
times past, present, or future. But he was limited to one
place and to one time — day-break to sunset. Furthermore, if we may put it so, the rights of the non-travelling
public were properly safeguarded from outside interference.
The wearer could see and hear what he wished, but could
neither be seen nor heard.

We propose to avail ourselves of this magic ring for the
purpose of this one chapter. And — after the hesitation
natural in making the important choice of our *when* and *where*
— we have decided on Greenwich in the county of Kent
on January the 26th, 1595.

Now that we have made this choice we feel that the reader
will call on us for some sort of justification ; will, indeed, ask
us what particular musical magic we may expect at that
special place and time. In reply to that we must allow ourselves a word or two of explanation.

The town of Greenwich stands on the river Thames, some

five miles below London Bridge. Here the Danish fleet anchored in the days of Ethelred, and here the sainted Alphege met his martyrdom. On the green slopes that lead upwards to Blackheath a Roman gentleman once had his villa; and from there his eyes must often have looked up past the great loop of the river to the heathen temple which then crowned the city of Londinium. A thousand years later the first Edward found the same spot delightful, and built himself a royal residence within a stone's throw of the dead Roman's house. From that palace, or "pleasaunce" as it was called, Henry IV dated his will; and thither came his son once or twice during his short reign. Nor has this town associations solely with royalty. For there lived at one time William Roye, the Franciscan, who helped Tyndale in his translation of the Bible; and earlier still through its streets often trotted the stout little poet with the downcast eyes and the nimble mind meditating the humors of his Canterbury Pilgrimage.

Greenwich then is both ancient and illustrious, well worth the unique opportunity of the magic ring. But — the reader may ask — what has this to do with music? To answer that question we must descend the hill and make our way back to the water's edge. For, as times changed and wealth increased, royalty no longer needed to live on the heights. It found a greater convenience in a residence near the river. So grew up the great *Palace of Greenwich*, with its stately water-frontage stretching east and west on the Thames. The place became the chief residence of the Tudor sovereigns. Here Henry VIII was born and married to his first wife. Here too were born his children Edward, Mary, and Elizabeth.

It would be pleasant to loiter here and recall some of its musical glories under Henry VIII; to recapture some at least of the sounds that were once heard in his long galleried rooms. But out of the one hundred and eighteen years of Tudor rule the magic ring will only give us back one poor day. And the reader is already asking with un-Arabian impatience why we have chosen this particular day.

Let us turn the ring and see what happens. . . . We are back in Tudor England. The Armada was destroyed seven years ago. It is eight since Mary Stuart met her fate at Fotheringay. Spenser is alive, and writing his *Fowre Hymnes* in this very place. Protestant Elizabeth has been on the throne for thirty-six uneasy years. She and her people have stretched their arms in many directions — to Greenland, to the Levant, to Virginia, even around the whole world.

But it is not the Elizabeth of political chicanery and naval enterprise of whom the ring is to give us a glimpse. It is the glorious Oriana, the inheritor of Henry VIII's musical traditions, the patroness of poets and composers. And to-day by good luck we are not likely to overhear any whisperings of policy or buccaneering. For the Queen is in residence at the Palace, and has promised her presence at the marriage of Lady Elizabeth Vere, daughter of the Earl of Oxford, with William Stanley, Earl of Derby. We have chosen — the reader must acknowledge — a happy day; for she will have music wherever she goes.

But there is more good fortune to come. The bridegroom's brother is something of a playgoer. And he has had an idea. He has probably noticed over and over again that a wedding is very good fun up to the end of the breakfast; and that then the hours till supper-time drag heavily. So he has suggested a little theatrical piece — a trifle to pass the afternoon — something with a pretty love story, quarrels, reconciliations, and so on — plenty of tomfoolery — classical dresses if you like, just for the pageant of it — and especially some good lines about the little old lady who will be sitting in front. Possibly all the little old gentlemen who have been writing these "good lines" for so many years past are growing tired of their subject. Or it may be just the other way about. At any rate, Stanley's brother, Lord Strange, has invited one of the "get on quickly" actors in his own company to string the thing together. This man is somewhat less than half the Queen's age and comes from Warwickshire.

We do not know who has "composed and arranged" all the music to be used on this busy day. Perhaps some elder members of the Lanier or Ferrabosco families. Or possibly for so notable an occasion the Queen's servants are to be mainly executants. Some big up-to-date composer like Mr. Dowland may have been brought in from the outside. Whoever he is he will have the services of an excellent librettist for his Songes and Ayres in the afternoon performance. He will also have at his disposal all the resources of a very complete musical establishment.

Her Majesty is indeed spending more than £1500 a year on her musical household, for every penny of which she is doubtless getting at least one shillingsworth of value. But in these hard times that is not to be wondered at. She cannot of course maintain an army of seventy-nine musicians in the way her father did. That was nothing but reckless extravagance. *Four* sackbutters were enough for her grandfather: her father had *ten*. At that rate she ought to keep *twenty-five*. Then there are the composers to be considered. And she is quite determined not to allow all that pickpocketing business of Cornysche and Fayrfax in *her* reign. Not that the patronage of artists is not a legitimate privilege of royalty. But it must be exercised within bounds. She recalls with pleasure how, soon after her accession, she promised old Dick Edwardes a reward for a capital play of his at Oxford. That was in '66, nearly thirty years ago. The poor man was already in a decline and died within a month — before she could do anything for him. Then again there is that white-elephant collection of instruments on which her father wasted his money. It takes half a dozen men even to keep them clean. There is that pair of long virginals and that other old pair with the double keyboard that cost a fortune merely to cart down to Greenwich. One little Italian spinet is all she has ever allowed herself. What *could* he have wanted with those endless "nests of cornetts," those "76 recorders," and "78 flutes and fifes"? There is some sense now in the "15 hunting horns." Today, for instance, when there are so many gentlemen staying in the Palace. . . .

But here we must interrupt Her Majesty's half-waking

thoughts. For the day is breaking, and with it we can for the first time test the musical powers of the magic ring. The hunt is up and taking its way over the Heath towards Eltham. From the noise they are making it is plain that his late Majesty's horns have been well looked after by his careful daughter. Each of the whippers-in has one of the old-fashioned English bugle-horns slung at his belt. These look not unlike their ancient model, the cow-horn; but are made of brass or copper wonderfully inlaid and enamelled. There is a metal mouthpiece at the smaller end, but even with this the player can only produce two or, at most, three notes — heavy, savage, and somber.

The Royal Huntsman himself has a silver horn of a shape that has been known in England for two centuries but has always been rather more popular in France. It winds completely round his body and has a bell projecting over his left shoulder. We can see that it is only a development of the other horn and — like that — tapers from bell to mouthpiece. The player, who is an expert, can get a good dozen notes out of the instrument. If folks are not too particular about one or two bad notes he can even play tunes. But these tunes will all be at the top of his compass. In fact, all his most showy hunting-calls have this character, that in the lower portion they jump by fifths, fourths, and thirds, while in the upper they are diatonic. But what a tone-quality he produces! Anything less soft and silky cannot be imagined. It is terribly rough, harsh, and unpleasant — more like the barking of a badly-blown trumpet. Clearly if Mr. Morley or Mr. Dowland has any hand in the arranging of this afternoon's program, such an instrument will not be allowed indoors.

However, we do not intend to follow the hunt. But as its notes grow sweeter and sweeter in the distance we will make our way back towards the Palace. Here everything is a flutter of anticipation. The maids of honor have finished their very substantial breakfasts of beef and beer, and the bride is being dressed for the ceremony. There is a full hour yet before the service. And as we do not wish to press the privileges of the magic ring beyond the bounds of propriety, we shall spend the time outside the Palace gates.

A dense crowd is already gathered in Church Street through which the bridal procession must pass to St. Alphege's. There is a general aspect of tarnished finery — of stout cloth that came some years ago from the best Cranbrook clothiers screaming with color, but has since then been much looked on by the sun. Music there is in plenty, but not at all the sort of music considered fit for royal ears. Indeed, the strolling players are making the most of their short license; for they know that recently they have twice been mentioned unpleasantly in the statute-book as "rogues and vagabonds." When authority appears they intend to disappear. So they make their musical hay *before* the sun of royalty shines.

Here is a lean fellow who has compassed a motion of the prodigal son.[1] He stands outside his box-on-wheels blowing a set of *Pan's pipes* just as showmen have done for two thousand years. With his right hand he is smiting a big *drum*, and at every smite a *bell* that hangs from a transverse cord starts jingling. In his left hand is a *clashpan*,[2] whose twin is secured to the top of his box. With these he marks the accents of his tune, hoping by the two to charm his prospective audience into the mental state necessary for the spending of ha'pence on the mixed object of piety and pleasure. And his method is sound. For he is only combining in his unconscious way the two instrumental elements which began to be developed many centuries ago into the service of the Christian religion and the cult of Isis. Hard by our "movie man" is a dancing-girl. As she dances she brandishes a *tymbyr*;[3] while her companion gives her a tune on the *pipe* and a tapped-drone on the *tabor*. The former is a sort of "penny whistle" of wood with two finger-holes in front and a thumb-hole behind: the latter is a shallow drum with a single snare-head. Farther down the street we can just hear the contesting din of a *bagpipe*, a *hurdy-gurdy*, and a Welsh singer with his *harp*.

Just by us is a little knot of townsfolk waiting impatiently

---

[1] A puppet-show.   [2] Cymbal.   [3] Tambourine.

for a ballad-singer to begin. In one hand he has his *crowd,*[1]
an awkward squarish sort of fiddle with five or six loose
strings. In the other he holds a short rudely-made bow.
With these he is to play the little phrases that give him
breathing-time during his long narrative. The people know
every note of his tunes — for he has only two or three — but
everybody is agog for the ballads themselves; one party
calling for *Adieu Sweet Heart* or *The Widow of Watling Street,*
and the other for *Sir Bevis* and *Clim o' the Clough.* The
singer motions for silence and puts his *crowd* against his
breast. At once the hubbub ceases. He plays over his
simple tune once and then begins :

> God prosper long our noble Queen,
> Our lives and safeties all ;
> A woeful hunting once there did
> In Chevy Chase befall.

The man is old and blind ; and he is sitting on a barrel-head
outside a tavern. Yet his singing moves many hearts —
"more than a trumpet." But the noblest of them all can
no longer hear it ; for nine years have gone by since Sidney
set the "outward seal" to his "inward glory."

But now our hour of waiting is drawing to a close The
Queen's marshalmen with the big "E. R." on their red liveries
have already opened the gates and are clearing a way for
the procession. We can just see a brilliant crowd of courtiers,
grouped in two lines down the broad steps of the main entrance. Their silks and satins make two streaks of vivid
aching color. One thinks of oriental butterflies. Everyone
is talking excitedly and absent-mindedly to his neighbor,
while keeping a wary eye on the little door behind the top
step — when suddenly the door opens and Oriana appears,
looking like a holiday Buddha. There is dead silence. It
is as if the cold January day had frozen all the butterflies
stiff.

The *Drums and Fifes* save the situation. For, as the pike-
men are to take her to the gate, their fifers are on duty and

---

[1] The bowed *crwth.* See page 23.

strike into *Sellenger.* Oriana likes her Drums and Fifes.
For one thing they don't cost her much; for another they are
almost the only visible link she has with her Plantagenet
predecessors.

But it is when she reaches the gate and the cavalry takes
up the escort, that she gets the music that is really dear to
her heart. All the rest of her musical acquirements have
something about them of the artificial and defensive, which
has been her normal mental state since Hatfield days. But
the *Trumpets and Kettle-Drums!* These she genuinely
admires. In a way it is a filial duty for her to do so. Did
not her father send all the way to Hungary to King Ludwig II
for these very drums? The drummer knows all about this
family-history just as well as she does. So he sits his horse
bravely and goes thump-whack-thump on either side of
him, quite certain that the queen's palfrey would as soon
think of shying at a peck of beans as at his drumming.

The man is a wonder. He contrives to make himself conspicuous even above the blaring of the brass. We can hear
the din of these trumpets right down at the Palace gates.
They play nothing but fanfares, repeating their passages
over and over again. The noise is just as rough and ugly as
that of the horns which we heard this morning, but more
biting, more martial. Each man's instrument is a long
cylinder of brass or silver, folded on itself into trumpet-shape.
The tube is not soldered into one rigid whole, but merely
bound together with ornamental cords and tassels; while a
silk banneret hanging from it is emblazoned with the royal
arms. All the instruments are of one pattern, but of two
sizes. And this has been the way now with trumpets for
about 250 years. The shorter small-bore instrument (the
clarion) can help best with the high notes : the large big-bore
(the *trump* or *trumpet* proper) with the lower.

Suddenly the trumpets and kettle-drums stop. A foot-
band of a dozen or twenty players that is marching behind
the cavalry is relieving the trumpeters. But what a weird
unearthly sound they are making — nearly as loud as the
trumpets and much more penetrating ! As they approach us

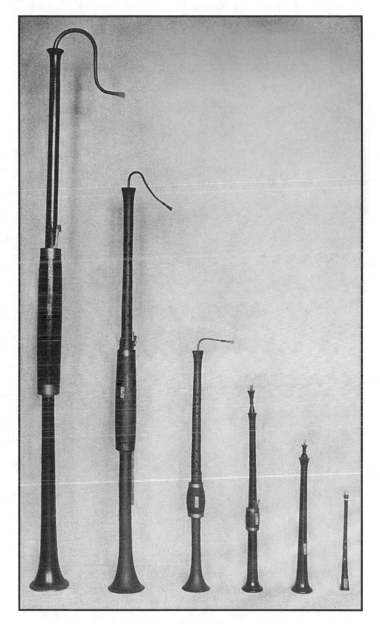

PLATE XXIV.   A FAMILY OF SHAWMS AND BOMBARDS

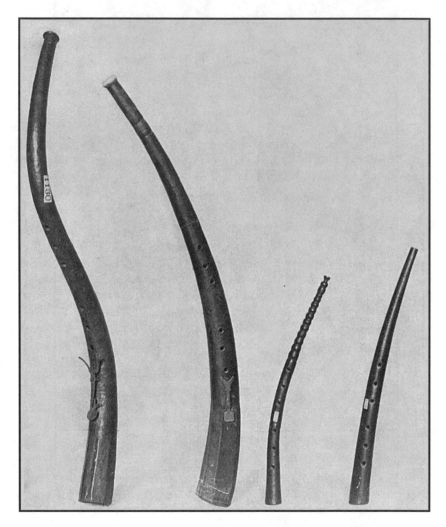

PLATE XXV.   CORNETTS

the buzzing and bumbling of the big instruments, and the skirling and shrieking of the little, become almost unbearable. A hive of giant-bees turned loose on us could not distress our ears more. We seem to be hearing a band of Highland pipers under a musical microscope. But this is infinitely more piercing and exciting. For the pipers have only their drones and a nine-note melody-scale; while these men are playing in full harmony, using a compass that extends from the highest notes of the flute down to the low notes of the double-bassoon. In such an excruciating noise we may be pardoned if we doubt the efficacy of the magic ring in allowing us to overhear anything we wish. But possibly we may just catch three words which an old-time Greenwich man is shouting in answer to a stranger's gesture of inquiry — "*The Royal Shawms.*"

However, here they come! Now they are just abreast of us! Let us slip into their midst and march with them as far as the church, keeping our eyes and ears open. We may learn something.

The first thing that we notice is that, though the instruments vary so grotesquely in size, they are all practically the same instrument and make the same kind of sound. "A straight conical wooden pipe bored with finger-holes" would describe them all. There appear to be four principal sizes — the *Discant, Alto, Tenor,* and *Bass* — corresponding to the four types of human voice. There are two or three players to each of these parts, and these four shawms vary from about 2 ft. to 6 ft. in length. The two largest of them are known as *Bombards.* But we must not overlook one little spry bandsman who is stepping out and doubling everything in the octave above. Here is a sort of "extra," and plays on the tiny *High Treble Shawm* less than $1\frac{1}{2}$ ft. long. There is no danger of our overlooking the other "extra," a huge brawny fellow with "Yorkshire" written all over his face. He is blowing the great *Double Bass Bombard* and is in some ways as important a personage as the Queen herself. His instrument is 9 ft. 8 in. long; and as — like all the others — it is in one straight piece, he has a second man in attendance to walk behind him and help with the porterage.[1]

All of these instruments — shawms and bombards — are blown with a big coarse double-reed. But the shawm-player prefers to place his lips not directly on the reed but on the widened rim or "flare" at the top of the pipe. This is of course out of the question for the three largest instruments. So a metal crook is led out from the end of the pipe, and the reed is "lapped" on to it with waxed thread. We need only keep our ears open to find out that all of these instruments have a good playing-compass of about a twelfth, and can at a pinch get up to the double octave. The three upper instruments have finger-holes, but no keys. The three lower have each got four keys as well as finger-holes. So that the compasses of the whole six are respectively:

We are here very much tempted to try opening up a conversation with the chief Discant-player — the *Master of the Shawms* — though that is of course impossible in his circumstances and ours. But we may be able to overhear him "talking shop" while cleaning his shawm in the band-room after playing the procession home. He will probably be complaining of the way some of the youngsters will persist in calling his shawm a "hautboy." He himself never heard the word till twenty years ago — it was in '75, when he went down to Kenilworth for the pageants there. If anybody questions him closely as to the reasons for using this new word he will allow grudgingly that there *is* another sort of shawm altogether. It is a poor, wretchedly weak, single-reeded affair; not even taper-bored; the second octave can't be got at all. It can never "come to anything." It

---

[1] The instruments in the illustration (Plate XXIV) are — from left to right — the Double-Bass, Bass, Tenor, and Alto Bombards, the Discant (or treble) Shawm, and the High Treble Shawm.

is a *naughty* instrument only fit for a yokel at a fair. And he would as soon think of putting one among his shawms as Dr. Bull would think of recommending one of those new "violins" to play in the Long Gallery after the Queen's supper.

However, the prophecies — even of a *Master of the Shawms* — do not necessarily come true. And while we have been indulging in these vain fancies the bridal party has entered the church. There is a full choir of boys and men from the Chapel Royal. The organist is sitting within a few feet of the spot where poor Mr. Tallis was buried more than nine years ago. If we look up the church towards him we may just catch a glimpse — through the scarlet liveries of the Chapel Royal boys — of six men standing between him and the choir. We wonder idly what they can be doing there. But, unless the cold January sun happens to send a reflection down the nave at the moment, we give them no more thought.

Now the service is beginning. We come to the bridal anthem. What an extraordinary quality the choir seems to have, especially in its upper and middle registers! This is a tone-color which we have never heard before. It sounds as if a big, sad, and superhuman "voice" was singing with each part. Sometimes these "voices" cease. We hear the choir alone or accompanied only by the organ. We prick up our ears and ask ourselves whether we are being cheated by an echo. But no! The "voices" begin again. There is something strange, mournful, even prodigious about this music. Has no one noticed it? We look up the packed church towards the chancel-rails. The little bride is hand-in-hand with her crimson-and-white-satin groom wondering only whether matrimony really can be as solemn as it sounds. Oriana is sitting bolt-upright, dreaming perhaps of might-have-beens and her "dear brother" waiting up in the north; or perhaps only thinking of the latitude and longitude of her wig. Suddenly the "voices" begin again, oppressively strong. There is a momentary shifting of the choirmen, and we see that the "voices" come from our six friends grouped round the organist.

Three of them — those that are making the sound least familiar to us — hold in their hands long curved instruments of gleaming polished ivory. They appear to be laboring terribly to control the tone and have to rest after every few phrases. These are the *Royal Cornettors*. The other three are playing on brass instruments with slides. One may call them simply trombones. These are the *Royal Sackbutters*. Together they make up the soft, rich, and solemn wind-ensemble which is used, not only in theatres, but also to support the choir in the great Abbeys and Cathedrals. Westminster, York, Durham, and Canterbury all maintain such bands of *Cornetts and Sackbuts*.

The former instrument is indeed an old English invention, and has been in use here for six hundred years. It is surprisingly simple — a cup mouthpiece at the end of a conical pipe bored with six finger-holes in front and a thumb-hole behind; with an extra "open key" for the larger instruments. This is of course the easiest way of increasing the natural compass of such an instrument; and is merely an idea borrowed from the flutes and reed-pipes. As a rule, the cornett is made of wood, or of wood covered with leather; but the Queen's large-hearted father always had a pretty taste in this direction; and it is his splendid carved-ivory cornetts to which we are now listening. We are not likely to hear the little "mute cornett" today. For that instrument is specially built to give a tame insignificant indoor tone. And this is done by leaving the upper end of the pipe unprovided either with cup or even rim, and gouging an *internal mouthpiece* out of the solid block.[1]

The cornetts are always made in sets (or "nests" as the chief cornettor would call them) and the larger instruments are showing a tendency towards a serpentine form; but any great increase of size is not much called for, as they are seldom played without the sackbuts. A "nest of cornetts" usually consists of three — the *Treble*, the *Mean*, and the *Great*. These have a compass of:

[1] The instruments in the illustration (Plate XXV) are — from left to right — the Great, Mean, and Treble Cornetts, and the Mute Cornett.

We have less to notice about the actual shape and appearance of the sackbuts. Nor is it any good our making an enquiry into their history. For no one will be able to tell us how the "slide" came to be applied to the long straight brass instrument which the old Kentishman Dan Michel called "the orible bosyne." Certain it is that some genius did turn the "bosyne" into a sackbut about two hundred and fifty years ago. And here we have our three modern sackbuts playing in front of our eyes — the *High* or *Discant*, the *Mean*, and the *Bass* or *Double*. But we cannot help remarking their tone-quality. It has nothing in common with the noisy blare of the horns and trumpets that we have already heard today. Both sackbutters and cornettors seem intent on producing a big round massive tone more like that of the human voice than a brass instrument. There is no attempt to "put an edge on it." And indeed if any one of the six players tried to do such a thing he would speedily find himself without a livery.

However, while we have been making these observations, the service has come to an end. There is much ringing of great bells in the tower and of little chime-bells in the church itself. Oriana is feeling very satisfied that — whatever her general objections to weddings — this special wedding has found her still unsurpassable. The little bride is feeling very proud and happy, but perhaps wondering at the bottom of her heart whether hawk-nosed old ladies who monopolize all the attention are quite in place at weddings. And so they come to the church-door, where stands the cream pony with the red velvet side-saddle. The Queen mounts. And the procession makes its way back to the Palace with much the same music as before.

We shall take leave to be absent from the wedding-breakfast. Not from any indifference towards the new Countess, but because on such occasions Her Majesty invariably commands the presence of twelve trumpets and a pair of kettledrums in the dining-hall. In this way she not only gratifies her own private tastes, but gains opportunities for those conversational misunderstandings and repudiations which are so necessary when ambassadors are present.

However, in this matter, she has not very much choice. The Shawms and Bombards are almost as loud as the Trumpets; and no one (out of Holyrood) would want to hear *them* indoors. The Cornetts and Sackbuts would give everybody the blues. While of course the Lutes and Virginals are out of the question. Even if her guests all sat mum the clatter of trenchers on the oak boards would drown their feeble tinkle. So in march the Trumpets and Drums; while a host of cooks, sewers, henchmen, seneschals, and serving-men bring on the banquet.

This is our opportunity to steal out into the long quiet corridors and peep into some of the innumerable little rooms to which they give access. There is not much furniture anywhere, and it is all of oak. But every gallery and chamber has its musical instrument or instruments. They are here by the dozen; though of course we are not in the musicians' wing of the Palace. There they must be counted by the hundred.

As we walk through the passages we come across half a dozen little toy-*organs* and *regals* — the latter generally furnished only with reed-stops. But most of the keyed instruments are of the mechanically plucked variety — *virginals, spinets, harpsichords,* and *clavicembalos.* Here against the wall are the two pairs of virginals, whose expense kept the Queen awake this morning. The next room — from its situation — evidently belongs to some one of importance. As we pass we hear the faint tinkle of very sweet and perfect fifths. If we dare draw back the tapestry and put our head inside we shall see that it is Her Majesty's room, and that the tuner is at work on her spinet — a little five-cornered Italian instrument adorned with the royal arms. Behind it, hanging on the wall, is her *polyphant,* a wire-strung cittern or guitar with twenty or thirty strings. Our curiosity is now whetted. Only this room is rather beyond our courage. So we hasten down one corridor and up another, select a room at random, and enter.

We are in a small square chamber, panelled and floored with oak. It has a table with two silver candlesticks, a couple of chairs, and a few dozen books arranged on a sort of dresser. In the window is a settle; and on it a jumbled heap of music. We turn it over and see that it is almost all manuscript — single-line parts of madrigals, ballets, and canzonets. But there are one or two printed books, such as Mr. Anthony Munday's *Banquet of Dainty Conceits*, published in '88; and some later things, such as Mr. Peter Phillips's madrigals that came out four years ago. Here is even a proof-copy of Mr. Morley's new five-part *Ballets*. Clearly the owner of this room is an advanced thinker. That locked case opposite, of stamped Spanish leather, evidently contains his favorite *gamba*. On the other side of the table is an open harpsichord, whose painted angels are thrown up into sombre magnificence by the dark oak background.[1] We draw up a chair and play a few notes. In the upper registers the tone is bright and interesting, though somewhat mechanical when compared — let us say — with that of the harp. In the middle and lower registers it has an incomparable gravity and severity. Its force is rather too great than too small for this kind and size of room.

But what is the method by which its tone is produced? The greater part of the instrument is obviously a hollow wooden resonating board with two fine "roses" or soundholes. Just above the keys are the two rows of wrest-pins by means of which the tension of the wires is regulated. These latter are strung from the pins to the curved bridge, and from there the frame where they are fastened. But between the wrest-pins and the bridge there is another double-line of little white objects. These are the *jacks*. If

[1] The harpsichord in the illustration (Plate XXVI) is Italian of the early seventeenth century. The wooden box-covers of the wrest-pins and jacks have been removed to show the action. These covers, in the original, are of the handsome black-and-white pattern seen underneath the keyboard.

we take one out we shall see that it is a weighted slip of wood, in the upper part of which is a *plectrum* — that is to say, a *plucker* — either of quill or of hard leather. The action of our finger on the key jerks the jack upwards, and brings the plectrum into contact with the wire. The plucking device in the jack is itself swung on a pivot and, as the player releases the key, a single white hog's bristle exerts a moment's pressure and so prevents the leather engaging the wire as the jack descends. All the parts of this mechanism are tiny and exquisitely made. The leather itself is no bigger than the Queen's nose on a coin. The keys are miniatures. And there is a compact device[1] by which, in the bottom octave, one runs downwards on the keys G—F—G-sharp—F-sharp—E and gets the sounds G—F—E—D—C. This saves space and increases the compass. The action of all these keyed plucked instruments sprang from the old *psaltery*, which was played by a plectrum held in the hand : just as the *clavichord* action — a metal *tangent* that pushes upwards at the string — sprang from the ecclesiastical *monochord*. In that instrument there was a single string and a movable bridge ; and the modern clavichord merely gives us a bridge to each string and a key to each bridge. We are not very likely to find many clavichords in the Palace just now, as they are not in the greatest favor. But if we do, we shall probably hear their owners still talking of them as "monochords."

However, we must not loiter any longer in this room. We had better make our way into the corridor, go down the staircase, and walk through the great gallery that runs the whole length of the building. We are now in the East Wing, where apparently the musicians have their quarters. In the main room the logs are blazing ; and on the table are scraps of lute-tablature altered and re-altered, with odds and ends of minnikins — the thin top-strings of the lute. There has evidently been a rehearsal here.

---

[1] Called the *short octave*. It was used also to continue the "white note" scale down from B to G. In that case the fingers touched the keys d—c— d-sharp—c-sharp—B, and got the sounds d—c—B—A—G.

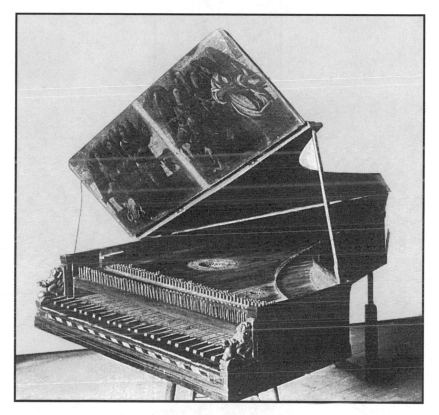

Plate XXVI. Harpsichord

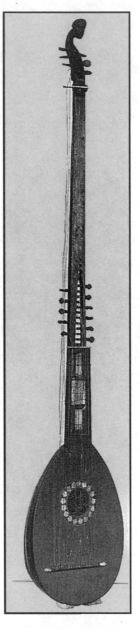

PLATE XXVII. CHITTARONE

Near the fireplace are the lutenists' boxes. We notice on them French and Italian as well as English names. If we open any of the boxes we shall find inside them some very lovely instruments. Their vaulted bodies are built up of strips of pine and cedar, and there are exquisite purflings and ornaments of ebony, ivory, and silver. In front is at least one beautifully carved and inlaid "rose"; while the necks are all "fretted," semitone by semitone. And it is this "fretting" which is represented on the untidy scraps of tablature which are lying about the room. Each lute has twelve strings of catgut tuned in six unison-pairs. But if we touch two or three lutes in succession we shall see that all players do not adopt the same tuning. The average lutenist seems to prefer for his six pairs of strings a system of fourths joined by a third in the middle.

The instruments are made in three chief sizes, but the *tenor-lute* or *theorbo* from Padua appears to be a favorite. If we take up one of these lutes and pass our hands across its strings, we shall become aware of a deliciously tender harmony. The instrument has no strength — only a sort of melancholy quietude. And this is due in some measure to the length of the strings. For much tension is out of the question in an instrument whose bridge is merely glued to the belly.

Here is a tall lute-case in the corner, reaching almost to the ceiling. From its appearance it has travelled far, over rough roads. Its owner's name suggests Italy. Let us take it out very gingerly. It is the latest thing in lutes — a big Roman *chittarone*[1] with seventeen strings — practically two instruments in one. For besides the usual *pairs-of-strings* that run up to the lower "nut," there is a second series of *single-strings* stretched to a second nut at the lute-head. These are the newly invented *diapasons*, a set of bass-strings

[1] Archlute or Basslute.

which hang free of the finger board, and can therefore only be plucked to give the one note of their full vibrating-length. This addition is naturally a great advantage in *consort* or ensemble playing; for it extends the compass diatonically downwards thus:

Diapasons

Before we leave the rehearsal room for Lord Strange's performance in the Hall we shall make free to open the huge oak cupboard that runs across the upper part of the room. This is a "boarded chest" as they call it; and we know very well that we shall find inside it a set of six viols. They are heavy, cumbersome instruments and they run downwards like a Noah's Ark procession from No. 1, the big *Double-Bass*, to No. 6, the *High Treble*. The favorite is No. 2, the *Bass Viol* or *Gamba*.[1] It is doubtless a choice specimen of this instrument which was under lock and key in the other room. It may have been by Gaspar di Salo. For the Italians are rapidly coming to the fore as viol-makers; and a new man called Andreas Amati is manufacturing a very small instrument which he calls a *violino* or *violin*. But the Queen's violists probably regard this as a rather cheap and not quite worthy attempt to vulgarize their dignified instrument.

The tone of the viols is somber and somewhat nasal. It lacks brightness altogether. Excellent for arpeggios and quiet vocal passages the instruments are apt to sulk unless continually coaxed by the bow. And the bow unfortunately has to be used with considerable caution. For the true viols have no fewer than six strings apiece. And in their tun-

[1] That is *Viola da Gamba* (leg-viol). The Italians also used the names *da spalla* (shoulder) and *da braccio* (arm) for the two next smaller viols. The instruments in the illustration (Plate XXVIII) are a somewhat odd lot. No. 1 is an old 7-stringed Double-Bass of poor and mixed design (guitar, viol, and violin). No. 2 shows the general shape of the Bass Viol (or gamba); but the stringing and fitting are modern. Nos. 3, 5, and 6 are Tenor, Treble, and High Treble Quintons. No. 4 is a true 6-stringed viol of characteristic sixteenth century pattern.

PLATE XXVIII. INSTRUMENTS OF THE VIOL FAMILY

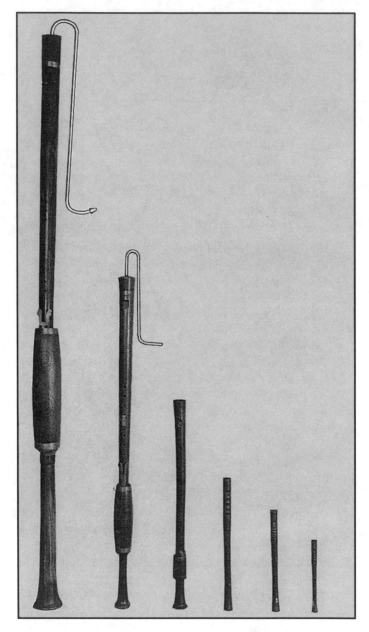

PLATE XXIX. A FAMILY OF RECORDERS

ing they follow the irregularities of the lutes by using a series of fourths joined together by a third. The *Bass-Viol* (No. 2), the *Tenor-Viol* (No. 3), and the *Discant-Viol* (No. 5) are usually strung thus:

But the makers are beginning to see the necessity of reducing the number throughout the whole viol-family; for the difficulties of bowing are very great. Accordingly, they are just introducing a modified type of instrument with five strings. They call these the *quintons;* and those players who use them are adopting a tuning which gives them perfect fifths, at any rate in the lower part of their compass.

This is interesting. For it shows that some change is in the air. We should like to have ten minutes' private conversation on the subject with Signor Amati. If we did he would first warn us that what he was about to say must not on any account be repeated to his best customers, the violists. Then he would probably give it as his opinion that his new *violino* with its simple regular tuning in fifths and its lovely caressing tone-quality is worth all the viols that have ever been made; and that all the talk about "vulgarizing" and "popularizing" is nothing more than professional stupidity.

However, this may or may not be mere advertising on his part. It is our business now to get back to the Hall as quickly as possible; for the lutenists and violists are beginning to drop in to their room by twos and threes. Some of them are taking their instruments out of the cases, fitting and tuning new strings. Others stand by the fire warming their stiff fingers and chaffing each other with scraps of theatrical jargon picked up at this morning's rehearsal. We can just distinguish the words "Nick the weaver" and "bloody blameful blade." . . .

In the Hall where the performance is to take place the company is already assembling. At one end a stage has been set up. We can see that it is nothing but heavy planking on trestles. At the back of this, within two feet of the end-wall, is a suggestion of Greek architecture, with a small pair of drawn curtains in the middle. Through these the actors are to enter, and the passage behind leads to their *tiring rooms*. We guess that the play is probably to be a gorgeous spectacle with antique costumes. But it is difficult to reconcile our guess with the humors of the bandsmen upstairs.

If we slip into any of the side-rooms we shall witness the same scene of confusion that has attended every first performance since theatricals began. We need not describe it. Lord Strange is by now cursing his own fatuity in ever having meddled with his brother's wedding arrangements. He feels himself at enmity with every living actor. Even the Warwickshire man — quietly busy in the property-room — seems to be avoiding him. His lordship is just considering whether he ought not to take some active notice of this — when br-r-r-r-r go the drums; and with an ear-splitting fanfare of trumpets the Queen enters. There is a moment of suspense while she takes her seat. And then, from the place where we are "behind the scenes," we can hear a man's resonant voice:

> Now, fair Hippolyta, our nuptial hour
> Draws on apace.

We wish we could follow every word of this play. But, as our object in being here is strictly musical, we must take the advantage of our privileged situation only in one direction. But that direction leads to some new viewpoints. For the author has provided plenty of opportunity for music. He has contrived some woodland fairy scenes, for instance. We peep through the curtains just as the fairies are about to make their first entrance and notice with dismay that half-a-dozen of our Shawm and Bombard friends of this morning are preparing to shatter our nerves again. However, our consternation vanishes when they begin to play. For, instead of the former piercing pandemonium, we have a sweet "warbling" tone-quality — woody and somewhat tame, it is true — but delightful to the ears.

These are the *recorders*, *fipple-flutes*, or *flûtes douces*, an instrumental squad which, time out of mind, has been known as the *dulcet* wood-wind in contradistinction to the *reed*, that is to say, the shawms and bombards.[1] The Queen has seven recorder players in her service, five Venetians, a Frenchman, and an Englishman. From where we are their instruments look as like the shawms as two pods of peas. There are the *Great Bass* and the *Bass Recorders* corresponding to the *Double-Bass* and *Bass Bombards*. The larger instruments of both families have much the same kind of bent metal crooks. Also we can hear that between them the six recorders have a compass from

But if we take a nearer view we shall see that in all the recorders the tone is produced by means of a fipple, not a reed. In other words the breath is directed against a sharp "lip" cut in the pipe itself. The little white object at the end of the metal crook is not a double-reed, but an ivory mouthpiece.[2] And this distinction in the tone-production causes the vast difference in actual sound.

[1] "That craftely begunne to pipe Both in doucet and in riede" (Chaucer, *House of Fame*, 1384). "The dulset, the dulsacordis, the schalme of assay" (Holland, *Howlat*, 1450).

[2] The instruments in the illustration (Plate XXIX) are — from left to right — Great Bass, Bass, Tenor, Alto, Treble, and High Treble Recorders. In the Great Bass Recorder the mouthpiece is lacking. Scientifically the fipple-flutes are the same as the flue-work of the organ. The strictly technical meaning of "fipple" is the inclined plane inside the pipe *above* the sharp "lip." This plane directs the breath on to the lip itself. But the word "fipple" is roughly used to include the whole mechanism — the inside plane, the sharp lip, and the outside bevel.

The music played by the recorders is practically four-part vocal music, with an octave-doubling at top and bottom. And this applies also to the viols and to the shawms. The cry indeed is all for *homogeneous tone-colors*. It is a simple vivid taste, consonant with the times. And to meet it these instruments have all been built "in families"; and play in *whole consorts*, as they are called. The spectators in front of us will tolerate a good deal of sameness in the texture of the music. They do not look for much flexibility or technique. But they do look for instrumental appropriateness. In fact one may almost say that they are *specialists in tone-color*. Lutes and viols for love-making; the horns for the chase; trumpets for war; the recorders for supernatural events; the solemn cornetts and sackbuts for heavy tragedy. That is what they expect.

We are not likely to hear the last-named group this afternoon, unless indeed the author intends to bring them in somewhere by way of burlesque. Nor shall we hear much of those timid combinations of *unlikes* which they call *broken consorts*. Out of doors they will occasionally mass their shawms, cornetts, and sackbuts; while indoors they are gradually being accustomed to the association of viols and lutes, viols and virginals, recorders and viols.[1] They also show a healthy dislike to the combination of instruments which have the same method of tone-production, such as virginals and lutes. But their musical taste runs mainly in the direction of *likes*, not of *unlikes*. And we can gauge the genuineness of this taste merely by looking at the color of their clothes.

But while we have been engaged in these philosophical reflections the play has been drawing to an end. It has been a wonderful experience. To Oriana in particular. Forty-five years of men's feigned adoration and her own deceit

---

[1] The accompaniments of the songs were usually played by lutes, viols, and virginals; while the instrumental force employed in the entr'actes depended solely on the character of the scene. In *Gorboduc* (1561) the five groups were as follows; violins — cornetts — flutes — hautboys — drums and fifes. In *Sophonisba* (1606) the four entr'actes were played respectively by cornetts and organs — recorders and organs — voices, viols, and organs — treble viol and bass lute.

have scorched and withered her heart. And now — at sixty-one — she thought herself beyond the reach of flattery. When she made her stately entry a few hours ago she intended to utter only the most formal compliments at the close of the performance. Once even, in the opening scene, she whispered, to ask her lady-in-waiting what was the mnemonic they had agreed on for the author's name — was it "S" or "B"? "S., ma'am," said the lady, "same as Lord Strange, ma'am." But that was three hours ago — before all this happened.

She makes *no* compliments to the bridegroom's brother; but rises and goes quickly with her lady upstairs to the tapestried room. She is a little bit flushed — for the first time in her life perhaps. And as she looks at the tiny spinet standing open on the table, the line about "the imperial votaress" comes into her mind. She is half inclined to cry, not being quite sure whether she feels very old or very very young — young enough to live forever. So she signs to the lady-in-waiting to ring the bell and, seating herself at the spinet, plays over Hugh Aston's *Ground* — the one that her father taught her. Then, as the tapestry is lifted, she says to the servant "Send Mr. Sha . . . "

But before we can learn what is in her mind another servant has entered with his tray of candlesticks. And we know that it is sunset; that we can neither see nor hear more; and that the Palace of Greenwich, with its strange sights and sounds, is for us a dream of the past. So, if the reader has grown tired of his long sojourn there, let them say:

> If we shadows have offended,
> Think but this, and all is mended,
> That you have but slumbered here;
> While these visions did appear.

CHAPTER 10

Song and Folk-Song

BEFORE proceeding to study the music of the third or modern period, we wish to ask the reader's attention to a subject which in a way knits all three periods together — *song*. In our first chapter we have already mentioned the bare fact that song was the latest and most complex of primitive man's achievements. It is a permanent element in musical history. One might almost say the only permanent element.[1] Before musical history begins, *it is*. And *it is* in the sense that it joins up civilized man to the savage.

Hitherto our history has dealt almost wholly with *artistic* music, that is, with music consciously formulated and developed by the most competent thinkers of each age. But, in the course of this history, it has been necessary to mention more than once the existence and influence of another body of music, which we have referred to as "secular music." This special term — accurate enough so long as *all* the artistic music was written to serve the church — becomes inaccurate about 1500 when professional composers began to divide their energies between church-music and lay-music. For though the art-music became split up into two channels, the stream of folk-music continued to flow alongside them as it had flowed from the dawn of time. A new differentiating term is therefore needed; and found in "folk-music."

We may view the history of artistic music as one vast cultivated field fenced off into three allotments — the *ancient, mediæval,* and *modern* — of which some parts are fertile and

---

[1] "All inmost things, we may say, are melodious; naturally utter themselves in Song . . . All deep things are Song. It seems somehow the very central essence of us, Song; as if all the rest of us were but wrappages and hulls." Carlyle, *The Hero as Poet.*

others sterile. But besides this cultivated crop there is another which grows without any care on the part of the farmer: and grows always, whatever the conditions of sunshine, rain, or general climate. These are not weeds. They are flowers whose colors and perfumes vary only as they are drawn from different parts of the field. But they all have this in common: that if the soil is anywhere deprived of the chemistry set up by their roots, the cultivated crop will probably be rank or sickly. It is well to fix this fact firmly in one's mind: that there always have been, are still, and possibly always will be two co-existent types of music — the wild and the cultivated, folk-music and art-music. But both of these types derive directly from their common ancestor, *song*. Therefore if we wish to put these broad facts of history into the simple form of a diagram, it will be something like this:

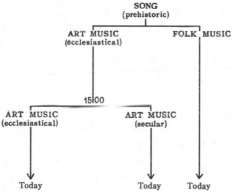

Now we have already dealt in the preceding chapters with the left-hand side of this diagram down to the year 1600. We shall have no more to say on that topic here, except in so far as it impinges on folk-music. But we wish to take the general subject of *song* and fill in some of the outlines which were necessarily left bare in the first chapter. We can then proceed to its derivative *folk-song*. And the reader will be better able to appreciate its importance and its relationships in the light of his present knowledge.

The history of song begins almost with the history of man.

In its first stages it is an interesting study, rather more in the domain of the ethnologist than the musician. It is concerned with antiquarian probabilities and with analogies from the surviving races of mankind. But in its later stages it is clearly within the musician's province. For he has at his disposal the materials for showing its growth in both the wild and the cultivated kinds, and also the interactions of the two varieties.

We have already seen in Chapter I how man stepped upwards from the level of a howling brute to the higher level of an articulate being, and next to the still higher level of a singing creature. These three words, *howling, speaking, singing,* in a measure comprise his whole history. But it is important to notice that they are not disconnected stages in a growth. The one does not cease when the other begins. The howling stage is not to the other two what the worm is to the chrysalis and the moth. It is rather a nucleus. The other two grow around it and are conditioned by it, even before they come into existence. Furthermore, it always remains in the center vitalizing the whole. And this is its overwhelming importance to us.

Let us take a commonplace instance. If you knock your elbow badly against the sharp corner of your desk, you utter a cry of pain. It gives you no relief to do this. You are merely resuming for a moment your savage ancestors' normal practice. You are in the howling stage. But you may include in your howl a word — "dash," let us say. You are now one step higher, in the speaking stage. But things are not yet so far advanced with you that you can express your emotion spontaneously *in song.* Your ancestors have only used that highly developed form of emotional expression for about 20,000 years (at a rough guess), a minute fragment in the whole span of time. It is man's most recent acquirement and is therefore not yet wholly natural to you. The desk knocks the civilization out of you, and you howl

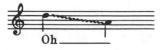

or you say

dash!

but you do not say

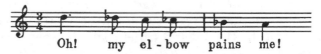

And even if you could hum these notes without the words it
would show that you were not very badly hurt — were indeed
somewhat outside the emotional field and able to view the
incident from a detached and semi-humorous standpoint.
These three illustrations then may symbolize for us the three
stages in the evolution of man which are the common heritage
of every human being — first the stage of howling; next the
stage of howling and speaking; and last the stage of howling,
speaking, and singing.

Of the first two stages we know very little. A few skulls
have been found of such a shape that their possessors could
certainly not have used their jaws to utter words. The date
at which these men lived has been guessed vaguely by geolo-
gists and others; let us merely say that it was very remote.
These were the people of the howling period. We may add,
that almost all remembrance of the fact that such people
ever existed had vanished long before the dawn of the earliest
civilization known to us. A single epithet which the most
ancient Greek poets applied to mankind seems to recall
dimly a period in which men could not articulate.[1]

The next period is nearly as blank to us. For though it
probably corresponds with the age of the bone and ivory
carvings found in caves, we have to rely solely on negative
evidence, such as the fact that even the most primitive musical instruments are not represented on the tusks and antlers.
How long this period lasted no one knows. But it is without
doubt the time when the first bow-string was twanged and

---

[1] Μέροπες βροτοί. The first word (mĕrŏpĕs) probably means *dividing the
voice;* that is, *articulating.* But the word may only imply a distinction between men and beasts.

the first reed blown into. It may very well be that one or other of these rudimentary instruments gave the first cue for breaking up and defining the long *glissando* howl. The pleasure produced by the plucked string and the desire to imitate it would account for much. Furthermore, it is probable that in such a process of imitation the governing condition would be the natural cadence of the speaking voice — a downward drop of a fourth.

At any rate when we come to the next period — that in which musical notes have been invented as a vehicle for words — we find a suggestive unanimity in the choice of 4-stringed instruments and 3-holed (that is 4-note) pipes. The earliest sacred chants, too, of which we have any record possess this 4-note character; and the Greek tetrachordal system is a hint in the same direction.

The first tunes were of course charms (*carmina* as the Romans called them); that is, incantations and magic formulæ. They were part of the stock-in-trade of the medicine-man; and as such were used to cure cattle disease, to insure success in war and the chase, and to bring fertility to the plough-lands.[1] We may be quite sure that, whatever was the actual succession of notes sung in such chants, they included the principle common to all savage races — repetition. This method of expression is universal in Asia, Africa, and Polynesia. It survives even in Europe. A Sicilian fisherman of the present day will repeat a single short song-phrase to the accompaniment of two guitar-chords throughout a whole evening, varying it emotionally from the plane of a dull lassitude to that of a wild frenzied excitement.

This simple type of chant or charm is the head-water from which all music flows. But, as we have said, it branches off into two main river-systems the (ecclesiastical) art-music and the folk-music. Of the two the former has by far the more varied course. The boat starts smoothly enough in charge of the medicine-man. He is succeeded by the pagan holy-boly, and the holy-boly by the monk or priest. As is

[1] The Roman *Song of the Arval Brothers* and the *axamenta* of the Salii were probably incantations of this sort.

natural in the circumstances their music preserves certain characteristics of simplicity, severity, and regularity. But at various points in its course this stream intersects with the other. And this occasional intersection produces, as we have seen, somewhat violent changes in its current.

Meanwhile, the broad stream of folk-music flows placidly on, fed by its own tributaries, and unconscious of the dangerous cross-currents which it causes when it meets the big official water-way. From the very first it serves two distinct purposes, the *lyric* and the *narrative*. Both are *poetical* forms and both demand music for their proper enforcement. But they demand a different sort of music. The lyric poem is short, vivid, emotional; and it asks for music clearly illustrating its special contents. The narrative is often quite unemotional and of enormous length. It asks for a short tune good enough to stand endless repetition, but not sufficiently hall-marked with character to be unsuitable in any part of the poem.

Narrative poems of this sort have existed from the earliest times. Till the invention of printing (and the happy thought some 300 years later of allowing people to read) they were practically the only means of disseminating secular fact and fiction. We must look to Greece for the first ballad-singers. There, in the most ancient times of which we have any accurate knowledge, we find the Homeric poems being recited — that is chanted or sung — by professional gilds of rhapsodists. The names of Alcæus, Sappho, Anacreon, and Pindar can scarcely be included in the line of folk-music; though they all probably relied a good deal on folk-tunes that had become popular since the Dorian migration. But a little later than Pindar's time, Aristophanes, in describing his own early years, recalls with pride an old song which was popular in his youth — *Pallas, Destroyer-of-Cities*.[1] This is one of the first folk-songs whose names we know. The type of music employed in these early songs must have been melodically simple and restricted. It must also have had a certain elasticity of rhythm; otherwise its repetition in the epic

[1] Παλλὰς περσέπολις.

poems under the conditions of a varying prosody would have been impossible. In the lyric poetry the "tune" probably fitted the words like a glove. Indeed, as we have already pointed out, the authors of these lyrics could never have conceived their existence apart from music.

In the countries of northern Europe we hear of ballad-singers as soon as we hear of the countries themselves. Tacitus tells us that in his time — the end of the first century A.D. — the German tribes had both short popular poems and the long narrative pieces in which they celebrated the deeds of their national heroes. From that time forward it may be said with confidence that every European country has produced a long succession of folk-singers, under such names as bards, skalds, gleemen, minstrels, ballad-singers, and so on.[1] Only partly within this succession are the German minnesingers and meistersingers and the French troubadours and trouvères. The former group began as folk-singers pure and simple, but degenerated into a highly artificial and useless class of musical carpenters. The latter also began with folk-song, but attempted, without any great intelligence, to form a sort of alliance between it and church-music. The only happy result of their efforts was the establishment of the rhyming stanza as a poetical form.[2]

But apart from these semi-artistic and not very successful movements, folk-song continued to flourish in its quiet persistent way right down to our own times. Most of the great musical crises of the professional "schools" have come and gone. And their comings and goings have been to the

---

[1] In England the professional bards of the great feudal families continued to exist well into the sixteenth century. William Peeris, who wrote a metrical *Chronicle of the family of Percy* for his employer, the fifth Earl of Northumberland (d. 1527), was one of the last. The most interesting of these metrical mixtures of fact and fiction is *The Song of the Lady Bessy* (*i.e.* Elizabeth, daughter of Edward IV). It deals with Bosworth and was probably written by Brereton, an adherent of the Stanleys, who himself took part in the action which he describes.

[2] The troubadours and trouvères were primarily song-composers. They wrote both the words and the music, but did not necessarily perform either. More than 2250 of their compositions have come down to us in manuscript. These are mostly to be found in the Bibliothèque Nationale at Paris, but others exist at Arras, London, Milan, Rome, and Siena. A *Bibliographie* has been published by Gaston Raynaud; and there are several special works on the subject by Pierre Aubry.

countryside singers no more than the falling of a leaf in autumn. These singers exist at the present day even in such an over-populated little place as England. Within an hour's journey of London, men can be found who sing narrative and other poems exactly as their forefathers have sung them for nearly a thousand years. It is true that they are mostly *old* people. But too much has been made of this point: too much has been said about the refusal of the young to learn the old songs, and about the probable extinction of the music in the next generation. One may reasonably ask whether the singers of such songs have not naturally always been old men since the days of Demodocus.

However that may be, it is plain that there has been a universal dependence of the people in all ages on *sung poetry*. And this presumes the existence of a vast mass of folk-music. The reader may well be asking where and what it is. Now these two questions cannot be answered by a brief statement in the one case or by a definition in the other. But enough can be said on both points to give him an accurate view on the subject.

Folk-song is a form of music orally transmitted. Each singer learns his poems and his tunes, twists and alters them to suit his own ideas, and passes on the result to his successor. It may be and probably will be slightly different from the music which he originally learnt. It is never written down [1] and yet is one of the most permanent things in the world. It is not the work of any one man or of any one period, though it can usually be employed for artistic purposes by composers of all periods. It is purely melodic; harmonic only by accident.[2] It is not self-existent; but exists for one of the two purposes, poetry or dancing. It is an *agglutination* formed by the sub-conscious artistic mind of a nation. But though a dozen generations and a hundred thousand repetitions may have gone to the shaping of one folk-tune, the result has two features very well worth attention. In the first place, the

---

[1] Except by "collectors," when it finds its way into printed books.

[2] An exception must be made of the Russian *horovodi*. These afford the only known instance of popular music which has developed into a rudimentary harmony without being written down.

folk-tunes of a nation show a remarkable homogeneity of style. And this means that underneath the myriad tiny acts of brain and muscle that are summed up in a single folk-song there is a real something, an impulse whose driving-force comes from the soil itself. The second point is that in all the best folk-songs there is precisely the same *ordered beauty* which we look for as the highest personal expression of the cultured composer. Design, balance, climax, and "points of repose" are identical in both. Only, in the one case, they are expressed in a few bars of melody, in the other by many bars of melody, harmony, and counterpoint.

These two last points suggest a somewhat wide field for reflection. It is a commonplace of history to say that during the nineteenth century the great symphonic and operatic schools of Germany held an unchallenged supremacy in most European countries. To German musicians this was a source of both pride and profit. But in these various countries there was a host of unhappy wretches breaking their hearts in the attempt to steal the German fuel and kindle it on their own altars. They had not observed what the Germans had thoroughly understood from the outset and what was in fact the source of their greatness — that wood for this special purpose must be cut in one's own forest. The result was that, when the time came for the sacrifice, no glint of sacred flame ever shot up from their altars; and the only satisfactory feature of the rite was that the priests themselves were usually suffocated in their own smoke.

Now, somewhere about the third quarter of the century various people in various countries of Europe, such as Denmark, Russia, and England, began to stop their superficial inquiries into the latest mental ingenuities of the German composers, and to ask themselves instead the much more serious question as to what was the fundamental factor on which the Germans depended for their inspiration. And the answer was "on their nationality." This led composers to a further inquiry — the perplexing search for the existence of a *musical sanction* for their national activity. This search was taken up eagerly in many countries and it resulted in the re-discovery of folk-song.

Not only was folk-song re-discovered, but its discovery gave composers exactly that final sanction for their efforts which they had before been groping for in vain. It made them at once free-born citizens of their own country. It gave them the right to wear their nationality proudly. Before that time all their efforts had not been much better than the antics of a clever juggler. They had been poised in the air on a borrowed wire. Now they were able to stand firmly on their own soil.

The point to be emphasized is that up to that time the composers of these countries had felt considerable doubts as to whether their soil was not merely a clod of black earth and nothing more. The discovery of folk-song showed them that inside the clod was a germ which produced wonderful wild flowers and renewed its vitality from its own soil. Furthermore, as people began to inquire more lovingly into this botany, they soon found out that it was a spontaneous vegetation, sometimes growing slowly and sometimes fast, but always under the laws of its own climate and not merely in response to the cultivation of the professional gardeners. Now, if anyone will consider these facts candidly, he will see that, as the natural growth of the wild flower alone justifies the toil of the gardener, so the folk-song sanctifies his art to the honest composer.

So far for the philosophy of folk-song. Let us now say a few words on the tunes themselves. These have become familiar in our concert-rooms either in accompanied or har-monized versions; and they are accessible in many well-known collections. Furthermore, they are being increasingly used as the bases for large symphonic works; and this tendency is particularly noticeable in Russia and Great Britain. Some of these tunes are of very great beauty and all are interesting. Their acquisition has not only rendered a special service to the composer, but has increased the general artistic wealth of the world. Folk-music is played and dis-cussed everywhere — often under conditions that would distress and horrify a genuine folk-singer. But as we have in a manner robbed him of his inheritance, or at any rate have secured a life-interest in his estate, we must take care at least to understand its proper administration.

Folk-song can be studied from one of two standpoints — the *historical* and the *artistic;* and both studies may be pursued along *comparative* lines. A tune may be valuable in the one case and valueless in the other. Even the historical associations of a tune are interesting. Thus we are glad to possess the tune to which "bonnie Prince Charlie" danced at his celebrated ball in Holyrood House; though the tune itself is no more than ordinary. But the main historical interest in folk-song is inductive. We examine a number of tunes belonging to one nation. And this examination gradually establishes in our minds three facts — first, the existence of a national type; second, the variation of this type in a larger or smaller degree from the *artistic* music of the nation; third, the *general* permanence of folk-music as a separate entity.

A judgment based on considerations of this sort always leads to the conclusion that the more intimately acquainted a nation is with its art-music the less interesting is its folk-music. Germany and England are the two best examples.

In Germany the people have been interpenetrated for centuries with the best works of their professional composers. Therefore, they have not been compelled to supply this vital necessity for themselves; or, if they have done so, they have worked under much the same conditions as their artists. Consequently when we examine German folk-song we learn little that is new. It is all summed up in their school of composition. From the German point of view this union is ideal. From the standpoint of the folk-song specialist it is just the reverse.

But when we turn to a country like England we find that secular music has mostly been the plaything of the rich townsman. The countryman has had to provide his own. Its folk-music is therefore the most interesting of all from the historical standpoint. It is strongly marked in type and widely divergent from the national art-music. Whatever the composers of each generation may have done with its tunes, it has clung to its antique modes of expression. We need not be surprised at hearing an old Somerset or Norfolk laborer sing a tune in exactly the same form as his Tudor forbears sang it; though the tune itself may have been borrowed by the composers of three or four different ages and dressed up by them into the fashionable idiom of their day. It is, then, the best possible example of folk-song as a permanent and separate type.

But there is another standpoint from which we can view folk-music — the artistic. And it is here that a few words of caution may be welcomed by the layman. A sort of glory or halo has of late been set round the subject. And this has at times become a nimbus of obscurity. The folk-lorists themselves — some of whom are better railway-travellers than musicians — are not guiltless in this matter. There has been a somewhat indiscriminate praise. Any tune that has a C for its first climax-note and an E for its second is hailed as a miracle of strength and subtlety. *Modality* and *masterpiece* become synonyms.

But there is nothing magic in the two words *folk-music*. They mean simply "music of the people." And the tunes of the people are to be judged by the same canons as those of the professional artist. A bad tune does not become good by having the word "folk" prefixed to it. If it is to be classed as "good" it must have beauty of expression and of organization — that is to say, of climax, balance, and proportion. Folk-song does not shirk the rigorous application of these laws. For, as we have already explained, the spring of its vitality lies in the one fact that it is a sub-conscious attempt of the people to achieve exactly the same sort of ends as those achieved consciously by the artists. One may add that the proportion of really beautiful tunes in folk-music is high. This is not to be wondered at. But it strengthens one's faith in human nature to know that the common folk instinctively drop what is bad and vulgar.

We had not intended to say anything at all as to the comparative merits of the various groups of folk-song. To do that adequately would require a large volume; for collections have been made from about two dozen nations. But as there is some consensus of opinion on this point even among musicians we shall permit ourselves to indicate briefly the character of two of the most interesting types — the Irish and the Russian — leaving the reader to pursue his own studies among any of the other groups.

The folk-music of Ireland is generally known as among the finest in the world. It has a *variety* unknown to any other country.[1] Every conceivable incident of human life from the cradle to the grave is reflected from its surface. And there is a corrresponding variety of substance in the tunes themselves. The best examples are astonishingly beautiful; and they have an incomparable perfection of form. They are never wandering or doubtful, unless intentionally so. And they rarely depend, as some English tunes do, on mere mathematical balance of design; though they generally include this special form of excellence.

The Russian folk-music is not less interesting, but it looks at life from fewer points of view. To say that it is the music of barbarians would be a woeful misstatement. But there is a grain of truth there nevertheless. A certain primitiveness and nearness to the soil runs through all the Russian songs. Man does not appear in them as the master of the world, but as its victim. They give utterance to a "yearning without hope," a thirst never to be slaked, a gnawing bitterness of heart. The word "destiny" seems to be written across them in letters of iron. Humor there is. But it is the black humor of the drunken headsman. All this music has force, color, and passion. Yet to a westerner, however conscious he may be of its merits, it always remains something of a nightmare.[2]

---

[1] The principal types are the songs, reels, jigs, caoines, marches, spinning-tunes, nurse-tunes, planxties, plough-songs, and whistles. The variety of subject in the songs alone can be seen merely by looking through the index of titles to the *Petrie Collection.*

[2] The long Russian narrative-songs in which Tchaikovsky took so much interest are known as *builini.* They are practically epics in blank verse, and have been sung by the peasants for a thousand years. The *piesni* are

The number of folk-songs at present in existence cannot be stated even approximately. But the reader will be able to appreciate its vastness when he is told that 5000 have been found in England alone. It is not our intention to print specimens of our particular taste in folk-song, for to do that comparatively as between nation and nation would be quite beyond the space at our disposal. But we propose to add one to the 5000 English tunes just mentioned — a lavender-girl's cry heard at Chelsea in three successive years about 1895, and never before printed.

Won't you buy my sweet la-ven-dar, la-ven-dar?

solo-songs, either laments for the dead or eulogies of the living. The *horovodi*, which we have already mentioned, are a sort of tentative choral singing, somewhat like the mediæval singers' counterpoint described on page 141.

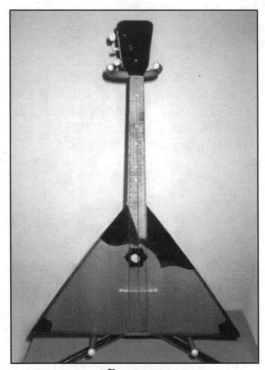

BALALAIKA

METELITSA ORCHESTRA - BALALAIKA PLAYERS

PLATE XXX. RUSSIAN FOLK INSTRUMENTS

METELITSA ORCHESTRA - ACCORDION & VIOLIN PLAYERS

METELITSA ORCHESTRA - DOMRA & MANDOLIN PLAYERS

PLATE XXXI. RUSSIAN FOLK INSTRUMENTS

UKELELE

BODHRANS

CELTIC HARP

PLATE XXXII. IRISH FOLK INSTRUMENTS

CHAPTER 11

The Secular Century

Up to the close of the Sixteenth Century there is only one composer of dominating figure, whose works are still alive and still intimately affecting musical ears and thoughts: Palestrina. The Seventeenth Century, while prolific in great men, contained no such overmastering personality. It was essentially a period of simmering experiment. The milk was rich, but it was only in process of being set, and the cream was yet to form. Secularism was in the air, and its atmosphere began to affect all arts alike. This interesting period saw the beginnings of what is called "absolute" music, *i.e.*, music independent of word illustration. Instrumental music began tentatively to take its place beside choral music, and to combine with it, as well as to assert itself independently of it. It also saw the first efforts at opera, at oratorio (in the modern sense), and their indispensable handmaid declamatory recitative: the birth of the overture, the concerto, the vocal aria, the literature of the organ and the precursors of the pianoforte. The organ challenged consideration on its own account; the harpsichord and its kindred developed the cramped lines of the Elizabethan masters into the extended suite and the sonata. The violin and other stringed instruments showed signs of becoming vehicles for individual solo display. The beginnings of instrumental chamber-music also are to be traced through the experiments of Italian and English masters. The latter were often surprisingly successful, and sufficiently numerous examples of them are extant to prove the value of their efforts. John Jenkins (1592–1678) wrote many chamber works, and may be said to have been one of the pioneers of the movement. It was carried to a high pitch of excellence by Henry Purcell, the only composer of his time, with the exception of Alessandro Scarlatti, who almost reached the position of a dominant master, and most certainly would have done so if his career had not been cut short in its prime.

The Renaissance (itself a reflection of the methods and tastes of ancient Greece) was not confined to architecture, painting, sculpture or letters, but deeply affected music as well. Its influence mainly showed itself in the development of monophony, the Greek method of musical expression as far as we know it, as distinct from polyphony: in other words, of the triumph of the single voice over the choral mass. Like all reforms and new departures, it often carried away the reformers and tempted them to run their new theories to death, even causing them to lose sight of that other side of Greek dramatic art which, when at its zenith in the hands of Æschylus, considered the chorus to be a vital part of the dramatic action and scheme. The chorus therefore became a shadow and the soloist had the field to himself. It may be said then that the Seventeenth Century had to carry on its shoulders the responsibility for those later troubles, the star system, and the exaggerated hero-worship of the individual performer.

The initiative of the new movement came from one house in Florence, the palace of Giovanni Bardi, Conte di Vernio.[1] This nobleman is credited with the first idea of opera, or rather with the first suggestion of applying the principles of the Greek Play to the conditions of the stage of his time, and of calling in the aid of music to assist in the presentation.

---

[1] The precursor of Italian Opera was the *Sacra Rappresentazione* of the Florentines. This was a species of Fifteenth Century mystery-play. It dealt with religious subjects, and was sumptuously produced. Music, dialogue, folk-dancing, and choral interludes all figured as part of the sacred representation. In its turn this type of religious performance gave way, under the pressure of the Renaissance, to a sort of pastoral tragedy based upon purely classical subjects. It was pagan — almost anti-Christian — and was first cultivated by Angelo Politian and his friend Lorenzo de' Medici. The greatest Italian artists, such as Leonardo, Raphael, and Andrea del Sarto, took part in the decoration of these tragedies; and music was always employed, either in the interludes or in the acts themselves. So began the long line of *Orfeo* dramas which more than a century later were to be revitalized by the new musical spirit of the Italian monodists.

Bardi summoned to his councils a large body of contemporary poets and musicians, Peri, Caccini, Vincenzo Galilei (the father of the famous astronomer), Rinuccini, Corsi and others, who wrote the *libretti* and the scores of various operas which were performed in his house. The most popular subject for their experiment was the compelling one of Orpheus, thereby emphasizing the Greek trend of their thoughts and aspirations. This movement rapidly affected the whole of Italy. Carissimi and Cesti at Rome, Cavalli and Legrenzi at Venice, Viadana at Rome and Mantua, all worked on the same line. Orazio Vecchi, of Modena, who aimed at a reconciliation between the polyphonic school of choral writing and the exigencies of dramatic effect, seems to have been more far-sighted than the Florentine reformers themselves.

In the midst of this party of progress there appeared a fire-brand, who carried the reform to revolution, and filled much the same rôle in early Italian times that Wagner and Berlioz did in the Nineteenth Century — Claudio Monteverdi of Cremona. He scorned tradition both with regard to voices and instruments, freely using unprepared discords (which were barred before his day) in his vocal work, and, besides adding orchestral accompaniment to sacred choral compositions, increased the number of instruments in his orchestra, and invented the *tremolando* on the strings which has affected all instrumentation down to our own times. He secured the coöperation of the Florentine poet, Rinuccini, with whose help he challenged the Liberal Conservatives of Count Bardi, and succeeded in imposing his masterful personality upon his audience. He, like some of his Red-cap successors, cared little for the admixture of ugliness with beauty, and considered that his innovations were superior to any necessity of sacrificing the former to the exigencies of the latter. The result was, as it remains still, that the man is forgotten as a composer, and is only remembered as an innovator. He had his uses, not only as a pattern of what can be done, but as an example of what to avoid. It was reserved for the genius of Gluck to use Monteverdi's discoveries, but to combine them with artistic beauty. We owe to the Italian the chord of the dominant seventh, which marks the division between his predecessors and his successors, and which has permeated all music since his day. Composers of his type usually rouse contemporary animosity, but their experiments often contain the germs of many a subsequent advance. It remains as difficult a task nowadays, as it was in the Seventeenth Century, to sift the chaff from the grain; but the process goes on, with the same human drawbacks as prevailed amongst our ancestors.

From Italy the movement soon spread to France. The son of a Florentine gentleman, Lorenzo de' Lulli, who developed musical gifts at an early age, was taken to Paris by the Chevalier de Guise, gained the ear of Louis XIV, and eventually became the master of the newly formed "Académie de Musique" (still the name of the Grand Opéra at Paris), for which he composed numerous operas and ballets, besides writing incidental music for the plays of Molière and other dramatists. Lully (to give him the French form of his Italian name) has one important achievement of far-reaching effect to his credit: the creation of the Overture. Before his time, the introductions to operas consisted of a few bars of irrelevant significance, little more than a flourish to call silence, and without the dramatic suggestiveness, which, for example, the trumpet calls which summoned the audiences to the Baireuth Theatre conveyed in full measure. He not only invented the idea, but laid down the form which was universally adopted down to the time of Gluck. It is true that the Lully Overture was a formal expression, having no inherent connection with the themes or ideas of the opera which it preceded; but the rough draft had to exist before it became possible to graft bigger ideas and more subtle meanings upon it; and for the inception of a movement, which was to result in the great dramatic overtures of Beethoven, Weber, and Wagner, we have to thank the Opera-Director of Louis XIV.

The operatic wave then rolled rapidly to other countries. First to England, where Henry Purcell in 1675, when only a

THE KING AT AGE 10

PLATE XXXIII.   LOUIS XIV OF FRANCE

PLATE XXXIV. PURCELL

boy of seventeen, showed a master hand in his setting of *Dido and Æneas*, a work which although only written for a girls' school, showed an astounding advance in dramatic treatment, and an instinct for music-drama far ahead of his time. The sailors' scene and the touching lament of Dido survive in their original freshness and characteristic appeal to the present day, and the whole opera (despite its antique trammels and trappings) can even now make its effect upon the stage. In his short and busy life of thirty-seven years, Purcell composed the music for no less than fifty-three operas and plays. He showed the way clearly to the treatment of the solo voice as a dramatic exponent of a situation in aria form, as distinct from recitative. The best known example of his powers in this respect is the scena, so amazingly modern even to our contemporary-era ears, "Ye twice ten thousand deities," from *The Indian Queen*. What had been a tentative experiment in the hands of Lully, became in his a vital force. He reached a point of realistic expression, which Handel did not attain to until he had deserted the opera for the oratorio. It is difficult for the superficial observer to distinguish between the relative dates of men who wore wigs: and it is too often assumed that Handel and Purcell belonged (owing to these monstrosities) to the same period. It is therefore important to remember that Handel and Bach were only ten years old when Purcell died; and that it would be as absurd to call Mendelssohn, Schumann, and Wagner the contemporaries of Beethoven, as to consider Purcell a contemporary of the two great Germans. The influence of Lully upon Purcell can be traced through Pelham Humphrey, his senior in the ranks of the Children of the Chapel Royal, who was sent by Charles II to work under the French master. Purcell, not having studied the Italo-French methods at their headquarters, grasped their principles without sacrificing his essentially English individuality, and improved upon them by reason of his inventive independence. Amongst lesser dramatic lights of his time, may be mentioned Banister and Blow.

Germany then began to show signs of the move. The

head center was at Hamburg, where Bernhard Keiser, a Saxon, took opera in hand, and was most successful during his life in raising it to a high pitch of excellence. During Keiser's reign at the Hamburg Theatre, a youth of seventeen entered the orchestra as a back-desk violinist, without any credentials to back him, and even posing as an ignoramus in technique. It was not long before Handel's self-assumed mask fell off and he became chief musician in the theater, producing operas of his own which even contained sufficiently good material to lay the foundations of the insatiable habit which grew upon him in later years, of using his own early work in his maturer compositions; a habit to which he subsequently added the use (without acknowledgment) of other men's brains. Our ancestors perhaps were not over-particular about this kind of annexation, but the only excuse for Handel's light fingers seems to be the statement (which is undoubtedly true) that he improved and immortalized what otherwise would have been lost and forgotten. These early operas of Handel seemed to have been a compound of Lully's theories with the German influence of Keiser, and shortly after their appearance, he left for Italy, where the center of specific gravity had shifted to Naples, mainly in consequence of the commanding genius of Alessandro Scarlatti.

Scarlatti, undoubtedly the greatest Italian composer of the Seventeenth Century, laid the first stone of the formal aria (first part, second part and *da capo* repeat of the first part), which ruled the world until the death of Handel. He introduced the orchestral *ritornello*, which we now colloquially term a symphony, and he elaborated the accompanied recitative, which has in Wagner's hand become the backbone of music-drama. He also led the way in making the Overture (which in Lully's works had a more or less stereotyped form) more independent and after the fashion of a Fantasia. This innovation, curiously enough, was ignored by Handel and only had its ultimate effect in later times. Alessandro Scarlatti's son, Domenico, is a much more well-known figure than his father, although he was not by any means his equal in importance. But if the father was one of the most prominent progenitors of modern opera, the son may truly be called the father of the modern pianoforte school. The list of Alessandro's pupils contains one name which links him with the great succession of German masters of the Eighteenth Century, that of Porpora, the first master of Haydn. It contains also the names of Leonardo Leo, a picturesque composer of great facility and charm, of Durante, who in his turn became the head of a less important line of young Italians (such as Jomelli, Piccini, and Paesiello), and of his famous son. Domenico's operas have all been forgotten, but his pieces "for the Gravi-Cenbalo" (one of the predecessors of the pianoforte) are as alive today as when they were composed. They have a striking individuality of their own, as marked indeed as that of Chopin. They are the work of an obviously perfect master of the instrument, abounding in devices (such as the crossing of the hands in rapid passages) [1] which are still an important part of the equipment of a pianoforte-composer, and they sparkle with a southern vividness and grace which was denied to his contemporaries of the north. The spread of his popularity outside his native country was not a little due to the enthusiasm of an Irishman named Roseingrave who was organist at Christ Church Cathedral in Dublin, and made the long journey thence to Naples for the sole purpose of knowing Domenico and seeing his artistic surroundings for himself.

In treating the clavi-cembalo as a medium for solo performance, Domenico Scarlatti was in some degree forestalled by a famous Frenchman, François Couperin, who was fifteen years his senior, and who may be said to have fixed the style of the *Partita* or "Suite de Pièces," a cycle of dances of the period, which became the model of a multitude of similar compositions. This type of extended piece in movements was adhered to and developed by Sebastian Bach, Handel, and many lesser luminaries. In the hands of the Frenchman, they were, however, destined, despite the native grace of their style, to remain music of his own age, and were denied

[1] These were facilitated by the double keyboard of the harpsichord.

the immortality which Scarlatti's daring Fantasias contained without straining after new effects or apparent effort in their production. The Italian still seems as much at home in a tail-coat and trousers as he was in trunk-hose. The Frenchman carries the mind back to wigs and rapiers. He holds, however, an abiding place in history as a master who possessed the art of idealizing the dance, and of materializing the use of ornaments, "agréments" as they were termed, which became so integral a part of harpsichord music, and were the parents of the modern pianoforte "passage." These devices were the inevitable result of the inability to sustain the sound of held notes upon the keyed instrument, which are still its chief drawback. The musician who is said to have invented them, de Chambonnières, was by profession an organist, and when he became a writer for and a famous player upon the harpsichord, he was most probably impelled to find a substitute for the long sounding notes to which his original instrument had accustomed him.

We have seen the reforms of Bardi and his coterie affecting dramatic music in the direction of emphasizing the solo voice, and the solo executant upon the harpsichord; they also, as a matter of course, affected the stringed instruments, especially the violin and the viol-da-gamba (a cousin of the violoncello), and the organ. Italy again was the leader in the formation of the great school of violinists which survived in that nation for many generations. The first of the race was Bassani of Padua, whose greatest pupil, Arcangelo Corelli, was destined to be known as the father of modern violin-playing. He was not merely a virtuoso, but a composer of striking merit; and he has won an imperishable name as a pioneer in the regions of chamber-music and of the treatment of the orchestra in Concertos. His influence upon Handel, who visited Rome as a young man when Corelli was at the zenith of his powers, was very marked. The German master, always impressionable, got many hints from him both in violin writing and in musical style, of which he did not, after his manner, fail to make the freest use in later life. Allusion has been made to the line of great violinists which started from Corelli. He had, amongst others, two pupils of great fame, Geminiani (the master of Dubourg, who came to England and was the leading violin of the orchestra when Handel produced the *Messiah* in Dublin), and Locatelli, the master of Leclair. Through another pupil of less fame, Somis, descended from master to pupil a great stock of world-known players, Pugnani, Viotti, Rode, Böhm and, greatest of them all, Joseph Joachim, and his contemporaries in the family tree, Hellmesberger, Ernst, Ludwig Strauss, Dont, and Rappoldi. From Viotti also descended de Bériot and Vieuxtemps, Baillot, Alard, Léonard, and Sarasate. Corelli, therefore, was responsible for nearly all the outstanding violinists in Italy, France and Germany for two centuries. His contemporary, Antonio Vivaldi of Venice, also a composer of the same stamp, but of less sure if more showy abilities, founded a school which contained one famous name, that of Tartini, the composer of several valuable works for his instrument of which the best known is the renowned *Trillo del Diavolo*, a piece which Tartini alleged to be a pale reproduction of a sonata played to him by the devil in a dream. From Tartini also was descended Dittersdorf, who played no small part in the development of the String Quartet at Vienna.

In the organ also Italy led the way. Girolamo Frescobaldi of Ferrara held much the same position in the development of composing for and playing that mighty instrument as Corelli did in the advancement of the violin. But he preceded the violin master by some eighty years. His compositions were at first of the pure vocal type of the Palestrina epoch, but he became affected, like the rest of his country, by the Bardi movement, and his later works are all in the direction of individualism. Through his German pupil, Froberger, he became the ancestor of the great German organ school which culminated in Johann Sebastian Bach. His style was daring, and indicative of the reliance he placed on the possibilities of his instrument as a factor, by itself, in musical life.

The movement in the direction of concerted chamber-music for strings and harpsichord, in which John Jenkins was one of the first to work, became more universal as the cultivation of solo playing increased. In this fascinating branch of music, Henry Purcell took the foremost place. His *Sonatas for two Violins, Bass, and Harpsichord* are so advanced in style and so daring in harmonic experiment, that they far exceed in value compositions in the same style which appeared fifty years after his death. *The Variations on a ground bass*, written some half a century before the *Violin Chaconne* and *Organ Passacaglia* of Bach are in their harmonic conception contemporaneous with them, and only lack the technical development of the instrument to take their place in the same rank. The final codas in these sonatas and the amazing progressions of which they consist belong rather to the twentieth century than to the Seventeenth. With the characteristic modesty of a great man, he ascribes the style of these chamber-works in his preface to them to the influence of "the most famed Italian masters," even going so far as to call them an "imitation," which, except as to their form, they certainly were not. He was nearer the truth when he added that "the attempt was bold and daring": he might have added that the boldness and daring were not beyond his powers. The skeleton was Italian, the flesh and blood were English. He has had to wait longer than the other great masters, both ancient and modern, in the circulation of his compositions through the medium of accessible print; but the efforts, though necessarily slow, of the Purcell Society helped greatly to bring to the world the surpassing genius and brilliant powers of a composer, British to the core, and instinct with all the finest qualities of his country. These sonatas are an epitome of his musical creed, as are Beethoven's string quartets of that master's phases of thought; and like the latter master they contain his most striking experiments in modernity of idea and progressiveness of expression.

A predecessor of Purcell, Christopher Sympson (or Simpson) played no inconsiderable part in the advancement of chamber-music. His magnum opus *The Division Violist*, published in 1659, the year after Purcell's birth, which was prefaced by laudatory verses, some of them contributed by John Jenkins, is a most interesting and valuable commentary upon the trend of the movement. His compositions for the viol-di-gamba are still played, and some of them were adapted by Piatti to the violoncello.

The Italian master to whom Purcell pays the compliment of "imitating" was probably Corelli, who wrote two kinds of concerted instrumental "sonatas," or as we should term them, "suites": the one founded on sacred models and derived from the music of the Church, the other in secular style and founded on the dance. But Corelli is the only outstanding name of his time amongst a number of disciples. Vivaldi, whose concertos owe their immortality to their adaptation by Sebastian Bach, had neither the grace nor the charm of his contemporary.

The scene then shifts to the North, and especially to Germany, where the policy of Martin Luther (who encouraged music as strongly as he discouraged painting) prepared the way for an outburst of the art, which came and dominated Europe for two centuries, a longer period of sovereignty than any other European country had enjoyed. If the art of painting which was showing equal signs of ascendency in Germany (as was evident from the master works of Dürer, Holbein, and Cranach) was strangled by the great Reformer, the sister art of music, upon which all artistic aspirations were then centered, profited by his one-sided influence. The Italian Renaissance was waning, and the German waxing. The Lutheran religion at once asserted its musical influence by the introduction of the Chorale, or hymn tune, of which it soon possessed a great collection, dignified and noble in character and melodious to a high degree. Upon this sure foundation the "Feste Burg" of North German music was solidly built. It is important to distinguish at once between the North and South of Germany, for the Protestant North was as distinct in aims and style from the South as were the Netherlands from Italy. The North was austere and solemn, the South lively and humorous. The North inclined to the Church, the South to the

Dance. Climatic conditions were reflected in their respective attitudes to the art.

If Palestrina may be termed the musical father of Italian sacred music, the musical father of North Germany was Jan Pieterszoon Sweelinck, a Dutchman born in 1562. Whether he visited Italy in early life or not (the point is doubtful), there is no question whatever that he closely studied Italian music, and was greatly influenced by such masters as Zarlino and Gabrieli, not to speak of Frescobaldi, the founder of organ-playing. His choral writing, while full of originality, shows in every bar his mastery of the methods of the Roman and Venetian schools; these he freely used, but showed a marked tendency toward getting rid of old trammels and of searching for new and free expression. He did not disdain to suck the brains of France. But his chief work as a pioneer was in his treatment of the organ, and in his initiative in applying and improving it upon the principles of Frescobaldi. He had one pupil, Reincke (or Reinken as he is best known), also a Dutchman, who went to Hamburg and became one of the apostles of the new religion. Reinken lived, like the painter Titian, to the great age of 99, long enough to have seen, heard, and endorsed the greatness of Sebastian Bach. Three other masters of the organ intervened between the days of Sweelinck and those of Sebastian Bach: Johann Jacob Froberger (b. 1605), Dietrich Buxtehude (b. 1637), a Dane who held office at Lübeck, and Johann Pachelbel (b. 1653) of Nuremberg. The two latter worked on the basis of the chorale in their treatment of the organ as a solo instrument. Buxtehude, whom Bach walked fifty miles to hear, had a great influence on the younger master, and so inspired him with his novel and progressive style that his work in the same line reflects the old master, for whom he showed such enthusiasm, from start to finish.

Johann Jacob Froberger, the eldest of the three, became a pupil of Frescobaldi, while he was still in the service of the Vienna Court, and came to London for a time, but returned to Vienna only to be dismissed for embracing the reformed religion. Some eighteen years after the birth of Sweelinck, three men were born in Germany within a short space of time, Heinrich Schütz (b. 1585), Johann Heinrich Schein (b. 1586), and Samuel Scheidt (b. 1587), all of whom worked on the principles of the great Dutchman, Schütz being (like him) a direct pupil of Gabrieli at Venice. Schein (a predecessor of Bach as Cantor of the Thomas School in Leipzig) added largely to the literature of the Chorale, and principally devoted himself to unaccompanied choral writing on the Italian model. Scheidt (the German Frescobaldi) made the organ his chief medium of expression. Schütz, the greatest of the "three S's" as they were termed, was wider in his sympathies and more experimental in his range. He wrote for the stage (early in life), but relinquished it for a determined effort to work out the principles of Peri and Caccini in the direction of Lutheran Church Music, anticipating the oratorios of Carissimi, and breathing the atmosphere of the Chorale so deeply, that he developed it into a scheme for accompanied chorus, mingled with dramatic recitative, to sacred words, upon which was built the Passion-music, a form idealized to its highest pitch by Sebastian Bach. Schütz's style was as progressive as his principles, and he may be called the first German creator of the North German School. His chief source of inspiration remained always the Chorale, which became, at all events for a considerable space of time, as important a factor (it might indeed be said an overpowering one) in the development of the German style as folk-song itself. If the descent of Bach were expressed in musical terms, it might be drawn up thus :

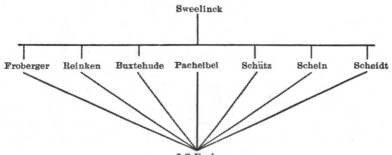

The Lutheran reform placed the Chorale on a still higher level, and religious enthusiasm preferred the solemn influence of the North to the light-hearted worldliness of the South. It remained for a later generation to combine the two, and as regards the German-speaking races, the church and the folk-song were as oil and water; the Catholics were on the side of sunny and lively open-air music, the Lutherans singing under dark skies and with what sun they had tempered by stained glass. So devoted were the northerners to the Chorales that they treated them in every conceivable shape and form, constructing ingenious variations on the themes for solo instrumental performance, and elaborating great vocal movements of which they were the backbone and center of interest. What Plain Song was to Palestrina and his school, the Chorale was to Schütz and his followers. They did not play with it or mix it with folk-song, as the Italians did when they used ribald ballads as the melodic basses of masses, and nearly wrecked the whole of music thereby. Nobility and dignity were the unfailing characteristics of the art in North Germany. The humor which pervaded Southern Germany, Italy, France, and the Netherlands and some of England was not temperamentally theirs, and never has made its way to them, except in spasmodic and exotic fashion.

The Seventeenth Century then was essentially a period of transition. It began with music based upon the old modes, of which composers had six at their command, the use of which was hemmed in by a mass of red tape rules and regulations, hampering all but the composers who were great enough to express themselves in terms of beauty within the limits set to them, and to make their wearers unconscious of the shackles which bound them. It ended with music based upon what are now termed keys, two of the old modes only (the Ionian and the Æolian), C-major and A-minor, transposed to various pitches, whose diatonic lines were in process of becoming pierced by the chromatic invader. Semitones, which were not a part of the scale, and were therefore termed "colored" or "chromatic," involving the use of accidentals to express them (a license rarely used in modal

times and then only under the most stringent rules), began
to make their way as independent factors in the harmonic
scheme, and revolutionized the whole outlook of music,
by enormously increasing its possibilities of vital expression.
When such a movement was in progress, it was inevitable
that its inception should be tentative, and it would have
been useless to expect any composer (however great his
genius) to be sufficiently equipped in the new methods to
stand out as a master in the first rank of creators. The
crooked ways had to be made straight, and the rough places
plain, before the men of the new régime should come to trav-
verse them with confidence. The absence of a world-famed
name, who could be classed with Palestrina of the old, and
Bach, Handel, Haydn, Mozart, and Beethoven of the new
ways, is not only not to be wondered at, but not to be looked
for. The Seventeenth Century masters, a numerous band of
high-minded and progressive artists, did their duty to the full,
and through their yeoman's service made the new forms of
music a possible and an abiding possession for the world.
Italy was the mother of them all, and having reared this
great family, was temporarily exhausted by the effort. But
hers be the praise of having permeated all Europe with her
steadfast devotion to the cause of progress. We have seen
the birth of opera, and of its main element, the dramatic
recitative; of the individual treatment of the voice, and of
the combination of instrumental accompaniment with it;
of the grouping of solo instruments in Chamber Music; of
the form of the vocal aria; of the concerto; of the possibilities of the organ and of the harpsichord as solo instruments;
of the foundation of the great school of violin playing; of
the dramatic treatment of sacred subjects, which evolved
the modern oratorio; of the appearance of the Chorale as
a dominant factor in its development in the countries which
had adopted the Reformed faith; and the experiments in
form which in a short time culminated in the Sonata, and its
family, the Symphony, the Overture, the String Quartet,
and the whole modern literature of Chamber Music. The
Seventeenth Century saw the parting of the ways between

music which depended upon voices and words, and music which existed by virtue of its own sounds alone, which we term "absolute music." With it began the reign of the virtuoso and its concomitants of good and evil influence. To the musical historian and student of evolution this period is perhaps the most fascinating, to the musician absorbed in contemporary developments, the least so. But we have the parallel in the respective interests and activities of the physiologist and the physician.

CHAPTER 12

The Eighteenth Century

DURING the Eighteenth Century the world began to profit by the wide-spread experimental activity of the Seventeenth. General activity began to crystallize into men of commanding power. The carbon had begun to be compressed into the diamond. The first rank composer, who was absent for so long, appeared, and not singly, but in surprising numbers. It was the age of Bach, Handel, Gluck, Haydn, and Mozart, and of the beginnings of Beethoven, of Schubert, and of Weber, each of them kings in their respective realms, few of them confined to any special line, but most of them supreme in some one of them. Choral work was the specialty of Handel, Operatic the exclusive domain of Gluck and of Weber, Instrumental the main occupation of Haydn, Song the chief feature of Schubert's short reign; while Bach, Mozart, and Beethoven covered the entire range of invention, absolute as well as composite. It can be seen at a glance that the center of gravity had shifted from Italy to Germany. England, which had produced in Purcell one of the greatest figures in the time of storm and stress, a composer who resembled Mozart in his easy grasp of every type of music ready to his hand and who was as much at home in the theatre as in the church, the platform or the chamber, relapsed into mediocrity. The few musicians she had were sound enough, one or two daring (like Blow), some poetical (like Jeremiah Clarke), but they shut themselves up in the churches, and did little else but produce services and anthems, far inferior in inventive genius and picturesque detail to their great predecessor. It is difficult to say if they would have produced in process of time another Purcell, but all chance of it was wrecked by the arrival in England of a great personality, who had little respect for any of them (a spirit which he did not scruple to show), who had sufficient perspicacity to adapt the style of Purcell to his own ends, and thereby be able to speak English fluently (if with a strong German accent), and whom we have to thank not only for immortal music of his own, but also for the decimation of the English School, — George Frederic Handel. During his long ascendency in England, which lasted long after his death in 1759, only one Englishman, born in the year of the Saxon's arrival in London (1710), raised his head, Thomas Augustine Arne. But though Arne wrote some immortal songs, one of them, "Rule, Britannia," as famous as and more British than any of Handel's, which the German did not scruple to copy in style and spirit in "See the conquering Hero comes" (written six years later), the Englishman never had a real chance against the overwhelming popularity of the foreigner, nor were the disheartening conditions under which he worked likely to make him aspire to great things. He was not Samson enough to tackle such a Harapha. English music therefore went into its shell and hibernated : putting out its head occasionally to see how many foreign visitors were about, and not destined to emerge for more than a century and a half.

Handel, after leaving Hamburg, had gone to Italy, a visit which lasted three years, where he devoted himself to opera, and to choral works which were cordially received. On his return to Germany in 1709, he became for a short time kapellmeister to George I (then Elector of Hanover), but removed to England a year later. Here, with the exception of a few short visits to Hanover, he remained until his death. He was the only great composer who was also an impresario. The only man, in later times, who resembled him in this combination of roles was not of the first rank in composition, however shrewd he was in business, Meyerbeer. Handel had a wonderful gift of adapting himself to current taste ; and it must be added that he did not do evil while following the multitude. He raised the taste which he followed, and

PLATE XXXV. GEORGE FREDERIC HANDEL

PLATE XXXVI.   CHRISTOPH WILLIBALD VON GLUCK

using it to his own ends, he placed it on a higher level. He
found Italian opera housed in London, and immediately set
himself to support it with his musical as well as his business
head. He wrote the opera of *Rinaldo* for it in a fortnight,
a feat which has been quoted as extraordinary, but which
when it is remembered that the original score is but a
string of songs, with only a violin line and a figured bass, is
not at all so surprising as Mozart's *tour de force*, when he
composed and fully orchestrated the overture to *Don Juan*
in one night, or Rossini's, when he finished the *Barber of
Seville* in thirteen days. The foundation of Handel's subsequent fame as a writer of oratorio was laid at Cannons, the
seat of the Duke of Chandos, a nobleman who had a private
orchestra and a body of choral and solo singers, and appointed
the composer the conductor and supervisor of his forces,
with much the same result to the world that Prince Esterhazy produced by his similar hospitality to Haydn. To this
period belongs the famous cantata *Acis and Galatea* and the
first of the oratorios, *Esther*. But the magnetism of the footlights was too powerful for him, and he became impresario
of the Italian opera, then dubbed The Royal Academy of
Music in imitation of the Paris Opera, except as regards the
preservation of national language and ideas. The usual
intrigues and squabbles arose; an Italian, by name Buononcini, captured half society and became an active rival; the
two parties flew at each other's throats, a battle ensued
which was repeated in history in the Paris days of Gluck and
Piccini, and after seventeen years of varying fortunes, perpetual bickerings and theatrical worries, Handel became a
bankrupt, and had a stroke of paralysis. Any ordinary man
would have collapsed under such a mental and bodily strain,
but, curiously enough, this catastrophe was only the dividing
line between the Handel we do not know much of and the
Handel who became a household word. All his greatest
works date from 1740, when he was no less than fifty-five
years of age, *Israel in Egypt*, the *Messiah*, *Samson* and the
amazing series down to *Theodora* and *Jephtha*. In two of
them, Handel grafted the dramatic style which he inherited

from his operatic experience upon the oratorio scheme: and these two works, *Semele* and *Hercules*, though far less known than the popular reflective oratorios of the type of the *Messiah* and less important from the point of view of the massive choral writing, which was his strongest point, are the most interesting of all the series. In them he showed the spirit of the explorer: and anticipated the dramatic recitative of Gluck so markedly and so successfully that it can scarcely be said to be less modern than the Austrian's innovations. In writing these oratorios Handel helped himself liberally to the works of other lesser luminaries, even appropriating whole movements without acknowledgement. As a critic once said of a literary proceeding of the same character, "he borrowed so unscrupulously, that it ceased to be plagiarism and became quotation." For example, the entire contrapuntal chorus "Egypt was glad" in *Israel in Egypt* was copied from an organ work of Kerl, the only change being a transposition of the key. Modern researches have resulted in the discovery of many more of these pilferings: not a few of them are obvious to the most superficial musician. It is a practical impossibility that he can have been ignorant of Bach's organ fugue in E-flat (known as *St. Anne's Fugue*) when he wrote what is to all intents and purposes a vocal version of it in the cantata *Acis and Galatea*, the famous chorus "Wretched lovers." The encyclopædic and unscrupulous brain of the composer may account to some extent for the extraordinary pace with which he finished score after score, and the meagerness of his orchestral writing was another help to rapidity of production. That Handel could have developed the treatment of the orchestra is evident from several scattered passages throughout his works, notably in *Saul*, in the *Messiah* (where he specifies the use of trumpets "behind the scenes" in the chorus "Glory to God"), and in his masterly treatment of the trombones in *Israel in Egypt*, which he did not trouble, however, to write into the score, but which were subsequently discovered in parts. For texture and the filling up of harmonies he trusted to the good taste of those who presided at the organ and the harpsichord. There is no record of any encouragement on his part to his English contemporaries. There is one of his contemptuous attitude towards them. To Dr. Maurice Greene, who brought to him a vocal composition for his opinion, he said, "Your music wanted air, so I did hang it out of the window": a singularly unjust criticism, for Greene, though not a strong writer, possessed a real gift of melody with a genuinely English flavor, of which the solo "Thou visitest the earth" is a very good example. As a man, Handel has left an unsullied record for uprightness and generosity. He was the second founder of the Foundling Hospital, to which he contributed largely, and one of the original founders of the Royal Society of Musicians. His works were almost innumerable. The library at Buckingham Palace contains no less than 105 volumes of his manuscripts, and there are seven more in the Fitzwilliam Museum at Cambridge, besides a quantity of interesting sketches.

While Handel was in the full glare of publicity, and was apparently sole master of the musical world, a contemporary greater, deeper, and mightier than he was at work in mid-Germany, writing for all time without a thought of his own aggrandizement, composing works far beyond the capabilities of musicians at his hand to produce with any approach to their requirements, which were predestined to temporary eclipse, only to shine with added luster a century and more after his death, Johann Sebastian Bach. A touching story, which throws some light upon his sufferings while striving to get some sort of realization of his ideas from his choristers, was told by Weinlig (a successor in the Cantorship of the Thomas School) to Richard Wagner. Wagner asked Weinlig if he had ever heard how the Church Cantatas were performed in Bach's time: Weinlig answered that his predecessor (who was one of Bach's choir) had told him that "he always thrashed us and it went abominably." Bach was a Thuringian and was born at Eisenach (near the Wartburg) of a race rich in musical associations. There were no less than fifty-three Bachs in the family tree compiled by John Sebastian himself and his son Philip Emanuel. The last male representative of this vast musical family died in 1846. All the chief members of it were musicians, or of musical leanings: some of them, of Sebastian's own time, have left compositions so striking as to have been attributed to the most famous of them all, such as the motet *I wrestle and pray* (Ich lasse dich nicht), which was the work of his cousin, John Christopher, Sebastian's senior by forty-two years. They all shone as organists. Sebastian's activities have been divided into three periods, corresponding with the cities where he sucessively held appointments, Weimar and Arnstadt, at the latter of which places he was organist, Cöthen, where he was Capellmeister, and Leipzig, where he was appointed Cantor of the Thomas School, a post which he retained until his death in 1750. His compositions, which covered every field, need not be tabulated here. His was a life which should be read for itself. One of his many gifts, which has been little commented upon, was that of decorative design, with which he amused himself while engraving the plates of his own compositions. The margins were often full of ornamentations of his own devising, especially the last of his large works, the *Musikalisches Opfer*, a most amazing specimen of contrapuntal skill, written upon a theme given to him by Frederick the Great. The engraving of this work he had to leave unfinished, owing to failing eyesight (he afterwards became totally blind), and it is a curious fact that the few concluding bars which were added by another hand contain a bad technical blunder. In Bach's hands the music of the period marked its climax of expression, the Chorale was idealized to its highest pitch, the combination of Orchestra, Chorus and Solo voices in the *Passions*, the *B-minor mass*, and the *Church Cantatas* became pillars of the house of musical art for all time, the principles of equal temperament were fixed for good in Clavichord work, the violin became a solo instrument which could speak unaided for itself, and the organ came finally into its own. All this immense range of work was accomplished by an unobtrusive, unadvertising man, of the highest moral force and of simple, deeply religious, and deep-feeling character, a personality who would have considered it the highest possible tribute to be called the worthy father of a devoted family. A great (perhaps the greatest) composer, but as great a man. It is odd that such a hero-worshipper and close student of human nature as Carlyle should have omitted from his Life of Frederick the Great the mention of the visit paid to the political monarch by the musical: still more so, as he confessedly knew all the details of the historic meeting. Perchance he classed Bach under that comprehensively contemptuous term, "fiddlers"!

Upon one department of the art Bach did not touch, the operatic stage. That in its development remained the property of the Latin race. Alessandro Scarlatti and Lully were the high priests of progress in that direction. The Operas of Handel were, as dramatic efforts, a dead letter. Individual songs and show pieces survive from the welter of notes he wrote down, some of them beautiful in themselves, but of no value as regards the advancement of operatic design. It is not a little curious that the only signs of a movement on his part towards true secular dramatic expression are to be found in the two oratorios mentioned above, *Semele* and *Hercules*. In the operas proper the characterization of dramatic figures is almost wholly absent. The subsequent effect of Handel's operatic writing, in so far as it relied upon songs calculated to show off their exponents' voices, showed itself in the growth in England of the so-called Ballad-opera; a class of which the well-known *Beggar's Opera* is a typical specimen. To this style English work, brought to heel by the compelling force of the Saxon immigrant, was forced to conform in order to get a hearing at all. Even Sheridan, the most brilliant dramatist and stage writer of his day, could not produce anything better than the obsolete *Duenna*, so throttled was he by the conditions which prevailed. But the *Beggar's Opera* had at least one virtue; it showed unmistakable signs of the British Folksong spirit, which was destined to break the foreign yoke, and to talk for and by itself. This infected Arne, who, despite the Handelian influence, remained an Englishman, as his air "Rule, Britannia" proves in every bar. Wagner's keen eye saw this, and his equally keen tongue said so. If it had not been for the misguided tastes of the higher members of society in England, which persisted in the adoration of the foreigner (even when unworthy of their favors), frowned on native efforts and imported everything they consumed down to the days of Mendelssohn (and later), the native effort would not have been crushed for so long a period, and native musicians would not have tried to speak foreign languages with a broken accent, in preference to their own sound, solid speech. The neighbor, France, did otherwise. She was too proud to forego her individuality, and too self-confident to borrow other men's goods. She had no Bach and no Handel, but if she was not blest with giants, she waited for them to come in their own good time, and was content with her own composers of more moderate but no mean stature. She fostered them, and got her reward in the steady growth of a distinctive French school, replete with qualities which are so valuable as to be indispensable; humor, daintiness, vividness, and poetry. She did not despise her Watteau, because he was not a Rembrandt, nor her Houdon because he was not a Michael Angelo. Therefore she has kept an even course down to our own day, definitely preserving her individuality, and encouraging her own composers to support her in doing so. Her chief musician of this period was Jean Philippe Rameau, born at Dijon in 1683, and therefore a contemporary of Bach and Handel. He came of a musical family (his father and his brother were organists). He spent a short time in Italy, where he gained the theatrical experience which afterwards resulted in the composition of not less than eighteen operas, for one of which, *La Princesse de Navarre*, Voltaire was his librettist. His innovations in harmony (on which he wrote a famous treatise) and in orchestration were of so progressive a character as to rouse the wrath of the Philistines, and the fight between the adherents of Lully and those of Rameau was well-nigh as fierce as the battles of the Gluckists and Piccinists in subsequent days. He led the way for Gluck's reforms, though he was not strong enough to carry them through himself. He knew his own limitations and lamented them. The novelty of his treatment of the ballet spread the knowledge and fame of his works far beyond the frontiers of his native land. His claveçin compositions also made their way, and are still proofs of his mastery of the keyboard, and, although not equal in daring to those of Domenico Scarlatti, or in strength to those of Bach, have an individual touch of their own which ensures their place in the world's musical literature.

After Rameau there sprang up a long line of French composers for the stage, many of whom are still far more than mere names, constituting a genealogy of writers which continues, still unbroken, to our own times. The first of Rameau's successors was Jean Jacques Rousseau (b. Geneva 1712), poet, musician, and ardent controversialist, whose pastoral *Le Devin du Village* had a success which lasted for 76 years. He was a mass of contradictions, decrying French music while he wrote it, fighting for Italian supremacy with one pen while supporting native art with the other, holding in fact much the same position in relation to the two countries which his native town occupies on the map. There followed in rapid sequence, Philidor (also a world-famous chess player), the author of some 21 operas, Monsigny, Gossec, Grétry, Dalayrac, Lesueur, Méhul, and many more who overlapped into the Nineteenth Century, and will be considered later. Most of these composers contributed to the repertoire of the Grand Opéra, or Académie de Musique as it is officially termed, but they were essentially the main supports of that much more typically French Institute, the Opéra Comique.

Meantime Italy was producing a great number of "little masters," most of whom are little more than names, but all of whom were contributing their quota to the preservation of their national art. Porpora, memorable as the master (task-master it might be said) of Haydn, Marcello of the *Psalms*, Tartini, Leo, Galuppi (the subject of a well-known poem by Robert Browning), Padre Martini, Jomelli, and one figure of great genius, whose death at the age of 26 robbed Italy and the world of what might have proved one of their most precious possessions, Giovanni Battista Pergolesi. Of him may be said with equal truth the words on the grave of Schubert, "Music has buried here a rich treasure but far more lovely hopes." His *Stabat Mater* remains a classic for all time, and his short dramatic intermezzo *La Serva Padrona* set the type of Italian comic opera which prevailed for a century after his death. In connection with all the Italian operatic composers of this period must be mentioned Metastasio (b. 1698), the poet and dramatist, who throughout his long life of 84 years supplied them all with libretti of fine quality, and while doing so had a great influence upon the whole future of the musical drama.

In Germany the king of the operatic stage was Johann Adolph Hasse (b. 1699 at Bergedorf), the husband of the famous singer Faustina Bordoni. Hasse, like Haydn, was a pupil of Porpora, but left him to study with Alessandro Scarlatti. On his return to Germany he became Director of the Dresden Opera-House, which dates the beginning of its fame in the musical world from his reign. Leaving the Elbe for the Danube in 1760, he took office at Vienna, but finding himself faced there by a personality too strong to resist with success he returned to Italy and died at Venice in 1783. That personality was no less a master than Christoph Willibald von Gluck (b. 1714), a South German educated at Prague, who was destined to rank with Weber and Wagner as a monarch of modern opera, and to be the first reformer and leader in the movement which led to its developments in the present day. Like Wagner he began with insufficient musical technique to back him, and only attained it after years of experience. He was never indeed remarkable for a certainty of workmanship equal to his mastery of dramatic effect. Therein lay a weakness which as a composer accentuated his inferiority to Mozart. Like Wagner also he began by writing operas of small merit in the Italian style, which had an ephemeral success in Italy, but only served to bring his name into prominence. A visit to London only resulted in failure, and led to the well-known gibe of Handel, that the new composer "knew no more counterpoint than his cook." This characteristic remark is, however, somewhat discounted by the less known fact, that Handel's cook is reputed to have been a very good musician. After his London visit, Gluck's powers began to grow and his eventually original style began by slow degrees to assert itself. He went to Vienna in 1746 and after producing several operas, all now forgotten but all showing unmistakable signs of his tendencies, he blossomed out after sixteen years of unceasing activity into a master-work, which will endure to the end, *Orpheus and Eurydice*. He had assimilated all the vital points of Greek tragedy, and applied them to the needs of his own time, not without a prophetic conviction of their prime necessity for the purposes and products of the future. The chorus became as important as it was in the days of Æschylus, and its counterpart and assistant in modern opera, the orchestra, ceased to be a mere vehicle of accompaniment, and added tone-color to the scheme, to balance the visible color on the stage. In a word, opera, instead of being a mere *mannequin* to show off the airs and graces of the performers, became a living entity in which the language, the action, the scenery, and the music went to make an artistic whole. This ideal was often departed from after Gluck's day, but it was aimed at more and more as time went on, always carped at by the featherheaded, always insisted on by the earnest-minded, until through the creations of the mature Wagner and the aged Verdi it became "fixed in its everlasting seat." What Gluck's aims were he has told us himself in the preface to *Alcestis* and *Paris and Helen*. Needless to say, a reformer of such marked type aroused an anger in proportion to his progressiveness. So savage were the attacks upon him in Vienna, that he betook himself to Paris armed with the score of *Iphigenia in Aulis* where he made propaganda as to his theories after the manner of Wagner himself, but more conciliatory and diplomatic in tone. He had also considerable assistance from Marie Antoinette, who had been his pupil in

Vienna. Here he challenged the Italian school, headed by Piccini, with *Iphigenia in Tauris* and routed his opponents. His victory was consolidated by the success of *Alcestis*, *Orpheus* (made memorable in much later days by the genius of Madame Viardot), and *Armida*, a spectacular music-drama which is still a stock-piece of the Paris Grand Opéra. Gluck, therefore, ceased to be a leader of German opera, and became the king of world-opera. He became as potent an influence in France as in Austria, and incidentally affected the musical stage in Italy. As a composer of absolute music he held no place : such of it as exists has mainly to do with ballet-music. His always insufficient mastery of the ground-principles of music *per se* told against him here. He knew it and left it alone, content with his only love, the theater. In two particulars, however, he laid the foundation of the success attained by his successors; the manipulation of the orchestra and the inclusion of many instruments for the sake of their color-qualities rather than their names, and the sub-ordination of the music for the solo-voice to the proper declamation of the words it has to enunciate. Of these two reforms, the second has been, curiously enough, the longer in becoming established; Italian influences, especially that of Rossini, having been all-powerful for a century after Gluck's time.

Simultaneously with the career of Gluck, Germany had developed another type of opera, which also had successors, called the "Singspiel." It was of ancient origin, dating in its inception as far back as the old Miracle Plays, but becoming secularized, and after the middle of the Eighteenth Century gaining a firm footing on all the German and Austrian stages. In some ways it resembled the French Opéra Comique, but had a distinct flavor of its own. The characters spoke as well as sang, and the whole plan was on a light basis, relying on comedy and even farce for its effects. The *Beggar's Opera* and its successors represented the style in England. Many distinguished German composers wrote the music for works of this stamp : J. Adam, Hiller, Ditters-dorf, and even the great Haydn himself, and in later times it was the chief means of expression of a clever and humorous master, Lortzing, who may be said to have carried the Singspiel in its pure form to its highest pitch of excellence. How the title of this type of opera affected even composers who worked on higher lines, is proved by the fact that Mozart gave both to the *Seraglio* and to the *Zauberflöte* the name of "Singspiel," a hopeless misnomer in all but the fact that the dialogue is spoken, and not set as recitative. Even Lortzing stepped at times over the bounds and embodied grand opera effects in his score. The Singspiel is a relative of the French vaudeville, and may be said to be the worthy ancestor of a degenerate descendant which we now (very improperly) call "comic opera," a form of entertainment often founded on the flimsiest plots, and mounted more for scenic effect, pretty (if scanty) dresses, and general fooling than for any artistic purpose. This lively, but often not enlivening, show had also its reformers in due time, who in their different ways did much to bring it more into line with the artistic side of music, Offenbach in Paris and Sullivan in London, whose collaborator, Gilbert, the Aristophanes of his day, and little inferior to his Greek prototype in genius and in wit, deserves a niche in history for the strong hand with which he, aided by his composer, swept dust and dirt and bad taste off the boards, and popularized cleanliness. But the discussion of this interesting development must be deferred to its proper place. It is therefore obvious that the influence of the Singspiel on the future of opera was very marked. Although its start was made on a side-track, it eventually moved so far in the direction of the main-line, that some of the most famous specimens of opera proper retain strong marks of its influence. Chief among them are the operas of Mozart, of Beethoven, and of Weber. Without losing its family characteristic, it married into the higher circles of art, with results that mutually affected both the direct and the collateral descendants.

CHAPTER 13

The Viennese Masters

IT was not long before the emancipation of music from the trammels of the stage and the sung word began to show itself in the rapid rise of instrumental, "absolute," music. The labors of Corelli, Purcell, Couperin, D. Scarlatti, J. S. Bach, and Handel began to tell both upon players and hearers. The foundations of the string quartet, the sonata, the symphony, and the overture were laid, and only waited for the builders; and they came, a great row of master-workers, who reared the edifice, decorated and embellished it, and furnished the interior no less sumptuously than its grandeur and proportions demanded. It was fit and proper that the first of these craftsmen should be a son of J. S. Bach, Carl Philipp Emanuel (b. 1714 at Weimar), the senior of Papa Haydn by fourteen years, who filled the gap between the days of his gigantic father, and the galaxy of genius which arose in the latter half of the Eighteenth Century. His was no overpowering talent; he is more a carrier of tradition and an experimenter in unfamiliar paths, than a great master. None the less he filled an invaluable role in musical history; he forged the link between the clavier suite and the pianoforte sonata, between the orchestral suite and the symphony, and in a neat and unobtrusive way indicated the new principles which he advanced by examples of his own work. Orchestration, which had been, in the hands of his father and the composers of the period, a conglomeration of solid blocks of sound, with scarcely any attempt at individual or variegated color, he began to resolve into its component parts, and so cleared the way for the new and rapidly developed system of instrumentation which is now universal. This great reform can be easily traced in his orchestral Symphonies, which, for all their slightness and semi-antique flavor, are ancestors of Beethoven's immortal Nine. He richly deserves the fame of a pioneer, for not only was he the founder of the Sonata and its embryo form, but he laid down the principles of technique for keyed instruments which have, subject to the modifications required by their subsequent development, prevailed ever since his day.

The first of the row of composers of the first magnitude to succeed him was Joseph Haydn (b. 1732 at Rohrau in lower Austria, on the borders of Hungary). He came of traders' stock; his father was a wheelwright. Both his parents were musical, and were as careful in imbuing him with the principles of personal neatness as of devout religion, characteristics which distinguished him throughout his long and honorable life. He even wrote his scores in full court dress, and inscribed his "Laus Deo" at the foot of each. His first master was his cousin Johann Frankh, who laid the foundation of Haydn's knowledge of the voice and of the various orchestral instruments. From the country he went to Vienna, where he became a scholar in the St. Stephen's Cantorei, and sang as a chorister both in the Cathedral and in the Court Chapel (still famed for the brilliance of its personnel and width of repertoire). After his voice broke, he fell on evil times and was almost a pauper; but through the aid of friends he was able to go on with his studies, the very first of which was devoted to the works of Emanuel Bach. The composition and production of a singspiel led to his acquaintance with Porpora, who took him to Hungary, and treated him more or less as a bootblack. But he met there no less a person than Gluck, who at once grasped the powers of the youngster (Haydn was then only twenty years old). He was not long in finding friends amongst art-loving amateurs in the aristocratic circles of Austria. Three in succession secured his services as director of their household music. Karl von Fürnberg gave him the opportunity for becoming closely acquainted with chamber-

music, and encouraged him to write string-quartets. The
first of a series, which reached the great number of 77, was
written at von Fürnberg's house near Melk. Count Morzin,
a Bohemian nobleman, was his next patron. Here Haydn
found himself in command of a small orchestra, and wrote
the first of his 125 symphonies. When Count Morzin gave
up his band, a third aristocrat came forward and with him
and his descendants Haydn remained in close relations for
the rest of his life. Prince Paul Esterhazy, who had noted
the composer's great gifts when he was still in Morzin's
service, promptly secured him as his Capellmeister, an
appointment in which Paul's brother Nicholas (who succeeded him in 1762) confirmed him. The private band was
enlarged and was at Haydn's beck and call every day in the
year. In these genial surroundings he wrote work after
work, and hence they spread all over Europe. In 1779
he visited Paris ; and in 1791, London. In the meantime, he
had as a pupil Edmund von Weber (whose half-brother Carl
Maria was the famous composer of the *Freischütz*), and had
got to know and to love Mozart; a friendship with the
younger master sprang up which had a mutual effect upon
both, the younger learning from the elder and, what is far more
surprising, the elder learning from the younger. The close
friendship and glowing appreciation which these two masters
preserved for each other without a cloud of difference or a
speck of jealousy is one of the brightest spots in the history
of the private lives of the great composers. There is one
parallel in England, though its details are lost for lack of a
careful chronicler of the period, the relations between John
Blow and Henry Purcell. The fact, however, that Blow
retired from his post as organist at Westminster Abbey to
make room for the younger master, and resumed the position after Purcell's death, tells the pretty tale without need
of further particulars ; and in later times we have another
example in the intimate relations between Schumann and
Brahms. When the individual greatness of one and all of
these men was of so outstanding a nature, it is easy to
imagine what party spirit they would have aroused in their

March 20th 1794

Geo Dance

PLATE XXXVII. HAYDN

PLATE XXXVIII.   FRANZ JOSEPH HAYDN

respective admirers, and how easy it would have been for irresponsible outsiders to poison the wells of their mutual friendship. They did not need, however, to be told even by an Iago to

> " beware of jealousy;
> It is the green-eyed monster which doth mock
> The meat it feeds on."

Their nature was too innately noble and too true to their art to be contaminated by any unworthy influences. If the history of all arts and artists contains a lamentable amount of intrigues, suspicions, and jealousies, it is redeemed also by illuminating instances of high-minded and unstinted mutual admiration, of which the episode of the bond between old Haydn and young Mozart is one of the most memorable.

In 1787 Haydn, after repeated invitations from W. Cramer, Salomon, and Bland, decided to visit England, and four years later he arrived in London with six new symphonies in his portfolio. His first appearance as conductor of his own works took place on March 11, 1791, in the Hanover Square Rooms, a concert-room of about the same size as the old Gewandhaus at Leipzig, which down to 1874 was the headquarters of orchestral music in London and was in existence as the dining room of a club until 1901, when it was pulled down. During his stay for a year and a half in England he was fêted in every quarter, visited the Universities, was given an honorary degree at Oxford, went to Ascot Races, became intimate with Herschel, with Bartolozzi the famous engraver, and with John Hunter the great surgeon. He returned to Vienna in the summer of 1792, meeting at Bonn for the first time the young Beethoven, then twenty-two years old, and was enthusiastically welcomed back by the Austrian public. Two years later he returned with six more new symphonies to London, where his success was even greater than on the occasion of his first visit. He himself openly stated that his fame in Germany was due to his reception in England, a home truth which has been experienced, though not often as honestly acknowledged, by not a few German composers of later date. His second and last English visit over, he returned for good to his native country, and although he had reached the age of 63 he started off upon new lines and ever progressive ideas, producing in the last fourteen years of his busy life the most important of his compositions, his finest quartets (notably the so-called *Kaiser quartet*, containing the Austrian hymn) and the oratorios *The Creation* and *The Seasons*. Both these choral works owed their inception to his English visit, and to the impression made upon him by hearing the rendering of Handel's oratorios at the Westminster Abbey commemoration and elsewhere. But Haydn's was too original a mind to copy Handel's style or to be hidebound by his conventions. It is enough to study the introduction to *The Creation* or to Winter in *The Seasons* to see the amazing strides in dramatic conception and in modernity of expression which the composer had made in his old age. The Representation of Chaos begins with a phrase as striking as, and very similar to, the Prelude to Wagner's *Tristan and Isolde*, and contains several passages which might have come from the pages of the music of the future.

The only parallel to this youthful inspiration in old age is the case of Verdi, whose greatest works, *Otello* and *Falstaff*, were written between the ages of 60 and 80. Both these men possessed the rare faculty of keeping their brains and hearts young and of preserving an open mind, a clear and matured insight, and a sympathetic outlook upon every development which made for experimental progress.

For these inestimable qualities alone, apart from his immortal works, Haydn occupies a unique position in musical history. Without him, it is unlikely that either Mozart or Beethoven would have reached the pinnacle of excellence which they attained. The way had been prepared for them by a universally loved and honored master, who had himself shown in no stinted manner his sympathies with sound progress and innovation, who had inculcated the supreme importance of perfect technical equipment, and, last but not by any means least, had idealized humor.

Twenty-four years after the birth of Haydn there was born at Salzburg the man whose brilliant genius conquered the world in the short space of the thirty-five years of life allotted to him, Wolfgang Amadeus Mozart. Of all composers that ever lived he was the most childlike in temperament, and has left behind him an aroma of simple yet fascinating kindliness, which impelled more than one musician to admit that if he were given the choice of meeting personally one great composer in the world to come, he would unhesitatingly name Mozart. Born in the Austrian Tyrol, he retained throughout his life the influences of Tyrolese folk-music, which peeps out at frequent moments even in such mature works as the *Clarinet Quintet*.

Wolfgang and his sister Marianne toured Europe as prodigies; but being blessed with a wise father they remained unspoiled by flattery, and undamaged by premature forcing. Their travels extended to Paris and to London, where (at the age of eight) he met John Christian (called the "English") Bach, and became the subject of a paper upon his physique and his abnormal brain development which was communi-

cated to the Royal Society. His stay in England lasted for
a year and a half, and he wrote his first symphony at a house
in Lower Ebury Street. Even his baby work shows an
astonishing instinct for putting down the right notes, and
technique, even of the more complicated kind, seems to have
had no difficulties for him. That his brain power was not
confined to music is proved by his excellence as a chess-
player and a mathematician. On his return he visited
Holland and returned to Salzburg through Paris and Switzerland. In 1769 he started with his father for Italy, where he
met every musician of note, and made great friends with an
English boy of his own age (Thomas Linley, the son of Linley
of Bath, famous as the father of the "nest of linnets," one
of whom became the wife of Richard Brinsley Sheridan).
It was during a visit to Rome that Mozart wrote out from
memory the *Miserere* of Allegri. He was made a "Maestro
di Capella" at Bologna when only fifteen years old, wrote and
conducted an opera for Milan which was repeated no less
than twenty times, was commissioned to compose another,
met old Hasse, who was so captivated by him that he
prophesied that the boy would relegate them all to oblivion.
Up to 1777 his life was one of combined travelling and success. The Archbishop of Salzburg was more irritated by
his growing fame than proud of it, and displayed his animosity
in such fashion that Mozart applied to be released from his
service, and was dismissed rather with a curse than a blessing.
Nowadays the chimes of the Tyrolese town avenge him by
ringing out his melodies every hour within ear-shot of the
Archiepiscopal Palace. He went with his mother to Mann-
heim, where he met the Weber family, of which the third
daughter, Costanze, was destined years later to become his
wife. He went on to Paris to find it in a fickle mood, lost
his mother there, and left it, discouraged, to return to Salzburg. There he devoted himself to composition and wrote
a vast number of works of every kind. His first great step
as a dramatic composer was made at Munich, where *Idomeneo*
was produced with the greatest success. His old foe, the
Archbishop of Salzburg, thereafter ordered him to Vienna,

PLATE XXXIX.   WOLFGANG AMADEUS MOZART

PLATE XL. WOLFGANG AMADEUS MOZART

apparently anxious to get some of his reflected glory, but
was not long in having him literally kicked out of his house,
accompanying his forcible exit with showers of verbal abuse
which have been immortalized in the records of his life.
Vienna, however, became his headquarters, attracting him
with the same irresistible magnetism which it exercised upon
Gluck, Beethoven, and Brahms. Here were written in
succession his great works for the operatic stage, *The Seraglio*,
The Marriage of Figaro, *Don Giovanni*, *Cosi fan Tutte*, and
(Beethoven's favourite) the *Zauberflöte*. He was fortunate in
his collaborator, da Ponte, an Italian with a consummate
talent for the construction of effective libretti. The success
of *Figaro* was immediate, that of *Don Giovanni* scarcely less
so. It is no small tribute to the artistic purity of Mozart's
work, that two plays which, in the hands of a less refined and
high-minded composer, might have been made impossible,
became so clarified and elevated in his, that no Mrs. Grundy
could find it in her heart to protest against a bar of them.
The power of delineating and differentiating the characters
is so strong, that *Don Giovanni* seems to be an epitome of
the composer's various moods and phases of thought. It is
almost possible to label movements from his instrumental
works with the names of Leporello or Elvira, Masetto or
Zerlina, Don Ottavio or Donna Anna, Don Juan or the Com-
mendatore. By the cruelty of fate, as his fame increased,
his worldly goods decreased, and after his greatest friend,
Haydn, left for London, his pecuniary embarrassments became more and more pressing. The curious anonymous
commission to write a *Requiem*, following on the chilling
first night of the *Zauberflöte*, seems to have preyed upon his
spirits, and after writing some and sketching most of his
greatest sacred work, he took ill of typhus[1] fever and died
in his thirty-seventh year. Vienna did no more than bury
him in a common pauper's grave, and not one of the many
colleagues to whom he was so unswervingly generous and
appreciative was present to do him honor. It was reserved

[1] Most probably typhoid, not typhus. Typhoid fever is still termed
"Typhus" in Germany, in common parlance.

for a later generation to erect the monuments and to collect and publish his enormous output of masterpieces.

It is a curious commentary on the subtle character of Mozart's creations, that almost every music-lover only reaches the point of adequate appreciation of his work, when his judgment has become matured. When one is a child, he speaks as a child; but when one is old, he puts away childish things; or rather, what we once imagined to be childish turns out to be mature. His simplicity of expression is so perfect that it gains with repetition. It is not the simplicity of a superficial or vapid mind, but the natural expression of a highly-trained and deeply sensitive one. The harmonic effects are never calculated even when they are most surprising, as in the Introduction to the *C-major Quartet*, or the slow movement of that in E-flat. The ingenuity of his canonic devices is so concealed, that an ignoramus can appreciate the music for itself without any idea of the complexity within. He wrote perfectly for the orchestra, but no less so for the human voice, and never crushed the latter with the former. He reached a point in symphonic work, with his last four works in that form, which has never been excelled within its own limits, although Beethoven climbed greater and larger heights when he enlarged frontiers which gave his predecessor sufficient room: but any observant eye can see in the *E-flat Symphony* the prototype of the *Eroica*. The string quartets are unsurpassable for workmanship, for charm, and for perfection of instrumental treatment. The most sympathetic, lovable, generous of composers, he richly deserved the recorded tribute of his brother Freemasons, "Orpheum vix superavit."

The third and youngest of the great trio was born in 1770 at Bonn on the Rhine, Ludwig van Beethoven. He was of Flemish-Dutch origin, as the "van" in his name, upon the use of which he was most insistent, clearly indicates. The family belonged to the neighborhood of Louvain, and afterwards to Antwerp; the last member of it died in that town during the last century. From Belgium to the Rhine was but a short distance, and the composer's grandfather and father migrated to Bonn, to join the Court Orchestra of the Elector of Cologne. He belonged therefore to the country of Sweelinck, and was the second great Dutchman to influence the cause of German art. His young days were passed in comparative poverty, which left its mark upon him throughout his life, and which no doubt is responsible for the dread of its recurrence which weighed upon him at its close. But his brilliant gifts found him friends, who helped him both in education and in pocket, notably an Englishman, Cressener, who was in the diplomatic service, and the Court Organist Neefe. He came to know his Bach when only eleven years old, mastering the 48 Preludes and Fugues even at that early age. In 1783 he went on the staff of the opera. His compositions so far were comparatively few, but sufficiently striking for his age to attract local attention. Four years later he visited Vienna, and met Mozart, who recognized the genius of the boy, and gave him some lessons. The illness and death of his mother recalled him suddenly to Bonn, where he made great friends with Count Waldstein, who became one of his warmest supporters. To the Count he dedicated the famous *Sonata in C-major* (Op. 53) in later life. Owing to the dissipations and consequent bad health of his father, he became virtually responsible for the care of his brothers and sisters, and found regular salaried employment in the Court band. He twice met Haydn at Bonn, when that composer was journeying to England, and had leisure enough to devote much time to composing and to sketching out his ideas. This habit of thinking upon paper, which is shown in the many sketch-books which are extant, became stereotyped throughout his life. It is possible by their means to follow practically every phase of a theme from its embryo form to its maturity. From them also we can arrive at the slowness of the process by which he attained perfection in the printed result. The thoroughness with which he followed this method can be best seen in the valuable printed collection which was edited and published by Nottebohm under the title of *Beethoveniana*. In it will be found such striking instances as the 18 sketches for the

"Invocation to Hope" in *Fidelio,* and the carefully finished studies for the final four bars of the variations in the *C-sharp minor quartet* (Op. 131), no less than fifteen in number, any one of them perfect enough for a less scrupulous composer, and not one of them the same as that which was eventually published. Some of the themes, which we know as specimens of Beethoven at his best, are in their first inception so commonplace and even "banal" that it is difficult to connect them with his name, or with their eventual beauty. We can follow the process from the felling of the tree to the polished and inlaid table. The very amount of music paper which Mozart and Schubert covered in the course of their short lives is a proof of the mental rapidity of their completed thoughts. The comparatively small output of Beethoven is a clue to the slow travail he endured in giving his creations to the world. He began working at the setting of Schiller's *Ode to Joy* in 1793, and it only came to fruition 30 years later in the *Ninth Symphony.*

Beethoven, following the advice of Count Waldstein, left Bonn at the close of 1792 and took up his residence at Vienna. He first made his mark there as a pianist, having very few works as yet to show, though many were in process of maturing. He at once set himself to study all the technique of composition, first with Haydn, and upon the latter's departure for England, with Albrechtsberger, a somewhat dry-as-dust musician, but a master of his craft, who taught most of the outstanding young musicians of his time. Haydn taught him the principles of the old modal counterpoint of the Palestrina tradition, a groundwork which shows itself throughout Beethoven's life, and of which a fine specimen occurs in the late *String Quartet in A-minor* (Op. 132). The exercises which he worked have been published with Haydn's corrections of his pupil's mistakes carefully marked. Albrechtsberger had a poor opinion of his mighty pupil, who was too fond of exercises in rebellion to suit his hidebound taste. It cannot be denied, that despite the assiduity with which Beethoven worked during his whole life at contrapuntal studies, he never attained the natural

Plate XLI.   Beethoven

PLATE XLII.   LUDWIG VAN BEETHOVEN

FROM SONATA, OP. 26.

ease of Sebastian Bach in coping with set fugue. He mastered its suburbs without capturing the citadel. There is a certain uncouthness in his fugal writing of which he never quite shook himself free, great as were the conceptions which underlie the form. He felt, as Tennyson once said of sonnet-writing, that it was "dancing in fetters." Bach danced all the same, and made the fetters invisible; and so also did Mozart in lesser and lighter fashion. To write such a complicated piece of quadruple counterpoint as the Finale of the *Jupiter Symphony*, and to leave the hearer in ignorance that any such complication exists, was a gift denied to his great successor.

In the social circles of the Austrian capital Beethoven made many friends, but he treated them one and all with a consciousness of his own equality with them, or rather superiority to them. His innate republicanism, which so horrified the courtly Goethe, and which made him angrily tear off the title page to the *Eroica Symphony* with its dedication to Napoleon, after he assumed the imperial purple, are instances of his uncomprising principles. Napoleon, once he became Emperor, was for Beethoven "the memory of a great man."[1] In later life his brother Johann left his card upon him with the word "Gutsbesitzer" (man of property) after his name, and Ludwig sent his back with "Hirnsbesitzer" (man of brains) written on the back. For all his roughnesses, and odd brusque ways, he was taken at his true worth by all the princes and courts whom he knew or at whose houses he was a frequent and honored guest, Lichnowsky, Erdödy, Odesschalchi, Rudolph, and many more, all of whom accepted the fact that the great composer might at any moment turn his back on them with language of unmeasured contumely. But his explosions were short and sharp, and he seldom failed to repent of them as warmly as he had indulged in them. And they had their sad explanation, the most trying physical ailment that could have befallen him, a deafness which began when he was twenty-eight years old and increased in intensity throughout his life. He was often on the brink of matri-

[1] See the heading of the slow movement of the *Eroica Symphony*.

mony, but never took the plunge. As he grew older he and his music became self-absorbed, his musical thoughts perforce came purely from within, as nature had denied him the faculty of being influenced from without. So far we may allow that the cloud of his terrible infirmity had for his successors a bright lining. All his great later creations were the expression of the man himself. Blind Homer, blind Milton, deaf Beethoven! The bodily failing made no difference to their immortality. Up to 1800 Beethoven's compositions were mainly of comparatively small dimensions or at least designed for less exacting and more restricted means of expression. From the beginning of the Nineteenth Century, he rapidly began to speak in wider forms and to write upon larger lines. The *1st Symphony* and a *Concerto* were performed on April 2, 1800, and the *Septet* was given at the same concert (which he gracefully prefaced with a Symphony by Mozart). The Ballet of *Prometheus* (containing the movement which developed into the Finale of the *Eroica Symphony*) was written in the same year, and was produced at the Burg Theatre in 1801. The so-called second period of his works began, Sonata followed Sonata, Quartet followed Quartet. The symphony proved to be but the first of a series of great and even greater masterpieces, which occupied him year after year until 1808, when he had completed eight. The ninth was not to come to the birth until fifteen years later, in 1823. The high-water mark of this prolific time was reached in the *Waldstein Sonata,* the *Rasoumoffsky Quartets* (op. 59), the *Eroica* and *C-minor Symphonies,* the *E-flat Pianoforte Concerto,* and his one Opera, *Fidelio.* This last work perhaps gave him more thought and more trouble than any other of his middle life. The libretto, originally by the Frenchman Bouilly, who also supplied Cherubini with the *Deux Journées* (both operas were on the rare subject of wifely devotion) attracted Beethoven so strongly, that although it had been twice set before by Gaveaux and Paër, he did not hesitate to adopt it himself. There is a legend that he heard Paër's version, and congratulated (?) that composer by saying

"I like your opera, and I will set it to music!" *Fidelio*
even after its appearance on the stage had to fight for its
life. It came out in the midst of war, was over the heads of
its mixed audience, and it was not until 1814 that revised,
rewritten, and much altered after the composer's manner, it
reappeared and came into its own. It remains to this day
the noblest, most ideal, most human, and most touching
opera in existence. No later work has surpassed or equalled
it in the dramatic qualities of the great quartet in the Prison
scene, the tenderness of the duet between Florestan and his
heroic wife, the delicate handling of the prisoners' chorus, or
the somber coloring of the digging of the grave. Rocco
stands out with Don Juan and Hans Sachs as one of the
typical figures of the operatic stage, to be ranked with those
of Shakespeare, Goethe, and Dumas *père* on the dramatic
boards. If less deft than Mozart in his handling of stage
effects, Beethoven draws more tears from the eyes than did
his great predecessor, and proves more deeply the root-
qualities of human nature. The story of *Fidelio* has often
been belittled on the score of the slightness and melodramatic
moments of its theme. But Beethoven knew better, and
saw that with all its drawbacks (and what opera book is
devoid of them?) it contained the germ of the finest quality
in human nature, self-sacrifice, and provided him with the
means of preaching a great sermon upon a small but piquant
text. A crust of bread has become in his hands the means
of stirring the world's emotions for two centuries. *Fidelio* is
seldom given, which is as well, for excessive repetition of
a very sacred thing is apt to dull its continuous appeal; but
it never disappears, or lies by for long, and when it is heard
the impression is as great as, or greater than, it was a hundred
years ago. When Beethoven the composer is compared (not
untruly) with Shakespeare the poet, the parallel is not a
little owing to the opera of *Fidelio*.

The year of the revival of *Fidelio* (1814) and of the great
success of the *Symphony in A* (No. 7) which was completed
six years before, marked the climax of his second and most
prolific period. Thereafter his deafness increased, and with

it came other troubles, domestic as well as bodily. The death of his brother Caspar left him with the charge of a nephew, to whom he was unceasingly devoted, but who was in every respect unworthy of his care, and ungrateful for it. He became involved in lawsuits, and consequent financial loss and worry. In spite of all these drawbacks, the philosophic and noble mind which had expressed its convictions in the famous "Will" (a letter written to his brother in 1802 when deafness was depressing him seriously) asserted itself, and the third period of the composer's creations began. He became more and more introspective, and progressive in consequence, more careless than ever of contemporary short-sightedness, more intense in his emotions, and more complex in his expression of them. To this period belong the greatest works of his life, the *9th Symphony*, the *Mass in D*, the last *Pianoforte Sonata* (Op. 111), and perhaps greatest of all, the five so-called *Posthumous Quartets*. These, the most intimate of his works and, until Joachim brought their appeal home to the most conservative, the most abounding in the quality known as "caviare to the general," give in themselves the closest clue to the workings and sympathies of his great mind. They are in a way an epitome of his career, and his expressions. They contain the idealizations of all his characteristics, his tenderness, his grim humor, his innate fun, his wealth of tragic sense, his depth of untrammelled religious feeling, his width of exploration. The language of four stringed instruments was for him his most eloquent means of expression, and he used it to say things which he never succeeded so markedly through orchestral or vocal channels in bringing straight home to the listener. Even when that expression is obscure, there is always the consciousness that the dark places are in the mind of the hearer, not in the brain of the maker; and the passing of years which brings with it greater capacity of understanding is throwing a clearer light upon them every day.

In 1826 his ailment increased, and he developed symptoms of dropsy. In his last days he got to know Schubert's songs and used about them the same expression which Tennyson in his old age used about Rudyard Kipling, "Truly Schubert has the divine fire." He died, as was fitting, in a thunderstorm, shaking his fist at the sky, on the 26th of March, 1827. Only eight days before he had written to Moscheles that he had in view the composition of a *10th Symphony*, a *Requiem*, and the music to Goethe's *Faust:* sketches for some of these are in existence. It is unfortunate for those who, with Wagner, claim that Beethoven's last expression in Symphony was reached when he wrote the 9th and introduced the human voice, to find that he intended to write another without its aid. The whole history of Beethoven's art points to the fact that he looked upon absolute music as his highest form of expression, the one with which he had the greatest sympathy, and whereby he reached the highest pinnacle of fame.

It is important to note that these three great masters all descended from Sebastian Bach :

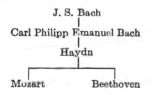

J. S. Bach

Carl Philipp Emanuel Bach

Haydn

Mozart   Beethoven

There was one department of the art in which Beethoven did not shine with the same luster, that of song-writing. Capable of writing instrumental miniatures, such as the *Bagatelles*, of unsurpassed beauty and finish, the vocal miniature which we term " song " apparently did not attract him to the same extent. No man, however great, is without his limitations, and Beethoven's lay here. There was, however, born in Vienna, in 1797, a master who was destined to attain to immortality in that very path of invention: Franz Peter Schubert. He came of peasantry stock in Moravia; his father was a schoolmaster. He was brought up in musical surroundings, and showed signs of exceptional natural gifts as early as Mozart did, but had not the same advantage of early training in contrapuntal technique, an omission which he lamented in later days, and set himself to make good not long before his death. But so ingrained was he with the innate sense of what was artistic, that only the sharpest eye can detect any lack of mastery in the workmanship of his ideas, save a certain lack of concentration in the presentation of them when he wrote in extended forms. This prolixity was idealized by Schumann under the poetical criticism of "heavenly lengths." His early education was at the "Convict," the school of the Imperial choristers. There, as if by accident, it was discovered that he was even then a composer; but was already conscious that the master whom he most revered, Beethoven, held the stage, and that he had but a remote chance of becoming known. None the less his irrepressible brain worked away, and he poured out compositions, mostly instrumental and many of them on extended lines, when he was in his early 'teens,—making also experiments in extended song-form, one of which contained no less than 17 movements. He wrote his first symphony in a month, while still at school, when only sixteen years old. What workmanship he had, he had picked up there by the light of nature. Salieri, who was one of the conductors, seems to have taken no practical interest in him, nor even marked what a genius was under his very nose: but he seems to have awakened to the fact when he heard the first performance of Schubert's *Mass in F* (No. 1) in 1814. One of Salieri's pieces of advice to the youth was to avoid tackling the poetry of Goethe and Schiller, a recommendation which turned out to be of negligible value, as was proved by no less than 121 of their poems being set by Schubert in the course of his short life. An unceasing flow of great songs now began, great even at this early period; *Gretchen am Spinnrade* was written at the age of seventeen. He set every poem which came in his way, wrote 8 operas in one year; as Schumann said, "He could have set an advertisement placard to music." A year later he had tossed off one of the greatest songs of the world, if not the very greatest, the *Erlkönig*. Vogl, the opera singer, at once produced it in public and it was encored four times. He told a pupil, who handed on the story to another writer, that Schubert used frequently to write songs on stray scraps of music paper in a Bier-Halle, crumple them up in his pocket, sometimes half in each, which the singer rescued after the composer had gone to bed. The year 1816 saw the composition of two Symphonies, one of them known as the *Tragic*, which were more important than any orchestral works he had hitherto attempted; but the vocal works of the same year, which included such masterpieces as the Harper's songs from *Wilhelm Meister*, *Sehnsucht*, and the *Wanderer*, were still far ahead of the instrumental. He composed them at such a rate that he even forgot that they were his own handiwork, when he heard them again. Vogl became one of his most intimate friends and supporters. In pianoforte works for two hands upon a large scale, such as the Sonatas, Schubert was not at his best, but he succeeded, as few if any men have, in producing a number of first-rate works for four hands, some of them, like the great *duo in C-major*, being obviously imagined as arrangements of an unwritten orchestral score. The greatest instrumental works date from 1822 to the close of his life in 1828. They may be summarized as follows:

1822   *The unfinished Symphony in B-minor*
1823   *Rosamunde*
1824   *The Octet*
        String Quartet in A-minor
1826   *String Quartet in D-minor*
1827   *Trios in B-flat* (for P. F., Violin and Violoncello)
1828   *Symphony in C-major*
        String Quintet in C-major

The *String Quartet in D-minor*, with the famous variations on *Tod und das Mädchen*, lay *perdu* for years, in consequence of a remark made by Schuppanzigh, the first violin, at the first trial of the work. He turned to Schubert and said, "But, Franzl, you can't write for the fiddle," and the little modest man without a word took away the parts and locked them up. Beethoven's sarcastic musical joke upon the fat violinist to the words, "Schuppanzigh ist ein Lump, Lump, Lump, wer kennt ihn nicht . . . den aufgeblasnen Esels-kopf. O Lump, O Esel, Hi-hi-ha," does not seem to have been ill applied.

Schubert's life is one which, though it has been invested by the enthusiastic pen of George Grove with an extraor-dinary interest and charm, cannot be said to be more than an unceasing record of composition, and a tragic lack of funds and general appreciation. He seldom went out of his native town and never far from it. His fame during his life was confined to his friends. He had no conceit, and allowed himself no time to develop it, or even to think about himself. He lived solely for his art, and thought of little else. When he first saw Beethoven he fled away from him in sheer fright; but when the great man was on his death-bed, Hüttenbrenner records that Schubert visited him twice: and on the first occasion Beethoven used the remarkable words, "You, Anselm (Hüttenbrenner), have my mind (Geist), but Franz has my soul (Seele)." Schubert's best and greatest *Symphony in C* he never heard: the task of playing it was said to be beyond the powers of the orchestra, which, in view of the fact that they had tackled the *9th Symphony* of Beethoven, may be dismissed as absurd. It is more likely that its novelty and the physical strain which its persistent rhythms put upon the executants made them restive, as were the players in the Philharmonic Society when Mendels-sohn brought the work to London. The autograph now in the Library at Vienna shows what merciless cuts were made in various trials of it — even the characteristic trombone passages being queried or omitted. As well might one of the Cherubs be cut out of the canvas of the San Sisto Madonna. He died, worn out, on November 19, 1828, aged only 31 years. Vienna honored his funeral slightly more than it did that of Mozart, and had enough sense of duty to lay his body near that of his chief idol, Beethoven. That Schubert's great fame was almost entirely posthumous is no doubt in a measure due to the exceeding shortness of his life. That it spread like wildfire after his death was the work of his successors in the ranks of the great, primarily of Robert Schumann and of Mendelssohn in the early part of the Nineteenth Century, who preached him with all the fire of youthful enthusiasm, Schumann with his pen, Mendelssohn with his bâton: afterwards of George Grove, whose pilgrimage with Sullivan to Vienna in 1867 resulted in many new discoveries amongst the piles of manuscripts which still lay under accumulations of dust. To this historical pilgrimage the world owes its belated knowledge of the *Unfinished Symphony* and the *Rosamunde* music. Grove had at his hand an excellent orchestra at the Crystal Palace (where he was Secretary); the conductor, August Manns, was as great a Schubert-worshipper as himself, and the new treasures were quickly brought to the hearing of the English musical public.

Within the space of 94 years (1732–1828) German music was the richer by four great masters of absolute music. There were also lesser lights in the same paths, and a star of the first magnitude in the dramatic firmament, whom we must consider in the next chapter, together with their contemporaries in other countries.

CHAPTER 14

The Contemporaries of Beethoven and the Development of Opera in Germany, Italy, and France

WHILE this extraordinary outburst of activity was taking place in Germany, an Italian was upholding the honor of his country and carrying on its great traditions, a master who was born four years after Mozart and outlived Beethoven by fifteen years, Luigi Cherubini (b. Florence, 1760), and who may be termed the last of the Italian classicists. This dignified and somewhat cold personality was privileged to see from a distant height the whole of the European art-world; he was open-minded enough to profit by much of it, independent enough to follow its principles without sacrificing his own individuality. It was no empty compliment that Beethoven paid, when he wrote that of all his contemporaries he valued him the most. During his life-time dramatic and absolute music began to drift apart; composers arose who specialized in each, rarely venturing on combining the two, a split which became more and more accentuated as the years of the Nineteenth Century passed by. Cherubini, like Haydn, Mozart, and Beethoven, was trained in the old Italian school of modal counterpoint, with which after Beethoven's death Germany, with the two exceptions of Wagner and Brahms, lost touch. His career began with church work, of which he wrote many specimens as a boy, but as early as 1780 he took to operatic writing, producing eleven operas in eight years. After a visit to London, he settled finally in Paris, 1788, and became the mainstay of the opera in that city, becoming in course of time the head of the Conservatoire and the guide, philosopher, and friend of a long series of

PLATE XLIII.   CHERUBINI

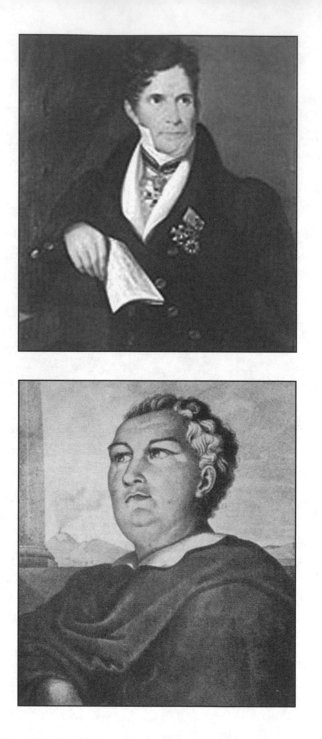

PLATE XLIV. GASPARE SPONTINI AND DOMENICO CIMAROSA

French composers for the stage. His aloof temperament was probably a strong factor in restraining him from Italianizing the French School, but his earnestness and high ideals undoubtedly helped to steady it, and to infuse it with sound principles. Many of his French operas had a great success, notably *Lodoiska* and *Medea*, but one, *Les Deux Journées*, known as "The Watercarrier," which was written to a libretto by Bouilly, the author of *Fidelio*, carried his fame to Vienna, whence it derived a long lease of life which is not yet exhausted. The similarity between the plots of Bouilly's two libretti has also affected the music which Beethoven and Cherubini wrote to them, and although the palm must be given to the former, there is no question that the Italian's work is also in its way a masterpiece. After 1809 Cherubini deserted the stage and resumed Church music, writing a great number of Masses, one of which, the *Requiem in C-minor*, ranks with the greatest of its kind. He also composed a considerable number of instrumental works, including several string quartets, which are models of chamber-music writing, and full of a charm and distinction which is all their own; owing much to the study of his contemporaries, but little to their influence. His *Credo* for eight unaccompanied voices is an astonishing masterpiece of writing upon the true old Italian lines. It is interesting to relate that he only became acquainted with Beethoven's Sonatas very late in his life, when Charles Hallé, then a young pianist studying in Paris, visited him frequently in the evening to play them for him.

During his eighty-two years of life, he saw his native Italy turning to a lighter and more superficial type of dramatic art than he himself sympathized with. The chief of the dramatic composers which arose in this period were Cimarosa (1749–1801), who was a rather pale reflection of Mozart, but had at least one enduring success in the opera of *Il Matrimonio Segreto;* and Spontini (1774–1851), a curious, masterful, grandiose figure, who, without being a compelling genius himself, had a great influence on the later development of German opera. Spontini had a great veneration for

Mozart, and did much to carry on the principles of Gluck. His opera, the *Vestale*, still lives with several of his overtures, a form in which he reached great distinction. As a writer for the orchestra he is conspicuous for his love of highly-colored, not to say noisy, effects, which, although they have been thrown into the shade by the big orchestral battalions of the present day, are not a little responsible for the exaltation of color over design, and for the use of instrumental leger-de-main to conceal lack of invention, which has since Wagner so hypnotized the superficial hearer. Spontini's active life was spent partly in Paris and eventually in Berlin; with his native Italy he had little to do. Nevertheless he was to the German mind, then awakening to the consciousness of its own powers, one of the chief centers of foreign influence, and as such was anathema to the arising patriots. From the day that Weber won the battle of the *Freischütz*, Spontini's star began to set. The next Italian to arise was of a far livelier, not to say flippant type, Gioachino Rossini (1792–1868). Witty, lazy, ready with his pen, he was the spoilt child of Europe throughout his life. He was one of the pioneers of the star system, and did not care how much the celebrated singers of his day interlarded his works with their alterations and embellishments for their own aggrandizement, though he was caustic enough to twit them for it. He knew his Mozart, however, and could be serious if and when he chose. He wrote operas incessantly until 1829, when he was thirty-seven years of age, and then stopped suddenly. His two greatest works, the *Barber of Seville* and *William Tell*, were his last serious contributions to the stage. In the former he worked on the lines of Mozart, though in a thoroughly Italian spirit, and with a power of *buffo* writing in which he excelled. In the latter he scaled almost without effort the heights of Grand Opera, and showed himself capable of being the peer of his contemporary, Meyerbeer, excelling him indeed both in vocal treatment and in sincerity of utterance. When he wrote, his pen went like a whirlwind. When Donizetti was told that the *Barber of Seville* was written in a fortnight, he answered that "it was not surprising, as Rossini was so lazy." From the day that *Tell* came out in 1829 (Rossini was then only 37 years of age), he was practically silent until his death in 1868; amusing himself with music paper sometimes and his friends always with inexhaustible wit. He could be satirical, as on the occasion when a young composer brought him a funeral march which he had written in memory of Meyerbeer. After hearing it, Rossini said: "Charming, charming! But would it not have been still better, if you had died, and Meyerbeer had written your funeral march?" He never would travel in a railway, and even posted with four horses from Paris to pay a visit to a friend in Frankfort. His compositions are nearly all operatic, or vocal. He wrote 46 operas, 9 cantatas, a *Stabat Mater* and *Mass*, and some fugitive vocal pieces. His purely instrumental works are (with the exception of the overtures to his operas) very few, although amongst them are, curiously enough, six string quartets. Three other Italian composers for the stage arose and attained considerable success during Rossini's life: Gaetano Donizetti (1798–1848), the composer of 63 operas, some of which (*e.g. Lucrezia Borgia, Lucia di Lammermoor, The Daughter of the Regiment*) still survive where prima donnas who can still vocalize exist. He was a facile writer, with considerable melodic grace and charm; Vincenzo Bellini (1802–1835), a still more gifted composer, who in his short life made several striking successes such as the *Puritani, Sonnambula,* and *Norma,* and had the advantage of an unsurpassable cast of great singers, Grisi, Mario, Tamburini, Rubini, and Lablache, to interpret them; Mercadante (1797–1870), the third of the group, was the least important of them, though he possessed a distinct facility in *buffo* writing.

But in spite of the great vogue of his two younger compatriots, Rossini remained master of the field. His long residence in Paris, his generosity and bonhomie, and, above all, the amazing success of his masterpiece, *William Tell,* an opera as superior to all his other works as Verdi's *Otello* is to the *Trovatore,* gave him an influence in Paris (then the

center of musical life) comparable to that of his Italian predecessor, Lulli. He, although not himself a technical trainer
of composers, attracted to his style all the pupils of Cherubini, and changed the face of French music. He became in
fact a link between the later schools of the two Latin races.
Tell set the model of Grand Opera : the *Barber of Seville* that
of Opéra Comique. Gluck and Cherubini were equally, for
the time, snuffed out. Monsigny (1729–1817), Gossec
(1733–1829), Grétry (a Belgian, 1741–1813), Dalayrac
(1753–1808), Lesueur (1763–1837), Méhul (1763–1827), the
composer of *Joseph and His Brethren,* which still lives, and
Boieldieu (1775–1834), the composer of the famous *Dame
Blanche,* upheld the essentially French banner of Opéra
Comique ; but the last of this succession of French masters
showed signs of the Rossini influence, which began insensibly
but continuously to affect the pure Gallic style. Auber
(1784–1871), even with all his inborn Parisian gaiety, could
not avoid the infection, though he preserved an individuality
of expression which has ensured a long life to such masterpieces as *Fra Diavolo,* and *Masaniello.* His training under
Cherubini stood him in good stead, and the technique which
he acquired under that great classical master gave him a
freedom of writing and a refinement of feeling which out-
shone his contemporaries Hérold (1791–1833), the composer of
Zampa and the *Pré aux Clercs,* Halévy (1797–1862), of *La
Juive* fame, and Adam (1803–1856), whose *Postillon de Long-
jumeau* still keeps the boards. It speak volumes for the
ingrained independence of French art and artists, that, though
their school of music was dominated in successive generations
by Italians, Lulli, Cherubini, Rossini, they kept in their
native paths, and never lost them even when alien growths
threatened to conceal them. In her hospitality France has
never shown herself niggardly to the stranger. She has
often asked him both to serve and to eat at her table. Her
banquet has been spread for all. But, admirable in her
knowledge of herself, she has always wisely ordained that
her guests shall feast with her only on her own severe conditions of respect and propriety.

PLATE XLV. ROSSINI

PLATE XLVI. CARL MARIA VON WEBER

GENEALOGY OF THE FRENCH OPERATIC SCHOOL

Lulli

Rameau

| Monsigny | Gossec | Grétry | Dalayrac | Méhul |

Cherubini

Rossini

| Boieldieu | Halévy | Auber | Adam |

We must now temporarily leave the French operatic school, to discuss the great movement which was so deeply affecting the stage in Germany, and which became a dominating influence for scores of years. The protagonist in this upheaval of national expression was a nobleman of Austrian descent, Freiherr Carl Maria von Weber (b. 1786). He was the nephew of Mozart's wife, Costanze, and half-brother of Edmund von Weber, who had studied with Haydn and Mozart. He himself studied with Haydn's brother Michael, and later with the Abbé Vogler, where he found himself the fellow pupil of another aspiring composer, whose later methods and aspirations sharply contrasted with his own, Meyerbeer. Weber's instincts were dramatic and his patriotic fervor soon led him to take up the cudgels for national, as opposed to exotic, art upon the German stage. After various experiments, of which the Opera *Silvana* is the best known, he hit upon a subject which brought him immortal fame, a story by Apel called *Der Freischütz*. The mixture of supernatural agencies and of simple burgher life appealed to him at once, though it was not until some years later (1817) that he began to work at it, and eleven years later (1821) that it appeared on the stage at Berlin. It was the first genuinely German opera that had been heard since *Fidelio*. The Italians, headed by Spontini and Rossini, seemed to have sole possession of the public ear. It came, like a bolt from the blue, on the 18th of June (Waterloo day), and conquered at once. Hitherto Weber had been chiefly known as an instrumental composer, and even pianist. His mastery of absolute music, founded on sound lines, had resulted in many remarkable works, all of them picturesque, most of them showing the feeling for the footlights which dominated him; but as an operatic composer he was not in the public eye until this great and sudden success placed him on a pinnacle for all time. In Berlin alone, where it took its turn in repertoire, the performances reached the number of 500 in half a century. It spread at once to England, where it became the rage: and Weber was commissioned to write another opera to an English text by Planché, *Oberon*, and to visit London to conduct it. In the meantime, however, he was at work on an opera which was to have far more influence on the German School than the *Freischütz*. The theme selected, *Euryanthe*, was unfortunate, for at any rate in its construction the plot was too involved and too ill put together to ensure success. For practical purposes it is a work which its inherent musical beauty does not allow to die, but which can never be universally attractive to the public. None the less it is the true ancestor of *Tannhäuser* and *Lohengrin*. But for it, it is safe to say that *Lohengrin* would never have existed. It laid down the principles of continuous music, of richly illustrative recitative, and of the subordination of everything to the dramatic effect. Lysiart and Eglantine are Telramund and Ortrud in other dresses. Adolar is the prototype of Tannhäuser and Walter von Stolzing, Euryanthe of Elsa. As a work of progressive art, it is alongside and not antecedent to the earlier works of Wagner; as music it is superior to them, alike in vivid picturesqueness, in melodic invention, and in absence of monotony. Weber was the last German composer who combined the branches of absolute and of dramatic music in his own output. . Even in his case the dramatic element predominated so markedly as to relegate his instrumental work to a second place. But his ease in manipulating pure music asserted itself in the masterly overtures to his operas, works which are even in themselves epoch-making, and which set a pattern which has been followed by most other operatic writers, when they have been sufficiently permeated with music *per se* to tackle it at all. His principles were to create an atmosphere which would typify the character of the play to follow, and to use its main features in epitomizing it. In carrying out this task he never lost sight of the value of form, and succeeded in using it to bring home the message of the story (itself "form" upon a larger scale) and to make its purport clear to the listener's ear, before the eye was called into play. The overtures to *Freischütz, Euryanthe,* and *Oberon* may, in a sense, be termed programme-music, but the programme does not interfere with the music, and they live without the adventitious aid of a knowledge of the story they illustrate. Each and all of them would remain as fascinating without any title at all.

The comparative failure of *Euryanthe* preyed upon Weber's health, and he developed symptoms of consumption. The invitation to London, for which he wrote *Oberon,* gave his life a flicker of returning activity, and he set out in the early months of 1826 for England, where he was the guest of Sir George Smart (so mercilessly and even unjustifiably satirized by Thackeray as Sir George Thrum). His appearance in the auditorium at Court Garden was the signal for an extraordinary outburst of popular enthusiasm. He conducted the rehearsals and the first twelve performances of the new opera, which was acclaimed by the big public, but neglected by the less musical leaders of society, still under the Italian thraldom. His illness rapidly increased, and he died at Smart's house on June 4, 1826. Eighteen years later his body was brought back to Dresden, where it was reinterred with great ceremony, Wagner conducting the music, and writing a work for the occasion.

In the movement for native opera Weber had two fellow-workers, Ludwig Spohr (b. 1784 at Brunswick) and Heinrich Marschner (b. 1796 at Zittau). Spohr was brought up as a violinist, but soon began composing as well, writing numerous works of every sort and kind, oratorios, symphonies, concertos, chamber-music, as well as operas. He was in politics an advanced radical, and in music a marked progressist, and had sufficiently wide sympathies to welcome the Wagner of the *Dutchman* and of *Tannhäuser* in his old age. Unfortunately his work was so soaked with sugary sentiment and so devoid of real backbone, that while it possessed qualities which attracted for the moment, it failed to retain its hold upon the musical public. A dinner consisting entirely of sweets was a novelty, but soon palled upon the public palate. Nevertheless Spohr had during his lifetime an astonishing quota of success, both in France and England, as well as at home. Although he was careful to adapt himself-to his surroundings, he was in no sense obsequious, and he was always an artist. Although his operas, seven in number, have failed (with the occasional exception of *Jessonda*) to keep the stage, he had a hand in building the edifice of German opera, which his personal popularity made more effective than the works themselves. His facility was extraordinary, and his orchestration had many features of interest both in accomplishment and in experiment.

Marschner, on the other hand, practically restricted himself to the stage. He was greatly influenced in style by Weber, but had a certain independence of his own, which is chiefly apparent in his opera *Hans Heiling*. *Templar und Jüdin*, an opera written on the subject of Scott's *Ivanhoe*, had a success which still keeps it in the German repertoire. Though he had the misfortune to be overshadowed by Weber, and to be less before the public than the virtuoso-composer Spohr, his qualities have ensured him a niche in the operatic Temple of Fame.

Contemporary with all these simple-minded men of high ideals, there was living a composer of vastly different stripe, clever to his finger-tips, opportunist of the deepest dye, cultivated, ambitious, and a master of his craft; a composer with great conceptions to his credit, who nevertheless has never gained the respect of great musicians, because he never hesitated to sacrifice principle to gain success : Jacob Meyer Beer, a name which he afterwards denationalized into Giacomo Meyerbeer, b. 1791 or 1794 of Jewish parents. His father was a rich banker of Frankfort. He was for some time a fellow-pupil with Weber of the Abbé Vogler, and was a close friend of the composer of the *Freischütz*, until his dalliance with Italian methods broke the bonds. An early visit to Italy, then under the thrall of Rossini, had appealed to the young man's innate desire for popularity at all costs, and resulted in Weber's historical words : "My heart bleeds to see a German composer of creative power stoop to become an imitator in order to win favor with the crowd." The rift was complete, and Meyerbeer betook himself to Paris, where he went to work as assiduously in assimilating French methods as he had those of Italy a few years before. He secured in Scribe the best librettist of the day, and in association with him wrote a series of works for the Grand Opéra, *Robert le Diable, Les Huguenots, Le Pro-phète, L'Africaine,* and for the Opéra Comique *L'Étoile du Nord* and *Dinorah.* These operas all still exist, and most of them show little signs of wearing out their powers of attraction : but they are one and all an amazing conglomeration of fine music, trivial detail, masterly orchestration, and a striving (so obvious as to be often silly) after effect. The great duet in the *Huguenots* (Act IV) could scarcely be bettered, but it shines out all the more because of its tawdry surroundings. Vulgarity hobnobs with nobility on equal terms everywhere. The listener is never sure that a great artistic moment will not be wrecked by some futile concession to the high notes and florid embellishments of a prima donna. In the case of Rossini this was part of his nature and came to him with the native air he breathed ; in that of Meyer-beer it was a concoction made to order. The Italian carried conviction, the German in question did not. It is not a little characteristic that Meyerbeer contrived to rule over two such vitally different kingdoms as the Hof-Oper in Berlin and the

Grand Opéra in Paris, and remain acceptable to both. Such adaptability is a little too artificial to give grounds for admiration; but to a man who could be at once so grandiose and so finnicking nothing was impossible. It is difficult to imagine how the composer of the Cathedral Scene in the *Prophète* could condescend to sit next the chief of the claque at the final rehearsal, and alter passages to suit his cue for applause, or to wander about the back of the stage to hear what the scene shifters said about his music. And yet for all his disregard of high ideals, and lack of self-sacrifice in the nobler interests of his art, Meyerbeer did a great work in developing the constructive side of opera, and showing how great effects of climax can be attained. It is to his credit that, though he could be trivial, he never would consent to be ugly. His worst characters are never delineated by uncouth or unmusicianly means. He had a certain sense of humanity which makes such figures as Marcel, Fidès, and Raoul de Nangis stand out as creations in musico-dramatic literature. He advanced orchestration, he knew to a nicety the limitations and capabilities of the voice, and he was not afraid of a big tune, even though it was not always a distinguished one. Upon the German school he had very little influence, upon the French a very considerable one, though his Parisian contemporaries and successors seem to have seen through his artificialities enough to steer fairly clear of them, aided therein by their own innate patriotism.

The consideration of this curiously cosmopolitan figure brings us back to the world of French music, with which he had so many sympathies, and in which he had so many friends. During his lifetime no less than five composers arose, who reached a world-wide fame: Hector Berlioz (1811–96), Charles Ambroise Thomas (b. 1811), Charles François Gounod (1818–93), Charles Camille Saint-Saëns (1835–21), and Georges Bizet (1838–75). To these must be added a sixth, who, although a Belgian and a native of Liège, was identified with Paris and the French school all his active life, Cèsar Franck (1822–90). Of these six Franck and Saint-Saëns are more particularly connected with the "new" French school, and will therefore be dealt with in Chapter XVI.

Berlioz, the most curious and uncanny personality in his era's music, is also the most interesting figure to be found in the history of the French School. He was a true product of the French Revolution, alike in his ways and in his music. As a man of literature, a critic, and a poet he had few equals. As a composer he had many superiors. He re-belled against convention, he had no veneration save for the very greatest, no regard for tradition as such, no sympathy with anything short of the grandiose. His scheme of work was always on the largest scale, and unfortunately he was not gifted by nature with the inventive qualities which alone could be adequate to carry it out. His music, as music, is seldom satisfying, always interesting, often bizarre, some-times ugly, but never irrelevant or lacking in conviction. He was a supreme egoist, with an unbounded belief in him-self, and as such imposed himself upon the world in a way which his contemporaries resented, but his successors could not fail to accept. For he was above all things in his art sincere to the core, and opened up paths which before his day were unexplored. He loved effect, but for its own sake, not, as Meyerbeer did, for the public applause. If he had been as great in musical invention as he was in conception and construction, he would have ranked as a master with the greatest. As it was, he is not far behind them in pic-turesqueness, and one of the greatest masters of the orchestra that ever lived. The only instrument which he himself played was the guitar, but he knew the capabilities of every other from the piccolo to the double-bass. His works not infrequently suggest that this knowledge dominated him to the exclusion of the music he wrote for it: and that the consideration of the instrumental effects he invented pre-ceded the ideas which they had to interpret. His works were comparatively few, but nearly all on a huge scale. Yet though his *Requiem* and his *Fantastic Symphony* necessitate the employment of an enormous number of instruments, he

could be equally effective in dealing with very moderate
forces in the *Enfance du Christ,* or parts of *Faust.* He was
capable of great charm when he chose, as in the Queen Mab
Scherzo from *Romeo and Juliet,* though the moments are
fleeting. He revelled in devils, and failed in angels. No
one has so nearly reached Goethe's conception of Mephistoph-
eles as he. A worshipper of Greek drama, his ideas of the
operatic stage came, as was but natural, direct from Gluck,
and he had little respect for any other stage writer save for
Weber, and in his case rather on account of his poetry of
utterance than his style. His operas, three in number,
have always been "caviare to the general." His symphonies
less so, though they, with the exception of *Harold in Italy,*
are more amusing for the conductor than attractive to the
hearer. He was admirably summed up by Dannreuther
in words which exactly convey his position in musical history,
and deserve repetition here. "He stands alone — a colossus
with few friends and no direct followers; a marked individuality, original, puissant, bizarre, violently one-sided; whose influence has been and will again be felt far and wide, for good
and for bad, but cannot rear disciples nor form a school."

Ambroise Thomas, an Alsatian from Metz, after gaining
the Prix de Rome, wrote several chamber works and choral
compositions, but soon devoted himself exclusively to operatic compositions, of which eighteen were brought out
at the Grand Opéra and the Comique. The best known are
Hamlet and *Mignon.* He was scarcely powerful enough for
grand opera, but was a worthy successor of Hérold in the
lighter type, which is indigenous to France. He succeeded
Auber as head of the Conservatoire in 1871.

Charles Gounod, a Parisian *pur sang,* was a curious compound of music and theology, picturesque and superficial
in both, endowed with a gift of melodic invention and a certain poetry which showed itself at its best in his first book
of songs, the well known *Vingt Mélodies.* He played with
the fringe of great things, but was clever enough to avoid
swimming in deep water. He was attracted to the lurid, but
was often "frighted with false fire." He produced one opera

which is an abiding success, *Faust*, and many others which are quite forgotten, though not devoid of a charm which was very far-reaching in its day, and was especially noticeable in *Mireille*.   Later in life he betook himself to oratorio writing, and produced (with much trumpeting) two works, the *Redemption* and *Mors et Vita*, both of them (to quote Carlyle) "poor husks of things," but sufficiently sentimental temporarily to capture the unthinking part of the English public, appealing alike to Catholics, Anglicans, and the Salvation Army.   In his own country these excursions into realms so foreign to himself and his countrymen had no success.   But his early songs and *Faust* remain, and prove his right to a high position in the French school.

Georges Bizet, the youngest and most shortlived of the group, was a genius of the first order.   He has to his credit two compositions of such compelling excellence, that they will long survive the bulk of contemporary work: the incidental music to *L'Arlésienne* and the opera *Carmen*. Like many great living operas, this masterpiece was a comparative failure at its first performance on March 3, 1875, and three months afterwards its composer was dead, aged only 38. No opera repertoire is now complete without it.   It struck a new note, which though essentially French had a deeper tone and a greater resonance than any heard since the days of Cherubini.   It was before all things sincere both in conception and in workmanship.

Into this center of Gallic activity there descended a German Jew who made for a space more noise than all the Frenchmen, and had the wit and the *savoir faire* to turn all the frivolities of the Second Empire to his own advantage and to exploit them accordingly.   Jacques Offenbach (b. 1819 at Cologne) came to study the violoncello in Paris in 1833, and soon adopted the double rôle of theatre manager and composer of light opera, of which he produced no less than 69.   He liked a *succès de scandale* and gloried in caricature.   He was in fact an opera-bouffe Meyerbeer, with the same faculty of feeling the pulse of his public.   He could write uncommonly pretty music when he chose, though he too often interlarded the beauties with vulgarity. He was however too much of an artist not to wish for one legitimate success in higher fields. He spent years in perfecting *Les Contes d'Hoffmann* with this purpose in view, but died in 1880, a year before his wish was fulfilled. The opera proved to be a worthy repentance for his earlier peccadilloes and has retained popularity of the better sort to the present day.

CHAPTER 15

The Post-Beethoven Period

WE must now retrace our steps to Germany, and note the developments which took place after the deaths of Beethoven and Weber. Here the streams of dramatic and of absolute music were of equal strength, and were flowing wider apart as their volume and force increased. The new school to which so many famous men belonged dated from 1809 to 1833: no less than four of them were born between 1809 and 1813, Felix Mendelssohn (b. 1809), Robert Schumann (b. 1810), Franz Liszt (b. 1811), and Richard Wagner (b. 1813). To these must be added one name, that of Frederic Chopin (b. 1809), who, although a Pole, was so intimately connected with the German masters (especially with Liszt) that he almost belongs to the same category as they. The eldest and the most immediately successful of this group, Jacob Ludwig Felix Mendelssohn-Bartholdy (to give him his full name), was, like Meyerbeer, of pure Jewish lineage and belonged to a family of bankers which stayed prominent in Berlin until run out by the Nazis. He was born at Hamburg on Feb. 3, 1809, and was with his brothers and sisters baptized as a Lutheran Christian. His family removed to Berlin when he was three years old, and he received a thorough education in classical literature, music, and drawing. Zelter, the friend of Goethe, was his master in composition. He wrote a great quantity of music, both vocal and instrumental, including no less than twelve symphonies, before he was fifteen, and made the acquaintance of Weber (who had a great influence upon him), of Spohr, and of Goethe, whom he several times visited at Weimar. He also paid a visit with his father to Paris, where he found himself surrounded by most of the well-known artists of the day, and received a most kindly and appreciative welcome from Cherubini. But France had little attraction for him, and he was too young to gauge the value of Cherubini's judgment, even calling him "an extinct volcano." The first works which really showed his mettle were the *Octet for strings* (1825) and the *Midsummer Night's Dream Overture* (1826). These two works represented his maturity, and he never surpassed them in later life. Similarly his *Seven Characteristic Pieces* for pianoforte solo strike a more important note than most of his later works for the instrument. Opera writing ceased to attract him after his early drawing-room experiments. An early meeting with Spontini, in which the older composer advised him to cultivate large ideas, a criticism not only kind but very much to the point, resulted in unpleasant relations between them. He devoted himself to the study of Sebastian Bach, and carried through, after many difficulties, the first performance of the *St. Matthew Passion* which had been given since Bach's death. For that achievement alone, the world owes him a great debt. He was fortunately in a social position which enabled him to accomplish many things which a man of lowlier birth and less means would have found difficult if not impossible: the same advantage gave him the opportunity of working without one eye upon the cupboard, and with a pen which could write what it liked, irrespective of publishers' requirements or limitations. His first visit to England, which was partly due to the advice of Moscheles, the pianist and friend of Beethoven, took place in 1829. He stayed in England for the greater part of the year, made his first appearance at the Philharmonic, attended many social functions, and went for a tour in Wales and Scotland, which resulted in the picturesque overture to the *Hebrides* or *Fingal's Cave*, the opening of which he sketched on the spot, and this journey was the genesis of the *Scotch Symphony*. His subsequent travels extended to the Tyrol, Switzerland, and Italy. In Rome he met, argued with, and was somewhat fascinated by Berlioz, then the holder of the Prix de Rome; on his return he came across

Mozart's son, an Austrian officer, at the house of Madame Dorothea Ertmann, the friend of Beethoven, in Milan. In 1831 he again visited Paris for the last time, and made friends with Chopin, Meyerbeer, and Liszt. Thereafter his journeys to London were frequent, and his influence there became almost paramount both upon the musicians and the public. His success as conductor of the Düsseldorf Festival in 1833 led to his acceptance of the chief musical directorship in that town; he produced there a vast mass of works by all the great masters from Palestrina and Bach to his own day. His worship for Bach expressed itself in a concrete form in the oratorio of *St. Paul*, which after long consideration and close work was given at Leipzig in 1836. In 1835 he had accepted the conductorship of the Gewandhaus concerts in that city, which became his headquarters for the remainder of his life. He gathered round him a large band of admirers and pupils, Sterndale Bennett (to whom he was deeply attached), Gade the Dane, Ferdinand Hiller, Robert Schumann and eventually Moscheles; labored incessantly for the production of the great and then unknown compositions of Sebastian Bach; and wrote a great number of works of every style except the operatic, a branch after which he, like Brahms, always hankered but which he never seriously tackled, though his efforts to obtain a sympathetic libretto were incessant. The incidental music to the *Midsummer Night's Dream* remains his only contribution to the modern stage, and is a worthy successor of Weber's *Oberon*, which was its prototype. His music to *Antigone* and *Œdipus Coloneus* and to Racine's *Athalie* is more fitted for the concert room than for the theater. After a short and not altogether agreeable experience of Berlin, whither the King of Prussia did his best to attract him, he returned to Leipzig and founded there in 1843 the Conservatorium of Music, which was for so long the center of musical education in Germany, and became international in its appeal. His later visits to London were increasingly successful; he introduced such famous players as Ernst, Joachim (then 13 years old), and Piatti to the London public. He began work at the *Elijah*, an oratorio, which eventually was produced at the Birmingham Festival on August 26, 1846, with a success which has continued, in England at least, for 150 years and more, and still possesses an extraordinary attraction for the British public. His favorite sister, Fanny Hensel, died suddenly in the summer of 1847, and the shock coupled with overwork speedily brought his short life to a close on November 4, 1847.

Mendelssohn is one of the only outstanding composers who had his greatest success in lifetime. His music, always finished to the smallest detail, always picturesque when written under inspiring conditions (Wagner called him a consummate landscape painter), and invariably careful not to outstep the limitations of his genius, does not, as a rule, retain its first appeal in subsequent repetition. His trick (and all composers are human enough to have tricks) was the dangerous one of perpetual and unvaried repetition of phrases and even of bars: a habit which was itself repeated in many of his works. This trick was of course seized upon by his admirers and imitators, and exploited to death, and it grew upon Mendelssohn as his years increased. He possessed great reverence for his predecessors but no great depth of invention or design in himself: he was always a supreme artist endowed with exceptionally good taste. With regard to his contemporaries, he was not so far-sighted, or at least did not show his appreciation for the best of them if he felt it; and it is difficult to imagine that so gifted a brain as his could be blind to the importance of the creations of Schumann, merely (as he went so far as to say) considering them amateurish, or could ignore the flashes of genius in early Wagner. But he was an out-and-out purist, and probably resented all attempts at experiment. In England he more or less crushed native individuality, not by Handelian methods, but by the glamour of his works. Few escaped his influence, until late in the nineteenth century. Oddly enough he himself keenly disliked being imitated, and his personal relations with the most prominent of his disciples were sometimes strained in consequence. His meteoric

PLATE XLVII.   FELIX MENDELSSOHN BARTHOLDY

PLATE XLVIII. SCHUMANN AND MADAME SCHUMANN

career, though of infinitely less value and less enduring influence than Mozart's, was a distinct factor for keeping the standard of the art on the highest possible level. Therein he reflected the high-souled nature which he most assuredly possessed.

The second of the group, Robert Alexander Schumann (b. 1810 at Zwickau), was a figure of greater fiber, deeper nature, and more epoch-making accomplishment, possessing also a greater humanity and a broader appreciation of his seniors and his juniors, which amounted at times to prophecy. Brought up in a literary atmosphere, and with a natural bent for philosophy, his early studies affected his compositions from his Opus 1 to his last. His devotion to music led him to desert every other interest, and he began by studying under Wieck with a view to becoming a pianist. Too much zeal in the muscular development of his fingers resulted in the permanent laming of his third finger, a catastrophe which had a happy result, for it turned him from the career of a virtuoso to that of a composer. His master was Dorn, then the opera conductor at Leipzig. He began by writing for the pianoforte, producing a number of novel and poetical works, which opened up a new horizon both in form, picturesqueness, and in technique, of which the first, *Papillons*, gave the keynote. His literary gifts impelled him to work for progress in the press as well as on music paper; and he founded the *Neue Zeitschrift für Musik* in 1834, writing for that paper for ten years, spreading the light of pure art, appreciating all that was best in everybody and merciless to what was worst. There has never been a more generous critic, or one who so completely combined the useful hints of a master with the functions of a censor. In this paper appeared the quaint humor of the "Davidsbund," a league of imaginary friends who were banded together to fight the Philistines,[1] most of them representing different phases of Schumann's own individuality, whom he christened Florestan, Eusebius, Master Raro, and some of

---

[1] "Philister" in German-student phraseology can best be rendered "stick-in-the-mud."

them his personal friends, Bauck, the painter, Zuccalmaglio the littérateur, and Mendelssohn. His criticisms began with a eulogium upon Chopin, then almost unknown, and ended with the famous pronunciamento about Brahms in 1853. He was during these twenty years unsparing in his appreciation of his many brilliant contemporaries, Mendelssohn, Hiller, Heller, Henselt, Bennett, Franz, and others; even including Berlioz (who in many respects was antipathetic to him) in his category of great men. In later life he expressed a lively interest in Wagner's *Tannhäuser*, taking up a far different attitude to that master than did his more prejudiced partisans and successors. From 1834 onwards Schumann's pianoforte works became more and more important, and in five years he had composed many which have become permanent classics, such as the *Fantasia* (Op. 17), the *Novelletten, Kreisleriana,* and the fascinating *Kinderscenen.* A visit to Vienna resulted in the composition of his *Symphony in B-flat,* and also (happily for the world) in the unearthing of Schubert's great *Symphony in C,* which he sent to Leipzig and which was first performed there under Mendelssohn's direction. In 1840 he married Clara Wieck, then grown up into a famous pianist, who was not only the most devoted of wives, but was also the chief means of spreading the knowledge of and love for her husband's creations. His first year of married life was signalized by an outburst of song-writing, which gave him a place beside Schubert in vocal literature. More symphonies and chamber-music followed; the celebrated *Pianoforte Quintet* appeared in 1842 and through the enthusiasm of Berlioz made its composer's fame known in Paris. The cantata *Paradise and the Peri* had a great success at its first performance in 1843 and set the composer's thoughts in dramatic and choral directions. He began writing the music to Goethe's *Faust*, wrote that to Byron's *Manfred,* and eventually completed *Genoveva,* an opera which belongs unhappily to the category of those which contain the best possible music, but have little attraction for the mass of the public. It was written on the lines of *Euryanthe* to a libretto, which a very little deft handling

PLATE XLIX.　ROBERT SCHUMANN

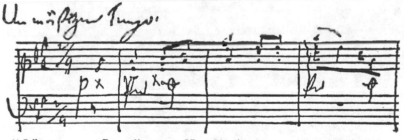

"LÄNDLICHES LIED" FROM NO. 20, ALBUM FOR THE YOUNG.

PLATE L. BRAHMS

would have made a stage success. It has moments (such as the march in Act 1) which are only comparable in depth of human feeling to Fidelio; but suffers throughout from the composer's dread of making effects for effects' sake, a dread which amounted to an obsession which led him to avoid effects altogether, however legitimate. Its inherent beauty of conception has however saved it from oblivion, and it still has its occasional moments of revival.

A disease of the bones of the skull began at this time to show itself, and though the progress was slow it was continuous and eventually affected the brain. He became more and more silent, and though far from lacking in appreciation of visits from his friends, took little or no part in the conversation. When living in Dresden in 1848, Wagner called upon him, and talked incessantly, while Schumann did not even attempt to get a word in. On leaving, his visitor said "Terrible man! one cannot get a word out of him!" and Schumann, turning to his wife, "Intolerable chatterer!" His last post was that of Capellmeister at Düsseldorf, where he remained until his brain complaint necessitated his confinement in an asylum near Bonn. There he died on July 29, 1856. His illness had not however seriously affected his creative work, for his *Symphonies in C, in E-flat* and *in D-minor* (a recast of an earlier work) all dated after the symptoms appeared, and even when in the asylum he composed one of his most beautiful themes, which Brahms transcribed outside the door and for which he afterwards wrote a set of four-hand variations, (Op. 23). It was in 1853 that Brahms arrived in Düsseldorf with a letter from Joachim, bringing with him his early pianoforte sonatas and the first set of songs. Shortly after his arrival Joachim received an envelope containing a card on which was written only "Das ist der, der kommen musste. R. Sch." "That is he who was bound to come." Shortly afterwards appeared the great article "Neue Bahnen," Schumann's swan song in the press. His literary activities ended as they began, in cordial appreciation of the work of others.

Amongst composers as such Schumann holds a first-rank position: if not a senior wrangler, he was so high in the first class as to be in the running for it; for his failure to attain the distinction his physical ailment was probably responsible. As a human being he was one of the noblest specimens in musical history — neither withholding his warm approval of the work of his fellows, nor resenting their too frequent lack of reciprocity.   When writing his three masterly quartets, he did not withdraw the dedication to Mendelssohn because that master said that he would be "much better employed in taking a walk" with him : on the contrary he never ceased in print and in conversation to show his reverence and admiration for him ; on one occasion, when he was entertaining Liszt at supper, and the lionized Hungarian used some disparaging expression about Felix, he rose from his chair (he was a very big and muscular man), seized Liszt by the shoulders and shook him, asked him how he dared to speak so of a great master, and stalked from the room : "a piece of bad manners," said Bendemann the painter (who was present), "but I honored him for it."   On the same occasion Wagner's comments on his future father-in-law were more biting in their sarcasm and less refined in their terms.[1]

If nature denied to Schumann the rôle of a virtuoso, and provided for him the career of a composer, it acted in precisely reverse fashion in the case of Franz Liszt (b. 1811 at Raiding in Hungary).   This extraordinary man, a mixture of nobility and charlatanry, of genius and of calculation, of high ideals and diplomatic methods, endowed with superhuman magnetism, with unfailing generosity, with supreme accomplishment and not a little humbug, practically brought all Europe to his feet before he was out of his 'teens.   He was a pianist "by the grace of God," for there is no record of any master of note in the direction of his studies save Czerny, whose influence must have been mainly technical, and whose pianistic methods he immediately outstripped.   He may almost have been said to survey mankind from China to Peru.   His sympathies were unbounded by prejudices or cliques.   He popularized Beethoven and the classics on the

---

[1] This incident was related by Bendemann to Joachim.

one hand, and Rossini, Donizetti, and the later Italians on the other. His transcriptions for piano included every master who came within his ken, and there were few, if any, who did not. After 1842, he made Weimar his head-quarters for life, where he settled as conductor of the Court orchestra, a post which he held for many years, and which he used to encourage as many rising men as he could find. When he retired from active direction, he made Weimar the center of a pianoforte school, the pupils of which have ever since permeated the artistic world. Weimar saw the production of Wagner's *Flying Dutchman, Tannhäuser* and *Lohengrin,* the last of which he produced for the first time, Joachim leading the orchestra, while its composer was still in exile in Switzerland. With equal hand he welcomed Berlioz's much-abused opera *Benvenuto Cellini,* Schumann's *Genoveva* and *Manfred,* and Schubert's forgotten *Alfonso and Estrella.* In the intervals of this strenuous work, he fre-quently visited Rome, which was his second home, and where, partly from his strong religious proclivities and partly (it was said) to avoid the restrictions of matrimony, he was ordained an Abbé. During this period he composed a great number of original works, which showed the result of his cosmopolitan interests, but which inherently were as super-ficial as they were brilliant. In writing he was always a virtuoso first and a composer afterwards. He started the principle of programme-music, which emphasized the pro-gramme at the expense of the music, producing a number of symphonic poems, which, while not devoid of poetic feeling (for that he could not fail to show), were lacking in the power of development and concentration which alone could make them live; two grandiose but unconvincing symphonies, *Dante* and *Faust;* two *pianoforte concertos,* which by virtue of their wonderful technical effectiveness still survive; a quantity of pianoforte works which are an admirable study in tech-nical writing for the instrument, and are necessities in the equipment of a player; and a series of *Hungarian Rhapsodies,* which, as the tunes were ready made for him and were red-olent of his native soil, remain his most valuable contribution to the art. In most of his work the complexion is rather artificial than natural. The deftness of his handicraft, and the world-wide experience which underlies it, cannot always conceal the rouge and the powder puff. To these meretricious developments more serious men in Germany were not blind, and a manifesto signed by Brahms, Joachim, and others in 1860 called public attention to them, and repudiated their principles and influence. This remarkable document was published prematurely and without the authority of the signatories : whether it would have ever seen the light after maturer deliberation in uncertain, but its authors fearlessly abided by their opinions therein expressed after it appeared in print. It marked the dividing line between the Wagnerians and Anti-Wagnerians and started the long war between them which oppressed Germany for a generation, and resurfaced occasionally for decades. Primarily it was not directed at Wagner, but at Liszt, whose pupil Hans von Bülow lived to become as warm a supporter and apostle of the purer school as he had been of the fascinations of Weimar. Too cultivated to be narrow-minded, and too cosmopolitan to be one-sided, Bülow, though not a composer of importance himself, is one of the most typical figures of true art in the history of the Nineteenth century. From Liszt's influence arose the exploitation of programme-music in the concert room, and the consequent confusion of dramatic and absolute music.

The fourth and greatest of the group, Wilhelm Richard Wagner, was born at Leipzig on May 22, 1813. He was also by virtue of educational descent the only one of the four who could claim that Sebastian Bach was his lineal musical ancestor, thus :

J. S. Bach
|
G. A. Homilius
|
Chr. Ehregott
|
Ch. Th. Weinlig
|
R. Wagner

Like Schumann, he began in an atmosphere of classical study, which he pursued at the Kreuz-school in Dresden. His knowledge of Greek enabled him to master the plays at first hand, and his early grounding laid the foundation of his enthusiasm for everything connected with the stage. Shakespeare, also, he read to such purpose that he soon tried his hand, when fourteen years old, at writing a tragedy himself. Weber and the *Freischütz* captured him as well, and music became an inseparable part of his scheme of life. A return to Leipzig to complete his schooling brought him in touch with the Gewandhaus concerts and with Beethoven. When at Leipzig University he found an excellent and sympathetic master in Weinlig, then Cantor of the Thomas School, who taught him counterpoint, undoubtedly upon the old Italian lines, an experience which gave him his knowledge of Palestrina and which fructified in *Parsifal*. He flew high and tried his hand at larger orchestral works, several overtures, and even a symphony, which he submitted to Mendelssohn, who took no notice of it and lost the score. In later years the parts were found and the music performed, but although showing flashes of the Beethovenian spirit, it is immature and not very interesting. In 1832 he turned to opera, writing his own libretto, a tragedy called *Die Hochzeit*. He was made chorus master at Würzburg, and wrote another, *Die Feen*. Neither opera reached the stage. In 1834 he first saw Wilhelmina Schröder-Devrient, the great soprano singer, at Leipzig, who for many years had a great influence upon him, both musically and politically. He wrote an opera on the subject of Shakespeare's "Measure for Measure," *Das Liebesverbot*, under the spell of her genius, brought it out at Magdeburg (where he had become conductor) in 1835, and had his first experience of a fiasco. He then married, and began to turn his eyes towards Paris. The book and two acts of *Rienzi* were finished when he started (in 1839) for France, taking England on his way, a roundabout journey which resulted in a stormy voyage of nearly four weeks and the inspiration of the *Flying Dutchman*. In Paris he remained until 1842, struggling to keep body and soul together, arranging other men's scores for pianoforte, fighting to get a hearing for his own, and composing his first great work of mark, the *Faust Overture*. Meyerbeer seems to have done his best to help him, but without any effect. Liszt snubbed him, when he called, which made him pen the bitter remark "Take Liszt to a better world and he will treat the angels to a Fantasia on the Devil." An odd beginning to what was to become a close friendship. He wrote many articles for the press, and submitted the draft of the *Flying Dutchman* to the Opera, which the authorities approved and gave to their own conductor, Dietsch, to set! His own music to it was written in seven weeks, a more remarkable feat than Rossini's *Barber*, when the complications and caliber of the orchestration are taken into account. He also began the consideration of *Tannhäuser*, and in the course of studying the literature of the subject, came across the legends of *Lohengrin* and of *Parsifal*. In 1842 Wagner returned to Dresden, where *Rienzi* had been accepted for production, and the opera had so great a success that it was closely followed by the *Flying Dutchman*, which did not at once make the same appeal to a public accustomed to the ways and tricks of Meyerbeer. Spohr, however, came to its rescue at Cassel, and gave it with great success four months later. Wagner never forgot his indebtedness to Spohr, who was the only leading musician in Germany who cordially welcomed him as a stage-composer. In Dresden he became Capellmeister, a post which he retained until the political troubles broke out in 1849. He produced *Tannhäuser* in 1845, not at once with success, but it nevertheless spread in time to Weimar, Munich, Berlin, and Vienna, and eventually had its terrible experience in Paris. Meantime he was at work on *Lohengrin*, making sketches for the *Meistersinger*, and beginning to touch the fringe of the *Nibelungen-lied*. Mendelssohn saw *Tannhäuser*, and characteristically praised (exclusively) a canon in the second *finale*. Schumann was far more appreciative, and made some very sound criticisms alongside his praise, foretelling with his usual deep insight the influence which the master would have in advancing German opera.

The general repertoire, however, at Dresden began to change
for the worse, and his interest in it to decline. He rebelled
against the powers that be in 1849 and had to fly the country,
taking up his abode in Zürich. Here he wrote a great
quantity of polemic literature which made him few friends
and plenty of enemies, and largely accounted for the shyness
with which his works were regarded, even delaying their
acceptance when their merits were admitted. Liszt saved
the situation for him by producing *Lohengrin* (in his absence)
at Weimar. Its success in Germany was comparatively
slow, it took nine years to reach Berlin and Dresden: outside Germany it was still slower, arriving in London as late
as 1875. He worked at the *Nibelungen*, completing it as
far as the end of the *Walküre*, and sketching *Siegfried*. A
call to London to conduct the Philharmonic concerts intervened during this period, and he spent one season in trying
to reform the orchestral style of playing, and to bring the
public back to the true reading of Beethoven and the classical
masters. For this devoted service he was badgered and attacked by nearly all the press, which was still bound by the
glamor of Mendelssohn's personality and rapid tempi, made
some close friends and a host of enemies, whom his trenchant
writings and sayings did not tend to conciliate. In London
the orchestration of the *Walküre* was completed. On leaving
England, he temporarily abandoned the *Nibelungen* for
Tristan, which occupied him until 1859. Political prejudices delayed its production until 1865. In 1859 he once
more went to Paris, and through the mediation of Princess
Metternich Napoleon III ordered a performance of *Tannhäuser* at the Opera. The intrigues against it were colossal.
Even the addition of a ballet failed to placate its antagonists,
who resented its being placed in the only possible situation
of which the plot admitted, the first Act. The failure was
as great as the opera : but it did the composer one service,
it restored his popularity in Germany, and hastened the
permission of the authorities for his return from exile.
After travelling all over Russia, Hungary, Bohemia, and the
leading cities in his own country as a conductor (which he

dubbed "a long series of absurd undertakings") he settled at Munich, where King Ludwig II invited him to reside. Here he was commissioned to complete the *Ring* and on June 10, 1865, *Tristan* was produced under Hans von Bülow's conductorship. Schnorr von Carolsfeld, the only Tristan possible at that time, died a month afterwards, and and it was not until four years later that the Vogls, husband and wife, sang in it at the first revival in Dresden. Political and musical intrigues drove him out of Munich, and he returned to Switzerland after the production of *Tristan* for a stay of seven years, completing there the *Meistersinger*, (produced under Von Bülow at Munich on June 21, 1868) and nearly all the rest of the *Ring*, irritating also half musical Europe by his acrid attacks in an otherwise most valuable prose essay upon conducting. King Ludwig having abandoned the idea of building a special theater at Munich for the production of the complete *Ring* (*Rheingold* and the *Walküre* had been given at the Court Opera in 1869 and 1870), Wagner turned his attention to Bayreuth, where the town authorities lent him every help, and he migrated to there in 1872; the foundation stone of the Festspielhaus was laid on May 22, 1872, and funds for its completion were raised all over Europe and America. In 1874 he finished the *Götterdämmerung* and on August 13, 1876, the house opened with three cycles of performances. Financially it was a failure in its first year, artistically it was an unquestioned success: so great, in fact, as to assure a monetary success also on practically all subsequent occasions. A less polemic attitude on the part of the composer would probably have prevented even a temporary set-back: but "he was ever a fighter," and could not help steeping his pen in gall. He came to London in 1877, and conducted a series of concerts from his works, which helped in a small degree towards diminishing the deficit. He was now at work at his last and in many ways his greatest work, *Parsifal*. It was produced at Bayreuth in 1882, and thereafter the theater, which had lain fallow for six years, became the center of an almost annual pilgrimage. Wagner died at Venice (in the Palazzo Vendramin) on February 13, 1883.

His life was one of the most stormy in musical history:
but for many of the hurricanes, he was himself responsible.
Like some other great men he had two strongly marked sides
to his character, and recalled that immortal double personality "Dr. Jekyll and Mr. Hyde." On the artistic side reams
could be, and have been, written, to prove his undoubted
wealth of conception, and strength of purpose. Like Bismarck, he set out to reach a certain predetermined point,
and did not care whom and what he trampled on in the
process. It was not in his nature to be satisfied with his
own ideals and to work for them without disparaging the
work of others as well. The main fact is that he got what
he wanted, and what German art wanted also, and this will
be remembered of him when his smaller-minded diatribes
are forgotten. If little dogs snapped at him, it might have
been wished by his admirers that the big dog had passed
them by (as he could well afford to) without a snarl. For
such developments in absolute music as have taken place
since his day, and of which he saw the beginnings, he had no
sympathy at all. He deprecated the intrusion of stage
methods into the concert room, and pointed his remarks by
lashing Berlioz for setting the example. It is a pity that his
warnings to his disciples and imitators have fallen upon
stony ground. He never mixed the two ingredients himself,
and even his overtures are, one and all, intelligible pieces
of musical design and effect, which would make their appeal
without the adventitious assistance of a title or an analysis.
It is curious, but not surprising in a man of his character,
that what he condemned in Berlioz, he tolerated, obviously
from personal motives, in Liszt, who in this respect was a
far more dangerous sinner against his principles than the
Frenchman.

Concerning Wagner's personal relations and private life,
it is happily unnecessary to dilate. His autobiography (a
possibly Bowdlerized version of the original), his published
correspondence with Liszt, and the numerous other books
which throw a light upon his character, supply sufficient
material to enable their readers to form an opinion for

themselves.   Perhaps the best advice to them is to ignore the Hyde and to study the Jekyll: and on the whole question to approach the matter in the same spirit as Sheridan's lovers in *The Critic* summed up their emotions:

> "Well, if we must, we must; and in that case
> The less is said the better."

The followers and imitators of Wagner have been legion. But from a general standpoint it would appear that the great outburst of German activity on the stage, which began with Gluck, ended for the time with Wagner: at any rate it cannot be denied that no German successor of the first caliber has appeared since 1883.   The same may be said of the realm of instrumental music in Germany since the death of Brahms in 1897, though he left still fewer imitators behind him.   Johannes Brahms was born in Hamburg on May 7, 1833.   He was of Low German stock.   The name is the same as the English Broom, or to give it its glorified form, Plantagenet.[1]   He also descended (educationally speaking) from Bach, as well as from Mozart: the genealogical tree shows also the connection of Beethoven with the race:

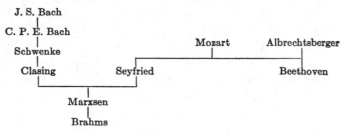

Brahms began his musical studies with Marxsen when only 12 years old, and received also a sound education in general literature.   He began his public career by touring as an accompanist with Réményi, a somewhat showy Hungarian violinist, whose playing, however, of his national dances infused the young man with an enthusiasm for their quality which influenced his work for the rest of his life.   In the course of his wanderings he came across Joachim, who

[1] Planta genista is the botanical Latin for the broom.

PLATE LI. BRAHMS

PLATE LII. FREDERIC CHOPIN

FROM PRELUDE IN E MINOR, OP. 28, NO. 4.

at once saw his great gifts, invited him to Göttingen, and
sent him to see Schumann at Düsseldorf, with the result
related above. Schumann's illness inspired him with one
of his greatest creations, the second movement of the *German Requiem*. He fell in also with two men who became,
with Joachim, his most powerful champions, Hanslick, the
critic of the "Neue Freie Presse" at Vienna, and Stockhausen,
the singer. After Schumann's death he accepted an en-
gagement at Detmold, where he buried himself in work, and
wrote a great number of important compositions with which
he emerged to public view in 1859. He visited both Liszt
and Wagner, and got well snubbed for his pains; Wagner
saying that he had no humor, an opinion which it would
have been equally true to give about Sydney Smith. Vienna
exercised its usual magnetism upon him, and he eventually
settled there for life. His record is one of quiet and most
uneventful hard work. He did not lay himself out to capture taste with eccentricity or theatricalism and was un-
failingly loyal even to those of his contemporaries who were
least sympathetic in their attitude to himself. He occasionally travelled in Italy, but never visited France or England, in spite of the many invitations which were showered
upon him from the latter country, where his music was as
much beloved as in his own. He discovered one composer,
Dvořák, and set him on his feet. He hated being lionized, a
quality which explained the comparatively restricted number
of his personal friends, and the devotion of those he had.
His compositions were not so numerous as those of Beethoven and Schubert, the two masters whom in symphony
and song respectively he most resembled: but their caliber
was big, and their contents finished *ad unguem*. He wrote
four symphonies, the greatest since the immortal nine, and a
quantity of chamber and orchestral music, besides pianoforte works which had a most individual technique and
texture. His vocal writing was not (except in his songs)
altogether free from uncouthness, and therein he resembled
Bach rather than Mozart. With opera he had nothing
active to do, though he had a great admiration for the opera

as an institution, and always tried (like Mendelssohn) to
get a libretto which would appeal to him, an effort in which
he never succeeded. His *German Requiem* (written in
memory of his mother) has made the round of the world, in
company with a work of smaller proportions but equal value,
the *Song of Destiny*. Of him it may be said, "Happy is the
man that has no history," for his life is summed up in his
immortal works. Hans von Bülow, who became his most
ardent champion, dubbed his first symphony "The Tenth,"
and formulated his famous musical "credo," which has been
crystallized into "the three B's," Bach, Beethoven, Brahms.

Contemporaneously with the first four of these great per-
sonalities, there appeared a romantic figure from Poland,
Frederic Chopin (b. March 1, 1809, near Warsaw), who
had a great influence upon and fascination for them all. His
father was a Frenchman. He studied with Joseph Elsner,
the director of the Warsaw School of music, and set out at
the age of nineteen to conquer Europe with his pianoforte
playing, backed by a number of amazingly original compositions for his instrument. He took Germany, France, and
England by storm, eventually taking up his abode in Paris.
He may be said to have invented as new a technique for the
pianoforte, as Domenico Scarlatti did for its predecessor a
century before. He hit the exact mean between sentiment and
sentimentality, having a sufficiently sound basis of technique
to prevent his more romantic moments from becoming too
saccharine. His time in Paris coincided with that of George
Sand, Alfred de Musset, Berlioz, and Liszt, the last of whom
profited throughout his career as a composer by the style
of his more original contemporary. He died early (in 1849),
leaving practically nothing except piano music and some
songs, but a name which will endure.

A few words may be spared here for two composers, neither
of them sufficiently lofty to be regarded as pinnacles of German art, but both eminent enough to rise well above the
level plain of kapellmeisterdom. These are the song-
writers, Carl Loewe and Robert Franz.[1]

[1] See page 358.

Loewe (1796–1869) was born at Loebejuen between Halle
and Cöthen. As a boy he sang in the choir at Cöthen, and
afterwards entered the theological faculty of Halle as a
student. But the greater part of his long life was spent at
Stettin, where he served the municipality as Musikdirector
and the church of St. Jacobus as organist. He travelled a
great deal in different parts of Europe, going so far afield as
Austria, England, Sweden, Norway, and France. In 1866,
under pressure, he resigned the position which he had held
at Stettin for over fifty years, and retired to Kiel, where he
died. He appears to have had something abnormal in his
constitution, if we may believe the tale that he was once in
a trance for six weeks.

Besides writing three technical works on singing and
church-music, he composed five operas (one of which was
performed at Berlin in 1834) and a large number of sacred
works. He had a special fondness for the unaccompanied
style of choral composition. But his one solid title to remembrance is his songs and ballads. All of these are earnest, musicianly works, and some are a good deal more than
that. He reached his high-water mark in the two ballads,
Edward and *The Erl-King*. The latter is a masterpiece,
dramatic and "telling" to the last degree, totally different
from Schubert's setting, yet equally picturesque and vital.
To have written it when Schubert appeared to have said the
last word on the subject is an achievement almost unique
in music.

Franz (1815–92) was born and died at Halle. He blossomed somewhat late. It was not until 1843 that his music
began to be noticed. In that year he published his first set
of twelve songs. These attracted Schumann's attention
and he, with characteristic kindness, encouraged the young
composer by an article in the *Neue Zeitschrift* (July 31).
Praise from such a pen naturally secured for Franz wide
recognition, and his work was welcomed both by Liszt and
by Mendelssohn. But, for all that, he suffered a good deal of
neglect, partly, no doubt, owing to his own timid disposition; and it was only after a considerable struggle that he

eventually climbed to the position of Königlicher Musikdirector at Halle. Already in 1841 there had been signs that
his hearing was not perfect. During his middle life this
weakness increased, accompanied — or perhaps caused —
by certain other disorders. By the time he was 53 he had
become totally deaf. Inability to work brought in its train
harassing pecuniary troubles. From the latter he was
rescued in 1872 by a fund and a series of benefit-concerts
which were instituted in Europe by Joachim and Liszt, and
in America by Otto Dresel, S. B. Schlesinger, and B. J. Lang.

The latter part of Franz's life was largely spent in editing
and arranging the works of the early masters for public
performance. On this subject he became an authority, and
he embodied his ideas in two literary works, the better
known of which is his *Open Letter to Eduard Hanslick* (1871).
He specialized on Bach and Handel, particularly the former. This is not the place to discuss the many interesting
questions that arise when a modern musician attempts to
supply substitutes for obsolete instruments, orchestral
wind-parts from an organ-sketch, and counterpoint from a
figured (or even an unfigured) bass. Suffice it to say that
Franz labored in a conscientious manner according to his
lights. He did not see eye-to-eye with the purists of the
Spitta school, and he had the disadvantage of working before the revival of the Bach Trumpet, the Oboe D'Amore,
and some other obsolete instruments of the eighteenth century. He was better on the contrapuntal side than on the
orchestral. In the latter field his enthusiasm often prompted
him to present Bach in modern clothes, and to conceal the
system of "orchestration in blocks" which was characteristic of the man and of his time.

As a song-writer Franz occupies a high place. He published 45 sets, making 257 songs in all. In the main he
continued the Schubert tradition without striking a distinctively new note of his own. This differentiates him from
Brahms. He had neither the dramatic force of Schubert
nor the burning intensity of Schumann. A certain timidity
and simplicity, a want of elasticity and passion are charac-

teristic of his style. On the other hand, he always shows a refinement, a certain admirable reticence, and a striking clarity of musical phrase. His successes only came occasionally. But when they did come they were amply deserved.

In England creative music was still suffering from the extinguisher applied by Handel, and later from the immense popularity of Mendelssohn. Nevertheless it was showing signs of life. William Sterndale Bennett (b. 1816), although always under the spell of his German friend, had an English touch of his own, which was conspicuous in his overture *The Naiads* and *The Wood Nymphs* and in such movements as the *Barcarolle* from the *4th Concerto*. It was a gentle stream, not a mountain torrent; but it reflected the quiet atmosphere of the English countryside. The most powerful of the English writers was Samuel Sebastian Wesley, the son of Samuel Wesley, who was a prominent champion of Sebastian Bach. S. S. Wesley (b. 1810), although exclusively devoted to Church music, had a genius for choral writing, and a grasp of new harmonic effects which were new to his day. His two anthems, *The Wilderness* and *Let us lift up our heads*, although written to suit the limited conditions of a Cathedral service, show an independence of thought and a mastery of climax which was well above the heads of his listeners. He was little touched by the Mendelssohn fever, and preserved to the full the traditions of his own country. It is not a little interesting to note that he aroused the interest of Liszt, whose name figures in the list of subscribers to his collected works. He proved that the spirit of Henry Purcell was not dead in England, and was one of the first extemporizers of his day.

T. A. Walmisley (1814–56), a contemporary of S. S. Wesley, was Professor of Music at Cambridge, and in his way rivalled his colleague in brilliancy. He was a devoted student of Bach, and as early as 1849 had mastered and disseminated the beauties of the *B-minor Mass*. His eight-part *Service in B-flat* is a masterpiece of English choral writing; and he prefaced it with a modest admission of his debt to the great church writers of the past, which contrasts very favorably and markedly with the famous diatribe which Wesley prefixed to his *Service in E.* Walmisley's part-song *Sweet flowers, ye were too fair* is one of the best specimens of its kind.

Robert Lucas (de) Pearsall (1795–1856) did yeoman's service in keeping alive the spirit of the English Madrigal School. He wrote little else but unaccompanied choral music, but his work can bear comparison with the best of his predecessors, both in style and in technical finish.

With the name of M. W. Balfe (b. 1805 at Dublin) and of Vincent Wallace (b. 1814 at Waterford), two composers of light opera not without a certain popular attractiveness and melodic grace, and of George Alexander Macfarren (b. 1813), a composer of great learning and erudition, who composed several light operas which had success, and some oratorios which had not, but who will be remembered as one whose mind (like Henry Fawcett's) triumphed over matter, for he too was blind, and as a patriotic worker for the English School, the record of England up to 1870 may be said to close.

CHAPTER 16

Nationalism. Modern Schools

"NATIONALISM" is a word awkwardly formed to express an idea the world found by the 18th century's end. Or rather it puts into eleven letters the *consciousness* of that idea's value to humanity. The thing itself has always existed. Chaucer was a nationalist: Scott was a nationalist. Neither of them would be alive today but for that one element in his art. But it may be questioned whether either of them would have admitted the possibility of this special immortality. Its bedrock-importance had not been agreed on or even discussed.

Most of Chaucer's literary life was spent in translating dull and artificial French verse. To his contemporaries he was "le grand translateur." Nobody reads his translations now, except under compulsion. Scott posed as a great mediævalist. He lived physically and mentally in a sort of museum. Every few months he invoiced and delivered to his patrons a selection from his stock of knights and warriors, crusaders and feudal barons; none of whom had any more vitality than Chaucer's French ghosts. Yet Scott was and is one of the greatest nationalists that ever lived.

These two statements need reconciliation. Let us observe first that every great artist — whatever his necessary pretences and accommodations — draws his vitality from the men and women, the rocks, rivers, and mountains of his own country; and not from those about which he has read. The less he needs to accommodate himself to his times the more easily will he be able to express himself. But this is hardly more than a personal incident. The point is that a man can work (and dream) only with those things that are "bred in the bone." So runs the canon of the Almighty. Chaucer's French abstractions are dull rubbish for the simple reason that when he was a child he never saw French abstractions walking down the Strand; but he *did* see very perfect gentle knights, cursing innkeepers, millers, and men-at-law.

Scott in every fiber and in every drop of his blood was a border-peasant. And everything he has ever written about the lowly Scottish folk is read today with as much zest as when it was first printed. It does not matter in what supposed age he places these humble Lowlanders. They remain live men and women — just as much alive as Shakespeare's Warwickshire-Athenians. But when he retires to his armory and returns with his stiff-jointed glittering puppets, we guess immediately that they are lay-figures and that they are in armor precisely to disguise that fact. The same criticism applies even to Shakespeare. So long as he allows his kings, princes, and dukes to play a part in the drama as men and women, so long are they alive. But the moment they take to behaving like disembodied and de-humanized princes and dukes, that moment they become insufferable snobs and prigs and bores.

But it may be asked, why should an artist labor under this restraint? All men are human. The artist sometimes secures *inter*national recognition. Why should he not draw his vitality from mankind at large, instead of from one fragment of mankind, the nation?

That is a dream or rather a nightmare — as the latter part of the twentieth century would show us. The nation of same-speaking and same-thinking people is the largest circle in which a man can work honestly. Even that circle is often too wide. An artist is more likely to begin in some inner concentric circle from which he may possibly bore outwards to the larger area of the nation and even in a few cases to the great world beyond the nation. He may become *international*, but only by first being *national*, or rather, *local*. Stupid people often ascribe Keats's power to his "pure Greek spirit." In doing so they are merely asserting the clumsy falsehood that he was not a great poet. We know that he was. But *that* part of him came from Hampstead Heath and Box Hill: the other part he got from Lemprière.

It must be confessed that in almost every generation there are two classes of men working and talking in opposition to each other — the nationalists and the denationalists. And the artistic health and productivity of any community increases exactly with its proportion of nationalists. The denationalists almost invariably have rank, wealth, and fashion at their backs. Indeed, but for the fact that they are a race of artistic eunuchs, the other party would never make any headway. But the people who *do*, generally get in front of those who *talk*. Only, in the next generation, the contest is sure to be renewed.

Thus there is a continual war between the two sides; the crossed swords that mark the various engagements are dotted all over the map of Europe. And these battles are usually fought out on some trivial pretext that masks the real issue underneath. In this way the subject of debate is often blurred and clouded beyond recognition. But it must be remembered that underneath all this smoke and crackling of thorns the original quarrel remains burning. It is the quarrel of the creative mind with the receptive, of the originator with the imitator, of the man who loves his country with the man who loves someone else's, of the vulgar (so called) with the truly cultured (also so called), of cloth with shoddy, and sterling with Brummagem.

This conflict is *general* in its nature. It is not applicable only to one art. In the field of music the two types — the nationalist and the denationalist — are clearly defined; though it must be said that the latter is almost always the product, or rather the victim, of his social surroundings. A man of this sort often begins with great natural talent. And if it were possible for him to exercise that talent *in a vacuum* he would no doubt achieve much. But he does not live in a vacuum. He lives on a closely packed planet throbbing with the highly developed and strongly differentiated groups of men which we call *nations*.

Let us say, he goes to Germany — the country whose technical proficiency is beyond question. There he masters all that the Germans can teach him. But when he returns home he does not set himself to answer any of the deeply important questions which we have already mentioned in discussing folk-song.[1] He does not ask himself whether after all his musical attainment is merely a brilliant sleight-of-hand which anyone can pick up with cleverness and application. He does not say, "I have learned so and so from the Germans; how did *they* learn it?" He accepts the German art of his day as a boy accepts a Christmas present of a box of conjuring tricks. He never honestly knows *why* the tricks are done, and so is never able to invent a new one. And in time the old apparatus, now worn smooth from constant use, begins to show the cogs and springs inside.

A man of the other type may go to Berlin or Vienna. He may learn there the Prussian and Viennese tricks as developed to suit the German hand. But when he returns home he begins to ask himself those very questions whose existence the cultured denationalist ignores to his dying day. He does not bring out his box of mechanical German toys and start them working merely to astound the natives. He may carry home with him a considerable knowledge of mechanics. But he brings home something more — the determination to build and run a steam-plough. And, as no one but a drunkard would try to drive a plough with the plough-share in the air, he puts it in the soil — the soil of his own native land.

We have made this comparison at some length for two reasons. In the first place, no lesson is more needed in England and America than the lesson of nationalism. Only by a fearless belief in itself can a people hope to possess an honorable music. And in this matter every single person who reads these lines is in some measure personally responsible. In the second place, the study of this force — nationalism — is interesting because it was the cracker that caused two or three slow fires (still burning in the musical world) and at least one big explosion.

[1] See pages 208–9.

We now intend to show how the consciousness of this new force helped to found or to develop some of the modern schools of composition. Taken "by and large," its effect was to *awaken* half a dozen nations to the possibility of imitating — not the German music — but the Germans. Hitherto they had either had little music of their own or had been mere translators of the Teutonic idiom. Now they proposed to pay Germany the compliment of adopting her national motto, substituting their own country's name before the *über alles*.

With the space at our disposal we cannot pretend to detail the application of this force in every case. But we can show its results in a rough general way by offering the reader groupings of the composers' names, and then indicating the various tendencies which these names connote.

If we take a bird's-eye view of these movements from about 1870 to the year 1920 we shall see at once that no two of them coincide artistically. This was to be expected from the very nature of the subject. But chronologically we can distinguish in the larger nations three groups of composers. First, a group whose pressure was exerted from about 1870 onwards. The members of this group were mostly born between 1840 and 1850.[1] Next, a group whose activities began between 1885 and 1890. And last, a group of twentieth-century men. To these three groups we shall generally prefix in brackets the name of some elder musician who — himself outside the period — may be looked on as the forerunner or inspirer of the newer movements.

The dates must not be pressed too closely; though they coincide with surprising exactness. Furthermore, they must be noted for what they are — "beginning" dates. The older men do not "down tools" because their apprentices are put on the pay-sheet. Very often they have combined the rôles of teacher and learner, or at any rate of teacher and observer. And the results have in some cases been little short of marvellous. A man like Saint-Saëns simply cannot be forced into the cramped dimensions of a catalogue.

[1] In the American list the composers are all a little later and do not fall so clearly into groups.

And what is one to do with Verdi, who spent the first fourteen years of his life as a contemporary of Beethoven, and outlived Tchaikovsky by eight? Finally it must be said that we have selected only a few representative names. The chief object of these groupings is to show national tendencies; and therefore the exclusion of many living composers' names is to be explained solely by the necessity of abbreviation.

GROUP	RUSSIA (Glinka)	ENGLAND ———	AMERICA (Paine)
1st	Balakireff Cui Moussorgsky Borodin Rimsky-Korsakoff Tchaikovsky	Sullivan Mackenzie Parry Thomas Stanford Cowen Elgar	Foote Chadwick Stillman Kelley
2nd	Liadoff Tanieff Arensky Glazounow	Delius Bantock MacCunn Wallace German Smyth (Miss) Somervell Davies McEwen Jones Monckton	Sousa Herbert MacDowell Parker Loomis Loeffler Beach (Mrs.)
3rd	Rachmaninoff Kalinnikoff Scriabine Stravinsky	Coleridge Taylor Holbrooke Hurlstone Vaughan Williams Scott Bridge Dale Bath	Converse Hadley Farwell Smith

RUSSIA

Russia is grouped with England and America for purposes of comparison. In many ways the two types of musical civilization — Slav and Anglo-Saxon — are violently differ-

ent. The one seizes greedily on a new idea, sucks it dry,
and throws it away before the other has had time to cut
the rind. Present the idea of folk-song to the Russian, and
he invents almost in a day a brilliant recklessly informal
method by which to exhibit his national music. Submit
the same idea to the Anglo-Saxon, and he begins a slow and
painful search among his old formulæ for the one that
seems best fitted to act as a crutch over the rough road.
The Russian jumps to the conclusion and then away from
it: the Anglo-Saxon crawls to the same conclusion and
settles there. These two mental types are the complemen-
tary colors whose union makes white.

But there is one striking similarity between the two. Both
were then possessed of great religious zeal. And in the essentials of religion the two had both arrived at much the same
conclusion. Furthermore, the texture of art in both countries was, so to speak, shot with the colors of religious emotion. We shall not understand either race unless we grasp the
fact that its musical revival was dependent on both church
and people — sacred- and folk-song.

The first figure of importance to Russian music is indeed a
church musician pure and simple — Bortniansky, who was
born in 1751 and died in 1825. He studied with Galuppi
and became to Russia very much what Palestrina was to
Rome. But the distinction of being the first great Russian
composer and the real forefather of the national movement
belongs to Glinka (04–57).[1] He was a pupil of the Englishman Field, an enthusiastic patriot, and an untiring student
of Russian folk-music. His two chief works are the operas
Life for the Czar and *Russlan and Ludmilla*. Of these the
former is saturated with the Slavonic spirit, and has always
been venerated by the Russians as a national inspiration.
Contemporary with Glinka, but scarcely holding his unique
position, is the composer Dargomiszky (13–69) who set
Pushkin's version of the *Don Juan* legend to music under the
title of *The Marble Guest*.

[1] The figures 18 are to be understood before the abbreviated dates in
this chapter.

But though the Russians during the first half of the century recognized Glinka as a national possession, the Russian school itself was hardly known to the rest of Europe. However, about 1880 certain tales began to leak out. It was said that there was a band of five national composers all working with a boiling zeal, and working directly in opposition to the German-Russian school which then held the field. These five men were externally as unlike any known school as could be imagined. In fact, only one of them could be called a professional composer in the sense in which western Europeans understand the words.

Balakireff (1836–1910) was a pianist; an ardent collector and utilizer of folk-song; and, through his personal acquaintance with Glinka, the link that connected the whole group with its founder. His influence and example fired Cui (35–1918), a major-general in the Russian service and a model of the most perfect anti-Wagnerite that has ever existed. Moussorgsky (39–81) was first a military officer, and then a government employee whose personal habits rendered him at times liable to sudden dismissal. He was a poet, a dreamer, and a sufferer. At 42 he died, leaving behind him a quantity of highly characteristic music. His best-known work is the opera *Boris Godounoff.* Borodin (34–87) was an aristocrat, a chemist and educationist by profession. In music his touch was strong and personal. His harmonies are broad and original while his counterpoint is somewhat more stringent than that of his fellow-workers. Outside Russia he is best known by his orchestral poem *In the Steppes of Central Asia.* His opera *Prince Igor,* like a good deal of Moussorgsky's music, was finished by the last member of this group — Rimsky-Korsakoff (1844–1908). This man was educated not for music, but for the navy, and held in later life the curious position of music-inspector to the Russian fleet. For all that, he was the most professional and in some ways the most nationalistic of them all. His symphonic work includes *Antar* and *Scheherezade,* and the two great *National Overtures* (one secular, the other sacred); while among his operas are *May*

Night, The Snow Maiden, Mlada, The Maid of Pskov, and *The Czar's Bride.*

The characteristic of all this group is a flaming nationalism, a defiance of traditional German methods, and, it must be said, a certain raggedness of texture, a want of cohesion, harmony, and unity. These shortcomings were just as apparent to the five composers whom we are studying as they are to us. They discussed them openly and accepted them as the necessary price of their freedom. To them, men like Seroff, Dargomiszky, the Rubinsteins, and even Tchaikovsky (40-93) were traitors. And the antagonism was not softened by the fact that the latter group gained a much easier acceptance in western Europe. Rubinstein, for instance, has always secured a tepid approval as a respectable member of the German school.

Here Tchaikovsky's position is peculiar. He had Jewish blood in him and was not so strictly national a composer as Rimsky-Korsakoff or Moussorgsky. His mind was more ordered and formal; his eyes less concentrated on one object, and therefore more able to take a wide international view of the field of music. Consequently he was the ideal instrument through which to announce the aims of the Russian nationalists to the outer world. To it he was pure Russian: to Russia he was semi-foreign. Hence comes the fact that — though he was four years junior to Rimsky-Korsakoff and contemporary with the whole group — his music appears to be of an older school than theirs. Of his individual works his six *symphonies,* his *Piano Concerto in B-flat minor,* his symphonic poems such as *Hamlet, Romeo and Juliet,* and *Francesca da Rimini,* and his chamber music are to be specially noted. Opera he wrote, but scarcely successfully. In fact, his operatic mind was about fifty years behind his symphonic.

We said above, that the Slav "jumps to a conclusion and then away from it." The second group of composers exemplifies this. For their tendency is on the whole away from the national ideals which we have just been describing. Liadoff (55–1914), eldest of the group, is chiefly known for his pianoforte works. Tanieff was a somewhat heavy theorist and Germanist of the Rubinstein type. Arensky (1861–1906) was a stronger composer than either, and made his mark with his opera *Nal and Damajanti*. The heavy-weight of this group was undoubtedly Glazounow (65-1936). He was a pupil of Rimsky-Korsakoff, but he never displayed the flaring national eagerness of his master. A certain ease of personal circumstance at some times caused his artistic aims to vacillate. On the technical side he is irreproachable. Solidity of utterance, a mastery of counterpoint that makes his orchestral work glow, and an occasional power of fantastic imagination are all to be found in his compositions. His *symphonies* and *overtures* and his ballets *Raymonda* and *The Seasons* are among his most successful works.

In the third group of composers Rachmaninoff (73–1943) was at first specially notable as a pianoforte writer. He studied composition with Arensky, and besides three or four operas had published fifty pianoforte works. Of these the most original are his series of *preludes* which have almost established a new *genre* in pianoforte-writing. But Rachmaninoff was by no means only a writer of pianoforte preludes. He contributed *symphonies*, some striking *pianoforte concertos*, and in especial the very remarkable orchestral work *The Island of the Dead*. Kalinnikoff was a man of great promise in the orchestral field. He wrote symphonies and symphonic poems. But his name is to be added to the list of composers who have been cut off almost before their life's work was begun. The two men who are perhaps most typical of twentieth century Russia are Scriabine (72–1915) and Stravinsky (82–1971). The former, a pupil of Tanieff, is associated in a not particularly Russian way with the ultra-modern developments of harmony. The latter first gained a somewhat broader reputation from his ballets, such as *Petrouchka* and *The Bird of Fire*. In these interesting works he shows a very original vein of musical creation and a complete command of orchestral expression.

ENGLAND

The national awakening in England is known there as the "*re*naissance," a convenient term which shows the movement not as a beginning, but as a resumption of national endeavor. England has no Glinka. For more than 150 years after Purcell's death (in 1695) the energies which might have been expended on secular music were devoted to the one object of eating up as much of the world as she could. Though this was an undoubtedly if temporarily successful exercise, it had the effect of drastically narrowing the concerns and interests of most of all classes of Englishmen in the period. As the Germans composed, the English conquered and claimed. In the lower stratum of this atmosphere, folk-song and a few semi-cultivated kinds of folk-song contrived to flourish : in the upper, music was contemptuously tolerated only so long as it was *expensive* and *foreign*. As a subject worthy of a gentleman's serious interest, we may see how it stood by turning over the pages of Boswell's *Johnson*. Even Macaulay — whose specialty was omniscience — could write a history of James II's reign without discussing Purcell.

This type of mind which assigns to musicians the status and rewards of a mountebank was universal in England. It is now something less than universal. But it would be a gross untruth to say that even now two Englishmen of equal ability could meet with equal success, if one of them was a musician. To the educated Englishman, a savant who deals with Greek manuscripts is a scholar (and a gentleman) : one who deals with musical manuscripts is a scholar (*but* a musician). If he is a symphonist he is wasting his time pitting himself against his superiors the Germans. If he writes opera he has overlooked the fact that it can't be sung in such a "vulgar" language as English. And whatever he is doing — symphony, opera, or chamber-music — he would be much better employed in the army, navy, or police forces.

This is the average line of the Englishman's thinking. And though there was a considerable difference between the social conditions of Dr. Johnson's day and those of 1870, we must not be surprised to find that the English school had to begin small. The names of the seven musicians who first tried to haul down the double-eagle and to bend on in its place the signal "England expects" are Sullivan, Mackenzie, Parry, Thomas, Stanford, Cowen, Elgar. Of these seven all luckily received their first musical training in Great Britain. Sullivan, Mackenzie, Thomas, and Cowen studied at the Royal Academy of Music. Stanford learned most of his business (except counterpoint) in Ireland. Their most impressionable years were thus spent in their native country. But they all followed up this earlier period with shorter or longer courses of continental study — much in the way that the best French composers have gone to Rome. In some cases — for instance, Parry and Elgar [1] — this period of foreign study and observation amounted to almost nothing. It is curious to note that Goring Thomas, the only one of them who wholly escaped the Teutonic influence, capitulated much more completely to the French traditions than they did to the German.

In judging the output of these men we must remember one important fact. They are not artistically analogous to Moussorgsky and Co., *but to Glinka.* They had to clear the forest and break the ground. And the difficulties of doing this in the stiff soil of England were enormous.

Sullivan (1842–1900) was one of the children of the Chapel Royal, then a student at the Royal Academy, where he was the first holder of the Mendelssohn Scholarship — a travelling prize similar to the *prix de Rome.* Returning to London he won early recognition with his music to *The Tempest.* But though he wrote a good deal of choral and orchestral music during his life (including the *Golden Legend* and the lively overture *Di Ballo*), it is as the musical founder of Savoy Opera that he became internationally famous. At the Savoy he set a standard of clearness, elegance, and graceful charm that was unknown before his day. He began the tradition of adequate orchestral accompaniment which has ever since been

---

[1] Elgar did some work at Leipzig. Parry was for a short and not very profitable time with H. H. Pierson (Pearson), the Anglo-German composer.

a feature of comic-opera in London.   On the æsthetic side
we owe him a lasting debt "for his recognition of the fact
that it was not only necessary to set his text to music which
was pleasing in itself, but to invent melodies in such close
alliance with the words that the two things become (to the
audience) indistinguishable." The long list of his works
begins with *Contrabandista, Cox and Box*, and *Trial by Jury*,
continues through *Patience, Pinafore, The Mikado, The
Yeomen of the Guard, The Gondoliers*, and ends with his half
completed work, *The Emerald Isle.*

Mackenzie (47–1935) was a Scotsman. He succeeded Mcfarren
(13–87) as Principal of the Royal Academy of Music.   Pre-
eminently an orchestral writer, he has a large quantity of
music to his credit.   And much of it is characterized by a
color and warmth of expression that, at the time of its
writing, was twenty-five years or so ahead of his European
contemporaries.   His *Britannia* overture, *La Belle Dame
sans Merci*, and his violin *Benedictus* and *Pibroch Suite* are
among his most played works.   A strong vein of romantic
Scottish feeling pervades a good deal of his music.   This is
particularly noticeable in the *Pibroch* and the *Rhapsodies*.
His incidental music to various stage-plays (such as *Ravens-
wood*) is admirable.   And it must be noted to his credit
that the opera *Colomba* was one of the earliest attempts of
the new English school to handle that form seriously.

Parry (1848–1918) showed the English side of the movement.
He was particularly associated in the public eye with choral
music on a big scale.   This, however, by no means exhausts
the list of his activities.   He composed much symphonic
and chamber music.   Under the heading "works for voice
and orchestra" he has no fewer than thirty-three entries.
This fertility is indeed characteristic of all the men of his
time.   Parry's work shows an extreme degree of consistence
and a constant nobility of ideal.   Sincerity is its keynote.
Nor is there wanting a certain admirable breadth and lyrical
fervor.   His best known works are *Blest Pair of Sirens,
The Glories of our Blood and State*, the *Symphonic Variations
in E-minor*, and the beautiful series of *English Lyrics.*   He

also made some work on the lines of Bach's *Church Cantatas*, looked at from the English point of view. Of these the most successful is the *Voces Clamantium* — a work which is in its way unique.

Goring Thomas (50–92) from his inherited tastes and long residence abroad became almost more French than English. He had a charming talent for melody and a great deal of natural dramatic perception. His best works are his operas *Esmeralda* and *Nadeschda*, and his cantata *The Swan and the Skylark*.

Stanford (1852–1924) is the man of widest achievement in this group. He has an opus-series that approaches 150. This includes nearly a dozen operas, seven symphonies, a mass of chamber music, several church-services that have become standard works, and more than a couple of dozen "choral and orchestral works." He approached subjects as far removed from each other as *The Eumenides*, *The Canterbury Pilgrims*, *Shamus O'Brien*, *Much Ado about Nothing*, and *The Critic*. Of all his works perhaps his *Irish Symphony* and *Irish Rhapsodies*, his choral ballad *The Revenge*, and his *Cavalier Songs* are at present most esteemed. But it may be questioned whether his *Stabat Mater* and his colossal *Requiem* will not eventually hold a higher place than any of these. An earnest collector, editor, and arranger of Irish folk-song, he always proved himself an upholder of his national artistic ideals — purity, clarity, and beauty of expression.

Cowen (52–1935) was a West Indian Jew, something more of an eclectic than any of the men hitherto mentioned. He was quite successful with his sets of *Old English Dances*, his *Scandinavian Symphony*, his oratorio *Ruth*, his suite *The Language of Flowers*, and his overture *The Butterflies' Ball*. He leans somewhat towards the lighter side of life and has been both over-praised and over-blamed. But he donated a distinct contribution towards English music.

Elgar (57–1934), the youngest of this group, reaped where the others had sowed. Cut off from his contemporaries by the circumstances of his religion and his want of regular academic training, he was lucky enough to enter the field and find the preliminary ploughing already done. His early works, such as *The Black Knight, King Olaf*, and *Caractacus*, had no great success; but with the appearance of the *Engima Variations*, the *Sea Pictures*, and the beautiful oratorio *Gerontius* he established a European reputation. After that he gave to the world among other works, the overtures *In the South* and *Cockaigne*, the *Pomp and Circumstance* marches, and the *Violin Concerto*. Neither of his two enormous symphonies would be genuinely successful. Nor can his later oratorios *The Apostles* and *The Kingdom* be said to rival *Gerontius*. Elgar is a master of orchestral decoration. His subjects, suavely indefinite, often lack distinction; but his treatment of them is strongly personal. A certain Aristidian air, a want of humor, and an inability to interest himself in English music as a part of music have combined to isolate him somewhat in the minds of his fellow-workers.

The men who comprise the second group — almost all pupils of the first group – were much less prolific; they had less of the revolutionary energy of their elders. Their technique, less decidedly German, was also a good deal more hesitating. They were less easily satisfied, less prone to take things for granted. But they shared the aims and ideals of the elder men; and this was the main source of hope to the English school.

Delius (62–1934) was English by birth, but Dutch-German-French by heredity, taste, and residence. For years he remained unknown to his country-men; but when the wave of nationalism began to mount high he came home on its crest. He composed a good deal of music mostly in the larger forms. *Brigg Fair, Appalachia*, the *Dance Rhapsody*, and the *Mass of Life* may be mentioned. His operas *Koanga* and *A Village Romeo and Juliet* received no success. Bantock (68–1946) was a Londoner and one of the strongest upholders of the English cause. He succeeded Elgar as Professor of Music at Birmingham University. Among his works are *Omar Khayyam, The Pierrot of the Minute, Sappho*, and *Fifine at the Fair*. MacCunn (1868–1916) made his name early with his symphonic poems *The Land of the Mountain and the Flood* and *The Ship o' the Fiend.* But most of his life was devoted to writing Scottish Opera (e.g. *Jeanie Deans* and *Diarmid*) and he had to pay the penalty of his connection with this musical Cinderella. The brilliant promise of his youth was never perhaps wholly fulfilled. This was only to be expected in the bitterly unpatriotic circumstances of the English musical stage. But by those who are familiar with these conditions his talents will always be held in kindly remembrance.

Wallace (61–1940) was a man whose mind had many facets. Besides being a composer he published two poetically philosophical books on music.[1] He was the first British composer regularly to write symphonic poems. His *Sister Helen, Beatrice, Pelleas,* and *Villon* are much played. Wallace's work, whether musical or literary, all bears the hall-mark of his vivid personality. German (62–1936) succeeded Sullivan at the Savoy, and had to his credit such works as *Merrie England, Tom Jones,* the *Henry VIII* and *Nell Gwynne* dances, the *Welsh Rhapsody,* the *Gipsy Suite,* the overture to *Richard III,* and the *Rhapsody on March Themes.* Miss E. M. Smyth (58–1944) was the amazingly Teutonic and forceful composer of the operas *Fantasio, Der Wald,* and *The Wreckers.* Somervell (63–1937) is best known for his graceful

---

[1] The English Renaissance men were accompanied and illustrated by a surprisingly wide *literary* movement. Almost for the first time since the days of Burney and Hawkins the English instigated an investigation into musical æsthetics and a systematic search in their own cathedral, college, and secular libraries. The existence of a vast store of madrigals, of church and instrumental music was scarcely suspected even by the professional musicians; and the treasure when unearthed came as a revelation to musical England. Little by little the worst features of continental indifference all disappeared and, with its disappearance, the English are taking a proper pride in their very considerable achievements. Among the many men who have written on this and allied subjects we shall select for mention the names of Sir George Grove, Sir Hubert Parry, Fuller Maitland, Barclay Squire, H. E. Wooldridge, Henry Davey, Ernest Walker, W. H. Hadow, E. J. Dent, Ernest Newman, Edward Dannreuther, D. F. Tovey, J. B. McEwen, Ebenezer Prout, Frederick Corder, Stewart Macpherson, Percy C. Buck, and Robin Legge. Among the pure antiquarians are Miss Schlesinger, E. J. Hipkins, and F. W. Galpin. In the special field of Greek music D. B. Monro first showed that it is not an essential of this study that the reader should have the sensation of swimming in glue. He has since been followed by H. S. Macran, Cecil Torr, Abdy Williams, and Wright.

songs and song-cycles, such as *Maud*. For some years he served as the official main-spring which keeps the clock of elementary musical education ticking. Charles Wood (66 –1926) was an Irishman, one of the soundest theorists in the country. His musical output is small, but its quality is fine and scholarly. He took a strong interest in folk-song, and composed a set of orchestral variations on the tune *Patrick Sarsfield.* In the realm of choral-music he achieved one or two successes such as his *Ballad of Dundee.* He had at least one admirable song to his credit, "Ethiopia saluting the colors." Walford Davies (69–1941) was a cool-blooded churchman of a very refined type. He utilized his talents to great advantage in his delightful work *Everyman.* McEwen (68 –1948) was the composer of a good deal of chamber music all characterized by a severe self-criticism, impeccable workmanship, and at times a certain curiously Scottish exaltation. His quartets in A-minor and C-minor are excellent. Of his symphonic poems, the Border Ballad *Grey Galloway* can hold up its head in any company. Stanley Hawley (1867–1916) specialized in the field of music for (spoken) recitation. He published over fifty of these com-positions, many of which show an alert and sympathetic sense both of music and poetry.

Finally, the names of Sidney Jones and Lionel Monckton must be mentioned. These are the two men, who, in prac-tice, kept vital the Sullivan tradition in London and made musical comedy there the "top-thing." Jones shone in a certain type of quaint and sparkling melody. He com-posed more than one extended finale well worth putting beside the masterpieces of the French school. Monckton was a tune-writer pure and simple. But his tunes have great variety. Some of them are in their way perfect. Vigor, lightness, originality, and formal balance are their best characteristics. He and Harry Lauder will probably be discussed scientifically by the Folk-Song Societies of the long-distant future.

In the third group, Coleridge Taylor (1875–1912) stands somewhat by himself. Half African by blood and very strongly influenced by the genius of Dvořák, he shows in his best work a warmth of coloring and a rhythmic insistence that are not at all English. His mind was quick and nimble, without being either deep or enterprising. He totally lacked *direction*. Among his best works are his *Hiawatha's Wedding Feast, Death of Minnehaha* (both choral), his *African Suite* and *Bamboula Rhapsodie* (for orchestra), and his violin *Ballade* and *Concerto*.

Holbrooke (78–1958) was a man of very different stripe, a pure Londoner, a somewhat cynical humorist, and a fighter who often said what the others only thought. His *Queen Mab* is perhaps his best work; but we must also mention *The Bells, Apollo and the Seaman, Three Blind Mice* (orchestral variations), and his big modern operas, such as *Dylan* and *The Children of Don*.

Hurlstone (1876–1906) is a greatly pathetic figure in the musical history of his country. As a scholar at the Royal College of Music he gave evidence of remarkable creative gifts. Their true development was only prevented by the physical weakness which ended his career before it was well begun. To the public he was then little known. But he has left behind him a considerable quantity of music, all of a fine earnest character. These include, besides songs, eight pianoforte and nine orchestral works. He was happiest in his chamber music. Four *sonatas*, two *trios*, three *quartets* (one of which is for pianoforte and strings), a *quintet* for pianoforte and wind-instruments, the *English Sketches*, and some other miscellaneous pieces make up his list. Most of these have been or are being published in London, and the public is now better able to appreciate its loss in the composer's early death.

Vaughan Williams (72–1958) was the man most closely allied with the national movement. Folk-music was to him a vital thing, not a toy. He employed it in almost all his orchestral work. His two symphonies, *The Sea* (choral) and *London*, are musical landmarks. Besides these, he composed *Norfolk Rhapsodies, In the Fen Country, Harnham Down, Boldrewood* (all orchestral), *Five Mystical Songs* (baritone, chorus and orchestra), the cantata *Willow Wood* (baritone, female chorus, and orchestra), and the six songs *On Wenlock Edge* (tenor voice, string quartet, and pianoforte). Cyrill Scott (79–1970) was the Narcissus of this group. But he often waited too long; and so caught only a distorted image of himself in the troubled water. His early work *Helen of Kirkconell* (baritone and orchestra), his *Aubade,* and his later *Pianoforte Concerto* may be mentioned. Gustav Holst (74–1934)– who was an Englishman for all his name — composed a good deal of music, orchestral, choral, and operatic; most of it on the large-scale modern pattern. His greatest successes were achieved with his Moorish tone-poem *The Street of the Ouled Nials,* the extraordinarily popular orchestral suite *The Planets,* and also with his elaborate works for voice and orchestra, such as *The Mystic Trumpeter* and *The Cloud Messenger.*

Frank Bridge (79–1941) was unrelated to Sir Frederick Bridge. He was a man of great technical resources, but he kept his technique as a means to an end. Among his biggest orchestral works are *The Sea,* the *Dance Rhapsodies,* and the symphonic poem *Isabella* (after Keats). He composed a great deal of chamber music, chiefly for strings, and has been particularly successful in the later revival of the *fancy* or *fantasy* form. His *Three Idylls* for string quartet are excellent. Dale (85–1943) was the chief representative of the chamber music school, and the author of a very remarkable *Pianoforte Sonata in D-Minor.* Bath (83–1945) was the leader of the anti-gloom crusade. His gay sprightly choral-ballads *The Wedding of Shon Maclean* and *The Jackdaw of Rheims* are great favorites in England. With his name may be coupled that of Balfour Gardiner, whose straightforward unaffected objects correspond somewhat with those of the American D. E. Smith. Friskin composed much work of a very earnest and promising character. With greater luck he might have achieved higher rank. His *Quintet in C-minor* and *Fantasy-quintet in F-minor* (both for pianoforte and strings), his five-part unaccompanied *Scottish Motets* (especially the third "Give ear, O Lord, unto my prayer"), and his *Pianoforte Sonata in A minor* all deserve mention.

Among others whose achievements we have not space to detail are Bell, the author of the orchestral work *Mother Carey* and the *Walt Whitman* symphony; Gatty (74–1946), who, with MacCunn, MacLean, Clutsam, and Holst, faced suffering for his devotion to English Opera; Dunhill (77–1946), who composed much earnest chamber-music, had written a theoretical work on his favorite subject, and — like the late Edward Mason — had been always ready to encourage English art by its public performance; Harty (79–1941), known both as a composer and conductor; Bax (83–1953), the musical counterpart of the "Celtic twlight" school of poetry; and Grainger (82–1961), whose happy knack in the arrangement of folk-song made popular his talent in many countries.[1]

AMERICA

The difficulty of discussing American music *in its relation to nationalism* is obvious. Other countries may have their various assortments of ethnic groups, but America is actually built of pieces of other nations, shifted in place via land, sea or air. The enormous immigration that comes to America in waves has produced violent changes and cross-currents in the national life. Composers who packed their trunks for Leipzig in their early years expecting on their return to write music for Americans found themselves in a foreign country.

Then, also, it is difficult for a stranger to make a personal acquaintance with American music. Its literary prophets are journalistic and fragrantly damp with rose-water. The proportion of it included in public orchestral concerts would be ridiculous were it not a scandal. The writer has sat out more than one third-rate performance of a dull resurrected antique, which should have been a first-rate performance of a live American work.

[1] For fuller details of the English movement see the author's "Modern Renaissance" in *The Art of Music*, volume 3, pages 409 to 444 (New York, National Society of Music).

The American composer deserves no less. He is earnest, able, and energetic. And if he cannot count on a sympathetic hearing at home it will go hard with him. He is likely to seek out a place elsewhere just as so many European composers and artists have done in America. There should be a happy reciprocation of artistic favor and friendship. In his own country, at least, his guests should encourage and foster his art, even if at times it may imply a temporary descent from the higher branches of the tree to the lower.

The American public too can help. Its personal and financial support gives many cities fine orchestras. But it can show a more lively and personal interest in the works performed at those concerts. A tepid and undiscriminating approval of the past is not sufficient. It should demand unceasingly some representation of itself through the medium of its own composers. From this demand will spring a vitality at present lacking in many concert-organizations. The American mind is unfettered and daring; and when once it recognizes the national importance of this spiritual union with its own interpreters (the composers), it will move freely and swiftly upwards. Concert-music is not a solemn mysterious rite to be accompanied by the reading of movie score credits between corporate sponsors' advertisements. No true American who gives the matter a moment's thought will "stand for" this. He knows that it is something deeper, nobler, and more personal. And he should have his part in it *as an American.*

If we put aside the early American hymn-writers, the men like Lowell Mason (1792–1872) and William Mason (1829–1908) who exerted a happy influence on the national taste, and those of the Theodore Thomas type whose main occupation was the production of European music in America, we may fairly claim J. K. Paine (1839–1906) as the founder of American music. Both by his personal example and by his music he set a standard which it is the task of all future American composers to uphold. His music to *Œdipus Tyrannus*, his *Tempest* fantasy, and his second symphony *Spring* were among his most successful works. With his name may be coupled those of J.C. Parker (28–1919) and George E. Whiting. The former was a Bostonian, an able musician, and the composer of a good deal of admirable sacred music, such as the *Redemption Hymn* and *St. John*. Whiting — the uncle of the scholarly and interesting composer Arthur Whiting (61–1936) — is best known as an earnest organist and writer for the instrument. He was a pupil of Best at Liverpool. His compositions include a *sonata* and various other pieces for the organ, and several choral works, of which the *Dream Pictures, A Midnight Cantata,* and *A Tale of the Viking* deserve mention. Dudley Buck (1839–1909) was and is much better known in Europe than any of these composers. Following in Parker's footsteps he wielded considerable influence as an organist and choral-composer. But his easy experience in these fields sometimes led him into shocking errors of taste; and without decrying his services one may fairly say that his angle of aim from the earth was remarkably *acute*.

Foote (53–1937) was the only American-born and American-trained member of the older group. He carried on Paine's traditions. He attuned himself resolutely to write the music that pleased himself, without following the fashion of the day. His biggest works are an orchestral *Suite* and a symphonic prologue *Francesca da Rimini*. In his songs he confined himself to *poetry* and never set *drivel*. He was one of the few prominent American composers who understood the bed-rock importance of English speech and song to American musical art.

Chadwick (54–1931), though Massachusettsian by birth, residence, and position was not so by pre-ordination. He had a directness of thought, a humor, and a power of seeing himself as others see him that smack more of London or Paris than of Boston. The desperate spectacled earnestness of that virtuous town is not his. An American historian accused him of "blending classical dignity with modern passion." He is not guilty. His blend is mellower and less pretentious. And he secured it by means of a sound technique that never gives his audience a moment's anxiety. His works have been much and should be more played in his own country. Among them may be mentioned : the two *Symphonies*, the *Rip van Winkle*, *Thalia*, *Melpomene*, and *Adonais* overtures; the choral-ballad *Lovely Rosabelle*; and many songs, such as the *Song from the Persian*, the *Bedouin Love Song*, and *Sorais' Song*.

"Stillman Kelley," his biographer says, "began his terrestrial career April 14, 1857, in Wisconsin." His spiritual career he began in Germany, to which place he later returned for a course of mental massage. His big works include a *piano quintet*, a *string quartet*, a suite made up from his early *Macbeth* music, and a *New England Symphony*,[1] a work "which" — biographer again — "was successful in Germany." The real un-*kultured* Kelley is probably the brilliant composer of the Chinese suite *Aladdin*, the *Gulliver* symphony, the *Christmas Eve with Alice*, and *The Lady Picking Mulberries*. Of this Kelley his country can never have too much. He died in 1944.

Van der Stucken (58–1929) was a Texan. Born of a Belgian father and a German mother he was sent to study first at Brussels under Benoit, and then at Leipzig. His early influences include personal acquaintance with Liszt, Grieg, and Sinding. He performed a great deal of conducting — as Capellmeister at the Breslau Stadt Theatre, then for eleven years in New York, and later still (from 1895 to 1908) at Cincinnati. He held an enviable and perhaps unique position as an American who had produced his fellow-countrymen's work on the continent. His compositions include a symphonic prologue to Heine's *William Ratcliff*, many songs of a pronouncedly German flavor, music to *The Tempest*, and an orchestral work which, in view of the composer's curiously mixed nationality, one may earnestly wish someday to be prophetic — *Pax Triumphans*.

Sousa (56–1932) comes midway in age between the first group and the second. His affinities were rather with his juniors. An American of Spanish-German descent, he developed a new and striking type of march. In addition to that he

[1] Written for the Norfolk Festival of 1913.

practically introduced to his countrymen the proper organization and treatment of the military band. His work is
peculiarly American, in that it could have been done nowhere else. In most European countries the military band was
supported by ancient tradition and present-day pride. In
America it had not had these advantages. Sousa's musical
gifts may be summed up by saying that he could do one
particular thing better than any contemporary. And this is
no small praise. He is certainly one of the most distinctive
figures in the country's musical history.

Victor Herbert[1] (59–1924) was to America what Sullivan was to
England and Chabrier or Messager to France. He had remarkable powers both melodic and constructional, and good
taste, which is rare in the American theatrical world. Besides many comic operas (all of which he treated as they should
be treated, *seriously*) he has one Red-Indian grand opera,
Natoma, to his credit.

MacDowell (1861–1908) was a pupil of Raff, but a much
abler composer than his master. In America the critics
see evidences of his Scottish ancestry in his music; but to
the Englishman his mind seems rather to have been tinged
with Scandinavianism. Neither view presents MacDowell
as a whole, for he elaborated a highly personal harmony and
method of musical speech which give him his position as
one of America's most original thinkers. His three pianoforte *sonatas* and two *concertos* and many of his smaller pieces
are common artistic property all the world over. His
larger orchestral works, such as *Hamlet*, *Ophelia*, and *Launce-
lot and Elaine*, are not so widely known.

MacDowell was one of the first to put on the gloves in the
fight between African and Indian folk-song.[2] He favored
the Native; and wrote his *Indian Suite* to support his
views. (The incorporation of a Native theme, however, should
not be interpreted as an endorsement of the indigenous music.)

---

[1] Born in Ireland.
[2] The African-American folk-music was minutely studied by Krehbiel in his
volume *Afro-American Folk-Songs*.

MacDowell has been seconded by a little group of original composers, some of whom have been ready to suffer a great deal for their gospel. The eldest members of this group are Gilbert and Farwell (72–1952). The former was a tenacious thinker, with a strong patriotic cast of mind. He never, however, confined himself to the one type of music, for among his published works are a *Comedy Overture* on African themes and a suite of five *Indian Scenes* all based on Native-American melodies. Farwell was more distinctly a disciple (if not the prophet) of the prairie-school. Almost all his work — even his *Cornell* overture — is founded on Native folk-song. He has a long list of compositions with such titles as *Ichibuzzi, Owasco Memories, Pawnee Horses,* and *Navajo War Dance.* Subsequently Cadman (81–1946)) then entered the ring with his *Four American Indian Songs.* [1]

It must be confessed that one finds some half-heartedness in this movement — though that does not apply to Farwell's work. The object of the composer often seems to use his folk-song title as a literary sign-post, but to hide the actual folk-song musically. And in general this is rather more characteristic of American composition than it should be. There is a certain hesitancy and distractedness of effort. If one glances through a history of American music that details the styles of the various composers one is surprised by the continual recurrence of the words German — African — Spanish — English — Indian — French — Japanese — Chinese, and even Balkan. Sometimes two or three of these descriptive epithets are applied to the same composer.

Furthermore, a wide gulf separates the *artistic* aims of the younger men from those of the older. On the other hand, the *personal* equality that exists between the two is one of the most delightful features of American musical life. In England any such free exchange of mind is as rare as roc's eggs.

Parker (63–1919) is known throughout America as the very

[1] He also wrote Greek, Persian, Japanese, and South Sea Island songs.

distinguished composer of *Hora Novissima, Mona,* and a great deal of fine vocal and organ music. As Professor of Music at Yale University he exercised a wise and happy influence on the artistic life of the country. His leanings were somewhat towards the reserved methods which idealize the best English music. But he was not lacking in a certain vivid sense of actuality and of response to his surroundings. His music shows both spontaneity and deep consideration.

Loomis (65–1930) was a prolific song-writer and has made a particular study of music for recitation and pantomine. D. G. Mason was more particularly a chamber-music composer of an earnest and scholarly type; while Ethelbert Nevin (1862–1901) was known chiefly for his drawing-room songs and piano pieces. Mrs. Beach (67–1944) was the American counterpart of the English Miss Smyth, though unlike the latter her efforts were not directed to opera. To Mrs. Beach's name may have been added that of a very sincere song-writer, Mrs. Lang.

No account of American music would be complete without the name of Loeffler (61–1935). But it is just with regard to such a man as he that one has to face the perplexing question of nationality. For Loeffler's real place was beside D'Indy and Debussy. He was a French thinker. His compositions all show an extreme fastidiousness of taste both in melody and harmony. His mind was orchestrally sensitive to a high degree. And, in this special branch of music, he enlivened his adopted country with such works as *La Mort de Tintagiles* (after Maeterlinck), *La Villanelle du Diable* and *La Bonne Chance* (both after Verlaine), and the Vergilian *A Pagan Poem.* The same difficulties of artistic nationality confront us when discussing Strube, except that he was a German.

Of the successive group of composers F. S. Converse (71–1940) gave the world two operas, *Pipe of Desire* and *Sacrifice,* and some orchestral music in the larger forms, such as the symphonic poems *The Festival of Pan* and *Ormazd.* His work is clever, somewhat "anxious," and technically interesting.

He has by no means been forgotten. Hadley (71–1937) was a conductor as well as composer. He has to his account a large number of big symphonic works, such as his *Youth and Life* symphony, his *Hector and Andromache* overture, and his *Lelewala* cantata. Besides these he composed chamber music, songs, and comic-operas. His musical personality was governed by a lively intelligence, confident in itself and happily opposed to boredom. J. A. Carpenter (76–1951) of Chicago was a musical enthusiast of a type that was rather commoner in Europe than in America. He was a well-to-do business man, only a part of whose energy was devoted to composition—in fact, an *amateur* of music in the best etymological sense. He gained great success with his compositions, both vocal and orchestral. Some of them show a highly unprofessional daring in attack and freedom of treatment. In his songs especially he explored over a wide field. Waller, Verlaine, Herrick, Tagore, Blake, and Stevenson were all given voice by his facile, sympathetic pen.

Amongst composers of the era there is a section with which we have not dealt — a section remarkable for its alarming mental precocity. And the resulting works, one must confess, are frothily complex and often dull. They represent almost nothing in life, and nothing at all in American life. From this category we must except — as a type, we hope — the name of D. S. Smith (77–1949) who, under the best influences at Yale, at least tried to find out what there is to say before trying to say it.

On the whole, it is more difficult to catch the note of nationalism in the American school than in the English. Some composers had difficulty representing her apart from Europe. The radical elements in America may never fuse enough to present the solid unbroken surface of a national style. But there are two features in American life which point to a very probable development in its school of composition. The first is the mixture of blood which is historically known to produce strong musical characteristics. The second is the *interiorizing* and democratic habit-of-mind which partly connotes the term *Americanism*. We cannot discuss the latter point here and we do not intend to risk any problems. But surprising things happen in suprisingly short periods of time. In the last century America has produced Ives, Copland and Glass; it may soon be time for a reevaluation of her classical music.

Group	Belgium (Benoit)	Norway (L. M. Lindemann)	Sweden (Berwald)	Finland (Pacius)	Denmark (J. P. E. Hartmann) (Gade)
1st	Blockx	Nordraak Grieg	Hallström Söderman	Wegelius Kajanus	Lassen
2nd	Gilson	Sinding	Hallen Sjögren	Sibelius Genetz Järnefelt Palmgren	Enna
3rd	Lekeu		Stenhammar Petersen-Berger Alfven		

BELGIUM

A good deal has already been said about the ancient Flemings. In the first part of this book they have been dealt with as the great experimenters and teachers of musical Europe; the modern representatives of the Flemings are the Belgians. It may therefore appear strange that they should figure in a group of nations striving to express their nationality in music. But the fact is that between the sixteenth century and the early nineteenth they had been completely subjected to French, German, and Italian influences. In the second quarter of the nineteenth century Belgium — like Poland and Greece — began a struggle for *political* independence. This was achieved in 1830–31, when she became a separate kingdom. At about the same time there began a struggle for *musical* independence. And nowhere was this struggle waged with a clearer consciousness of its importance than in Belgium.

The first man to unsheath the sword was Benoit (1834–1901), the celebrated director of the Flemish School of Music at Antwerp and composer of several fine secular cantatas, such as *The Scheldt, Lucifer,* and *War.* He was succeeded, as director, by Blockx (1851–1912), a strong nationalist composer, whose chief successes have been made with his cantatas *Ons Vaterland, De Klokke Roland,* and his opera *Herbergsprinses.* Contemporary with him is the church musician Tinel (1854–1912), whose trilogy-oratorio *Franciscus* (dealing with the life of St. Francis of Assisi) is very popular in Belgium. Tinel had something in common with Elgar.

Gilson (65–1942) composed a great number of music, operas, oratorios, overtures, folk-song fantasias, and works for voice and orchestra. Of all his compositions the symphonic poem *La Mer* and the dramatic cantata *Francesca da Rimini* are the strongest. Lekeu (70–94) died the day after his twenty-fourth birthday. He therefore had time to achieve little. But what he did showed great promise. He studied in Paris; but it was under the direct influence of the Flemish master Franck, who was there the center of an earnest circle of artists.[1] Among Lekeu's best works are his *Violin Sonata, Pianoforte Quartet* (finished by D'Indy), and his *Chant Lyrique* for chorus and orchestra. In the circumstances of his great talents, his lofty aims, and his early death, Lekeu was a Flemish counterpart of the lamented English composer Hurlstone. Before leaving this school of composers we shall add to the names mentioned above those of Sylvain Dupuis, Mestdagh, Van Duyse, Lenaerts, and Vlccshouwer.[2]

NORWAY

Norway can scarcely be said to have any founder-musician of the type of Benoit. But she had, on a small scale, a Bach family of her own. These were the Lindemanns, father and four sons, all of whom were composers and nationalists. One

[1] See page 344.

[2] A national movement scarcely exists in Holland. The country is merely a musical vassal of Germany. Hol, Röntgen, and, among the later men, Zweers, Diepenbrock, and Van t'Kruys may be mentioned.

son in particular (Ludwig Mathias, 12–87) undertook the systematic collection of Norse folk-song, and so directed the attention of his fellow-countrymen to their great treasure house of music. The position of Kjerulf (15–68) is curious. He lived in a time and place where the musical conditions were primitive and almost mediæval. He was therefore able to identify himself closely with the people and — if the contradiction may be allowed — consciously to write folk-song. At the same time he was quite aware of the artistic developments outside Norway. And this gave him a second and third line of attack — the art-song of the cultivated German variety, and the concert-ballad whose existence is only partly justified by the charms of the popular lady-vocalist.

Nordraak (42–66) was a composer with a fine sensibility and a deep belief in his own country. Many of his songs are household words in Norway. During his short life of twenty-four years he did one very good deed — he advised Grieg to avoid Gade as he would the plague. Most of Nordraak's contemporaries were of the type of Hjelm, Svendsen, and Selmer — men of lath and plaster who considered that the difference between Norse and German music lay in the title.

Grieg [1] (1843–1907) himself was educated at Leipzig; but after his meeting with Nordraak he decided not to become a Gade. He used his great talent first, last, and all the time to express the simplicity and the tender poetry of his own homeland. His gifts were not broad. They were exquisite and miniature-like; sometimes gnomish like himself. He was always a *singer*, whatever instrument or instruments he was writing for. His appeal is direct and convinces at a first hearing. This is apparent in all he wrote : the *Elegiac Melodies* and *Holberg Suite* (both for strings), the two *Peer Gynt* suites, the music to *Bergliot*, the *Piano Concerto*, and the three *Violin Sonatas*.

Sinding (56–1941) had the advantage of Grieg by thirteen years — an unlucky thirteen, for it gave him time to find out what Wagner would have liked Norse music to be. He tried hard

---

[1] Grieg was Scottish by descent. The name—spelled Greig—is common in Scotland.

in a desperate and self-conscious way to get back to Norway; and his friends have always claimed for him a place as a national musician. But the plain fact is that his works were all designed with the broad easy mastery that is now a commonplace in the great German school. Consequently any national sentiment that is introduced into them is apt to get lost in a corner. Sinding was more Norse than D'Albert was English. But D'Albert was not exactly a *norm* in this matter. At his best Sinding had a fluent expressive command of his material; but his style is often marred by a stupid fussy elaboration. His best known works are his two *Violin Concertos* and *Sonatas*. Ole Olsen (50–1927) was more strictly a Norse composer than Sinding; and in this category may be included the modern song-writers Halvorsen, Winge, Baker-Sunde, and Lie. Gerhard Schjelderup was a disciple and copyist of Strauss.

SWEDEN

The Swedish folk-song has neither the richness nor the character of the Norse. It has inspired less art-music. Sweden herself, trending mainly southward, has been more susceptible to the influences of her powerful neighbor across the Baltic. Her folk-music was collected and published by many scholars, such as Geijer, Afzelius of Upsala, Drake, and Arwiddson. But down to the first half of the nineteenth century her organized music was no more Swedish than the Boston Symphony Orchestra was American. It was imported for cash.

Berwald (1796–1868) was the first man to make a move in the right direction. His music is not heard at the present day, but it drew his countrymen's attention to the existence of their sagas as a possible subject for musical treatment. More distinctively national than he is Hallström (1826–1901) who did a good deal for the Swedish school, such as it is. He wrote a great many operas, in the best of which he used the Swedish folk-song with judgment and effect. One may mention *The Viking's Voyage* and *The Mountain King*.

Söderman (32–76) specialized in the choral-ballad with orchestral accompaniment, a style of music wholly congenial to the Swedish nature.

Hallen and Sjögren (53–1918) are somewhat in the same category as Sinding — good Swedish spring-water just sufficiently colored with the Rhine-wine to be unpleasant. Both made attempts to do for Sweden what Greig did for Norway. Stenhammar (71–1927) and Petersen-Berger were home-grown operatic composers, physically pupils of the last two musicians, spiritually of Richard Wagner. Alfven (72–1960) was a classicist who burnt incense at the shrine of Brahms. His symphonies and chamber music are therefore well spoken of and not much played.

The Swedish music is disappointing. It is tepid. On the rare occasions when it is heard outside Sweden it strikes one as insincere. But, as most of it is imitative, there is a ray of hope here. The national attitude of mind must be considered. This is less based on love of German *kultur* than on fear of Russian. When the Swedes are rid of these distractions they will be able to look for inspiration to themselves and to the songs of their own romantic land.

FINLAND

Finland was for a time a satellite of the Russian empire. From its position on the *eastern* side of the Gulf of Bothnia, that would seem to be its natural destiny. But ancient association and intermarriage have affiliated it rather with the Swedes on the opposite side of the water. However — as anyone knows who has ever spoken to a Finlander — its thoughts and aspirations are neither with Russia nor with Sweden, but with Finland. The people have always shown a strong love for the natural features of their country, great pride in their language, and an abiding sense of their own nationality.

The Finlanders possess a folk-poetry of both the narrative and lyric kinds.[1] Their national epic the *Kalevala* may be

[1] See page 205.

compared with the *Iliad*, the *Nibelungenlied*, *Beowulf*, or the narrative-poems that make up the ballad-groups of the English border. They also have short poems, descriptive or emotional, which are sung to the accompaniment of the copper-strung *plucked* instrument called the *kantele*. But Finland has this special advantage: that its folk-music and poetry are still matters of common daily delight to its people.

Curiously enough the art-music of Finland takes its rise not from a Finlander, but from a German. This man, Pacius (09–91), was a rare bird of a very happy migration. He came from Hamburg and seems to have possessed the unique faculty of being able to identify himself with the people among whom he lived. His successors were Collan, Linsen, and Ehrström. Faltin, who founded the Helsingfors Choral Society, was a classicist of the German type. But Wegelius (1846–1906) and Kajanus (56–1933)—both cultured men of strong personality — asserted the national claims both on the literary and the musical side. The latter was one of the first to treat subjects from the *Kalevala*.

In the next generation there were at least four composers whose vivid interest in their national art did honor to themselves and to their country. Of these the first three are Genetz, Järnefelt (69–1958), and Palmgren (78–1951). The choruses of the first and last-named are imbued with the true spirit of folk-song. The fourth member of this group is Sibeliis (65–1957). He studied both in Berlin and in Vienna. But on his return to Finland he asserted his position as an uncompromising nationalist. In fact, he may well be quoted as a prime example of that type.[1] To him Finland owes much of her present-day musical fame. His compositions have been played all over the world. We need only mention among his best known works the suite *Karelia*, *The Swan of Tuonela* (from the *Kalevala* epic), the *Elegy*, and *Finlandia*.

Finnish music is in a healthy condition. The same spirit that fights against Russification fights for its own artistic

[1] See page 306.

ideals. And in spite of the remoteness and comparative poverty of the country it has made good progress. All friends of the little nations must wish well to Finland.

DENMARK

Denmark is not so interesting from the national point of view. Down to the middle of the nineteenth century her main aspiration was to copy the doings of her great southern neighbor. But the events of 1864 made that *kultur* less popular. Her first national composer — or rather *somewhat* national composer — was J. P. E. Hartmann (1805–1900). A man who was eight years junior to Schubert and outlived Wagner by nearly twenty, had time to make his mark. It was not a very distinct mark that he made, but at any rate he was the first Danish composer to introduce a Scandinavian flavor into his music; and it is satisfactory to record that his greatest success was made with a Danish opera on the pretty subject of *Ib and Little Christina*.

Gade (17–90), though of the same generation as Hartmann, was his son-in-law. He caught Mendelssohn's ear with a work which, characteristically enough, was not called *Ossian* but *Echoes of Ossian*. A long residence in Leipzig followed. He returned to Copenhagen in 1848 a decided Germanist, but with that politely external patriotism which caused him to give an occasional dash of "local color" to his compositions. In fact, if Parry's theory [1] of song-writing be the correct one, Gade was the wisest composer that ever lived. He left a mass of chamber, symphonic, and choral music, including a cantata *Comala* which is Ossianic somewhat in the Johnsonian sense. His *Crusaders* had some vogue after its first performance at Birmingham; but even the English choral societies have now given it up.

Not much can be said about Lassen (1830–1904). He was a protégé of Liszt and a devout follower of Wagner. He wrote

---

[1] "Composers of different nations impart the flavors of Slav, English, Norwegian, and French to their songs, but make them, if they have any sense, on the same general terms as the great Germans." *Art of Music*, page 292.

a good deal for the stage — either opera or incidental music; but he is chiefly associated with a particularly sweet type of drawing-room song. Enna (60–1938) was a much bigger man. He studied with Gade and then devoted himself mainly to operatic composition. He made his first success with *The Witch;* but after the production of *Cleopatra, Aucassin and Nicolette,* and *Lamia,* he specialized in fairy-opera based on Hans Andersen's tales. Of these he composed half a dozen, of which *Ib and Little Christina* and *The Match-girl* may be mentioned here.

BOHEMIA

Bohemian music may almost be summed up in two words — Smetana and Dvořák. It is true that the Dusseks, Kalliwoda, and Tomaschek were Bohemians by birth; but they did nothing towards the foundation of a national school. Indeed, the only man that can challenge Smetana's claim to the dignity of founder is Frantisek Skraup (01–62), whose simple songs and popular operas (such as *Dratinek* and *Udalrich and Bozena*) brought him into particular prominence as a Bohemian composer. But Smetana (24–84) was the first serious artist who consciously worked to gain that title.

In early life he came under the influence of both Schumann and Liszt, but he seems to have set himself the definite task of becoming a national composer. His best work is confined to Bohemian subjects, and he labored at these under great physical disabilities, till deafness and then complete nervous collapse ended his career. His best known works are the comic-opera *The Bartered Bride* and the series of symphonic poems *My Fatherland,* illustrating Bohemian places and events. After these come the string quartet *From my Life* — one of the most individual and haunting pieces of modern chamber music, — the operas *Dalibor, Libussa, The Devil's Wall,* and the comic-opera *The Kiss.* Smetana's nationalism, whether considered musically or otherwise, is earnest, but not quite spontaneous. If it had been, he could never have tempted fate with a first opera called *The Brandenburgers in Bohemia.* There was something literary and considered about his attitude. Consequently the music, though always suave and charming, often lacks personality.

This criticism can certainly not be made of his pupil Dvořák (1841–1904), all of whose music strikes the note of a violent egotism. The external events of his life were a sojourn in Prague, then in England, then in the United States, and finally a return to his native country. At first his music reflected the colors of Wagner's harmony. But this tinge soon disappeared. It is interesting to recall the fact that his earliest recognition came from Brahms. During his stay in England he produced his *Stabat Mater, Husitska* overture, and *The Spectre's Bride* — perhaps his best work. But he only liked the English so long as they were willing to "feed out of his hand." And by this time there were a good many hard-thinking musicians in that country. Criticism on a dull cantata, *Saint Ludmila,* apparently fixed his determination to cross the Atlantic. His stay in America was signalized by the production of the *F-major Quartet* and the *New World Symphony.* And the composition of these works was accepted by musical America as Dvořák's lesson to it in nationalism.

A great deal of misconception has gathered round this point, and it may be as well to state the facts of the case. In the first place, on the thematic side Dvořák did not generally employ pre-existing folk-song at all. Even in the works which he wrote in Europe he rarely used Bohemian melodies. His plan was rather to saturate himself with the folk-music and then to produce original music in very close alliance with its spirit. Going to America he was apparently able to repeat this process with the music which he considered most characteristic of the country — the African-American music, and that element of folk that has its origin in Ireland. Dvořák's success in doing this was beyond all question. But it was a success achieved by his wonderful capacity to absorb a new nationality and to reproduce it in its own idiom. There is not a single bar of plantation folk-song in the *F-major Quartet;* while, in the *New World Symphony,* beyond a somewhat shadowy reference to "Yankee Doodle" the only fragment of folk-music is to be found in the little G-major tune which is first heard on the flute. The opening notes of this melody are taken from the plantation-song "Swing low, sweet chariot." [1]

Dvořák's music is rated higher in America than in Europe. Its good points are a strong rhythmical basis that makes a direct and elemental appeal to the hearer; a fascinating type of melody, and a certain witchery of outline in the passage-writing. Against this we must put a glare, a coarseness, and an undeniable superficiality. Many of his works disappoint at a second hearing. Technically he was rather clever than profound. He appears to have written chiefly at the piano, and consequently some of his pieces — such as the last movement of the *New World Symphony* — are staring examples of loose, ill-considered construction. One must, however, set against this a constant and inexhaustible flow of melody. This special faculty — melodic invention — is at bottom the differentiating factor between the composer and the compiler. And Dvořák had it in much the same degree as Schubert.[2]

His industry was amazing. Even in opera, which is not generally considered his special *forte,* he has seven compositions to his credit. His only thorough-going disciple was Coleridge Taylor, who never swerved in his worship of the

[1] The information in this paragraph has been kindly furnished by Mr. H. E. Krehbiel who, from his association with Dvořák at the time these works were written, speaks *ex cathedra.*
[2] For Liszt and Chopin, representatives of the Hungarian and Polish schools, see chapter XV.

Dvořákian idiom. Dvořák had various American pupils and protégés among the younger men — none of them, one thinks, quite whole-hearted in their devotion.[1]

GROUP	ITALY (Verdi)		FRANCE (Franck)	GERMANY (Wagner)
1st	Boito Sgambati		Lalo Saint-Saëns Délibes Massenet Chabrier Fauré D'Indy Messager	Cornelius Goldmark Bruch Goetz
2nd	Martucci Mascagni Leoncavallo Puccini		Bruneau Charpentier Debussy	Humperdinck Strauss Weingartner D'Albert Wolf
3rd	Perosi Wolf-Ferrari		Ravel Schmitt	Hausegger Reger Schoenberg

At the period which we are now discussing the three great nations, Italy, France, and Germany, had attained a complete consciousness of their musical nationality. They must therefore be treated from a somewhat different standpoint. Their artistic methods are to be taken for granted; and though there are some curious interactions between them, their struggle for national musical expression may be considered as already settled. The three lists of composers given above should therefore be looked on not as the wave-crests of an uncharted sea, but as tributaries that broaden the expanse of three ancient and well-known rivers.

ITALY

The period's history of musical Italy might almost be threaded on the later life of Verdi (1813–1901). Essentially

[1] Loomis, Arnold, Rubin Goldmark, Shelley, Hopkins, Fisher.

PLATE LIII. VERDI

PLATE LIV. GIACOMO PUCCINI

it is an unexpected assimilation and adaptation of German methods to Italian needs. Donizetti (1797–1848) died when Wagner was a man of 35. Neither he nor Bellini (01–35) shows any trace of German influence. But the inimitable Verdi was keenly aware of the fact that Italian music, if it was to survive, could not stand still. Born at Roncole, he began as an operatic composer of not the highest type, became the artistic symbol of the *risorgimento*, and so passed through the mellow richness of his middle life to the artistic splendors of his amazing old age — if indeed he can be said to have had an old age.

He was bred of the people. Steeped in Italian folk-song during his youth, he never lost touch with it to his dying day. His sincerity of purpose, his immense melodic gifts, and his infallible knack of hitting the nail on the head not by calculation as in the case of Meyerbeer, but by intuition, at once gained the hearts of his people. He trained them, as he trained himself, to appreciate the greater and deeper qualities of the art as his tale of years grew and his experience widened. He resembled Haydn in his power of assimilating new ideas in old age without loss of individuality. And he is perhaps the only composer in history who wrote his greatest work when nearly an octogenarian.

His early operas, though often raw to the verge of vulgarity, are always the sincere expression of his convictions. He wrote himself, as it were, into refinement. He possessed an exceptional power of individual characterization which lent great force to his ensembles, such as the famous quartet in *Rigoletto* and the second scene in *Falstaff*. His orchestration, at first rather noisy than sonorous, became in later days a model of finesse, coupled with a force which could be even volcanic without disturbing the voice which it accompanied. His vocal writing was always that of a master of the *bel canto*. Better than any great composer since Mozart he knew the value of the human voice and its proper treatment both on and off the stage. He was exacting, but never demanded of it the impossible, or approved its maltreatment on dramatic grounds.

He wrote twenty-eight operas. Of these, twenty-two (including *Rigoletto, Il Trovatore,* and *La Traviata*) may be classified under his first period; four (*Un Ballo in Maschera, La Forza del Destino, Don Carlos,* and *Aïda*) under his second, or transition, period; and two (*Otello* and *Falstaff*) under his third, or mature, period. He also wrote a considerable amount of instrumental music, of which only one string quartet has seen the light. Of his remarkable sacred choral works, the *"Manzoni" Requiem* belongs to the *Aïda* period; the *Stabat Mater* and *Te Deum* to that of *Otello*. While fully alive to the reforms effected by Wagner in Germany he never went beyond adopting such of them as seemed to him sound for carrying out his own designs. He had no sympathy with excessive length. His practical experience taught him not to risk stage-waits. He kept the musical interest centered in the voice, not in the orchestra. He did not wholly ignore the gospel of *leit-motivs*, but he was no slave to it. For the portrayal of individual men and things he trusted to larger means of characterization rather than to short musical mottos. As a result he is never dull; and of all operatic composers he gives the least opportunity for cuts.

The man through whose mind a knowledge of the German achievements filtered to his countrymen was Boito (42–1918). His one opera *Mefistofele* was in its way a challenge and a revelation to Italy. And his influence, exerted also through the younger men and through his work as Verdi's librettist,[1] permeated the country for decades after his passing. With his name may be linked that of Sgambati (1843–1914), round whom grew up a group of absolutists and Germanists such as Bossi (61–1925), Pirani, Martucci (1856–1909), and Franchetti (60–1942).[2] These men widened the musical outlook of Italy; but none of them had, in this matter, Verdi's broad selective gifts.

Mascagni's career is almost too familiar to bear repetition.

---

[1] In *Otello* and *Falstaff*.
[2] Franchetti's Teutonism actually went the length of a complete opera (*Germania*) glorifying Germany.

Born in 1863 he won a publisher's prize while still in his early youth with *Cavalleria Rusticana,* and later drew about half a dozen blanks. Leoncavallo (58 –1919) was another "lucky strike" man. His *Pagliacci* was his third attempt at opera, and its success equalled that of *Cavalleria.* There are admirable pages in *Pagliacci* with both melodic and harmonic distinction of a properly theatrical type. But the composer was afterwards unable to recapture this mood. His flaring early success was somewhat in the nature of a disability. He also had the German Kaiser as librettist. . . .

Puccini (58 –1924) was a pupil of Ponchielli. Through five years Mascagni's senior he made his artistic success later. In every respect he was a musician of a much higher type. He had refinement, technical variety, great warmth of feeling, and a strong sense of the theater. Like all true composers he was not afraid to trust his emotions to a tune. His many successes include *Manon Lescaut, La Bohème, Tosca,* and *Madama Butterfly.* Other operas and composers of minor importance are *Andrea Chénier* of Giordano, *A Basso Porto* of Spinelli, and *Adriana Lecouvreur* of Cilea.

The two names to be mentioned in the next group of composers are Perosi (72–1956) and Wolf-Ferrari (76–1948). The former was a churchman with an official position at the Vatican, which he gained through the success of his trilogy *The Passion of Christ.* His goals were generally sound — in the main a return to Palestrina's solid style. But as Italian choral singing is somewhere near the "absolute zero" of European taste, many preliminary concessions have to be made. Wolf-Ferrari was half-German, half-Italian, and his music sounds like it. He composed some early operas: *Cenerentola, Le Donne Curiose,* and *Il Segreto di Susanna.* Of his later works a sacred cantata-setting of parts of the *Vita Nuova* and his opera *The Jewels of the Madonna* became a great success. But neither he nor Perosi can, by the ordinary standards of enlightenment, be said to approach the first-class.[1]

FRANCE

The musical godfather of the new French school was Franck (22–90), a Liégeois musician who settled in Paris and became a French citizen. He began his artistic career as an organist, and was so much absorbed in his instrument that his whole technique was affected by it throughout his life. But his position at the Conservatoire and the personal devotion which he inspired there, made him eventually the greatest power in his day's France. He never wrote an unworthy bar nor faltered for an instant in his artistic aims. He was progressive always, but within the bounds of reason. In singleness of purpose and in disregard of worldly considerations he resembled John Sebastian Bach — and that, although the conditions of Parisian life were so much more distracting than those of sleepy Leipzig. But here the resemblance ceased. He was too self-critical to be prolific; and his works, always interesting and sometimes beautiful, are comparatively few for his length of life. Among the best of these are his great *D-minor Symphony*, the *Prelude, Aria, and Finale*, the *Prelude, Chorale, and Fugue* (both for pianoforte), the *Symphonic Variations* and *Les Djinns* (both for pianoforte and orchestra).

Franck died before the days of his European fame. But, as we have already hinted, his influence was exerted not so much by his actual compositions as by the example of his simple earnest life. A band of enthusiastic young Frenchmen gathered round him and cultivated a lofty idealism which was certainly at that time a strange plant in Paris. Among these pupils were such men as Vincent D'Indy, Pierre de Bréville, and Guy Ropartz. Thus a nineteenth century Fleming established a new tradition in France, and in so doing merely repeated there what his forefathers had done in the sixteenth century and the Italian Lulli in the seventeenth. But the French school (more strictly so called) persisted.[1] Lalo was almost exactly contemporary with Franck; about fifteen years junior to the latter were Délibes, Massenet, and Saint-Saëns; and ten years later still comes Saint-Saëns's pupil Fauré. There were thus two semi-independent currents in the French river. We shall take the Belgian side of the stream first.

D'Indy (51–1931) was a Parisian born and bred. But his life showed the influence not only of Franck, but of Liszt and Wagner. A wide-minded man of somewhat radical sympathies, he was for a time of some twenty years looked up to as the live-center of French inspiration. Opera was not his chief stronghold, though he did prove himself with at least two large pieces in that kind, *Fervaal* and *L'Étranger.* His orchestral poems include *Sangefleurie, La Forêt enchantée,* and the Assyrian *Istar.*

Debussy (62–1918) was the most interesting figure of modern France. His earliest work, *L'Enfant Prodigue,* gave little evidence of the curious shadowy cast of his mind. But the influence of the English poet Rossetti turned him towards the road which he has devotedly followed ever after. The first work in which he showed the elusive and nebulous traits with which we are now familiar was a translation (or rather a perversion) of Rossetti's *The Blessed Damozel.* Later still came the orchestral *L'Après-Midi d'un Faune* and *Nocturnes;* piano pieces such as *Les Estampes, La Cathédrale Engloutie, Berceuse Heroique;* and songs such as the *Proses Lyriques.* Debussy's talent was miniature, strange, subtle, and evasive. He saw everything through a pearl-grey mist. It was scarcely an accident that his first success was made with *The Blessed Damozel;* for his atmosphere was never that of France, but of England, where a floating vapor softens every outline and turns the commonest prose into poetry.

On the technical side, Debussy's experiments in harmony and instrumentation have sound knowledge to back them, even if at times eccentricity overbalances beauty. In his

[1] For Berlioz, Thomas, Gounod, Bizet, and Offenbach, see chapter XIV.

orchestration he was a model of economy, obtaining a maximum of effect with a minimum of forces.

We have said nothing so far of his opera *Pelléas et Mélisande*, perhaps the most admired and disliked work ever written. To some it is the acme of monotony, to others the quintessence of poetry. It certainly lacks direct and convincing orchestral melody. But one must remember that Debussy's object in writing it was to do over again what Gluck and Wagner had done before him; to reform opera by getting rid of parasitic vocal phrases and restoring the drama to its proper position of superiority. And when we reflect that the composer was born in Paris two years before Meyerbeer died, we must allow him to have had some strength of mind and more good fortune.

Very little of the work of the next French school has been famous out of France; but a few pieces have made the names of Ravel (75–1937), Schmitt, and some others known. Ravel's famous *Bolero* and his pianoforte pieces *Ondine, Gibet*, and *Scarbo* are quite familiar to concert-goers. As far as one may judge, these younger men attempted to get outside Debussy's somewhat limited field of activity. In their subjects and their treatment they displayed greater freedom, and they were not merely riding his hobby-horse "the whole-tone scale" to death. Schmitt's music showed a certain spiritual alliance with the reserved style of the English school. His four orchestral sketches, *Pupazzi*, very promptly made their way across the Atlantic.

We must now return to the saluting point and pass in review some of the composers of the French school who were uninfluenced by the Franck tradition. The two chief names here are Saint-Saëns and Massenet. Saint-Saëns (35–1921) was a Parisian whose length of service and dexterity of talent were phenomenal. Like Franck he began as an organist. But he then covered more ground than any of his contemporaries, and he became famous not only as an organist but as a composer of orchestral, chamber, and operatic music. He had the eclectic interests of Renaissance man. He appreciated everything good that has ever been written and could beat most composers at their own weapons. Once (before he had heard of the English Renaissance) he even adopted the Handelian style as being appropriate to that backward country. One may add that since those days his many English friends and admirers were then able to change his views on that topic. The real Saint-Saëns was a man of a hard, polished technique, able to plan wisely without self-illusion, and to finish the work to the last nail's breadth. Less experimental and daring than Berlioz, better equipped technically than Gounod, and more powerful in gauging effects than Thomas, he possessed an astonishing faculty for making his music "come off" in performance. His aim was often just short of the noblest; but it must be said in candor that his best work showed much more the spirit of the ancient Greek than the modern French. An early supporter of Wagner, he would never be affected by his style, though he has profited by his tenets. His literary gifts are as striking as his musical endowment. In this respect he resembled Berlioz, Bruneau, and others of his brilliant compatriots. His *Danse Macabre* and his symphonic poems *Phaëton* and *Le Rouet d'Omphale* were far the best of his day. And in constructing them he never sacrificed intelligibility to "programme." Besides these works one may select from his long opus-list the *Africa* fantasia, the *G-minor Concerto* (both for pianoforte and orchestra), and the *B-minor Violin Concerto*. He has written a great deal of operatic music including the very successful Biblical Drama *Samson and Delilah*.

Massenet (1842–1908) first came into French prominence with the concert-dramas *Eve* and *Marie Madeleine*, both sacred subjects viewed from the modern secular standpoint. Since then he turned out a long series of operas on various topics and in various styles. The majority of these exhibit a thinness of texture and a rather stupid sensuality with which an Anglo-Saxon cannot pretend to sympathize. Perhaps his best works are *Le Jongleur de Notre-Dame* and *L'Esclarmonde*. But *Hérodiade*, *Werther*, *Manon*, and *Thais* must be noted. Among his orchestral works the *Scènes*

Pittoresques had been most successful. A large part of Massenet's time had been devoted to teaching composition at the Conservatoire, and he had a long list of distinguished pupils. Of these we shall mention two presently.

Lalo (22–92), Franck's contemporary, was a comic-opera writer, who made a great success with *Le Roi d'Ys*. His fiddle-concertos and his *Symphonie Espagnole* are delightful works, full of refined and haunting melody. Délibes (36–91) is best known by his charming ballets *Coppélia* and *Sylvia*, and by his operas *Lakmé* and *Le Roi l'a dit*. Chabrier (41–94) was in his way a genius — brilliant but erratic. His comic opera *Le Roi malgré lui* and his rhapsody on Spanish tunes *España* are certainly the two best things of their class ever produced. His music forecasts that of Charpentier.

Both Bruneau (57-1934) and Charpentier (60-1956) were pupils of Massenet. The former was a realist, a busy journalist, and in his music something of a slasher. His early operas *Le Rêve* and *L'Attaque du Moulin* first brought him into prominence. Since then he composed his *Messidor, L'Ouragan,* and a few others. His texts are taken from Zola and this has not been altogether an advantage. Charpentier, one of the youngest of this group, came latest into his kingdom. He was a man of one idea, but as he did crystallize that idea into the opera *Louise* the world can pick no quarrel with him on that score. The position and talents of the composer can be estimated from the common title given to his work *The French Meistersinger*.

Messager was another delightful comic-opera writer. *La Basoche* was one of his earliest successes but *Véronique* is his masterpiece. Fauré (45-1924) who succeeded Dubois (37-1924) at the Madeleine was a pupil of Saint-Saëns. His string quartet music and his songs have an elusive charm that foreshadows the later Debussy. Curiously enough he wrote the incidental music for the (spoken) production of *Pelléas et Mélisande*. Widor (45-1937) was known throughout the world as the composer of the eight massive *Symphonies for Organ* as well as the *Symphonie Romaine* and the *Symphonie Gothique* for the same instrument. Besides this he contributed a certain amount of secular music, including the very successful ballet *La Korrigane*. Dukas (65–1935) composed that much-played symphonic poem *L'Apprenti Sorcier*. The position of Madame Holmès (1847–1903) as an energetic woman-composer corresponded with that of Miss Smyth in England and Mrs. Beach in America; while Mademoiselle Chaminade (61–1944) was probably the only feminine composer in the world who never relied on the loud pedal.

GERMANY

The technical developments of modern Germany are based mainly on the achievements of Richard Wagner. But the composers of that happy musical country are able to draw their inspiration from Mozart, from Schumann, and from Brahms; at the same time recognizing sanely that the last word in art is not with any of these men. We must therefore be prepared to find that the most imposing figures of the second group — such as Richard Strauss — still built up their modern structures on the foundation laid by these men. This statement may appear questionable on a mere exterior inspection of the later "modern" German work. Nevertheless it is true. And the particular glory of the German music lies in the fact that it is a natural growth and a completely satisfactory embodiment of their nationality.

The Germans of 1900 were eclectics as far as their own country was concerned. They inherited a double patrimony — the classical and the romantic. As far as the rest of the world is concerned they were Germans pure and simple. Except in a few isolated cases there is not a trace of foreign influence. It is a big school that mirrors for us both the good and the bad sides of the German character.

The four members of the "old guard" who will be mentioned here are Cornelius, Goldmark, Max Bruch, and Goetz. Cornelius (24–74) was an operatic composer, who in his early years came under the influence of Liszt. His one great work is the deft and delightful opera *The Barber of Bagdad* which has been played thousands of times in Germany, and suggested to Wagner some points of humorous characterization in the *Meistersinger*.

Goldmark (1830–1915) was a Hungarian Jew, but his music and associations are wholly German. His greatest successes were : his opera *The Queen of Sheba;* his overtures *Sakuntala, Penthesilea,* and *Prometheus;* and his symphonic-suite *Rustic Wedding.* In addition to these he wrote symphonies and a violin concerto which is still played. Later in life he abandoned the rich oriental style of opera with which his name was connected and tried his wings in the western air. Among these extra-Asiatic flights may be mentioned his *Götz von Berlichingen, Merlin,* and his setting of Dickens's "Cricket on the Hearth" (*Heimchen am Herd*). But in all these works his genius was "brailed," if one may use the old falconer's term, by the subject. And he will probably survive as the composer of *Sakuntala* and *The Queen of Sheba.*

Max Bruch (1838–1907) cannot be classified either as a romantic or a classical composer. He had all the structural elements of form and design, with a wide vein of poetic gold running through his nature. His *Violin Concerto in G-minor* was his masterpiece. But he also produced a number of works similar to, but larger than the *choral-ballads* so popular in England. These may have been suggested to him by his residence as conductor in Liverpool. Among these big epic works are *Odysseus, Achilleus, Das Lied von der Glocke;* and (for male voices) *Frithjof, Salamis, Leonidas,* and *Normannenzug.*

The name of Goetz (40–76) sounds like an echo from the past. Yet he was the youngest of the group — and the least happy in the circumstance of his early death. High hopes were built on his few achievements, as they all showed the working of a refined and very musical intelligence. But he has left us nothing beyond his *Symphony in F* and his comedy-opera "The Taming of the Shrew" (*Der Widerspänstigen Zähmung*).

The eldest member of the second group is Humperdinck (54–1921) the devout Bayreuther who grew famous overnight by devising the algebraic formula (Wagner + folk-song + fairy-

tale) = (Success). His *Hänsel und Gretel* is an amazing
mixture of fact and fancy, invention, borrowing, adaptation,
and theft. Æsthetically it is a thing of never-fading charm
and technically a masterpiece of the (old style) counterpoint.
It seems almost libellous to say anything against a work that
has delighted millions; but one must record the fact that
outside Germany the association of the Wagnerian technique
with such a simple little story is looked on as almost criminal.
An epic on "Mary had a little lamb" would be as natural.
However, one can't "argue with an earthquake." Of
Humperdinck's other works, such as the cantata *Das Gluck
von Edenhall*, and the operas *Dornröschen, Saint-Cyr*, and
Die Königskinder, only the last has been successful.

The other post-Wagnerian opera composers — such as
Kistler (1848–1907), Bungert (46–1915), and Schillings —
seem to be more post-Wagnerian than pre-anybodyelsian.
But an exception must be made of Kienzl (57–1941) and his work
Der Evangelimann. Siegfried Wagner (69–1930) was Wagner
jun. — not Wagner II.

Richard Strauss (64–1949) was brought up like all good Germans
on a diet of Mozart, Beethoven, Schumann, and Brahms.
His *Horn Concerto* shows the earlier influence : his *Symphony
in F-minor* and his six-part *Wanderer's Sturmlied* the later.
But there are passages in the symphony that presage the
Strauss-to-be. The turning points in his career were his
acquaintance with Ritter (an enthusiast for Berlioz and
Wagner) and his sojourn in Italy. The first-fruits of this
new way-of-life were seen in his symphonic fantasia *Aus
Italien.* Then followed a series of enormous symphonic
poems *Macbeth, Don Juan, Tod und Verklärung, Till Eulenspiegel, Also sprach Zarathustra, Ein Heldenleben, Sinfonia
Domestica*, and the variations for cello, viola, and orchestra
known as *Don Quixote.* In addition to these he also produced a number of songs, a setting of *Enoch Arden* for
speaking-voice with pianoforte accompaniment, and a long
list of operas : *Guntram, Feuersnoth, Elektra, Salome*, and
Der Rosenkavalier.

Most of these works exhibit some point or other of the

amazing technical resource associated with the composer's name. As a contrapuntist, harmonist, and orchestrator Strauss was beyond question the freest and ablest musician of his age. But it is the merest nonsense to talk of him as a wild revolutionary. That he was not and never had been. He was a man of great industry and courage with broad conceptive and executive powers; but quite definitely and down to the smallest technical details a composer in touch with the past. His powers as a melodist have been over-depreciated both in Germany and England; while his very modest attempts to improve the haphazard constitution of the orchestra just brought on him a ridiculous storm of abuse. His most elevated works are *Tod und Verklärung* and *Also sprach Zarathustra;* but a certain elvish streak in his character (which often marrs his best work) has given enduring life to that masterpiece of lucid form, wit, and orchestral workmanship *Till Eulenspiegel.*

Strauss's artistic path was, on the whole, to be a smooth one. His purely technical advances would not be attacked in the way Beethoven's and Wagner's were. Indeed, in most European countries his talent in this direction was to be warmly recognized from the first. But one must chronicle the fact that a certain section of musical Europe challenges him on a much more serious question, regarding much of his music as the output of a diseased and harmful personality. The present writer, without agreeing with such a charge, thinks that it should be mentioned.

Mahler (1860–1911) was a Bohemian by birth, but purely German as an artist. He studied with Bruckner (24–96) at Vienna and spent most of his life in attempting to do for the symphony what Strauss has done for the symphonic poem. To the non-German mind his symphonies may be described as simplicity decked in the robes of mechanical complexity. Weingartner (63–1942) was an author, conductor, and composer. Among his operas are *Malawika, Sakuntala, Genesius* (on an early Christian subject), and three Æschylean one-act tragedies. But none of these had ever the success of his two symphonic poems *King Lear* and *The Elysian Fields* (after

Böcklin). His best work found him as an interpreter of Beethoven and Brahms.

D'Albert (64–1932) has a record both as a great pianist and as a composer. He started as a Scotsman (Glasgow), but grew as German as Von Tirpitz. He was a man of great gifts, both executive and creative. Among his most interesting works are his *Cello Concerto* and his operas *Cain* and *Tiefland*. The Viennese composer Wolf (60–98) we mention here not for his very few works in the larger forms, but for the exquisite songs with which he has enriched the modern world.

In the following group of composers Siegmund von Hausegger (72–1948) was a protégé and fellow-worker with Strauss. He was never successful in the operatic field, but his symphonic poems such as *Barbarossa* and *Wieland der Schmied* have been well spoken of, though criticized for their diffuseness. One would like to hear his enormous *Barbarossa* played before Frank Bridge's tiny string *Lament* (marked *Catherine, aged 9, "Lusitania," 1915*). It would teach more than one lesson.

Reger (73–1916) was one of the "intellect for its own sake" brigade. He has even used a theme crab-wise as the fifteenth-century pundits did.[1] Beethoven also did this. But there is this difference: that Beethoven selects a tune which is recognizable backwards, while Reger overlooks this fundamental necessity. His variations *On a theme by Bach, On a theme by Beethoven* (for two pianos), and *On a theme by Mozart* (for orchestra) all exhibit abundant technical and especially contrapuntal talent.

The name of Schoenberg (74–1951) became known for what may be considered almost a new type of music–a music which is founded, not on the direct harmonic forms that have come down to us, but on extensions and adaptations of those forms. Much will be said in our next chapter about how his innovations affected others. The composer repeatedly announced the *naturalness* of this mode of expression to himself; and it may be fair to accept that announcement as artistically

[1] See page 156.

honest. Composers who have tried altering his harmonies will understand this point. Among his published works are the *Five Pieces* (for orchestra), the *Kammersymphonie*, the *Sextet* (for strings), and the two *String Quartets* (one with vocal accompaniment).

CHAPTER 17

"Twelve-Tone" Music and Other Innovations

Since the close of the period dealt with in our previous chapter there have been revolutions upon revolutions within classical music. European and American composers have further altered the former rules of harmony, melody, rhythm and form, almost to the point of being unrecognizable in kind from the music of a hundred years ago. Western classical music has responded, not only to the music around it, such as jazz, Eastern, and folk musics, but also to poets, artists, filmmakers, and historical events of the modern era.

The innovations of Schoenberg proved prophetic for many twentieth-century composers. Schoenberg himself chose to consider his "atonal" or "pantonal" (incorporating all tonalities) compositions not revolutionary, but evolutionary. Nevertheless, the works of Schoenberg and his disciples produced discomfort in many musicians and listeners who were accustomed to the safety of the tonal center. By the time of his death in 1951, Schoenberg had refined his twelve-tone system and defined the "rules" for composing in this new fashion. Schoenberg's atonal disciples include Von Webern and Berg. He also, briefly, taught the American composer John Cage.

Another composer who, at close to the same time as Schoenberg but in America, was working on music free from conventional tonality was Charles Ives (1874-1954). Ives derived some inspiration for his music of multiple simultaneous keys and meters from his father, who experimented in daring ways with his marching bands. Ives in his early years won few admirers around his Danbury, Connecticut home. Even when the American conductor Nicholas Slominsky premiered several of the composer's works in cities around the nation of his birth, the reception was generally hostile. However, Ives did find an audience for his works in Europe, and gradually his music appreciated in esteem and respect in his native country. He won the Pulitzer Prize for his *Third Symphony* in 1947, although he had largely stopped composing almost three decades before.

Another notable American composer of the early twentieth century was George Gershwin (1898-1937). Gershwin began his musical career in a quite different fashion than that of Ives; he found his fame as a Tin Pan Alley songwriter and composer of light opera before achieving success with his "serious" compositions as well. Gershwin was an innovator, but in a very different way from Ives; Gershwin for the most part adhered to accepted rules of tonality and harmony, but brought them to life using inspiration from African-American folk music and pop songs. His most famous orchestral composition is *Rhapsody in Blue*, which when conducted properly contains the uniquely exciting sound of an orchestra "swinging" in jazz fashion.

A composer who also made use of the folk idioms of his native land was Béla Bartók (1881-1945). Naturally, the Hungarian Bartók had a much different vein of native folk music to mine than the American Gershwin. Bartók pursued it ravenously, touring the Eastern European countries collecting and notating songs. The scales, harmonies and rhythms that he heard would later be incorporated in his own distinctive music. Distinctive indeed, for Bartók did not slavishly reproduce folk songs in a formal setting, but worked their sounds into his own experiments with the modern and atonal. Bartók escaped war-ravaged Europe by coming to America in 1940; he was often unhappy in his new environment, but nevertheless composed some of his greatest music during his stay, including the famous *Concerto for Orchestra*.

The Bavarian composer Carl Orff (1895-1982) was also shaped by his native surroundings in eastern Europe. His most famous work is the *Carmina Burana,* for which he adapted love songs, drinking songs and feast songs for a piece of musical theater.

Like Orff, Igor Stravinsky (1882-1971) frequently incorporated his music into the theatrical world. Stravinsky's early works had caused both acclaim (*Petrouchka, The Firebird*) and rioting calamity (*Rite of Spring*, which enraged the audience with brutal rhythms and avoidance of melody). The composer was little more inclined to steer clear of controversy when he continued his career in America after 1940, shocking the musical establishment with works such as

Cantata (1952) and *Septet* (1953), which experimented with serialism.

Whereas some composers were prompted by World War II to flee Europe, the Russian composer Dmitri Shostakovich was caused by the war to write such patriotic war-victory programs as his *Symphony no. 7 (Leningrad)*. The foremost composer of Soviet-era Russia, Shostakovich had to cope with official repression, including public attacks and criticism from Stalin himself. After Stalin's death in 1953, Shostakovich found slightly more creative leeway, and included in his *Symphony no. 13* a setting of words that attack anti-semitism.

One nation that was not even mentioned in our previous chapter produced one of the twentieth century's most outstanding composers. Heitor Villa-Lobos (1887-1959) was born in Rio de Janeiro, Brazil, and celebrated with his music the unique culture of his nation. As dedicated a nationalist as Sibelius or Grieg, Villa-Lobos collected folk-songs from the vast country of Brazil and used them in his compositions. He also played a greatly decisive role in the music of Brazil by presenting a revolutionary musical education plan, which was accepted by the Department of Education of the State of São Paolo. Following his efforts in São Paolo, Villa-Lobos organized and directed the introduction of the study of Music and Choral Singing to the State of Rio de Janeiro. The prolific composer's roughly 2000 works include *Uirapuru* and the Bach-inspired *Bachianas Brasileras*. Villa-Lobos continues to influence the music of his native land (and of others) through his advancements in musical education.

Technology, as it accelerated its pace of advancement in the twentieth century, also changed the face of classical music. One composer who made early use of electric and electronic instruments was Edgar Varèse (1883-1965). Varèse created compositions for such uniquely modern instruments as the theremin, a purely electronic device that reacts in tone and amplitude to the position of the player's hands in the air around it. This innovative composer's most famous works include *Ionisation* and *Déserts*. Varèse was born in France, but like Bartók and Stravinsky came to live in America, and in fact composed virtually all of his mature music in his adopted country.

Varèse's fellow native of France, Pierre Boulez (born 1925), is not only a composer but a developer of sophisticated electronic equipment for use in musical applications. He has composed such avant-garde works as *Le Soleil des eaux* and *Memoriales* and conducted such orchestras as the London Symphony Orchestra and the New York Philharmonic-Symphony Orchestra.

The American John Cage (1912-92), who also utilized electronic devices in his compositions, was a composer whose interests ranged from architecture to mycology. His influences included such diverse factors as social critic Marshall McLuhan, poet Walt Whitman, and Zen Buddhism. His most notorious work is *4'33"*, a composition for which the pianist sits down at the piano and plays nothing for four minutes and thirty-three seconds. The noises created by the audience form the music. When the composer was studying under Schoenberg, Cage felt it became apparent that his own sense of harmony was completely lacking. Cage therefore devoted his music to chance, exotic percussion, and observance of no strict time. He experimented with compositions for electronic keyboards, toy pianos, and "prepared piano," which he assembled using various noisemaking items attached to the strings of an ordinary piano.

German composer Karlheinz Stockhausen (born 1928) began working in electronic music in the early 1950's. He has composed major works on tape, including *Telemusik* and *Hymnen*. While he often employs electronic devices in his compositions, he has also been known to give the performers of his music a great deal of freedom in their interpretations, even to the point of determining the form of the piece. In recent years, he has worked on his *Licht* series, intended to be of seven parts, one for each night of a week.

America claims another native-born composer of brilliance in Philip Glass (born 1937). Glass is a distinctly post-modern figure who incorporates a great deal of Indian and Eastern music in his eclectic works. He is also post-modern in the way his music is presented; while the classical community distrusted his work, Glass booked his ensembles in rock clubs, and he has been successful not only as a composer but as a recording artist. Glass is much associated not only with the merger of Western and Eastern classical musics but also with minimalism, a hypnotic brand of composition featuring a high degree of repetition. His most notable works include

Einstein on the Beach, Glassworks, and the soundtrack to the Martin Scorcese film *Kundun*.

Elliott Carter (born 1908), also American, is only ten years the junior of Gershwin, yet he recently observed his 90th birthday with his music being celebrated all over Europe and America. Like Gershwin, Carter also invokes the spirits of jazz players in his music, although he as the composer controls every aspect of it, unlike jazz with its improvised solos. Carter has been honored with the U.S. National Medal of Arts and twice with the Pulitzer Prize. His prominent works include *Double Concerto, Piano Concerto* and *String Quartet #3*.

Indelibly stamped upon the memory of patriotic America is the music of Aaron Copland (1900-1990). Like Gershwin, Copland in his early years was much influenced by jazz and composed pieces such as *Music for the Theater* and *Piano Concerto*, which were described by the composer as "symphonic jazz." However, Copland gained his greatest fame with works such as *Appalachian Spring* and *Rodeo*, which incorporated folk music in their simple, yet moving melodies and evocations of the great American landscape. Copland had a mutually rewarding friendship with the conductor Leonard Bernstein, who led the New York Philharmonic in performances of Copland's music that brought it to a large audience.

Classical music faced challenges in the twentieth century as other forms of music, such as jazz and rock, came to be considered suitable for "serious" appreciation and some audiences were left bewildered by distinctly modern styles. However, there has not been a lack of talented composers or performers, and as long as there are brilliant artists working in the field, classical music will not cease to be produced or enjoyed.

PLATE LV.   PHILIP GLASS

THE CHIEF NAMES IN MUSICAL HISTORY

The following list contains all the most important writers of and on music. Proper names not in common use are enclosed in brackets without inverted commas and without the prefix "or." Executants, as such, are excluded. C.F.

A

Adam, Adolphe-Charles. 1802–56.

Adam de la Hale (or Halle). c. 1230–88.

Adam von Fulda. c. 1450–?.

Afzelius, Arvid August. 1785–1871.

Agricola, Alexander. ?–1522.

Agricola, Martin. 1486–1556.

Alayrac. See Dalayrac.

Albeniz, Don Isaac. 1860–1909.

Albert, Eugène (Francis Charles) d'. 1864–1932.

Albrechtsberger, Johann Georg. 1736–1809.

Alcuin. 735–804.

Aldrich, Henry. 1647–1710.

Alembert, Jean le Rond d'. 1717–83.

Alfven, Hugo. 1872–1960.

Allegri, Gregorio. 1584–1662.

Alypius. 4th century B.C.

Ambros, August Wilhelm. 1816–76.

Ambrose (Saint, of Milan). 333–97.

Anerio, Felice. 1560–1630.

Anerio, Giovanni Francesco. 1567–1620.

Animuccia, Giovanni. c. 1500–71.

Anonymous, of the British Museum. 13th century (?)

Aquinas, Thomas. 1227–74.

Arcadelt, Jacob. c. 1514–c. 1570.

Arensky, Anton Stepanovitch. 1861–1906.

Aristides Quintilianus. 2d century A.D.

Aristotle. 384–322 B.C.

Aristoxenus (of Tarentum). 4th century B.C.

Arne, Thomas Augustine. 1710–78.

Arrigo Tedesco. See Isaak.

Aston, Hugh. ?–1522?

Astorga, Emmanuele. 1681–1736.

Attwood, Thomas. 1756–1838.

Auber, Daniel-François-Esprit. 1782–1871.

Audran, Edmond. 1842–1901.

Avison, Charles. 1710–70.

B

Bach, Carl Philipp Emanuel ("Bach of Hamburg" or "of Berlin"). 1714–88.

Bach, Johann Christian ("English Bach"). 1735–82.

Bach, Johann Christoph. 1642–1703.

Bach, Johann Sebastian. 1685–1750.

Bach, Wilhelm Friedemann ("Bach of Halle"). 1710–84.

Baini, Giuseppe. 1775–1844.

Balakireff, Mily Alexejevitch. 1836 (Dec. 31. O.S.)–1910.

Balfe, Michael William. 1808–70.

Banister, John. 1630–79.
Bantock, Granville. 1868–1946.
Bardi, Giovanni, Conte del Vernio. Late 16th century.
Bargiel, Woldemar. 1828–97.
Barnett, John. 1802–90.
Bartók, Bela. 1881–1945.
Basiron, Philippe. 15th century.
Bath, Hubert. 1883–1945.
Beach, Mrs. H. H. A. 1867–1944.
Bedos de Celles (Dom François). 1706–79.
Beethoven, Ludwig van. 1770–1827.
Bellermann, Johann Friedrich. 1795–1874.
Bellini, Vincenzo. 1801–35.
Benedict, Julius. 1804–85.
Benedictus. See Ducis.
Benet, John. ?–1614.
Bennett, William Sterndale. 1816–75.
Benoit, Pierre-Léonard-Léopold. 1834–1901.
Berchem (or Berghem), Jachet de. c. 1500–80.
Berlioz, Hector (-Louis). 1803–69.
Berwald, Johann Friedrich. 1788–1861.
Billings, William. 1746–1800.
Binchois, Gilles (or Gilles de Binche). ?–1460.
Bishop, Henry Rowley. 1786–1855.
Bizet, Georges (christened Alexandre-César-Léopold). 1838–75.
Blithman, William. ?–1591.
Blockx, Jan. 1851–1912.
Blow, John. 1648–1708.
Boccherini, Luigi. 1743–1805.
Boëllmann, Léon. 1862–97.
Boethius, Anicius Manlius Torquatus Severinus. c. 475–c. 524.
Boieldieu, François-Adrien. 1775–1834.
Boito, Arrigo. 1842–1918.
Bononcini (or Buononcini), Giovanni Battista. 1660–1750.
Bononcini (or Buononcini), Marc' Antonio. c. 1675–1726.

Borodin, Alexander Porphyrjevitch. 1834–87.
Bortniansky, Dimitri Stefanovitch. 1752–1825.
Bossi, Marco Enrico. 1861–1925.
Boulez, Pierre. 1925–.
Bourgault-Ducoudray, Louis-Albert. 1840–1910.
Boyce, William. 1710–79.
Brahms, Johannes. 1833–97.
Bridge, Frank. 1879–1941.
Bridge, John Frederick. 1844–1924.
Bruch, Max. 1838–1907.
Bruckner, Anton. 1824–96.
Brumel, Antoine. c.1480–c.1520.
Bruneau, (Louis-Charles-Bonaventure-) Alfred. 1857–1934.
Buck, Dudley. 1839–1909.
Bull, John. 1563–1628.
Bülow, Hans (Guido) von.1830–94.
Bungert, August. 1846–1915.
Burney, Charles. 1726–1814.
Busnois (or de Busne) Anthoine. ?–1492.
Buxtehude, Dietrich. 1639–1707.
Byrd, William. 1542–1623.

C

Caccini, Giulio (called "Romano"). c. 1546–c. 1615.
Cage, John. 1912–92.
Calcott, John Wall. 1766–1821.
Cambert, Robert. c. 1628–77.
Campagnoli, Bartolommeo. 1751–1827.
Campenhout, François van. 1779–1848.
Campion, Thomas. ?–1619.
Capella, Martianus Minucius Felix. 5th century A.D.
Carey, Henry. c. 1685–1743.
Carissimi, Giacomo. c. 1604–74.
Carolan. See O'Carolan.
Caron, Philippe (or Firmin). 1420?–?.
Carpentrasso, Il. See Genet.
Carter, Elliott. 1908–.
Cassiodorus, Magnus Aurelius. 5th century A.D. (?).
Cavalieri, Emilio del. c. 1550–c. 1599.

Cavalli (or Caletti-Bruni),
Francesco. c. 1600–76.
Cellier, Alfred. 1844–91.
Certon, Pierre. ?–1572.
Cesti, Marc' Antonio. 1620–69.
Chabrier, Alexis-Emmanuel.
1842–94.
Chadwick, George Whitfield.
1854–1931.
Chambonnières, Jacque Champion de. Middle 17th century.
Chaminade, Cécile (-Louise-Stéphanie). 1861–1944.
Charpentier, Gustave, 1860–1956.
Cheney, Miss Amy Marcy. See
Beach, Mrs.
Cherubini, (Maria) Luigi (Carlo
Zenobio Salvatore). 1760–
1842.
Chilston. Middle 15th century.
Chopin, (François-) Frédéric.
1809–49.
Chrysander, Friedrich. 1826–
1901.
Cifra, Antonio. c. 1575–c. 1636.
Cilea, Francesco. 1867–1950.
Cimarosa, Domenico. 1749–
1801.
Clarke, Jeremiah. c. 1669–1707.
Clay, Frederick. 1840–89.
Clément, Jacques ("Clemens
non Papa"). ?–c. 1558.
Clementi, Muzio. 1752–1832.
Coleridge Taylor. See Taylor.
Combarieu, Jules-Léon-Jean.
1859–.
Compère, Loyset. ?–1518.
Converse, Frederick Shepard.
1871–1940.
Cooper, John ("Coperario").
Late 16th century.
Copland, Aaron. 1900–1990.
Corder, Frederick. 1852–.
Corelli, Arcangelo. 1653–1713.
Cornelius, Peter. 1824–74.
Cornysche, William. ?–1524.
Corsi, Jacopo. c. 1560–?.
Costa, Michele (or Michael).
1810–84.
Cotton, John ("Johannes Cotto" or "Cottonius"). 11th–
12th centuries.

Couperin, François. 1668–1733.
Coussemaker, Charles-Edouard-
Henri de. 1805–76.
Cowen, Frederic Hymen. 1852–1935.
Cramer, Johann Baptist. 1771–
1858.
Cristofori, Bartolommeo. 1653–
1731.
Croce, Giovanni. 1557?–1609.
Croft, William. 1678–1727.
Crotch, William. 1775–1847.
Cui, César Antonovitch. 1835–1918.
Czerny, Karl. 1791–1857.

D

D'Albert, Eugen. See Albert.
Dalayrac, Nicolas (or Alayrac,
Nicolas d'). 1753–1809.
Dale, Benjamin. 1885–1943.
Danican-Philidor. See Philidor.
Dannreuther, Edward. 1844–
1905.
Dargomiszky, Alexander Sergievitch. 1813–69.
Davey, Henry. 1853–.
David, Félicien-César. 1810–76.
Davies, Henry Walford. 1869–1941.
Davy, Richard. 15th and 16th
centuries.
Debussy, Claude-Achille. 1862–1918.
De Koven. See Koven.
Delattre, Roland. See Lasso.
Délibes, Clément-Philibert-Léo.
1836–91.
Delius, Frederick. 1863–1934.
Dent, Edward James. 1876–1957.
Dering, Richard. ?–1630.
Des Près, Josquin. 1445–1521.
Diabelli, Antonio. 1781–1858.
Dibdin, Charles. 1745–1814.
D'Indy. See Indy.
Discantus Positio Vulgaris,
Author of. 12th century.
Ditters (von Dittersdorf), Karl.
1739–99.
Donizetti, Gaetano. 1797–1848.
Dowland, John. 1562–1628.
Dubois, (Clément-François-)
Théodore. 1837–1924.
Ducis, Benoit ("Benedictus
Ducis"). c. 1480–?.

Dufay, Guillaume. ?–1474.
Dukas, Paul. 1865–1935.
Dunstable, John. ?–1453.
Durante, Francesco. 1684–1755.
Dussek, Johann Ladislaus. 1761–1812.
Dvořák, Antonin. 1841–1904.

E

Eccles, John. 1668–1735.
Edwardes, Richard. 1523–66.
Eitner, Robert. 1832–1905.
Elgar, Edward William. 1857–1934.
Elvey, George (Job). 1816–93.
Emmanuel, Maurice. 1862–1938.
Engel, Karl. 1818–82.
Enna, August. 1860–1939.
Eratosthenes (of Cyrene). 276–195 B.C.
Expert, Henri. 1863–.

F

Faltin, Richard Friedrich. 1835–.
Farrant, Richard. ?–1580.
Farwell, Arthur. 1872–1952.
Fauré, Gabriel-Urbain. 1845–1924.
Fayrfax, Robert. 1460?–1529.
Ferrabosco, Alfonso. c. 1580–1652.
Festa, Costanzo. ?–1545.
Festing, Michael Christian. c. 1680–1752.
Fétis, François-Joseph. 1784–1871.
Févin, Antoine de. 1490?–1516?
Févin, Robert de. 15th and 16th centuries.
Field, John. 1782–1837.
Frink, Henry Theophilus. 1854–1926.
Flotow, Friedrich Freiherr von. 1812–83.
Foote, Arthur William. 1853–1937.
Ford, Thomas. c. 1580–1648.
Forkel, Johann Nikolaus. 1749–1818.
Franchetti, Alberto. 1860–1942.
Franchinus Gafurius. See Gaforio.
Franck, César-Auguste. 1822–90.

Franco of Cologne. Late 12th century.
Franco of Paris. Early 12th century.
Franz, Robert (born Knauth; father, Christoph Franz Knauth, adopted his second name as surname in 1847). 1815–92.
Frescobaldi, Girolamo. 1583–1644.
Froberger, Johann Jacob. c. 1605–67.
Fux, Johann Joseph. 1660–1741.

G

Gabrieli, Andrea. 1510?–86.
Gabrieli, Giovanni. 1557–1612.
Gade, Niels Wilhelm. 1817–90.
Gaforio (or Gafori), Franchino ("Franchinus Gafurius"). 1451–1522.
Galilei, Vincenzo. c. 1533–c. 1600.
Gallus, Jacobus. c. 1550–91.
Galuppi, Baldassare (called Il Buranello). 1706–84.
Garland, John ("Johannes de Garlandia"). 13th century.
Gaspar. See Weerbecke.
Gaspari, Gaetano. 1807–81.
Geijer, Erik Gustaf. 1783–1847.
Geminiani, Francesco. c. 1680–1762.
Genet, Eléazar (called "Il Carpentrasso"). c. 1475–c. 1532.
Genetz, Karl Emil Moritz. 1852–.
Gerald ("Giraldus Cambrensis"). 1146–1220.
Gerber, Ernst Ludwig. 1746–1819.
Gerbert (von Hornau), Martin. 1720–93.
German, Edward (born Jones). 1862–1936.
Gershwin, George. 1898–1937.
Gevaert, François-Auguste. 1828–1908.
Ghiselin, Jean. 15th and 16th centuries.
Gibbons, Orlando. 1583–1625.

Gilbert, Henry F. 1868–1928.
Gilson, Paul. 1865–1942.
Giordano, Umberto. 1867–1948.
Giraldus. See Gerald.
Glareanus, Henricus (properly Heinrich Loris, or Loritus). 1488–1563.
Glass, Philip. 1937–.
Glazounow, Alexander. 1865–1936.
Glinka, Michael Ivanovitch. 1804–57.
Gluck, Christoph Willibald (Ritter von). 1714–87.
Godard, Benjamin (-Louis-Paul). 1849–95.
Goetz, Hermann. 1840–76.
Goldmark, Karl. 1830–1915.
Gombert, Nicolas. c. 1495–1570.
Goss, John. 1800–80.
Gossec, François-Joseph. 1734–1829.
Goudimel, Claude. 1505–72.
Gounod, Charles-François. 1818–93.
Graun, Karl Heinrich. 1701–59.
Greene, Maurice. 1696–1755.
Gregory (Saint, "The Great"), born c. 540. Pope from 590 to 604.
Grétry, André-Ernest-Modeste. 1741–1813.
Grieg, Edvard Hagerup. 1843–1907.
Grossi. See Viadana.
Grove, George. 1820–1900.
Guido d'Arezzo. 990–1050.
Guilmant, Alexandre-Félix. 1837–1911.
Gungl, Joseph. 1810–89.

H

Hadley, Henry Kimball. 1871–1937.
Hadow, William Henry. 1859–1937.
Hahn, Reynaldo. 1874–1947.
Hale (or Halle). See Adam.
Halévy, Jacques-François-Fromental-Elie. 1799–1862.
Hallén, Anders. 1846–.
Hallström, Ivar. 1826–1901.
Hamerik, Asger. 1843–1923.
Hanboys, John. 15th century.

Händel (or Handel, Handl). See Gallus.
Händel, Georg Friedrich (semi-Anglicized by him "George Frideric Handel"). 1685–1759.
Hartmann, Johan Peder Emilius. 1805–1900.
Hasse, Johann Adolph. 1699–1783.
Hatton, John Liptrot ("Czapek"). 1809–86.
Hauptmann, Moritz. 1792–1868.
Hausegger, Siegmund von. 1872–1948.
Hawkins, John. 1719–89.
Haydn, (Franz) Joseph. 1732–1809.
Haydn, Johann Michael. 1737–1806.
Heller, Stephen. 1815–88.
Helmholtz, Hermann Ludwig Ferdinand. 1821–94.
Henderson, William James. 1855–.
Henry VI. 1421–71 (acc. 1422).
Henry VIII. 1491–1547 (acc. 1509).
Henselt, Adolf von. 1814–89.
Herbert, Victor. 1859–1924.
Hermannus Contractus (properly Hermann, Graf von Vehringen). 1013–54.
Hérold, Louis-Joseph-Ferdinand. 1791–1833.
Hervé (properly Florimond Ronger). 1825–92.
Heyden, Hans. 1540–1613.
Heyden, Sebald. 1498–1561.
Hiller, Ferdinand von. 1811–85.
Hiller (or Hüller), Johann Adam. 1728–1804.
Hipkins, Alfred James. 1826–1903.
Hobrecht. See Obrecht.
Hofmann, Heinrich (Karl Johann). 1842–.
Hol, Richard. 1825–.
Holbrooke, Josef. 1878–1958.
Hollingue. See Mouton.

Holmès (properly Holmes), Augusta Mary Anne. 1847–1903.
Holst, Gustav von. 1874–1934.
Hook, James. 1746–1827
Horsley, William. 1774–1858.
Hothby, John. ?–1487.
Hubay, Jenö. 1858–1937.
Hucbald. c. 840–c. 930.
Hucbald, Pseudo–. Early 9th century?
Hullah, John Pyke. 1812–84.
Humfrey, Pelham. 1647–74.
Hummel, Johann Nepomuk. 1778–1837.
Humperdinck, Engelbert. 1854–1921.
Hurlstone, William Yeates. 1876–1906.
Hykaert, Bernard. 15th century.

I

Indy, Paul-Marie-Théodore-Vincent d'. 1851–1931.
Isaak, Heinrich ("Arrigo Tedesco"). ?–1517.
Ives, Charles. 1874–1954.

J

Jachet. See Berchem.
Jackson, William ("of Exeter"). 1730–1803.
Jadassohn, Salomon. 1831–1902.
Jahn, Otto. 1813–69.
Jannequin, Clément. 16th century.
Järnefelt, Armas. 1869–1958.
Jelinek, Franz Xaver. 1818–80.
Jenkins, John. 1592–1678.
Jensen, Adolf. 1837–79.
Joachim, Joseph. 1831–1907.
Johannes (Chrysorrhous) Damascenus. c. 700–60.
John (of Fornsete). Early 13th century.
Jommelli, Nicola. 1714–74.
Jones, Edward. 1752–1824.
Jones, Robert. 16th and 17th centuries.
Jones, William (of Nayland). 1726–1800.
Josquin. See Des Près.

K

Kajanus, Robert. 1856–1933.
Kalliwoda, Johann Wenzel. 1801–66.
Kastner, Johann Georg. 1810–67.
Keiser, Reinhard. 1674–1739.
Kéler-Béla, Albert (or Albert von Kéler). 1820–82.
Kelley, Edgar Stillman. 1857–1944.
Kelly, Michael. 1762–1826.
Kerle, Jacques de. 16th century.
Kerll, Johann Caspar. 1621–93.
Kiel, Friedrich. 1821–85.
Kienzl, Wilhelm. 1857–1941.
Kiesewetter, Raphael Georg ("Edler von Weisenbrun"). 1773–1850.
Kinkeldey, Otto. 1878–.
Kistler, Cyrill. 1848–1907.
Kjerulf, Halfdan. 1815–68.
Klindworth, Karl. 1830–.
Knight, Joseph Philip. 1812–87.
Korbay, Francis Alexander. 1846–.
Koven (Henry Louis) Reginald De. 1859–.
Krehbiel, Henry Edward. 1854–
Kuhlau, Friedrich. 1786–1832.
Kullak, Theodor. 1818–82.

L

Lachner, Franz. 1804–90.
Lalo, Édouard (-Victor-Antoine). 1823–92.
Lambillotte, Louis. 1797–1855.
Lanier, Nicholas. c. 1588–c. 1665.
La Rue. See Rue.
Lasso, Orlando di (properly Roland Delattre). 1520–94.
Lassen, Eduard. 1830–1904.
Lawes, William. 1582–1645.
Lawes, Henry. 1595–1662.
Layolle, François de. Early 16th century.
Le Bossu d'Arras. See Adam de la Hale.
Leclair, Jean-Marie. 1697–1764.
Lecocq (Alexandre-), Charles. 1832–1918.

Legrenzi, Giovanni. c. 1625–90.

Lekeu, Guillaume. 1870–94.

Leo, Leonardo. 1694–1746.

Leoncavallo, Ruggiero. 1858–1919.

Leonel (or Lionel). See Power.

Lesueur, Jean-François. 1764–1837.

Liadoff, Anatole. 1855–1914.

Liapounow, Serge Michailovitch. 1859–1924.

Lindblad, Adolf Fredrik. 1801–78.

Lindemann, Ludwig Mathias. 1812–87.

Linley, Thomas. 1725–95.

Liszt, Franz (or Ferencz). 1811–86.

Locatelli, Pietro. 1693–1764.

Locke, Matthew. 1632–77.

Loder, Edward James. 1813–65.

Loeffler, Charles Martin Tornov. 1861–1935.

Logroscino, Nicola. c. 1700–63.

Loomis, Harvey Worthington. 1865–1930.

Loris (or Loritus), Heinrich. See Glareanus.

Lortzing (Gustav), Albert. 1803–51.

Lotti, Antonio. c. 1667–1740.

Löwe, Johann Karl Gottfried. 1796–1869.

Lully (or Lulli), Jean-Baptiste de. 1633–87.

Luther, Martin. 1483–1546.

Lwow (or Lvoff), Alexis von. 1799–1870.

M

MacCunn, Hamish. 1868–1916.

MacDowell, Edward Alexander. 1861–1908.

McEwen, John Blackwood. 1868–1948.

Macfarren, George Alexander. 1813–87.

Machault, Guillaume de. c. 1300–77.

Mackenzie, Alexander Campbell. 1847–1935.

Magnus. See Perotinus.

Mahler, Gustav. 1860–1911.

Maitland, John Alexander Fuller. 1856–.

Mansfeldt. See Pierson.

Marcello, Benedetto. 1686–1739.

Marchettus (or Marchetto) of Padua. 13th century.

Marenzio, Luca. 1560–99.

Marpurg, Friedrich Wilhelm. 1718–95.

Marschner, Heinrich (August). 1795–1861.

Martianus. See Capella.

Martini, Giambattista ("Padre Martini"). 1706–84.

Martucci, Giuseppe. 1856–1909.

Marx, Adolf Bernhard. 1799–1866.

Mascagni, Pietro. 1863–1945.

Massé, Félix-Marie (called Victor). 1822–84.

Massenet, Jules (-Émile-Frédéric). 1842–1908.

Mattheson, Johann. 1681–1764.

Mayseder, Joseph. 1789–1863.

Mazas, Jacques-Féréol. 1782–1849.

Mazzocchi, Domenico. c. 1590–c. 1650.

Méhul, Étienne Nicolas. 1763–1817.

Mendelssohn, Felix (properly Jacob Ludwig Felix Mendelssohn-Bartholdy). 1809–47.

Merbecke (or Marbeck). 1523–c. 1581.

Mercadente, Francesco Saverio. 1795–1870.

Mersenne, Marie. 1588–1648.

Merulo (properly Merlotti), Claudio (called "da Coreggio"). 1533–1604.

Messager, André (-Charles-Prosper). 1797–1856.

Meyerbeer, Giacomo (properly Jakob Liebmann Beer). 1791–1864.

Meyer-Helmund, Erik. 1861–.

Monsigny, Pierre-Alexandre. 1729–1817.

Monte, Filippo de (or Philippe de Mons). 1521–1603.
Monteverde (or Monteverdi), Claudio (Giovanni Antonio). 1567–1643.
Moore, Thomas. 1779–1852.
Morley, Thomas. 1557–1602?
Morales, Cristobal. 1512–53.
Mornington. See Wellesley.
Moscheles, Ignaz. 1794–1870.
Moszkowski, Moritz. 1854–1925.
Moussorgsky, Modest Petrovitch. 1839–81.
Mouton, Jean (properly Jean de Hollingue). 1475?–1522.
Mozart, Johann Georg Leopold. 1719–87.
Mozart, Wolfgang Amadeus (christened Johannes Chrysostomus Wolfgangus Theophilus). 1756–91.
Muris, Johannes de. 14th century.

N

Nanini, Giovanni Bernardino. ?–1624.
Nanini, Giovanni Maria. c. 1540–1607.
Nápravnik, Eduard. 1839–1916.
Neri, Filippo. 1515–95.
Nešvera, Joseph. 1842–.
Nevin, Ethelbert. 1862–1901.
Newman, Ernest. 1869–.
Nicolai, Otto. 1810–49.
Nordraak, Rikard. 1842–66.
Notker (or Notger, called Balbulus). ?–912.
Nottebohm, Martin Gustav. 1817–82.

O

Obrecht (or Obreht, Hobrecht, Obertus, Hobertus), Jakob. 1430?–1500?
O'Carolan, Turlogh. 1670–1738.
Odington, Walter ("The Monk of Evesham"). ?–c. 1316.
Odo (of Cluny). ?–942.
Offenbach, Jacques. 1819–80.
Okeghem (or Okekem, Okenghem, Ockenheim), Jean (or Johannes) de. c. 1430–1513.

Olsen, Ole. 1850–1927.
Onslow, George. 1784–1852.
Orff, Carl. 1895–1982.
Orlandus Lassus. See Lasso.
Ornithoparcus (properly Vogelsang), Andreas. 16th century.
Ouseley, Frederick Arthur Gore. 1825–89.

P

Pachelbel, Johann. 1653–1706.
Pacini, Giovanni. 1796–1867.
Pacius, Friedrich. 1809–91.
Paër, Ferdinando. 1771–1839.
Paganini, Niccolò. 1782–1840.
Paine, John Knowles. 1839–1906.
Paisiello, Giovanni. 1741–1816.
Palestrina (properly Giovanni Pierluigi Sante, called "da Palestrina"). 1514 or 1515–94.
Palmgren, Selim. 1878–1951.
Parker, Horatio William. 1863–1919.
Parry, Charles Hubert Hastings. 1848–1918.
Pearsall, Robert Lucas de. 1795–1856.
Pepusch, John Christopher (or Johann Christoph). 1667–1752.
Pergolesi, Giovanni Battista. 1710–36.
Peri, Jacopo (called "Il Zazzerino"). c. 1560–c. 1630.
Perosi, Lorenzo. 1872–1956.
Perotinus, Magnus. 12th century.
Petersen-Berger, Olaf Wilhelm. 1867–1942.
Petrus Platensis. See Rue.
Pettrucci, Ottaviano (de). 1466–1539.
Philidor, François-André Danican-. 1726–95.
Philippe de Mons. See Monte.
Philippe de Vitry. See Vitry.
Philipps, Peter. ?–1633?
Piccini (or Piccinni, Picini), Nicola. 1728–1800.
Pierné (Henri-Constant-) Gabriel. 1863–1937.

Pierson (properly Pearson), Henry Hugo ("Edgar Mansfeldt"). 1815–73.

Pipelare, Matthäus. 15th and 16th centuries.

Pirani, Eugenio. 1852–.

Pirro, André. 1869–.

Planquette (Jean-) Robert. 1850–1903.

Plato. 429–347 B.C.

Playford, John. 1623–93.

Plutarch. c. 50–c. 120 A.D.

Ponchielli, Amilcare. 1834–86.

Porpora, Niccolò Antonio. 1686–1766 or 1767.

Porta, Costanzo. 1530?–1601.

Portugal (or Portogallo) Marcos Antonio ("Portugal da Fonseca"). 1762–1830.

Potter, Philip Cipriani Hambly. 1792–1871.

Power, Lionel. Middle 15th century.

Prätorius (or Praetorius) Michael. 1571–1621.

Près. See Des Près.

Proske, Karl. 1794–1861.

Prout, Ebenezer. 1835–1909.

Ptolemy (or Claudius Ptolemaeus). 2nd century A.D.

Puccini, Giacomo. 1858–1924.

Purcell, Henry. 1658–95.

Pythagoras. c. 582–c. 500 B.C.

Q

Quantz, Johann Joachim. 1697–1773.

R

Rachmaninoff, Sergei Vassilievitch. 1873-1943.

Raff, Joseph Joachim. 1822–82.

Raimondi, Pietro. 1786–1853.

Rameau, Jean-Philippe. 1683–1764.

Ravel, Maurice. 1875–1937.

Ravenscroft, Thomas. c. 1582–1635.

Redford, John. Middle 16th century.

Reger, Max. 1873–1916.

Regino (of Prum). 9th and 10th centuries (died 915).

Regis, Jean. 15th century.

Regnart (or Regnard), Jacob. 1540–1600.

Reicha, Anton. 1770–1836.

Reichardt, Johann Friedrich. 1752–1814.

Reichenau, Hermann von. See Hermannus.

Reimann, Heinrich. 1850–.

Reinecke, Carl (Heinrich Carsten). 1824–1910.

Reinken (or Reinke, Reinicke), Johann Adam. 1623–1722.

Reissiger, Karl Gottlieb. 1798–1859.

Reissman, August. 1825–.

Remi (of Auxerre). 9th century.

Reyer (properly Rey), Louis-Étienne-Ernest. 1823–1909.

Reznicek, Emil Nicolaus Freiherr von. 1861–1945.

Rheinberger, Joseph (Gabriel). 1837–1901.

Richter, Ernest Friedrich (Eduard). 1808–79.

Riemann, Hugo. 1849–.

Rimbault, Edward Francis. 1816–76.

Rimsky-Korsakoff. 1844–1908.

Rinuccini, Ottavio. 1562–1621.

Rockstro (properly Rackstraw), William Smyth. 1823–95.

Rolland, Romain. 1868–.

Romano, Giulio. See Caccini.

Romberg, Andreas (Jacob). 1767–1821.

Ropartz, Guy J. 1864–1955.

Rore, Cipriano da. 1516–65.

Roseingrave, Thomas. 1690–1766.

Rossini, Gioachino Antonio. 1792–1868.

Rouget de l'Isle, Claude-Joseph. 1760–1836.

Rousseau, Jean-Jacques. 1712–78.

Rubinstein, Anton Gregorovitch. 1830–94.

Rue, Pierre de la ("Petrus Platensis"). ?–1518.

S

Sacchini, Antonio Maria Gasparo. 1734–86.
Sachs, Hans. 1494–1576.
Sagittarius. See Schütz.
Saint-Saëns, Charles-Camille. 1835–1921.
Salieri, Antonio. 1750–1825.
Sarti, Giuseppe ("Il Domenichino"). 1729–1802.
Scarlatti, Alessandro. 1659–1725.
Scarlatti, Domenico. 1683 (or 1685)–1757.
Scharwenka (Franz) Xaver. 1850–1924.
Scheidemann, Heinrich. 1596–1663.
Scheidt, Samuel. 1587–1654.
Schein, Johann Hermann. 1586–1630.
Schillings, Max von. 1868–.
Schindler, Anton. 1796–1864.
Schneider (Johann Christian) Friedrich. 1786–1853.
Schoenberg, Arnold. 1874–1951.
Schubert, Franz (Peter). 1797–1828.
Schulz, Johann Abraham Peter. 1747–1800.
Schumann, Robert (Alexander). 1810–56.
Schütz, Heinrich ("Sagittarius"). 1585–1672.
Schytte, Ludwig (Theodor). 1850–1909.
Scott, Cyril Meir. 1879–1970.
Scriabine, Alexander Nicolaievitch. 1872–1915.
Selmer, Johan. 1844–1910.
Seroff, Alexander Nicolaievitch. 1820–71.
Sgambati, Giovanni. 1843–1914.
Shield, William. 1748–1829.
Shostakovich, Dimitri. 1906–1975.
Sibelius, Jan. 1865–1957.
Simpson (or Sympson), Christopher. ?–1677.
Sinding, Christian. 1856–1941.
Sjögren (Johann Gustav) Emil. 1853–1918.

Skraup, František (or Franz Skroup). 1801–62.
Smart, George (Thomas). 1776–1867.
Smart, Henry. 1813–79.
Smetana, Friedrich (or Bedrich). 1824–84.
Smith, David Stanley. 1877–1949.
Smith (or Schmidt) John Christopher. 1712–95.
Smith, John Stafford. 1750–1836.
Smyth, Ethel Mary. 1858–1944.
Södermann, August Johan. 1832–76.
Sokolow, Nicholas. 1858–.
Solovieff, Nicolai Pheopentovitch. 1846–.
Somervell, Arthur. 1863–1937.
Sorge, Georg Andreas. 1703–1778.
Soriano (or Suriano), Francesco. 1549–1620.
Sousa, John Philip. 1856–1932.
Spinelli, Niccola. 1865–.
Spitta (Johann August) Philipp. 1841–94.
Spohr, Ludwig (or Louis). 1784–1859.
Spontini, Gasparo (Luigi Pacifico). 1774–1851.
Squire, William Barclay. 1855–.
Stainer, John. 1840–1901.
Stamitz, Karl. 1746–1801.
Stanford, Charles Villers. 1852–1924.
Stcherbatcheff, Nicolas de. 1853–.
Steffani, Agostino. 1655–1730.
Steibelt, Daniel. 1765–1823.
Stenhammar, Wilhem, 1871–1927.
Stockhausen, Karlheinz. 1928–.
Storace, Stephen. 1763–96.
Stradella, Alessandro. c. 1645–81.
Strauss, Johann (Jr.). 1825–99.
Strauss, Johann (Sr.). 1804–49.
Strauss, Richard. 1864–1949.
Stravinsky, Igor. 1882–1971.
Strong, George Templeton. 1855–1948.
Strube, Gustav. 1867–.
Stucken, Frank (Valentin) van der. 1858–.

Sullivan, Arthur Seymour. 1842–1900.
Suppé, Franz von. 1820–95.
Suriano. See Soriano.
Svendsen, Johan (Severin). 1840–1911.
Sweelinck, Jan Pieterszoon. 1562–1621.
Sympson. See Simpson.

T

Tallis (or Tallis, Talys), Thomas. c. 1510–85.
Tanieff. 1856–1915.
Tansur, William. c. 1700–83.
Tartini, Giuseppe. 1692–1770.
Taubert (Karl Gottfried) Wilhelm. 1811–91.
Taylor, Edward. 1784–1863.
Taylor, Samuel Coleridge. 1875–1912.
Telemann, Georg Philipp. 1681–1767.
Thalberg, Sigismund. 1812–71.
Thayer, Alexander Wheelock. 1817–97.
Thomas, Arthur Goring. 1850–92.
Thomas (Charles-Louis-), Ambroise. 1811–96.
Tiersot, Jean-Baptiste-Elysée-Julien. 1857–.
Tinctoris, Johannes (or John Tinctor, properly Jean de Vaerwere). 1446–1511.
Tinel, Edgar. 1854–1912.
Tomaschek, Johann Wenzel (properly Jan Václav Tomášek). 1774–1850.
Tovey, Donald Francis. 1875–1940.
Traetta, Tommaso (Michele Francesco Saverio). 1727–79.
Traetta (or Trajetta), Filippo. 1777–1854.
Troutbeck, John. 1832–99.
Tchaikovsky, Peter Ilyitch. 1840–93.
Tudway, Thomas. c. 1650–1730.
Tunsted (or Tunstede, Dunstede), Simon. ?–1369.

Turle, James. 1802–82.
Turnhout, Gérard de (properly Gheert Jacques, called Turnhout). c. 1520–80.
Tye, Christopher. c. 1500–85.

U

Utendal (or Utenthal, Uutendal, Outendal), Alexander. ?–1581.

V

Valentini, Pietro Francesco. c. 1570–1654.
Vanderstraeten, Edmond. 1826–95.
Van der Stucken. See Stucken.
Varèse, Edgar. 1883–1965.
Vecchi, Orazio. c. 1551–1605.
Vehringen, Hermann Graf von. See Hermannus.
Verdelot, Philippe. ?–1567?
Verdi (Fortunio) Giuseppe (Francesco). 1813–1901.
Viadana, Ludovico da (properly Ludovico Grossi). 1564–1645.
Vicentino, Nicola. 1511–c. 1576.
Vieuxtemps, Henri. 1820–81.
Villa-Lobos, Heitor. 1887–1959.
Viotti, Giovanni Battista. 1753–1824.
Virdung, Sebastian. 15th and 16th centuries.
Vitry, Philippe de (or Philippus de Vitriaco). ?–1316.
Vittoria, Tomaso Ludovico da (properly Tomas Luis de Victoria). 1540?–1613.
Vivaldi, Antonio. c. 1675–1743.
Vleeshouwer, Albert de. 1863–1940.
Vogler, Georg Joseph ("Abbé Vogler"). 1749–1814.
Volkmann (Friedrich) Robert. 1815–83.
Voss, Gerhard Johann. 1577–1649.

W

Waelrant, Hubert. c. 1517–95.
Wagner, (Wilhelm) Richard. 1813–83.
Wagner, Siegfried. 1869–1930.

Wallace, William. 1861–1940.
Wallace, William Vincent. 1814–65.
Walmisley, Thomas Attwood. 1814–56.
Webbe, Samuel. 1740–1816.
Weber, Carl Maria (Friedrich Ernst) Freiherr von. 1786–1826.
Weckerlin, Jean-Baptiste-Théodore. 1821–1910.
Weelkes, Thomas. ?–1623.
Weerbecke, Gaspar van. c. 1440–?
Wegelius, Martin. 1846–1906.
Weingartner, (Paul) Felix. 1863–1942.
Wellesley, Garret Colley, Earl of Mornington. 1735–81.
Werckmeister, Andreas. 1645–1706.
Wesley, Samuel Sebastian. 1810–76.
Westphal, Rudolf (Georg Hermann). 1826–92.

Whiting, Arthur Battelle. 1861–1936.
Whiting, George Elbridge. 1842–.
Whyte, Robert. ?–1574.
Widor, Charles (-Marie). 1845–1937.
Wieniawski, Henri. 1835–80.
Wilbye, John. 1574–1638.
Wilhem (properly Bocquillon, Guillaume-Louis). 1771–1842.
Willaert (or Wigliardus, Vigliar, Vuigliart), Adrian. 1480?–1562.
Williams, Ralph Vaughan. 1872–1958.
Wilson, John ("Jack Wilson"). 1594–1673.
Wolf-Ferrari, Ermanno. 1876–1948.
Wolf, Hugo. 1860–1903.
Wooldridge, H. Ellis. 1854–.
Wormser, André (-Alphonse-Toussaint). 1851–.

Z

Zarlino, Gioseffe. 1517–90.

INDEX

In the case of subjects and composers mentioned many times in the book, the principal reference will be found under the conventional sub-heading " discussion of." C. F.

A

Absolute Music, 232, 246, 261, 272, 273, 295.
Accent and Quantity, 81.
Accordion, origin of the, 33.
Adam, A. C., 270, 271.
de la Hale, 132, 153.
J., 244.
von Fulda, 153.
Added accompaniments, 300.
Ad organum faciendum, 124.
Æschylus, 218, 243.
Æterne rerum, 79.
Afzelius, 333.
Agincourt Song, 148, 164.
Agréments, 224.
Agricola, 153.
Alain, 150.
Alard, 225.
Albeniz, 344.
Albert, E. d', 333, 340.
discussion of, 353.
Albrechtsberger, 256, 296.
Alcæus, 69, 205.
Alcuin, 91.
Alfven, 330.
discussion of, 334.
Alle psallite cum luya, 135.
Alliterative poem, quoted, 23.
Amati, Andreas, 194, 195.
American School, 322.
table of composers, 308.
Anacreon, 205.
Andrea del Sarto, 218.
Anerio, the two, 172, 173.
Animuccia, 175.
Antiphon, 80.
Apel, 271.

Arabian Instruments, 23.
Arabians, 10, 11, 23.
Arcadelt, 146, 160.
Archilochus, 69.
Archlute. *See* Chittarone.
Arensky, 308.
discussion of, 312.
Aria, the, 217, 221, 222, 231.
Arian Psalmody, 79.
Aristophanes, 205, 245.
Arne, 234, 239.
Arras, MSS. at, 206.
Ars Cantus Mensurabilis, 125.
Articulation, 7.
Arwiddson, 333.
Assyrian Instruments, 19, 20.
Assyrian Sculptures, 20.
Assyrians and Babylonians, 10, 11.
Aston, 166, 167, 171, 199.
Aubry, 206.
Aulos, the, 39, 40, 71.
discussion of the, 41.
Authentic and Plagal Modes, 92.

B

Babylonians. *See* Assyrians.
Bacchylides, 66.
Bach, C. P. E., 237, 261, 296.
discussion of, 246.
Bach family, the, 237, 331.
Bach, J. C., 237, 251.
Bach, J. S., 98, 109, 221, 223, 225, 226, 227, 228, 229, 231, 233, 236, 240, 241, 246, 255, 257, 261, 282, 283, 290, 296, 297, 300, 301, 344, 353.
discussion of, 237.
Bagpipe, Assyrian, 19.

Bagpipes, 42, 43, 73, 119, 182.
Baillot, 225.
Baker-Sunde, 333.
Balakireff, 308.
  discussion of, 310.
Balfe, 302.
Ballad-Opera, 239, 244.
Ballad-Poetry, 205, 206, 334, 335.
Ballad-Singers, 65, 183, 205, 206, 207.
Ballet, 241, 244, 258, 348, 349.
Ballet (or Ballade), the ancient
  vocal, 138, 191.
Banister, 221.
Bantock, 308. discussion of, 317.
Bardi, 218, 219, 224, 225. *See also*
  Monodists. Monophony.
Bartók, Bela, 356.
Bartolozzi, 249.
Basiron, 152.
Bassani, 224.
Bass Viol. *See* Viola da Gamba.
Bateson, 166, 171.
Bath, Hubert, 308.
  discussion of, 321.
Bauck, 286.
Bax, Arnold T., 322.
Bayreuth, 220, 294, 350.
Beach, Mrs., 308, 349.
  discussion of, 328.
Bedingham, 150.
Beethoven, 4, 221, 226, 231, 233, 245,
  247, 249, 251, 253, 262, 263, 264,
  266, 267, 282, 283, 288, 291, 293,
  296, 297, 308, 351, 352, 353.
  discussion of, 254.
Belgian School, 330.
  table of composers, 330. *See also*
  Flemings. Flemish.
Bell, W. H., 322.
Bellini, 269, 341.
Bells and Bell-chimes, 189.
  Chinese, 31, 32, 37.
Bells, Egyptian, 16.
Bells on drums, 182.
Bendemann, 288.
Benedictus, the early, 79.
Benet, 150.
Benet, John, 166, 171.
Bennett, W. Sterndale, 283, 286.
  discussion of, 301.
Benoit, 325, 330, 331.
  discussion of, 331.

Berlioz, 219, 276, 282, 286, 289, 295,
  298, 347, 351.
Berlioz, discussion of, 277.
Berwald, 330.
  discussion of, 333.
Best, 324.
B-flat, the, 94–6, 104, 108.
Bharata, 26.
Biblical Instruments, 20.
Binchois, 152, 153.
Birds, songs of, 3.
Bishop (organ builder), 77.
Bismarck, 295.
Bizet, 276.
  discussion of, 279.
Black Notation, 100, 106, 113.
Bland, 249.
Blithman, 172.
Blockx, 330.
  discussion of, 331.
Blow, 221, 233, 248.
Boar's Head Carol, 148.
Boethius, 91.
Bohemian School, 337.
Böhm, 225.
Boieldieu, 270, 271.
Boito, 340.
  discussion of, 342.
Bologna, MSS. at, 148.
Bombards. *See* Shawms.
Bordoni, 242.
Borodin, 308. discussion of, 310.
Bortniansky, 309.
Bossi, 342.
Boswell's *Johnson*, 313.
Bouilly, 258, 267.
Boulez, 358.
Bowed stringed-instruments, origin
  of, 23, 147.
Brahms, 151, 248, 253, 266, 283, 287,
  290, 300, 334, 338, 349, 351.
  discussion of, 296.
Bréville, Pierre de, 344.
Bridge, Frank, 308, 353.
  discussion of, 321.
Bridge, Frederick, 321.
British Museum, MSS. at, 125, 163,
  167.
Browning, Robert, 241.
Bruch, Max, 340, 349.
  discussion of, 350.
Bruckner, 352.

Brumel, 154.
Bruneau, 340, 347.
Bruneau, discussion of, 348.
Buccina, the, 71, 72.
Buck, Dudley, 324.
Buck, P. C., 318.
Buckingham Palace, MSS. at, 237.
Bull, 166, 168, 171, 172.
Bülow, Hans von, 290, 294, 298.
Bungert, 351.
Buononcini, 235.
Burleigh, H. T., 326.
Busnois, 146, 152.
Buxtehude, 228, 229.
Buysine, the, 71.
Byrd, 146, 166, 171, 172, 173.
    discussion of, 168.
Byron, 286.
Byzantine notation, 101, 108.
Byzantine scales and modes, 90, 99.

C

Caccini, 219, 229.
Cadman, 327.
Cage, 358.
Cambridge, MSS. at, 167, 237.
Canon, 152, 292.
Canto fermo, 153.
Carissimi, 219, 229.
Carlyle, 239.
    quoted, 200.
Carolsfeld, Schnorr von, 294.
Caron, 152.
Carpenter, J. A., 329.
Carpentrasso. *See* Genet.
Carter, 359.
Castanets, 16.
Cavalli, 219.
Caxton, 163.
Certon, 146, 162.
Cesti, 219.
Chabrier, 326, 340.
    discussion of, 348.
Chadwick, 308. discussion of, 324.
Chamber Music, 231, 263, 267, 286,
    354. *See also* Sonata. String
    Quartet. Suite.
Chambonnières, 224.
Chaminade, Mdlle., 349.
Chandos, Duke of, 235.
Charlemagne, 102.

Charles II, 170.
Charpentier, 340, 348.
    discussion of, 348.
Chaucer, 102, 303, 304.
    quoted, 23, 78, 145, 178, 197.
Chiavette, 95, 109.
Chiavette transportate, 110.
Chilston, 141.
Ch'in, the, 33.
Chinese, 10, 11.
    instruments, 37.
    lüs, 28, 29, 31, 32, 37.
    ritual instruments, 32.
    ritual music, 30.
    scale. *See* Scale, pentatonic.
    tone-systems, 28, 29.
Chittarone, the, 193.
Chopin, 223, 281, 283, 286.
    discussion of, 298.
Chorale, the, 227, 228, 229, 230, 231,
    238. *See also* Luther. Lutheran.
Chorus in drama, 218, 243.
Chorus in Greek drama, 65.
Chorus (the instrument), 24.
Chromatic kind, the, 57.
Chyfonie-à-roue. *See* Hurdy-gurdy.
Cicero, 49.
Cifra, 173.
Cilea, 343.
Cimarosa, 267.
Clappers, the, 31, 36.
Clarinet, origin of the, 186.
Clarion, 23, 184. *See also* Trump.
    Trumpet.
Clarke, 233.
Clasing, 296.
Claspan. *See* Cymbals.
Clavicembalo, 190, 223.
    origin of the, 192.
Clavichord, origin of the, 192.
Clef-signs, evolution of the, 111.
    the modern, 112.
Clef, the, 105. *See also* Chiavette.
Clemens, 146, 160.
Clonas, 69.
Clutsam, George, 322.
Collan, 335.
Comedy, origin of, 65.
Comic Opera, 245, 314, 319. *See
    also* Opéra Comique. Singspiel.
    Savoy.
Compère, 155.

Complete-system, the Greek, 27, 51, 55, 56, 62, 107.
Concerto, 231, 258, 289.
Conductus, 129, 143.
Confucian Ceremony, the, 30.
Consorts, 198. *See also* Orchestration.
Conspectus of eight centuries, 141–3.
Constantine Copronymus, 75.
Contrapuntal School, 143, 145, 146–57.
  deformities of the, 155, 353.
Converse, F. S., 308.
  discussion of, 328.
Copland, 359.
Corder, Frederick, 318.
Corelli, 225, 246.
  discussion of, 224, 227.
Coriun, the, 24.
Cornelius, 340.
  discussion of, 349.
Cornett, 180, 187–9, 198.
  the Chinese, 37.
  the mute, 188.
Cornu, the Roman, 71.
Cornysche, 166, 180.
  discussion of, 167.
Corsi, 219.
Cotton, John, 124.
Council of Trent, 175.
Couperin, 223, 246.
Cowen, 308, 314.
  discussion of, 316.
Cramer, W., 249.
Cranach, 227.
Cressener, 255.
Croce, 146, 162.
Crowd. *See* Crwth.
Crwth, 19, 21, 23, 183.
Ctesibius, 72, 74.
Cui, 308.
  discussion of, 310.
Custos, the, 109.
Cymbals, 182.
  Chinese, 37.
  Egyptian, 16.
  Hebrew, 21.
  Indian, 26.
Czerny, 288.

D

Dalayrac, 241, 270, 271.
Dale, B. J., 308.

Dale, B. J., discussion of, 321.
Danish School, 336.
  table of composers, 330.
Dan Michel, quoted, 189.
Dannreuther, E., 278, 318.
Da Ponte, 253.
Dargomiszky, 309, 311.
Davey, Henry, 169, 318.
Davidsbund, the, 285.
Davies, H. Walford, 308.
  discussion of, 319.
Davy, Richard, 166, 167.
De Bériot, 225.
Debussy, 328, 340, 348.
  discussion of, 345.
Declamatory Recitative, 217, 222, 231, 236. *See also* Monodists. Monophony.
Délibes, 340, 345.
  discussion of, 348.
Delius, 308.
  discussion of, 317.
De Musica Mensurabili Positio, 125.
Denmark. See Danish.
Dent, E. J., 318.
Derby, Earl of, 179.
De Speculatione Musicæ, 125.
Des Près, Josquin, 90, 109, 142, 143, 146, 155, 161, 162, 166.
  discussion of, 153.
Deus Creator, 79.
Diapasons, the lute, 193.
Diaphony. *See* Organum.
Diatonic kind, the, 51.
Diepenbrock, 331.
Dies Iræ, 83.
Dietsch, 292.
Discant, 125, 140, 143.
Discantus Positio Vulgaris, 125.
Dithyramb, the, 65, 66.
Dittersdorf, 225, 244.
Donizetti, 268, 288, 341.
  discussion of, 269.
Dont, 225.
Dorn, 285.
Dot, the, 116.
Double-pipes, Egyptian, 17.
  Greek, 43.
Double-reed pipe, the Graeco-Roman, 42.
Dowland, 166, 168, 171, 172, 180, 181.

Dowland, discussion of, 169.
Drake, 333.
Dresel, 300.
Drums, 182.
and fifes, 183, 198.
and trumpets, 190, 196.
Drums, Assyrian, 19.
Chinese, 31, 35, 36, 37.
Egyptian, 16.
Hebrew, 21.
Indian, 26.
Roman, 72.
See also Kettle-Drums.
Dubois, 348.
Duborg, 225.
Dufay, 142, 143, 146, 149, 153, 166.
discussion of, 151.
Dukas, 349.
"Dulcet and reed," 197.
Dulcimer, Assyrian, 19.
Chinese, 37.
Dumas (père), 259.
Dunstable, 88, 90, 142, 143, 145, 146, 152, 153, 154, 176.
discussion of, 148.
Duple time, 136, 143.
Dupuis, 331.
Durante, 223.
Dürer, 227.
Dussek, 337.
Dutch School, 331.
Dutch, the, 151.
Duyse, van, 331.
Dvořák, 297, 319, 320.
discussion of, 338.

E

Edward VI, 178.
Edwardes, 166, 180.
Egyptian instruments, 15.
Egyptians, the, 10, 15.
Ehregott, 290.
Ehrström, 335.
Elegy, the Greek, 67.
Elgar, 308, 314, 317.
discussion of, 316.
Elizabethan Composers, partial list of, 167.
See also English School (Elizabethan). Oriana.

Elizabeth, Queen, 166, 168, 171, 178–99.
Elsner, 298.
Encina, Juan del, 162.
England, early Vocal School, 127.
faburden in, 140.
in the year 1400, 144.
want of continuity in, 146.
English School (Contrapuntal), 147.
English School (Elizabethan), 165, 173.
table of composers, 166.
English School (Modern), 313.
table of composers, 308.
English Writers (Modern) on music, 318.
Enharmonic kind, the, 59.
Enna, 330.
discussion of, 337.
Erdödy, 257.
Ernst, 255, 283.
Ertmann, Madame, 283.
Esterhazy, Prince, 235, 248.
Ethos of Greek music, 63, 69.

F

Faburden, 128, 136, 143.
discussion of, 138.
Faltin, 335.
Farrant, 166.
Farwell, A., 308.
discussion of, 327.
Fauré, 340, 345.
discussion of, 348.
Fawcett, 302.
Fayrfax, 166, 180.
discussion of, 167.
Fayrfax Book, the, 166.
Ferrabosco, 168, 180.
Festa, 158, 161.
Févin, A. de and R. de, 155.
Fiddle, 77.
Chinese, 37.
Troubadour and Minnesinger, 78.
See also Violin. Violin Family. Violin Schools.
Field, John, 309.
Fifes, the, 180, 183, 198.
Figured bass, 100, 300.
Final close, 96, 137–8, 152, 163. *See also* Occurse.

Finnish School, 334.
  table of composers, 330.
Fipple. *See* Flutes.
Fisher, 340.
Fistula, the Roman, 71.
Fitzwilliam Virginal Book, the, 172.
Flageolet, 16. *See also* Flutes. Re-
  corders.
Flemings, the, 146.
  characteristics of the, 151.
  in Italy, 158.
Flemings, the modern, 330, 344.
Flemish School (15th century), 151.
  (16th century), 161, 167.
Flutes, 180, 188, 198.
  Assyrian, 19.
  Chinese, 31, 35, 37.
  douces, 197.
  Egyptian, 16.
  fipple, 197.
  Hebrew, 21.
  Indian bamboo, 26.
  Indian nose-, 26.
Flue-work, 42, 43, 197.
Folk-Song (Folk-Music), 10, 200.
  African/African-American, 326, 338.
  and art-music, 200, 208, 209.
  as a musical sanction, 208.
  description of, 207.
  discussion of, 209–13.
  Dvořák's use of, 338.
  effect of, on art-music, 159, 204.
  English, 9, 209, 210, 211, 309.
  Finnish, 334.
  German, 210, 229.
  Greek, 22, 79, 205.
  Hungarian, 289.
  Irish, 9, 212, 338.
  Italian, 22, 79, 212, 341.
  lyric and narrative, 205, 334, 335.
  Norse, 332.
  Native-American, 326, 327.
  Russian, 207, 209, 212, 309.
  Spanish, 9.
  Swedish, 333.
  See also Ballad-Singers. National-
    ism. Song.
Foote, Arthur, 308.
  discussion of, 324.
Forest, 150.
Franchetti, 342.
Franck, 277, 331, 340, 345, 346.

Franck, discussion of, 344.
Franco of Cologne, 113, 125.
Frankh, 247.
Franz, 286, 298.
  discussion of, 299.
Frederick the Great, 238, 239.
Free Organum. *See* Organum.
French   School   (15th   century),
  153.
French School (16th century), 146,
  162.
French School (Modern), 344.
  table of composers, 340.
Frescobaldi, 225, 228, 229.
Friskin, James, 321.
Froberger, 225, 228, 229.
Fugue, 257.
Fürnberg, Karl von, 247, 248.

G

Gabrieli, A. and G., 146, 162.
  G., 173, 228.
Gade, 283, 330, 332, 337.
  discussion of, 336.
Gafori, 152.
Galilei, 219.
Galpin, F. W., 74, 318.
Galuppi, 241, 309.
Gamba. *See* Viola.
Gardiner, Balfour, 321.
Garland, John, 125.
Gaspar di Salo, 194.
Gaveaux, 258.
Geijer, 333.
Geminiani, 225.
Genealogical Trees,
  Bach from Sweelinck, 229.
  Brahms from Mozart and Bach,
    296.
  French Operatic School, 271.
  Viennese School from Bach, 261.
  Wagner from Bach, 290.
Genet, 155.
Genetz, 330.
  discussion of, 335.
George I, 234.
German, Edward, 308.
  discussion of, 318.
German School (15th century), 152.
German School (Modern), 349.
  table of composers, 340.

Germany, North and South, 227, 229.
Gershwin, George, 356.
Ghiselin, 155.
Gibbons, 146, 166, 171, 173.
    discussion of, 169.
Gigue, 78.
Gilbert, Henry F., 327.
Gilbert, W. S., 245.
Gilson, 330. discussion of, 331.
Giordano, 343.
Giotto, 151.
Giraldus Cambrensis, 128.
Glass, 358.
Glazounow, 308.
    discussion of, 312.
Glinka, 308, 310, 314.
    discussion of, 309.
Gluck, 88, 219, 233, 235, 236, 240, 241,
    247, 253, 267, 270, 296, 346.
    discussion of, 242.
Goethe, 257, 259, 261, 262, 278, 281,
    286.
Goetz, 340, 349.
    discussion of, 350.
Golden Age, the, 143, 145, 146, 158–
    76.
Goldmark, Karl, 340, 349.
    discussion of, 350.
Goldmark, Rubin, 340.
Gombert, 162.
Gongs and gong-chimes, Chinese,
    31, 35.
Gongs, Indian, 26.
Gorboduc, 198.
Gossec, 241, 270, 271.
Goudimel, 142, 143, 172, 174.
    discussion of, 162.
Gounod, 276, 347.
    discussion of, 278.
Gradual, the, 80, 81.
Grainger, P. A., 322.
Granados, 344.
Grand Opéra, 220, 241, 244, 268, 275,
    276, 278, 279. *See also* Opera.
Greek art and Greek theorists, 60,
    70.
    complete-system, 27, 51, 55, 56, 62,
    107.
    influence on Berlioz, 278 ; on Keats,
    304 ; on the 17th century, 218,
    219 ; on the 18th century, 243 ;
    on Wagner, 291.

Greek instruments, 40–9.
    magadizing, 40, 119.
    melodies, 10, 67.
    modes, list of, 93.
    musical art, 38–40.
    music and meter, 67, 68.
    music, ethos of, 63–5, 69.
    nomoi, 66.
    notation, 61–3, 100 ; examples of,
    61, 62, 89.
    poetical and musical forms, 65–7.
    tone-system, 50–60.
Greene, Maurice, 237.
Gregorian Chant, 81, 95, 175. *See
    also* St. Gregory.
Grétry, 241, 270, 271.
Grieg, 325, 330, 332.
    discussion of, 332.
Grisi, 269.
Grove, George, 264, 265, 318.
Guiding March, the Chinese, 30,
    32–5.
Guido d'Arezzo, 128, 143.
    and the Organum (old style), 123.
    improvements in notation, 105.
    solmization and hexachords, 107,
    108.
Guise, Chevalier de, 220.
Guitar, 9, 27.
    Chinese, 37.
Gymel, 138, 140, 168.

H

Hadley, H. K., 308.
    discussion of, 329.
Hadow, W. H., 318.
Halévy, 270, 271.
Hallé, 267.
Hallelujah, the early, 79, 81.
Hallen, 330.
    discussion of, 334.
Hallström, 330.
    discussion of, 333.
Halvorsen, 333.
Handel, 221, 222, 223, 224, 225, 231,
    233, 239, 240, 242, 246, 250, 300,
    301, 341.
    discussion of, 222, 234–7.
Handel's "borrowings," 222, 236.
Hanslick, 297, 300.
Harmonics. *See* Overtones.

Harmonium, origin of the, 33
Harmony, 98, 141, 154, 161, 163, 164, 168, 345, 346, 353.
Harp, Assyrian, 19.
  Egyptian, 17.
  Hebrew, 21.
  Welsh, 182.
Harp-type, the, 17.
Harpsichord, 190, 191–2, 217, 223, 224, 231.
  and strings, 225.
  origin of the, 20, 192.
Hartmann, J. P. E., 330.
  discussion of, 336.
Harty, Hamilton, 322.
Hasse, 242, 252.
Hausegger, Siegmund von, 340.
  discussion of, 353.
Hautboy, first mention of the word, 186.
Hautboys, 198. *See also* Shawms.
Hawley, Stanley, 319.
Haydn, Joseph, 151, 231, 233, 235, 241, 242, 244, 246, 253, 255, 256, 261, 266, 271.
  discussion of, 247.
Haydn, Michael, 271.
Hebrew instruments, 21.
  Temple Songs, 10, 11, 22, 82.
Heller, 286.
Hellmesberger, 225.
Helmholtz, 99.
Hengrave Hall, 170.
Henry IV and VI, 147.
Henry V's Chapel, members of, 147.
Henry VII, 167.
  sackbutters of, 180.
Henry VIII, 163, 165, 167, 178, 179, 199.
  musical instruments of, 180, 181, 188.
  sackbutters of, 180.
Hensel, Fanny, 284.
Henselt, 286.
Herbert, Victor, 308.
  discussion of, 326.
Hermannus Contractus, notation of, 104.
Hero of Alexandria, 73, 74.
Hérold, 270, 278.
Herschel, 249.
Hexachords, the Guidonian, 108.

Higden's *Polychronicon*, 163.
Hiller, F. von, 283, 286.
Hiller, J. A., 244.
Hipkins, E. J., 318.
Hjelm, 332.
Hocket, the, 130, 139.
Hol, 331.
Holbein, 227.
Holbrooke, Joseph, 308.
  discussion of, 319.
Holland, quoted, 197.
Holmès, Madame, 349.
Holst, Gustav von, 322.
  discussion of, 321.
Holyrood House, 190, 210.
Holy Trinity, the, 113, 114, **126.**
Homer, 65, 205, 258.
Homilius, 290.
Hopkins, 340.
Horace, 71.
Horn, Hunting, 71, 180, 181, 198.
  Indian, 26.
  Roman (cornu), 71.
Hothby, 141, 149, 150.
Houdon, 240.
Howling, speaking, singing, 4–6, 202–4.
Hucbald, 120, 128, 143, 151. *See also* Pseudo-Hucbald.
  notation of, 104.
Humperdinck, 340.
  discussion of, 350.
Humphrey, Pelham, 221.
Hungarian School, 288.
Hunter, John, 249.
Hurdy-gurdy, 77, 119, 182.
Hurlstone, W. Y., 308, 331.
  discussion of, 319.
Hüttenbrenner, 264.
Hydraulus, the, 72–5.
Hymns, the early, 82.
Hymn to Confucius, 31.
Hymn to St. John, 108.
Hypo- and hyper-modes, 54, 94.

I

Iamb, the, 66, 67.
Indian instruments, 26, **27.**
  Plain-Song, 26.
  rāgs, 25.
  scales, 24.

Indians, the, 10, 11, 24.
Indy, Vincent d', 326, 331, 340, 344.
  discussion of, 345.
Italian School (Modern), 340.
  table of composers, 340.
Italian Schools (Ancient). *See* Palestrina. Roman. Venetian.
Ives, Charles, 355.

J

James I, 165, 168.
James II, 313.
Jam surgit hora tertia, 79.
Jannequin, 162.
Järnefelt, 330.
  discussion of, 335.
Jaydeva, 26.
Jenkins, 217, 225, 227.
Jewish. *See* Hebrew.
Joachim, 225, 260, 283, 289, 290, 297, 300.
John of Fornsete, 132, 133.
Jomelli, 223, 241.
Jones, Sidney, 308.
  discussion of, 319.
Jordans, the, 77.
Josquin. *See* Des Près.
Julian the Apostate, 75.

K

Kaiser, the German, 343.
Kajanus, 330.
  discussion of, 335.
Kalevala, 334, 335.
Kalinnikoff, 308.
  discussion of, 312.
Kalliwoda, 337.
Kantele, the, 335.
Keats, 304, 321.
Keiser, 222.
Kelley, E. Stillman, 308.
  discussion of, 325.
Kerl, 236.
Kettle-drums, 184, 190.
  Arabian, 23.
  Egyptian, 16.
  Hebrew, 21.
  Indian, 26.
  See also Drums.
Keyed stringed-instruments, origin of, 147, 192.

Keys, balanced, ancient use of, 74.
Kienzl, 351.
Kinesias, 69.
Kipling, 261.
Kistler, 351.
Kithara, the, 9, 39, 53, 71.
  discussion of the, 47.
Kjerulf, 332.
Kommoi, the, 65.
Kratzenstein, 33.
Krehbiel, H. E., 326, 330.
Kruys, van t', 331.
Kytson, 170.

L

Lablache, 269.
Lady Nevell's Booke, 172.
Lalo, 340, 345.
  discussion of, 348.
Lambillotte, 116.
Lang, B. J., 300.
  Miss, 328.
Langland, quoted, 144.
Lanier, 180.
La Rue. *See* Rue.
Lassen, 330.
  discussion of, 336.
Lasso, Orlando di, 142, 143, 146, 173.
  discussion of, 161.
Lauder, Harry, 319.
Layolle, F. de, 155.
Le Bossu d'Arras. *See* Adam de la Hale.
Leclair, 225.
Legge, Robin, 318.
Legrenzi, 219.
Leier, 78. *See also* Hurdy-gurdy.
Leit-motives, 342.
Lekeu, 330.
  discussion of, 331.
Lenaerts, 331.
Leo, 223, 241.
Léonard, 225.
Leoncavallo, 340.
  discussion of, 343.
Lesbos, 66, 67.
Lesueur, 241, 270.
Letter Notation, 100. *See also* Byzantine. Greek. Notation.
Lhéritier, 155.

L'homme armé, 156.
Liadoff, 308.
  discussion of, 311.
Lichnowsky, 257.
Lie, 333.
Lindemann, L. M., 330, 332.
Linley, 252.
Linos-song, the, 66.
Linsen, 335.
Liszt, 281, 283, 288, 292, 293, 295,
  297, 298, 299, 300, 325, 336, 337,
  345, 349.
  discussion of, 288.
Lituus, the Roman, 71, 72.
Locatelli, 225.
Loeffler, C. M. T., 308.
  discussion of, 328.
Loewe, 298.
Loomis, H. W., 308, 340.
  discussion of, 328.
Lorenzo de' Medici, 218.
Lortzing, 245.
Louis XIV, 220.
Ludwig II (of Bavaria), 294.
  (of Hungary), 184.
Lully (Lulli), 221, 222, 239, 240, 270,
  271, 344.
  discussion of, 220.
Lüs, the Chinese, 28, 29, 31, 32, 37.
Lute, the, 169, 190, 193, 198.
  ancient Roman, 71.
  Arabian, 23.
  Egyptian, 17.
Lute-type, the, 17, 24.
Lutheran Music, 229, 230.   *See also*
  Chorale.
Luther, Martin, 22, 175, 227.
Lyra, 78.   *See also* Hurdy-gurdy.
Lyre, Assyrian, 19, 21.
  Hebrew, 21.
  Greek, 21, 40, 47.
  See also Kithara.

M

Macaulay, 313.
MacCunn, 308, 322.
  discussion of, 317.
MacDowell, 308.
  discussion of, 326.
McEwen, 308, 318.
  discussion of, 319.

Macfarren, 302, 315.
Machault, 153.
Mackenzie, 308, 314.
  discussion of, 315.
MacLean, Alec, 322.
Macpherson, Stewart, 318.
Macran, H. S., 318.
Madrid, MSS. at, 162.
Madrigal, the, 160, 161.
  the early, 138.
  the modern, 302.
Madrigalists, Elizabethan, 165.
  Flemish, 160.
  Roman, 172.
  Venetian, 161.
Magadis (magadizing), 40, 119.
Magdeburg organ, 75, 76.
Magnificat, the early, 79.
Mahler, 352.
Maitland, J. A. F., 318.
Mandolin, 27.
Manifesto of 1860, the, 290.
Manns, August, 265.
Marcello, 241.
Marenzio, Luca, 146, 172, 173.
Marie Antoinette, 243.
Mario, 269.
Marschner, 274.
Martin le Franc, 149.
Martini, 241.
Martucci, 340, 342.
Marturiai, the, 90, 91.
Marxsen, 296.
Mary, Queen, 161, 178.
Mary Stuart, Queen, 179.
Mascagni, 340.
  discussion of, 342.
Mason, D. G., 328.
  Edward, 322.
  Lowell, 323.
  William, 323.
Massenet, 340, 345, 346, 348.
  discussion of, 347.
Measured music, 125, 143.
Méhul, 241, 270, 271.
Meistersingers, 206.
Mendelssohn, 221, 240, 264, 265,
  286, 288, 291, 292, 293, 298, 299,
  301, 336.
  discussion of, 281.
Mercadente, 269.
Merkham, 150.

Mese (Greek tonic), 44, 55–7, 65.
Messager, 326, 340.
 discussion of, 348.
Mestdagh, 331.
Metastasio, 242.
Methods of study, 10, 69.
Meyerbeer, 234, 268, 269, 271, 277, 279, 283, 292, 341, 346.
 discussion of, 274.
Michael Angelo, 240.
Micrologus, 123.
Midas of Agrigentum, 42.
Midsummer Night's Dream, A, production of, 179–99.
Mi-Fa (the semitone interval), 9, 108.
Milan, MSS. at, 206.
Milton (father), 171.
 (son), 169, 258.
Minnesingers, 206.
Minot, quoted, 23.
Missal, the, 80.
Mithras, 79.
Modal counterpoint and Beethoven, 256.
 and Wagner, 291.
Modal-system, discussion of the mediæval, 163.
Modena, MSS. at, 148, 150.
Modes, Arabian, 23.
 Byzantine Church, 91.
 Greek, 10, 45, 92; description of, 52–7; list of, 93; tonic-pitch of, 55–7, 65, 92.
 hypo- and hyper-, 54, 94.
 Indian. *See* Rāgs.
 mediæval, 10, 230; list of, 93.
 modern, the two, 57, 97, 230.
 transposed, 95, 122.
 See also Scales.
Monckton, Lionel, 308.
 discussion of, 319.
Monochord, the, 192.
 the Greek, 41.
Monodiai, the, 65.
Monodists, 10, 88. *See also* Bardi. Declamatory Recitative. Monophony.
Monophony, 218. *See also* Bardi. Declamatory Recitative. Monodists.
Monro, 64, 318.
Monsigny, 241, 270, 271.

Monteverdi, 219.
Morales, 146, 162.
Moral value of music. *See* Ethos.
Morley, 141, 146, 166, 171, 173, 181, 191.
Morton, 150.
 discussion of, 169.
Morzin, Count, 248.
Moscheles, 261, 282, 283.
Motet, the, 129, 134, 143.
Motion, contrary, 124.
 similar and oblique, 122, 123.
Moussorgsky, 308, 311, 314.
 discussion of, 310.
Mouton, 155, 161.
Mozart, 231, 233, 235, 242, 245, 248, 249, 251, 255, 256, 257, 258, 259, 261, 264, 266, 267, 271, 285, 296, 297, 341, 349, 351, 353.
 discussion of, 251.
Mundy (or Munday), 171, 172, 191.
Music, definition of, 7.
 printing and publishing of, 163.
Musica Enchiriadis, 120.
Musica ficta, 96, 138, 164.
Musical instruments, 7.
 Biblical, 30.
 groupings of, 18.
 See also Bowed. Keyed. Orchestra. And under names of instruments.
Musset, A. de, 298.

N

Nāgarī, 26.
Nakers, 23.
Nanini, the two, 172, 173.
Napoleon I, 257.
 III, 293.
Naqqareh, 23, 26.
National characteristics, 227, 230.
Nationalism
 American, 322, 329.
 and folk-song, 208, 310.
 beginnings of, 142.
 Belgian, 330.
 Bohemian, 337, 338.
 Danish, 336.
 discussion of, 303.
 Dvořák's lesson in, 338,
 English, 313.

Nationalism — *continued*
Flemings and Italians, 158.
Flemish, 344.
French, 270, 344.
German, 337, 306, 349.
Italian, 341.
Norse, 331.
Russian, 311.
Swedish, 333.
See also Folk-Song.
Nay, the Egyptian, 16.
Neefe, 255.
Neidhardt, 98.
Netherlands. *See* Dutch. Flemings. Flemish.
Neue Zeitschrift für Musik, 285, 287, 299.
Neumes, 100–3, 105–7, 112.
Nevin, E., 328.
Newman, Ernest, 318.
Nomoi, the Greek, 66, 67, 79.
Nordraak, 330, 332.
discussion of, 332.
Norfolk Festival, 325.
Norwegian School, 331.
table of composers, 330.
Notation, 99.
B-flat, 94–6, 104, 108.
black, 100, 106, 113.
Byzantine, 110.
clef and clef-signs, 105, 111, 112.
See also Chiavette.
development of, 117.
dot, the, 116.
flat, sharp, and natural, 108.
Greek, 61–3, 100; examples of, 61, 62, 89.
Guido's improvements in, 105.
mediæval and modern, 99–118.
modern signs, 112, 115.
staff, the, 105–7.
white, 100, 115.
Notations, table of various, 100.
obsolete mediæval, 103–5.
Notker (or Notger) Balbulus, 83.
Nottebohm (*Beethoveniana*), 255.
Nunc Dimittis, the early, 79.

O

Oboe. *See* Hautboy. Shawms.
Oboe, Chinese, 37.

Oboe d'Amore, 300.
Obrecht, 146, 152.
Ocarina, Assyrian, 19.
Chinese, 31, 36.
Occurse, the, 124. *See also* Final Close.
Odesschalchi, 257.
Odington, Walter, 125, 132, 133.
Odo of Cluny, description of the organistrum, 77.
obsolete notation of, 104.
Offenbach, 245.
discussion of, 279.
Okeghem, 146.
discussion of, 153.
Olsen, 333.
Olympus, 66.
Opera, 235, 236, 239, 242, 252, 258, 266, 267–80, 286, 291–4, 315, 318, 322. *See also* Comic Opera. Grand Opéra, Opéra Comique. Savoy. Singspiel.
beginnings of, 217, 231.
precursor of, 218.
Opéra Comique, 241, 244, 270, 275, 278, 279, 280, 348. *See also* Comic Opera. Savoy. Singspiel.
Oratorio, 235, 236, 250, 279.
beginnings of, 217, 231.
origin of the word, 175.
Orchestration, 18, 198, 219, 236, 243, 244, 246, 254, 268, 274, 276, 277, 300, 345, 346, 352.
Ordines, the, 134.
Orff, 356.
Organ, the, 217, 224, 231, 238.
origin and development of the, 72–7.
Schools, 225, 228.
small, 190.
theatrical use of the, 75, 198.
Organistrum, the, 77.
Organum, free, 129.
(new style), 123, 143.
(old style), 120, 139, 143.
Oriana, Triumphs of, 166, 169, 172.
names of contributors to, 171.
Orphic legends, 66, 67, 219, 243.
Overtones (or harmonics), 39, 99.
Overture, the, 220, 222, 231, 246, 273, 282, 291.
Oxford, MSS. at, 148, 167.

P

Pachelbel, 228, 229.
Pacius, 330.
  discussion of, 335.
Paër, 258.
Paesiello, 223.
Paine, J. K., 308.
  discussion of, 323.
Palace of Greenwich, the, 177.
Palestrina, 79, 142, 143, 146, 151, 155,
  157, 162, 172, 173, 217, 225, 228,
  230, 231, 256, 283, 291, 309, 343.
  discussion of, 174.
Palmgren, 330.
  discussion of, 335.
Pandoura, the ancient, 71.
Pan's pipes, 8, 182.
  Chinese, 37.
  Greek, 41, 60.
  origin of the organ, 73.
Papal Decree, the, 136, 139, 175.
Parabasis, the, 65.
Parker, Horatio, 308.
  discussion of, 327.
  J. C. D., 324.
Parodos, the, 65.
Parry, 308, 314, 318, 336.
  discussion of, 315.
Parthenia, the, 66.
Partita. *See* Suite.
Passion Music, 229, 238, 282, 343.
  earliest example of, 167.
Pearsall, 302.
Peeris, 206.
Peñalosa, 162.
Perfect and imperfect time, 113,
  114.
Pergolesi, 242.
Peri, 219, 229.
Period, the ancient, 13.
  the mediæval, 85.
  the modern, 215.
Periods, the three, 11.
Perosi, 340.
  discussion of, 343.
Petersen-Berger, 330.
  discussion of, 334.
Petrucci, 163.
Philharmonic Society (of London),
  264, 282, 293.
Philidor, 241.

Philippe de Vitry, 137.
Philipps, 166, 171, 191.
Philo of Alexandria, 72.
Philoxenus, 69.
Phrynis, 69.
Pianoforte, 7.
  origin of the, 20.
  passages and technique, 224, 285,
    288, 289, 297, 298.
Piatti, 227.
Piccini and Piccinists, 223, 235, 240,
  244.
Pierson (or Pearson), H. H., 314.
Pindar, 42, 69, 88, 89, 205.
Pipe and tabor, 182.
Pipelare, 155.
Pipes, Egyptian, 16.
  Indian, 26.
  See also Aulos. Reed-pipe.
    River-reeds.
Pirani, 342.
Pitch, 7. *See also* Tonic pitch.
Plagal modes, 92.
Plain-Song, Indian, 26.
  origin of the Catholic Christian,
    10, 11, 22, 79.
  See also Gregorian Chant.
Planché, 272.
Plural-melody, discovery of, 87,
  119.
Polish School (16th century), 162.
  (modern), 298.
Politian, 218.
Polyphant, 190.
Ponchielli, 343.
Popes
  Gelasius I, 80.
  Hadrian I, 102.
  John XXII, 136, 139, 175.
Porpora, 223, 241, 242, 247.
Porta, 161.
Possessoris organ, the, 74.
Power, Lionel, 141, 150.
Programme Music, 289.
  earliest example of, 172.
Prolation, 113, 114, 137.
Proses, the early, 82.
Prosodia, the, 66.
Prout, Ebenezer, 318.
Psaltery, 192.
  Assyrian, 19.
  Hebrew, 21.

Pseudo-Hucbald, 192.
  obsolete notation of, 103.
Ptolemy, 92.
Puccini, 340.
  discussion of, 343.
Pugnani, 225.
Puknon, the, 59.
Purcell, 147, 170, 218, 227, 233, 234, 246, 248, 301, 313.
  discussion of, 220, 226.
Pushkin, 309.
Pythagoras, 15.

Q

Quantity and accent, 81.
Queen Elizabeth's Virginal Book. *See* Fitzwilliam.
Quen of Evene, 131.
Quintons, the, 195.

R

Rachmaninoff, 308.
  discussion of, 312.
Racine, 283.
Rāgs, the Indian, 24, 25, 58.
Rameau, 271.
  discussion of, 240.
  theoretical work of, 98, 240.
Ram's-horn trumpet, 21.
Raphael, 218.
Rappoldi, 225.
Ravel, 340.
  discussion of, 346.
Reading, the Abbey of, 132.
Rebec, 24, 78.
Recorders, the, 197, 198.
Redford, 172.
Reed-pipe, 8, 60, 67, 188.
  Egyptian, 16.
Regal, the, 190.
Reger, Max, 340.
  discussion of, 353.
Regis, 152.
Reinken, 228, 229.
Rembrandt, 240.
Réményi, 296.
Renaissance, the English, 313, 318, 347.
  the German, 227.
  the Italian, 153, 227.

Reynaud, 206.
Rhythm, fundamental importance of, 3, 7.
Ribera, 162.
Riemann, Hugo, 11, 42, 111.
Rigveda, 26.
Rimsky-Korsakoff, 308, 311, 312.
  discussion of, 310.
Rinuccini, 219.
Risorgimento, the, 341.
Ritornello, the, 138.
  the orchestral, 222.
Ritter, 351.
River-reeds, 8. *See also* Reed-pipe.
Rivers, Lady, 170.
Rode, 225.
Roman instruments, 71–5.
  neumatic notation, 101.
  origin of organum, 120.
  tone-system, 71.
Roman School (16th century), 172.
  table of composers, 174.
Rome, MSS at, 206.
Rondel (or rota), 129, 132, 143.
Röntgen, 331.
Ropartz, 344.
Rore, Cipriano da, 146, 161.
Rossetti, D. G., 345.
Rossini, 235, 244, 269, 270, 271, 275, 288, 292.
  discussion of, 268.
Rota. *See* Rondel.
Rousseau, J. J., 241.
Row the bote, Norman, 148.
Roye, 178.
Rubible (rubybe, ribibe), 78.
Rubini, 269.
Rubinstein, N. and A., 311.
Rudolph, 257.
Rue, Pierre de la, 154.
Russian School, 308.
  table of composers, 308.

S

Sackbut, the, 71, 187–9, 198.
Sackbutters, 190.
Sacramentary, the, 80.
Sacra Rappresentazione, 218.
Saint Alphege, 178.
  Ambrose, 79.
  Dunstan, 149.

Saint Edmund's College, MSS at, 147.
Evroult, 106.
Gall, antiphonary of, 102; singing-school at, 83.
Gregory, 79, 80–2, 102. *See also* Gregorian Chant.
Hilary of Poitiers, 79.
Panteleemon, 101.
Philip Neri, 175.
Saëns, 276, 277, 307, 340, 345, 348; discussion of, 346.
Salieri, 262.
Salomon, 249.
Salvation Army, 22, 279.
Salzburg, Abp. of, 252.
Sāman Chant, 26.
Sanctus, the early, 79.
Sand, George, 298.
Sappho, 69, 205.
Sarasate, 225.
Sārñgadeva, 26.
Savoy Opera, 245, 314, 318.
Scale, Chinese chromatic, 29.
  early Byzantine, 90.
  Greek diatonic, chromatic, and enharmonic, 9, 90.
  invention of, 7–9.
  pentatonic, 8, 29, 35, 60.
Scales, reed-pipe, 60.
  transposed, 95, 122.
Scarlatti, Alessandro, 218, 223, 239, 242; discussion of, 222.
  Domenico, 224, 241, 246, 298; discussion of, 222.
Scheidt, 229.
Schein, 229.
Schiller, 256, 262.
Schillings, 351.
Schjelderup, 333.
Schlesinger, Kathleen, 318.
  S. B., 300.
Schmitt, 340.
  discussion of, 346.
Schoenberg, 340.
  discussion of, 353.
Schola cantorum, 81.
Schröder-Devrient, 291.
Schubert, 69, 78, 233, 242, 256, 260, 286, 289, 297, 299, 300, 336, 339.
  discussion of, 261.

Schumann, 221, 248, 262, 265, 281, 283, 284, 289, 291, 292, 297, 299, 300, 337, 349, 351.
  discussion of, 285.
Schuppanzigh, 263, 264.
Schütz, 229, 230.
Schwenke, 296.
Scolia, the, 66.
Scott, Cyril M., 308; discussion of, 321.
  Walter, 274, 303, 304.
Scriabine, 308.
  discussion of, 312.
Scribe, 275.
Script, 5.
Sê, the Chinese, 33, 34.
Secular forms, Greek, 65, 66.
Sellenger's Round, 184.
Selmer, 332.
Sequences, the early, 82.
Seroff, 311.
Seyfried, 296.
Sgambati, 340, 342.
Shakespeare, 259, 291, 304, quoted, 196, 199, 249.
Shawms and Bombards, 43, 184–7, 190, 197.
Shêng, the Chinese, 31, 32, 33, 43.
Sheridan, 239, 252.
  quoted, 296.
Shophar, the Hebrew, 22, **71.**
Short octave, the, 192.
Shostakovich, 357.
Sibelius, 330.
  discussion of, 335.
Sidney, Philip, 183.
Siena, MSS at, 206.
Simpson, 226.
Sinding, 325, 330, 334.
  discussion of, 332.
Singers, abuses in Church Service caused by, 130, 138, 174.
Singspiel, 244, 245, 247. *See also* Comic Opera. Opéra Comique. Savoy.
Sistra, Egyptian, 16.
Sjögren, 330.
  discussion of, 334.
Sketches, the Beethoven, 255.
Skraup, 337.
Smart, 273.
Smetana, 337.

Smith, D. S., 308, 321, 329.
  Sidney, 297.
Smyth, Miss, 308, 328, 349.
  discussion of, 318.
Södermann, 330.
  discussion of, 334.
Somanātha, 26.
Somervell, 308.
  discussion of, 318.
Somis, 225.
Sonata, the, 217, 226, 231, 246, 255, 258.
Song, 6, 200.
  earliest types of, 204.
  lyric and narrative, 205, 334, 335.
  modern, 261, 262, 263, 279, 286, 297, 299, 300, 353.
  repetition in, 204.
  See also Folk-Song.
Song of the Lady Bessy, the, 206.
Songes and Ayres, 169, 180.
Sophonisba, 198.
Sousa, 308.
  discussion of, 325.
Spanish School (16th century), 146, 162.
  (Modern), 343.
Speech, 5, 202.
Spenser, 179.
Spinelli, 343.
Spinet, the, 190.
  origin of the, 20, 192.
Spohr, 281, 292.
  discussion of, 274.
Spontini, 267, 282.
Squire, W. B., 318.
Stabat Mater, 83.
Staff, the, 105–7.
Stanford, 308, 314.
  discussion of, 316.
Stanley, 150.
Stasima, the, 65.
Stenhammar, 330. discussion of, 334.
Stockhausen (singer), 297.
Stockhausen (composer), 358.
Stone-chimes, the Chinese, 31, 32.
Stove, 150.
Strange, Lord, 179.
Strauss, Ludwig, 225.
  Richard, 333, 340, 349, 353; discussion of, 351.
Stravinsky, 308.

Stravinsky, discussion of, 312, 356.
String Quartet, the, 225, 226, 231, 246, 250, 254, 256, 258, 260, 263, 267, 288, 348.
Strube, G., 328.
Stucken, F. V. van der, 325.
Suites de Pièces (or Partita), 217, 223, 246.
Sullivan, 245, 265, 308, 314, 318, 236.
  discussion of, 314.
Sumer is icumen in, 127, 143, 147, 149.
  discussion of, 132–4.
Sumphoneia, the, 19.
Svendsen, 332.
Swedish School, 333.
  table of composers, 330.
Sweelinck, 161, 229, 255.
  discussion of, 228.
Symphonic Poem, the, 289, 351.
  in England, 318.
Symphonie-à-roue. *See* Hurdy-gurdy.
Symphony, the, 231, 246, 249, 254, 256, 258, 259, 260, 261, 263, 264, 265, 277, 278, 282, 287, 297. *See also* Ritornello, the orchestral.
Sympson. *See* Simpson.
Syrinx. *See* Pan's pipes.
Syrinx (= speaker), 41.

T

Tablatures, 100, 116, 118, 192.
Tabor (or taborne), 23, 282.
Tallis, 141, 146, 166, 169, 173.
  discussion of, 168.
Tambourine, 182.
  Arabian, 23.
  Egyptian, 15.
  Roman, 72.
Tamburini, 269.
Tanieff, 308.
  discussion of, 312.
Tappster, Dryngker, 148.
Tartini, 99, 225, 241.
Taverner, 166, 167.
Taylor, S. C., 308, 339.
  discussion of, 319.
Temperament, equal, 98, 238.
  unequal (Arabian), 23.
Tennyson, 69, 257, 260.
Terpander, 49, 53, 66.

Tetrachords, Greek, 50–5, 57, 58, 60, 204.
Indian, 25.
Thaletes, 69.
Thāt, 27.
Theatrical forms, Greek, 65.
Theorbo, 193.
"The three B's," 298.
"The three S's," 229.
Thibaut, 101.
Thomas, A. Goring, 308, 314; discussion of, 316.
C. A., 276, 347; discussion of, 278.
Theodore, 323.
Tibia, the Roman, 71.
Tiger-box, the Chinese, 32, 36.
Timotheus, 69.
Timpan, origin of the, 20.
Tinctoris, 149, 152.
Tirpitz, von, 353.
Tisias, 69.
Tomaschek, 337.
Tones and semitones, 9, 104, 230.
Tone-system, Arabian, 23.
Chinese, 28, 29.
Greek, 50–60.
Indian, 4, 25.
mediæval and modern, 90–9.
origin of mediæval, 10, 41.
Roman, 71.
Tonic-pitch in Greek music, 55–7, 65, 92.
Tonic Sol Fa, 100, 104.
Torr, Cecil, 60, 318.
Tovey, D. F., 134, 318.
Tragedy, origin of, 65.
Tremolando, invention of the, 219.
Trevisa, 163.
Trigon, 20.
Triple time, 125, 143.
Troubadours, 138, 206.
Trombone, the, 71. *See also* Sackbut.
Trouvères, 138, 206.
Trump, 23, 184. *See also* Trumpet.
Trumpet, 184, 198.
Assyrian, 19.
Bach, 300.
Chinese military, 37.
Egyptian, 16.
Greek, 40.
Hebrew straight, 21.
Indian, 26.

Trumpet, ram's-horn, 21.
Roman, 71.
Trumpets and drums, 190, 196.
Tchaikovsky, 212, 308, discussion of, 311.
Tuba, the Roman, 71.
Tunsted, 141.
Tye, 166, 173. discussion of, 168.
Tymbyr (or tymbre), 23, 182. *See also* Tambourine.

V

Valentini, 173.
Varèse, 357.
Vecchi, 219.
Vehringen. *See* Hermannus.
Venetian School, 146, 161.
publishing, 163, 166.
Veni redemptor, 79.
Verdelot, 161.
Verdi, 243, 250, 269, 308, 340.
discussion of, 341.
Vere, Lady Elizabeth, 179.
Viadana, 219.
Viardot, Madame, 244, 276.
Vielle à manivelle. *See* Hurdy-gurdy.
Vienna, MSS at, 148.
Vieuxtemps, 225.
Villa-Lobos, 357.
Vīnā, the, 26, 27.
Viola da Gamba, 169, 191, 224, 227.
Viol family, the, 78, 194, 198.
Violin, the, 198, 217, 238.
family, the, 77, 78, 194.
Schools, 224–5.
Viotti, 225.
Virdung, 152.
Virginal, the, 190, 198.
origin of the, 20, 192.
Vitruvius, 70, 72, 74.
Vittoria, 142, 143, 146, 162, **173.**
Vivaldi, 225, 227.
Vleeshouwer, 331.
Vogl, 262, 263.
Vogler, the Abbé, 271, 275.
Vogls, the, 294.

W

Wagner, Richard, 88, 219, 220, 222, 240, 242, 243, 250, 266, 267, 272, 273, 274, 281, 284, 286, 287, 288,

289, 290, 297, 332, 334, 336, 338, 340, 341, 342, 345, 346, 347, 349, 350, 351, 352.
Wagner, discussion of, 290.
    Siegfried, 351.
Waldstein, Count, 255, 256.
Walker, Ernest, 318.
Wallace, Vincent, 302.
    William, 308; discussion of, 318.
Walmisley, 301.
Waltham Abbey, 168.
    MSS at, 141.
Watteau, 240.
Weber, Carl Maria von, 220, 233, 242, 245, 268, 274, 275, 281, 283, 291.
    discussion of, 271.
    Costanze, 252, 271.
    Edmund von, 248, 271.
Weelkes, 166, 171.
Weerbecke, Gaspar van, 154.
Wegelius, 330.
    discussion of, 335.
Weingartner, 340.
    discussion of, 352.
Weinlig, 237, 290, 291.
Werckmeister, 98.
Wesley, S. S., 301.
Westphal, 44.
White Notation, 100, 115.
Whiting, Arthur, 334.
    George E., 324.
Whyte, 166, 168.
Widor, 348.
Wieck, 285.

Wieck, Clara, 286.
Wilbye, 142, 143, 146, 151, 166, 168, 171, 173.
    discussion of, 170.
Willaert, 160, 161.
William the Monk, 141.
Williams, Abdy, 318.
    R. V., 308; discussion of, 319.
Willis, 77.
Winchester Organ, the, 75, 76.
Wind-bells, Chinese, 47.
Winge, 333.
Wolf, 340.
    discussion of, 353.
Wolf-Ferrari, 340.
    discussion of, 343.
Wood, Charles, 319.
Wooldridge, 129, 318.
Wright, 318.
Wynkyn de Worde, 163.

Y

Yankee Doodle, 339.

Z

Zampogna, the, 19.
Zarlino, 146, 162, 228.
    theoretical work of, 97.
Zelter, 281.
Zola, 348.
Zuccalmaglio, 286.
Zweers, 331.